# Redeemer—Friend and Mother

# Redeemer
## Friend and Mother

---

## Salvation in Antiquity
## and in the Gospel of John

J. Massyngbaerde Ford

**Fortress Press**
**Minneapolis**

REDEEMER—FRIEND AND MOTHER
Salvation in Antiquity and in the Gospel of John

Cover and book design by Joseph Bonyata
Cover art: "Figure in Glory," Albert Gleizes. Copyright © 1997 Artists Rights Society (ARS), New York / ADAGP, Paris. Used by permission.

---

Library of Congress Cataloging-in-Publication Data

Ford, J. Massyngbaerde (Josephine Massyngbaerde)
    Redeemer—friend and mother : salvation in antiquity and in the
Gospel of John / J. Massyngbaerde Ford.
        p.  cm.
    Includes bibliographical references.
    ISBN 0-8006-2778-4
    1. Bible. N.T. John—Criticism interpretation, etc.
2. Salvation—Biblical teaching. 3. Suffering of God—Biblical
teaching. 4. Jesus Christ—Crucifixion—Biblical teaching.
5. Friendship—Religious aspects—Biblical teaching. 6. God—
Motherhood—Biblical teaching. 7. Salvation—Comparative studies.
I. Title.
BS2615.6.S25F67    1997
226.5´06—dc21                                                              96-51001
                                                                                CIP

---

The paper used in this publication meets the minimum requirements of American National Standard for Information Sciences—Permanence of Paper for Printed Library Materials. ANSI Z329.48-1984.

Manufactured in the U.S.A.                                    AF 1-2778

02  01  00  99  98  97    1    2    3    4    5    6    7    8    9    10

# Contents

# Abbreviations

| | | | |
|---|---|---|---|
| *Ap. John* | *Apocalypsis Joannis* | Ps. | Psalm |
| *B.T. Hullin* | *Tractate Hullin, The Talmud of* | Pss. | Psalms |
| | *Babylonia* | Prov. | Proverbs |
| *B.T. San.* | *Sanhedrin,* | Eccl. | Ecclesiastes |
| | *The Talmud of Babylonia* | Song of Sol. | Song of Solomon |
| *Const Apost* | *Apostolic Constitutions* | Isa. | Isaiah |
| *Hag.* | *Haggadah* | Jer. | Jeremiah |
| Sanh. | Sanhedrin | Ezek. | Ezekiel |
| *Sifre Deut.* | *Sifre on Deuteronomy* | Dan. | Daniel |
| Cyril, *In Jo* | *Commentarii in Joannem* | Hos. | Hosea |
| Epictetus, *Man.* | *The Manual of Epictetus* | Mic. | Micah |
| Eratosthenes, *Catast.* | *Catasterismi* | Nah. | Nahum |
| Eusebius, *HE* | *Historia Ecclesiastica* | Zech. | Zechariah |
| Florus, *Hist* | *Romane Historie* | | |
| Herodotus, *Hist* | *Historiae* | Matt. | Matthew |
| Hyginus, *Fab* | *Fabularum liber* | Mk | Mark |
| Jerome, *Ad Gal* | *Comentarii ad Galathas* | Lk | Luke |
| *Af Eph* | *Comentarii ad Ephesios* | Jn | John |
| Justin Martyr, *Dial* | *Dialogus cum* | Rom. | Romans |
| | *Tryphone Judaeo* | 1 Cor. | 1 Corinthians |
| Lucian, *Toxaris* | *Toxaris vel amicitia* | 2 Cor. | 2 Corinthians |
| Melito of Sardis, *Frag.* | *Fragmenta* | Gal. | Galatians |
| Philo, *Gig* | *De gigantibus* | Eph. | Ephesians |
| | | Phil. | Philippians |
| **Biblical** | | Col. | Colossians |
| OT | Old Testament | 1 Thess. | 1 Thessalonians |
| NT | New Testament | 1 Tim. | 1 Timothy |
| MT | Masoretic Text | Heb. | Hebrews |
| LXX | Septuagint | 1 Pet. | 1 Peter |
| RSV | Revised Standard Version | Rev. | Revelation |
| Gen. | Genesis | | |
| Exod. | Exodus | Bar. | Baruch |
| Lev. | Leviticus | Ecclus. | Ecclesiasticus |
| Num. | Numbers | 4 Esd. | 4 Esdrae |
| Deut. | Deuteronomy | 1 Macc. | 1 Maccabees |
| Josh. | Joshua | 2 Macc. | 2 Maccabees |
| Judg. | Judges | Q | Qumran |
| 2 Sam. | 2 Samuel | Sir. | Sirach |
| 1 Kgs. | 1 Kings | Tob. | Tobias |
| 1 Chron. | 1 Chronicles | Wisd. Sol. | The Wisdom of Solomon |

**Journals**

| | |
|---|---|
| *BiblSacr* | *Bibliotheca Sacra* |
| *BTB* | *Biblical Theology Bulletin* |
| *Bull Litt Eccles* | *Bulletin de litterature ecclesiastique* |
| *BZ* | *Biblische Zeitschrift* |
| *CBQ* | *Catholic Biblical Quarterly* |
| *EstBibl* | *Estudios Biblicos* |
| *ET* | *Expository Times* |
| *Journ Evang TheoSoc* | *Journal of the Evangelical Theological Society* |
| *JSNT* | *Journal for the Study of the New Testament* |
| *JSOT* | *Journal for the Study of the Old Testament* |
| *NovTest* | *Novum Testamentum* |
| *NTS* | *New Testament Studies* |
| *RAC* | *Revue de l'Art Chretien* |
| *Rexp* | *Review and Expositor* |
| *TU* | *Texte und Untersuchungen zur Geschichte der Altchristlichen Literatur* |

**Other**

| | |
|---|---|
| B.C.E. | Before the Common Era |
| c. | *circa* |
| C.E. | Common Era |
| chap. | chapter |
| chs. | chapters |
| col. | column |
| cols. | columns |
| comp. | compiled by |
| d. | died |

| | |
|---|---|
| ed. | editor |
| rev ed. | revised edition |
| esp. | especially |
| ET | English Translation |
| Fr. | French |
| frag. | fragment |
| Gr. | Greek |
| Hebr. | Hebrew |
| LCL | Loeb Classical Library |
| MG | Migne Graeca |
| n. | note |
| nn. | notes |
| No. | number |
| OUP | Oxford University Press |
| p. | page |
| pp. | pages |
| par. | pagagraph |
| PL | Patrologia Latina |
| Pref. | Preface |
| Repr. | Reprint |
| SBL | Society of Biblical Literature |
| serm. | Sermon |
| Syr. | Syriac |
| trans. | translation |
| v. | verse |
| vv. | verses |
| Vat. City | Vatican City |
| vol. | volume |
| vols. | volumes |

# Introduction

A BRIEF NOTE IN DR. SANDRA SCHNEIDER'S ARTICLE on the footwashing in John[1] sparked my interest in friendship in this Gospel. She observed the lack of research in this field. I reflected again on Jesus' remarkable and strategically placed statement in John 15:15, namely, that he no longer regarded the disciples as servants but as friends. It is a key text in the Farewell Discourses. This stimulated me to look into the idea of redemption in John, for surely redemption is restoration of friendship with God and with the universe. I had noted the absence of expiatory and sacrificial language in John in contrast to the rest of the New Testament. Could we, I asked, express redemption in terms of friendship? Would this be understandable in the Greco-Roman world in which our Gospel was born? Would this be a more attractive model of redemption than satisfaction, expiation, or victimization? Therefore I turned to classical materials on friendship and began to compare them to the Johannine text with its rich Judeo-Hellenistic background. But I noticed that friendship in antiquity meant a mating of souls, a shared experience of life, the deep commitment to community, "going to calamity's depths for a friend,"[2] often dying for him or her. Friendship embraced relationships with the gods and goddesses and the earth, as well as humanity.

But a friend must "feel" for the Other; there is a spiritual and emotional component to true friendship. We could certainly predicate this emotion of the human Jesus, but could we predicate it also of God per se? I found that the God portrayed in the Hebrew Scriptures is certainly an emotive, empathetic God, and that this divine aspect was developed in many rabbinic and mystical traditions, particularly as represented by the feminine aspect of Yahweh, the Shekinah. But I was also interested in some modern Christian systematic theological studies, especially those that discussed the *pathos* or anguish of God. At the beginning of this century Miguel de Unamuno, the Salamancan philosopher (1846–1936), was

1

ahead of his time. Much of his work, including the deeply moving *El Cristo de Velázques*, is devoted to the positive and godlike nature of suffering and also to the innate attraction of divinity for humanity and vice versa. They are not polar opposites but possess a mutual lure, the one for the other. Unamuno developed the theory of God's profound anguish. This theme has been resumed by a number of contemporary theologians, e.g., Elizabeth Johnson, LaCugna, McFague, and Moltmann. Many theologians still present this *pathos* as the anguish of God the Father. But is the paternal model an adequate one to express the whole *pathos* of God? To me this model seemed to suggest a suffering related to one outside himself. The feminine model was needed in concert with the masculine. Male and female together, not separately, reflect the image and likeness of God and fully reveal the divine *pathos*. However, even this was not entirely satisfactory. It was imperative to find a model that fused and rose superior to these two. This is provided in the model of friend, the father as friend and the mother as friend, that carries us beyond the simple parental image. So both together, with the addition of friendship, could be the working model for redemption.

It was now incumbent on me to inquire about the nature of Jesus' death. Quite simply one can ask, Why could not Jesus die in his bed?, "drawing up his feet" like Jacob (Gen. 49:33)? The answer appears to lie in the necessity of a friend to share the whole experience, joyful and sorrowful, of the Other, and this led Jesus, not by a masochistic choice of his own or by a sadistic choice of his Father's but as a consequence of his mission, to join in death with those who were deprived of the privileges of life in its fullest earthly meaning. The incarnate Jesus comes as the friend of humankind, and thus he allows himself to undergo the *pathos*, not of a select few, but of all representative sections of humanity. He suffers as the sage, as rejected teacher, as charismatic healer and exorcist, as son and brother, as master betrayed by one of his chosen. The crucifixion enables Jesus' friendship and compassion to empathize most profoundly with the broadest spectrum of humanity, especially the depersonalized humanity of the slave and, in some cultures, woman in the ancient world. The cross represented the most obscene death not only on a physical but also on a psychological, familial, societal, and spiritual level. This is why I have devoted so much space to it. I suppose today Jesus might have been a victim of the concentration camps or a Hiroshima survivor suffering the excruciating aftermath of the nuclear bomb. Jesus truly dies as one who "goes to calamity's depths" for his friends.

Thus I devote the first part of my book to (1) a survey of models of redemption, in order to provide a context for our discussion; (2) an examination of the *pathos* of God under the image of Father; (3) under the image of mother; and (4) in the whole process of crucifixion: I discuss the crucifixion of women in this section. Last, I investigate the concept of friendship and heroic suffering in antiquity as a model for Christian redemption.

The second part of my book deals with select sections of the text of John's Gospel. My intent here is to search for both the friendship motif and the feminine imagery pertinent to redemption. Friendship as the interpenetration of spirits, and the friend as the second self, explains much of the theology of the Prologue of John. But interwoven with the friendship theme is feminine imagery, especially of birth and nourishment.

The friendship motif is continued and reaches its climax in the Farewell Discourses, on the cross, and in the Johannine Pentecost. Schneider and Rohden see the footwashing as a friendship text, but I add a reflection on Herman's seminal book *Ritual Friendship*. The footwashing is a *semeion* (revelatory sign) that predicts and encapsulates all that will transpire in the passion, death, and resurrection of Jesus. Jesus' statement about friendship with the disciples (John 15:15) is a solemn statement betokening their redeemed relationship with God.

The Farewell Discourses are also important for their "trinitarian" theology, which enables John to raise the concept of friendship to its climax, from the human level to the divine. In the Farewell Discourses, Jesus emphasizes not only his union with God but also the fact that the Christian community has an ontological association with the godhead. The friendship that Jesus offers is an acceptance of the hospitable invitation of God to mingle our lives within the very communal friendship relationships of the Trinity. Jesus prayed that we might be one even as he and the Father are one. We share the trinitarian life and glory. But glory is not success; it is a new mode of existence, and it can involve suffering as well as joy. However, suffering takes on a new complexion. It is not negative and unproductive. Christian suffering is the pangs of childbirth that herald the rebirth of humanity. This is the very image that Jesus uses in John 16:21, and that is implied in John's special account of the soldier piercing Jesus' side.

But we must inquire further. How are these images, friend and mother, continued, implemented in the passion and on the cross? The friendship theme is seen not only in the human Jesus' heroic endurance of shame and suffering but also in the heroic endurance of shame and suffering by God per se, by all three persons in the Trinity. In this way the true meaning of God as sovereign is that of the friendly servant monarch first discussed by the Greek philosophers. The product of this divine suffering is the transmission of the Spirit, which causes our souls (ourselves) to be soul-mates of the incarnate God. Here there is an interpenetration of spirits, divine and human, a clasp of the right hand of fellowship by God and humanity. But John does not omit the feminine symbolism in the passion. The small group of women with the beloved disciple, standing not at a distance but near the cross, are the prototypes of God's true friends. Then by a startling inversion of images the man on the cross gives birth in a mystical sense. John shows this through the striking symbolism of the piercing of the side of Christ and the effusion of blood and water. The image comes from childbirth. The one born is the Christian community represented by Jesus' mother, aunt, and intimate friends, Mary and the beloved disciple, perhaps identified with Lazarus. The wound from the side and breast-feeding become of paramount importance in Syriac texts and later in medieval texts.

The final "redemptive scene" in John's Gospel is the second bestowal of the Spirit, the Johannine Pentecost (John 20). Here again we have trinitarian symbolism: the Son, the Father who sent him, and the Spirit. It is important that this bestowal of the Spirit is associated with Jesus' showing his wounded body to the disciples. The first transmission of the Spirit, the principle of life, is intimately associated with the pangs of birth. The second bestowal of the Spirit on the disciples (the early church and ourselves) transforms them into co-redeemers with Christ. The Christian community has power to absolve from sin through the sharing of the Spirit with others.

Finally, I wish especially to emphasize that redemption is a cooperative experience; unlike the earlier theories, the modern ideas of redemption do not place the whole onus on God. Instead, redemption is covenant partnership, friendly, ecstatic cooperation.

I have taken the liberty of combining in my discussion ancient, medieval, and contemporary literature at many points. I realize that this may seem inappropriate to some readers, but as a biblical scholar I have sought to express some of the modern theological tenets in biblical terms. It seems to me that there should be a greater marriage between biblical studies and systematic theology. I am grateful for some perspicacious comments on my earlier material that my friend and colleague Professor LaCugna gave me. I have added the medieval texts at certain points because they show that this feminine imagery is not the invention of twentieth-century feminists but rather an age-old tradition of deeply committed men and women who pondered the meaning of the biblical texts and especially the humanity and crucifixion of Jesus.

I selected the Gospel of John because, unlike the Synoptic Gospels, it does not see Jesus' death as "ransom" (Mark 10:45) or the Eucharist as Jesus' blood poured out for the remission of sin, or speak of the necessity of Jesus' death in so explicit a way. Further, John portrays the passion as a unique event that reveals the true meaning of glory and that invites participation on the part of the reader. Thus I believe that John's Gospel is a fertile field for the study of redemption. It appeals to Christians of various persuasions, and I hope that it will especially appeal to women to play their redemptive part in the body of the church.

Finally I wish to express deep appreciation to my three graduate assistants, Mr. Richard Rivers, Ms. Susan Graham, the Rev. Jeremy Williams, who have worked uninstintingly on bibliographies and the text; and Ms. Stacey Wendlinder, who worked on some of the indices; and to our two secretaries, Ms. Sherry Reichold and Ms. Cheryl Reed, who have shown me unfailing patience and worked with much diligence.

# PART 1

# 1

# Models of Redemption

H<small>OW DO WE CONCEIVE OF</small> G<small>OD</small>?
What image comes to our minds when we speak of a Redeemer God?
Is the God of the Hebrew Scriptures a contrast or a complement
to the God whom Jesus Christ "interprets" (John 1:18)[1] for us in
the New Testament?[2]

How can we explain humanity made in the image and likeness
of God?

How does God reveal him or herself to us in the twentieth
century?

Do new insights into redemption help us to understand
the Eucharist better?

In this essay I shall seek to find some answers to these questions.[3]

## *The Concept of God*

In 1 Kings 19:1-18 we find the prophet Elijah hiding in a cave on Mount
Horeb (Sinai). He awaits a theophany, a revelation of the presence of God.
On this same mountain God had revealed him or herself to the chosen
people, established the divine covenant, and had given the Ten Commandments. The biblical writers indicate that on that earlier occasion the presence of the deity had been accompanied by thunder, lightning, volcanic
eruption, and possibly earthquake (Exod. 19:16-25).[4] It is reported as a
terrifying experience (contrast Heb. 12:18-24). Elijah expected a similar
theophany. To his surprise it was wholly other (different), it came in a still,
small voice, a whisper. The message of this passage is an encouragement to
look for new ways in which the divine revelation occurs, age after age.[5]

God has many "faces," including human faces, in this world. Here we
see "through a mirror darkly" (1 Cor. 13:12). However, as time proceeds

and as she walks among many diverse cultures, she grants us flashes of insight, as it were, whirling the kaleidoscope of the mystery of God tantalizingly before our eyes. It is for us to catch the color and to paint our own portrait of God which, though respecting tradition, will throw into high relief a God whose commandment, as Deuteronomy 30:11-14 says, is "something very near to you, already in your mouths and in your hearts. . . ." The biblical text is not static,[6] but polyvalent; it "speaks in tongues," each tongue the dialect of the serious and open reader. The reader with his or her cultural background and the text with its rich history meet in an embrace of friendship to bring forth new knowledge of God.

I have caught two colors: (1) of redeemer-friend and (2) of redeemer-mother. They are colors rich, blood red, refracting a thousand hues, eager, in Cicero's words, to go to "calamity's depth" for their beloved. It is thus that I choose to see this God as our redeemer, the friend and mother par excellence.[7] However, before I do so, I should like to give a very brief overview of theories of soteriology, that is, the study of redemption.[8]

## Definitions of Salvation/Redemption

### Salvation

We may provisionally define "salvation" as the result of that dynamic action of the triune God that brings to humankind, animals, and the whole creation the fullness of their being, the totality of their potential. It recreates them so that they reflect more vividly the image and likeness of God. Sin comprises fracture of relationships. Salvation brings healing to that fracture so that the relationship between God and humanity, between human beings themselves, and between humanity and creation is restored.

Salvation (yš)[9] connotes "wide" or "spacious," the absence of the bonds of the captive, of the slave and the oppressed, and full *shalom* (wholeness and harmony), a *shalom* not only of the individual but of the community and the universe. Hence it is that the prophets dream of utopias (e.g., Isa. 11:1-9)—lambs feeding with lions, children playing with vipers, abundant fertility, and luxuriant living. The later prophets, especially those of the New Testament, anticipate the resurrection as a cosmic event[10] that will bring a perfect communion of saints, that is, new ranges of personal relationships within a renewed cosmos.

### Redemption

Redemption is the process by which we acquire or regain this cosmic and spiritual *shalom*. According to Paul we are saved from God's wrath, from sin, from death, and from the law. The cross, always to be closely linked to the resurrection, triumphs over the agents of human bondage and over every adverse or hostile cosmic element. The entire ministry of Jesus, earthly and exalted, must be considered within the purview of redemption.[11] Reconciliation is the unique and wondrous work of the Spirit. Redemption[12] is the means by which this "re-creation" is implemented, and it involves all the persons of the Trinity. However, the work of redemption requires humanity's full cooperation with the deity:[13] it is a cooperative venture.

## *The Doctrine of Redemption*

It is not the intention of this author to give a full historical or exegetical treatment of redemption/salvation but to furnish a brief survey and then to make two new approaches. The reader is referred to the brief but useful study by John McIntyre.[14]

The church has never formally defined the doctrine of redemption as she has those of Christology and of the Trinity.[15] Further, forgiveness of sin has not always been attributed specifically to Jesus' death. For example, in the Nicene Creed forgiveness is associated with baptism and the Holy Spirit rather than the death of Jesus.[16] The Chalcedonian Creed predicated forgiveness on the incarnation. McIntyre contends that this absence of a definite soteriology may be due to the fact that the theology of redemption was so deeply embedded in the various liturgies that associated it with Jesus' words at the Last Supper (8–9).[17] He states that "the atonement[18] effected by the death of Christ was more integral to the *worship* of the church than to the *thought-life* of its theologians."[19] Thus, instead of being defined, redemption was reflected in the *consensus fidelium* of the worshiping community and was not a prerogative of the clergy. However, when people lost their full participation in liturgy, this led to the idea of the priest representing the people and may well have given rise to the concept of redemption by representation, that is, that Jesus, like the priest, represented the people and shed his blood for them.[20] This also meant that the teaching about redemption fell, for the most part, into the hands of males and scholars rather than all the people.

Another reason for the absence of formal doctrines on soteriology may be found in the fact that in the early church there were no sustained major heretical treatises against established soteriological views.[21] However, McIntyre points out the importance of these questions to the reformers. They composed vernacular liturgies in which all the faithful could participate. They produced soteriological statements because of the vast theological literature on the death of Jesus and the Eucharist. This was done especially in their confessional statements and catechisms (for children and adults) and also through their theological treatises. McIntyre also mentions the emphasis on the attributes of God and its importance for atonement.[22] Some fifty works on the atonement were produced in Europe in this period. Thus theories about redemption were given great prominence from the time of the Reformation.

There are several crucial questions that constantly occur when one discusses redemption: (1) How can we understand Jesus' insistence that he *must* (*dei*) suffer and die?[23] This is seen particularly in the three predictions of his passion, death, and resurrection in Mark 8:31; 9:31; 10:45; and parallels.[24] (2) Could God have forgiven human sinfulness without the suffering of Christ? (3) Was Christ free to die for humankind, or did his filial obedience make his death obligatory?[25] (4) Was God under a necessity to save his creatures in order not to nullify his purpose in creation? In other words, was God free? (5) Why was Jesus' death penalty, "crucifixion," the most obscene of capital punishments? (6) What positive fruits were brought to humankind by Jesus, the redeemer?

## Models of Soteriology

McIntyre[26] expounds thirteen models of soteriology.[27] I shall use some of these but shall explicate them with patristic material and also add several others. One must say, however, that many of these theories overlap and can be distinguished rather than separated from one another.

### Ransom[28]

One of the most popular theories of redemption explained Jesus' death (life,[29] as "ransom," literally, a "buying back." The *locus classicus* for Jesus' life as ransom is Mark 10:45[30] (cf. Matt. 20:28) where Jesus says that the Son of humanity will give his life as a ransom (*lytron*) for many (*anti pollōn*). This appears to be linked directly to Isaiah 52:13–53:12, especially verses 9 and 10 (see LXX), which concern the Servant of the Lord. However, "ransom" in Mark 10:45 does not have the sacrificial and expiatory tone that it acquired later.[31] We may quote Irenaeus, who appears to emphasize ransom from captivity rather than "ransom" in a sacrificial sense:

> . . . redeeming us by his blood in accordance with his reasonable nature, he gave himself as a ransom for those who had been led into captivity (Irenaeus, *Against Heresies* 5.1.1).

Lyonnet observes that nowhere in the New Testament do we learn to whom the price was paid.[32] However, the fact that *lytron, apōlytron,* and *exagorazein* (*agorazein*) were used in the discussion of Jesus' redemptive work, especially his death on the cross, led many writers to think in terms of payment made either to God or the devil as our ransom from sin and for our salvation. Stock[33] observes:

> Redemption exemplifies how legal concepts may be turned into religious concepts, and these in turn both give rise to further social legislation and serve as the model for an even higher form of the same concept.

One theory that was influential throughout many centuries was the "rights of the devil." According to this, the devil was master or mistress of sinners; sin brought persons under his or her control.[34] For this reason it was necessary either to "buy off" the devil[35] or to lay a snare for him or her.[36] Augustine (*Sermons* 181.5 and 263.1) speaks of Christ's cross as a trap (*muscipula*) for Satan, for he did not realize that he was crucifying the sinless one; hence he was thwarted. However, Augustine claims that the devil cannot really be our master.[37] Rather he is our tormentor and he serves divine justice in punishing sinners.[38] Augustine says:

> In this redemption the blood of Christ has been given on our behalf as the price; the devil, however, by accepting it, was not made richer but was bound so that we might be freed from his fetters. . . . (*On the Trinity* 13.15).

The ransom-diabolical right theory, though popular, was never the official teaching of the church. It is an unattractive model; it reads almost like a financial transaction. Today most Christians would not wish to countenance a "commercial" transaction on the part of God or Christ or humanity, and many would question the existence of an individual character named the devil.

### Deliverance from Bondage

A model close to that of "ransom" is that of "redemption": deliverance from psychological and spiritual bondage and debt (cf. Eph. 1:7, 14; Col. 1:14). Here there is not such a clear stress on buying back. Rather it is redeeming from sin, the law, and death rather than from a personal agent of evil, the devil (although in some texts both "sin" and "death" are personified). Two important texts from Paul have been very influential in this theory and are the subject of monographs by Lyonnet and Sabourin (see bibliography). These texts are:

> Christ redeemed us from the curse of the law, having become a curse for us—for it is written, "Cursed be every one who hangs on a tree"(Gal. 3:13).

and

> For our sake he made him to be sin who did not know sin, so that we might become the righteousness of God in him(2 Cor. 5:21).

As an example of this model we may quote three illustrative texts from Athanasius, who says that one who was true God and a true human being had to pay humanity's debt. The first text associates this deliverance with the incarnation:

> All men being lost according to the transgression of Adam, his flesh before all
> others was saved and liberated, as being the Word's Body; and henceforth we,
> being incorporate with it, are saved after its pattern (*Against the Arians* 2.61).

The second makes a clear link between the death of Jesus and deliverance. The debt is paid to death.

> Whence by offering unto death the body he himself had taken as an offering
> and sacrifice free from any stain, straightway he put away death from all his
> peers by the offering of an equivalent. For being over all, the Word of God nat-
> urally by offering his own temple and corporeal instrument for the life of all
> satisfied the debt by his death (Athanasius, *On the Incarnation of the Word* 9).

The third example shows not only the liberation but the bestowal of a graced righteousness.

> The Word himself bearing our sins in his body on the tree, we humans were
> redeemed from our own affections, and were filled with the righteousness of
> the Word (*Against the Arians* 3.31).[39]

Again liberation from bondage is an incomplete model in that the positive fruits of salvation are not fully expressed. We are reluctant to see a God who wishes to be "paid off," who records our sins or debts like a creditor.

### Satisfaction and Substitution[40]

A starker form of the redemption model is found in the theory of satisfaction and substitution. It was felt that humankind could not satisfy the wounded honor of an offended God. For example, Jerome, referring to Marcion's[41] concept of God, describes him as bloodthirsty, cruel, and vindictive.[42] Or as Diognetus expressed it a little more mildly:

> And when the cup of our iniquities was filled, and it had become perfectly
> clear that their wages—the punishment of death—had to be expected, then
> the season arrived during which God had determined to reveal henceforth his
> goodness and power. O the surpassing kindness and love of God for man!
> . . . Of his own accord he gave up his own Son as a ransom for us [see Rom.
> 8:32; 1 Tim. 2:6; Matt. 20:28; Mark 10:45]—the saint for sinners, the guiltless
> for the guilty, the innocent for the wicked [1 Pet. 3:18], the incorruptible for
> the corruptible, the immortal for the mortal! Indeed, what else could have
> covered sins but his holiness [Ps. 84:3; 1 Pet. 4:8; James 5:20]? In whom could
> we, the lawless and impious, be sanctified but in the Son of God alone? O
> sweet exchange! O infathomable accomplishment—[Rom. 11:3; Eph. 3:8]. O
> unexpected blessings—the sinfulness of many is buried in one who is holy, the
> holiness of one sanctifies the many who are sinners [Rom. 5:17-19]![43]

It is understandable that this type of teaching, though acceptable in a feudal, class-conscious, and militant[44] society, is difficult for contemporary Christians. One cannot see God as a "bloodthirsty victor" or think of divine honor being appeased or the innocent suffering for the guilty. The theory is dependent on a very different model of God and of human nature.

### Christ as Sacrifice and Victim[45]

The theories of satisfaction and substitution tend to lead to Jesus being seen as a "victim" and his death as a bloody sacrifice offered to God. Augustine understands 2 Cor. 5:21 to mean that Christ became a sin offering, "In this sinless victim are found the moral requirements [cf. Heb. 7:26] corresponding to the physical integrity and the ritual 'purity' of the animal victim [see Num. 6:14]." Seeing Christ's solidarity with humankind Augustine says:

> What hanged on the tree [see Gal. 3:3], if not the sin of the old man, which the Lord for our sake received in the mortality of the flesh? . . . Our old self would not have been at the same time crucified, the apostle says elsewhere, if in this death of the Lord, had not hanged the image (*figura*) of our sins, that the sinful body might be destroyed, and we might no longer be enslaved to sin (Rom. 6:6) (Augustine, *Sermon on Galatians* 3.13; cf. *Against Adimantus* 21).

Augustine also explains Romans 8:3 in the light of Leviticus 4:29 (imposing one's hand on the sin offering).The teaching of Cyril of Jerusalem is similar. He says:

> According to the Scriptures then, Christ has been made a victim (*sphagion*) for our sins. Hence the very wise Paul writes: him who knew no sin God has made to be "sin"...that is, God made him a victim for the sins of the world [cf. Isa. 53; 1 Pet. 2:24; Rom. 5:10 f.]....In fact the word of God, good and merciful, was made flesh, man, that is, like us who are under the yoke of sin; he has accepted our lot [cf. Heb. 2:5] and has given his life in exchange [*antallagma*] for the life of all (*Letters* 41).[46]

Further, Ambrosiaster sees salvation/redemption in two stages: Christ causes reconciliation by his human life and teaching, but he also offers himself as a victim through a sacrificial death, rescues us from the devil, and makes us righteous.[47]

Gregory of Nazianzus says that Christ became sin (*autoamartia*) and a curse. He speaks about Jesus consuming evil in himself "as fire consumes wax" (*Oration* 30.5–6). For a contemporary reading of victimage into New Testament texts see Duncan Derrett.[48] He sees Jesus striding through God's wrath and offering an expiatory sacrifice. Derrett thinks that this is predicted in the Old Testament and seen to be fulfilled in the Gospel of John.

However, it is with Anselm (one of the first to write a whole treatise on redemption) that we find the doctrine of satisfaction gaining favor and almost monopolizing the doctrine of redemption. In *Cur Deus Homo?* (*Why Did God Become Human?*) Boso, Anselm's interlocutor, asks:

> What justice is it to deliver the most just man of all to death in the sinners' stead? . . . If God cannot save sinners otherwise than by condemning the just, where is his omnipotence? But if he could but would not, how are we to defend both his wisdom and his justice?[49]

Anselm answered that Christ's death was a *voluntary* one, but the world could not be saved in any other way. However, Christ's obedience was more important to God than his suffering. Anselm finds the solution to the problem in the theory of satisfaction. We must, however, see all this against the background of the weight placed on penance, which was so emphasized in the Middle Ages. The church's penitential system rested on the idea of satisfaction: voluntary penance in union with Christ's suffering was thought to diminish punishment in the world to come. Again the idea of making satisfaction to God for his offended honor must be seen in the light of the system of feudal lords (and ladies). The "mathematical" approach to sin and reparation can be seen in the idea that the smallest sin requires satisfaction "of infinite magnitude."[50] But no human being, save the incarnate God, can accomplish this. Anselm sees Christ's death in this light:

> There is nothing more severe and arduous that a man can suffer for the honor of God, freely, and not as a matter of due, than death; and there is no way in which a man can more entirely give himself up to God than when he delivers himself up to death for His honor. . . . It is needful, therefore, that he who would make satisfaction for man's sin should be one who can die, if he wills to do so.[51]

Anselm also considers the gravity of sin, the punishment owed, obstacles to the sinner's rehabilitation, and the ethical requirements of satisfaction. Speaking in legal terms, he says that God could not reward Christ with something he already possessed, so the reward was given to humanity (Anselm, *Why Did God Become Human?* 2:9). Sabourin[52] observes that Anselm does not pay sufficient attention to the importance of conversion; for him satisfaction is owed to the *wounded honor* of God. Anselm works from reason rather than revelation. We may compare Peter Lombard: "This is the price of our reconciliation which Christ offered to the Father so that he may be appeased,"[53] and "Christ is the priest; he is also the victim and thus the price of our reconciliation, who offered himself on the altar of the cross, not to the devil, but to the Trinity on our behalf, to meet more than sufficiently the price" (*Sentences* 3, Distinction 20.3).

With this theory our difficulties increase. Is God a feudal lord, insulted by his serfs and demanding appropriate appeasement? How are we to interpret the teaching of Jesus on forgiveness, especially in the light of such parables as the prodigal son, in which no satisfaction is required of the repentant sinner?

## Jesus as Scapegoat

The theory of sacrifice and victim sometimes includes the idea of Jesus as the scapegoat. On the Day of Atonement (Lev. 16:1-43) the Jewish high priest took two goats; one he offered to God, and upon the other, representing the people, he laid the sins of the nation. This became known as the scapegoat.

> Laying both hands on its head, he shall confess over it all the sinful faults and transgressions of the Israelites, and so put them on the goat's head. He shall then have it led into the desert by an attendant. Since the goat is to carry off their iniquities to an isolated region, it must be sent away into the desert (Lev. 16:21-22).

This ceremony is called the Azazel rite.[54] Milgrom points out that the fact that the high priest lays two hands (not one) on the goat shows that this is not a sacrifice, rather it "serves as a transference function."[55] The goat is given to Azazel and the confession of sin[56] implemented "to trap the sins by exposing them, by calling them by their name, and thus preventing their escape or concealment."[57] But Milgrom argues that the purpose is to release sin, not entrap it. The evil is banished to the wilderness or netherworld, where the demon Azazel was thought to dwell.[58] The purpose was to remove the goat (and sin) from human habitations.[59]

The typology of the scapegoat was taken up by a number of early Christian writers. Tertullian (*Against Marcion* 3.7), speaking about the humiliation, suffering, and mockery of Christ, offers an interpretation of the two goats on the Day of Atonement and opines that they symbolize Christ's two natures and his first and second coming. He says:

> One of the goats was bound with scarlet (between its horns), and driven by the people out of the camp into the wilderness, amid cursing, and spitting, and pulling and piercing, being thus marked with all the signs of the Lord's own passion. . . (*Against Marcion* 3.7.7; cf. *Against the Jews* 14.7).

Justin Martyr (*Dial* 40) and Cyril of Jerusalem give a similar interpretation.

Within the last two decades the sacrificial aspect of Christ's death and the idea of Jesus as scapegoat have been questioned by the anthropologist René Girard and others.[60] Girard discusses sacred violence in religion and literature and traces the sacrificial system, and particularly the scapegoat ritual, back to the effort of communities to reduce conflict and mimetic rivalry. He sees sacrifice as collective murder.[61] He avers that the "victimage mechanism" is the basis of religion.[62] Societies seek to resolve mimetic rivalry, which might reach a disastrous intensity.[63] To this end they often transfer the violence onto an animal or person.[64] In this way the community strengthens its unity at the expense of a victim that cannot defend itself, cannot wreak vengeance or cause fresh conflict.[65] Normally only an arbitrary victim can implement this role.[66] The victim breaks the cycle of violence. It acquires a sacred character in that it is "held responsible for the renewed calm in the community and for the disorder that preceded this return. It is even believed to have brought about its own death."[67] However, the effect of the ritual is only temporary and thus there must be repetition of the sacrifice.[68] This vengeful imitation might be perpetuated through generations.[69] As Burton Mack states:

> It is "generative" or collective violence that can transform the "monstrous double" (veneration and rejection, mimesis and difference) into a savior. . . . Only by retaining a fictional or mythic account of the event can the community avoid the truth about itself, which would destroy it. The mythic account casts the victim as savior and the event of his [*sic*] death as sacrifice. Rituals of sacrifice are instituted to substitute for the real thing. Thus the circle closes.[70]

We can see this principle at work especially in the ritual vis-à-vis the scapegoat.[71] This victim is seen to satisfy vengeance, not only human vengeance but also divine.[72] Thus the

> supernatural disguises themselves have a role in protecting human beings from their own violence. By linking an infraction with the notion of divine vengeance rather than with intestine rivalries, religion provides a twofold defense against them: it envelops them in an imposing mystery, and guards against the mistrust and suspicions that would inevitably result from a less mythic view of the threat they pose.[73]

When, however, Girard turns to the Christian Scriptures to examine the death of Jesus, he opines that the Gospels "only speak of sacrifices in order to reject them." He quotes Matthew 5:23-24 to support this.[74] He further avers that the Gospels never suggest that Jesus' death is a sacrifice although it does bring salvation to humankind.[75] *So the Gospels disengage themselves from the scapegoat phenomenon.* They force the founding mechanism to become visible and thus prevent its repetition.[76] Girard repudiates the idea of God requiring the death of his beloved Son; rather the New Testament (save for the Apocalypse) presents a God "who is foreign to all forms of violence".[77]

> Thus mankind [*sic*] no longer has to base harmonious relationships on bloody sacrifices, ridiculous fables of a violent deity, and the whole range of mythological cultural formations.[78]

We cannot see the Father of Jesus as one who is not only violent but

> . . . of unequalled violence, since he not only requires the blood of the victim
> who is close to him . . . but he also envisages taking revenge upon the whole of
> mankind for a death that he both required and anticipated.[79]

There is no secret agreement between the Father and the Son with
regard to self-sacrifice.[80] Rather, the redemptive aspect of the passion lies
on a different plane.[81] Jesus himself directed all his actions against violence, but in pursuing this course,

> Jesus himself stands accused of unnecessary violence, offensive language,
> immoderate use of polemics, and failure to respect the "freedom" of his inter-
> locutors.[82]

He is ready to go to death for his convictions and to reveal a God of love
and friendship, not of violence. Jesus does become a victim but his death is
planned by human beings, not God.

> It is absolute fidelity to the principle defined in his own preaching that con-
> demns Jesus. There is no other cause for his death than the love of one's neigh-
> bor lived to the very end, with an infinitely intelligent grasp of the constraints
> it imposes. "Greater love has no man than this, that a man lay down his life for
> his friends" (John 15:13).[83]

The *people, not God,* choose him as a scapegoat. Girard remarks on the
words of Caiaphas about one person dying for the nation in this light
(John 11:47-53).[84] Girard sees the sacrificial aspect of Christianity only in
the Epistle to the Hebrews.[85] The present writer must add that the Epistle
to the Hebrews, deliberately or not, omits all reference to the scapegoat
when it discusses Jesus fulfilling the high priestly office on the Day of
Atonement.[86]

However, it is not only anthropologists who have questioned the sacrificial nature of Jesus' death and especially the ideology of the scapegoat.
Schwager[87] answers *Violence and the Sacred,* 1977, but he writes before
Girard's *Things Hidden from the Foundation of the Earth,* 1987. Schwager
points out that, even though many acts of violence (more than 600 passages) occur in the Old Testament, there is much condemnation of violence against human beings in the law and the prophets.[88] Then he turns to
the question of the violence of God.[89] He admits that approximately 1,000
passages speak of God's violent anger[90] but this is always a consequence of
human deeds, and God does not appear to take pleasure in killing.[91]
Schwager also admits that mimetic rivalry does play an important role in
the Old Testament.[92] He also demonstrates the prophetic objection to hyp-
ocritical worship including sacrifice. Sacrifice alone cannot lead to God.[93]
He admits that there are many texts that show enemies uniting against an

individual, but he does not find sufficient evidence of the projection of collective guilt onto an individual.[94] Rather, in many texts it is God who
comes to the aid of the person in distress and unmasks the violence of the
mob,[95] so the process of revelation overcomes human violence.[96] He finds
the Isaiah Servant passages unclear, whether God transfers the crimes of
many onto the Servant or whether the people themselves do so.[97] However,
it is the Christians, not the Jews, who assign a special significance to the
Servant of Yahweh.[98] Schwager questions Girard's hermeneutics with
regard to the New Testament.[99] He particularly states that, unlike Girard's
scapegoat, Jesus is not a random victim. The actual impetus for the violence unleashed against Jesus was his "exalted claims about himself,"[100]
according to John's Gospel his claim to be Son of God.[101] Thus, although
Girard is right to some extent, his views need to be modified.

The concept of Jesus as scapegoat is losing favor in the present time
and, as we shall see, there is renewed effort to come to grips with the suffering of Christ and the idea that this suffering was willed by God and a
sacrifice for the sake of the people.

The result of sacrifice, propitiation, and expiation[102] was atonement or
reconciliation (*katallagē*). The blood of the victim was thought to convey
atoning power thus reestablishing right relationships with God. Earlier
writers spoke about the broken relationship as the wrath of God, but today
we should speak instead of human alienation. There is no need for God to
reconcile him or herself to humankind. Reconciliation effects a change of
heart and creates a personal and often intimate relationship with God.[103]

### Example and/or the Moral Theory

A very different theory of redemption, namely, the "moral theory" that
Christ is our supreme example or role model, was propounded by Peter
Abelard.[104] Abelard was a highly controversial figure who expounded the
doctrine of atonement in his commentary on Romans. He says:

> Thus our redemption is that loftiest love inspired in us by the passion of
> Christ, which not only frees us from the slavery of sin, but also gives us the
> true freedom of the sons of God, that we may be wholly filled not with fear,
> but with love of him who has displayed such grace to us. . . . He testifies, there-
> fore, that he came to extend among men this true liberty of love (on Rom.
> 3:26). It is to be noted that the Apostle here clearly expresses the mode of our
> redemption through the death of Christ, viz., when he says that he died for us
> to no other end than that true liberty of love might be propagated in us,
> through that loftiest love which he displayed to us (on Rom. 5:5).

But Abelard ran the risk of being accused of Pelagianism, that is, the
belief that a person can take the initial steps towards salvation by his or her
own efforts rather than divine grace. Another theologian, Peter Lombard
(1100–1160), tried to reconcile the older theories with those of Abelard. He

rejected the idea of God's attitude being unchangeable (immutable). Thomas Aquinas (1225–1274) shows knowledge of the three main theories: Christ as a sin offering, Christ as taking on our sinful nature, and Christ considered as a "sinner." However, he distinguished between the curse of guilt and the curse of penalty. Christ suffered the curse of guilt because many of his contemporaries saw him as guilty and the curse of penalty because he assumed mortality.

## Liberation Theology

There are three contemporary approaches to redemption that are engaging the attention of many scholars today, namely, liberation, feminist, and ecological theology. They seem to be more attractive to the modern person. Each of these sees Jesus as the great liberator. The chief biblical texts on which these theologies are founded are: (1) the exodus tradition (often designated the "first redemption"); (2) the rescue and restoration after the Babylonian exile; (3) Luke 4:16-30, Jesus' inaugural homily (according to Luke) in which he proclaims himself as redeemer or liberator for the oppressed.[105]

In these models there is a concentration not only on the passion and death of Jesus but upon his entire ministry, his healing and teaching, and his empathy with the oppressed of every station.[106] These are all essential elements in the process of redemption, whereby God brings us to the fullness of salvation. In these theologies, Jesus is seen as the friend of sinners and of the underprivileged. The theology of the cross is alive in contemporary confessors and martyrs, men and women. Liberation theology is a critical reflection on historical praxis in the light of the Word. E. Dussel explains it as

> a rational consequence of prophecy, which springs from reality, human, social, historical, for contemplating from a worldwide point of view the reports of injustice which obtain from the center to the periphery of the impoverished population.[107]

Here there is no trace of appeasement and satisfaction of an aggrieved God, nothing of the rights of the devil, no scapegoat theory, and little emphasis on punishment and ritual sacrifice. However, "ransom," in the sense of rescue from socially, economically, and spiritually underprivileged situations; restoration of the dignity of the human person; and just distribution of wealth and land resources are the central issues. God shows an option for the poor. So the liberation theologian appeals to God's great deeds in rescuing the chosen people from slavery in Egypt, from deportation to Babylon; and she or he emphasizes Jesus' prophetic role as healer and seeker of justice. Here she or he finds the model for redemption in the contemporary world. Jesus is seen as a friend of the poor.[108]

Thus in liberation theology injustice is rethought in the light of the faith and the earthly life of Jesus and of the first Christians. It encompasses both human sciences and a rich spirituality, often formed in base Christian communities.[109] The crucified Christ is seen in the suffering of the under-privileged, the imprisoned, the tortured, the homeless. Redemption means *befriending* the disadvantaged and helping them to realize their full poten-tial for salvation in every way. Liberation theology befriends not only the poor but also the land, sea, and air. It is, therefore, cosmic in scope.

### Feminist Theology

In 1975 much furor was caused by the depiction of a female figure on the cross in St. John the Evangelist's Church in New York.[110] This, however, was not the only such presentation of a Christa, for an Australian artist, Arthur Boyd Tucker, portrayed a young (pregnant) woman on the cross (*Crucifixion*, Shoalhaven, 1979–1980). He said, "I do not believe it is enough to say he represented all of us, I do not wish to separate the idea of suffering by allowing just the male to be seen. There has been an awaken-ing consciousness of the potential and force of women in our time."[111] There is also an African Christa available in which a child emerges from her side.[112] Later I shall discuss the crucifixion of women in antiquity, but for the present I am concerned to sketch briefly a feminist approach to redemption in general. A sacrificial death of Jesus is not only disturbing for scholars like Girard but particularly for feminists. In the provocative book *Christianity, Patriarchy, and Abuse*,[113] several women address the question of the violence of God and especially the problem of his apparent willingness to sacrifice his son on the cross. One could ask how this differs from offering a child by holocaust to the god Molech (e.g., Lev. 20:2-5). Elizabeth Bettenhausen presents us with a student's rewriting of Luke 22:54-65 (the arrest and mockery of Jesus) in which the soldiers as well as jeering at the Christa figure also rape her.[114] Bettenhausen (78) asks:

> Would we ever construe gang-rape as a salvific event for other women? What sort of a god would such an event reveal?

Whereas the present writer has certain reservations about this approach, one must grant that the point is well made. The women scholars in this book question the redemptive nature of suffering, the idealization of victimage and of passive submission, which "*reinforces the scapegoat syn-drome for women.*"[115] They question the satisfaction theory of Anselm, especially because it represents God as despotic. They also address the bloody nature of Christ's death. The real blood that is life-giving is women's blood, but this has been defamed and declared unclean; "the reli-gious imagery of Jesus' blood carries an implied, silent devaluation of women."[116] They conclude:

We must do away with the atonement,[117] this idea of a blood sin upon the whole human race which can be washed away only by the blood of the lamb. This bloodthirsty god is the god of the patriarchy who at the moment controls the whole Judeo-Christian tradition.[118]

Jesus did not choose the cross but was put to death for his convictions; his death was unjust. It was not an "acceptable sacrifice." "Suffering is never redemptive, and suffering cannot be redeemed."[119] The cross is tragedy, and God's reaction to it is grief, not triumph. Rita Nakashima Brock also questions the image of the Father who allows his only beloved Son to die on the cross. She queries the intervention of the Father with his reward of resurrection after the punishment is inflicted. Can these really be celebrated as salvific?[120] For her Jesus is the "symbol of woundedness,"[121] and it is our calling to imitate his redemptive work.

> To trust in the fragile Child, to challenge the powers of destruction with love, interdependence, care, and compassion, we must be courageous. But it is absolutely necessary—and a little Child will lead us.[122]

The contributors to this book do not repudiate all suffering, for they recognize a distinction between voluntary and involuntary suffering.[123] Jesus' suffering was a consequence of his love. It is seen

> in his passionate love of right relations and his refusal to cease to embody the power-of-relation in the face of that which would thwart it. It was his refusal to desist from radical love, not a preoccupation with sacrifice which makes his work irreplaceable.[124]

Another of the influential authors in feminist theology is Sallie McFague. In her *Models of God* she discusses God as mother (chapter 4), as lover (chapter 5), and as friend (chapter 6). Another feminist writer, who has particularly addressed the subject of redemption in her book *Feminism, Redemption and the Christian Tradition,* is Mary Grey. She refers to some of the "constants" that Schillebeeckx believes should be present in any theology of redemption:[125] (1) the relationship between "human bodiliness, nature, and the ecological environment;" (2) the dimension of mutuality and communion; (3) institutional structures; (4) time-space categories; (5) the relationship between theory and praxis and (6) between religion and parareligion. Grey's focus is on mutuality and communion. She asks how women are to be redeemed, what is authentically redemptive for them.[126] She repudiates the passive, submissive suffering of women. Grey's answer is redemption (1) from a passive acquiescence in her inferior status;[127] (2) from her position as victim;[128] and (3) by embracing responsibility.[129]

She quotes Elizabeth Cady Stanton: "Self-development is better than self-sacrifice!"[130]

Grey sees "relating" as the core of redemption, "right relationship is at the heart of the redemptive process."[131] She advocates *self-transcendence*, which means "the ability to reach out creatively beyond physical and mental boundaries in a process of evolution"[132] so that one reaches a "new existence of being." She agrees with Whitehead when he suggests that God is "the poet of the world, with tender patience leading it by his own vision of truth, beauty, and goodness."[133] However, God per se is intimately concerned with the redemption of the world, she or he is a fellow sufferer, a vulnerable God. McFague would go so far as identifying the world with the body of God.[134] Grey contends that women can play an integral part in this redemption, not by attaining power but by transforming it.[135] Women actively engage in the birth-growth-death (resurrection) cycles of nature and humanity.[136] Bonding together they can create "the cosmic matrix of novelty" in which they experience the Spirit of God.[137] They realize that darkness is a time for transformation[138] and sense the redemptive process within themselves,[139] the very presence of the suffering God.

In the last section of her book, Grey examines atonement[140] from a feminist perspective (chapter 7). She has argued that "this dynamic quality of mutuality-in-relating can be part of divine creative-redemptive energy in a process of world transformation."[141] Atonement does emphasize a movement towards wholeness and unity, and from this point of view it is acceptable. She quotes Daniel Day Williams, who would like to see the doctrine of atonement in the context of human love, which seeks to heal broken relationships. Grey thinks that process thinkers provide a framework for this. She also quotes Meland who speaks about

> renewal of the creative act in human life by which the sensitive nature which is God is made formative and fulfilling in our purpose. Whatever happens in life to open up our natures to the tendernesses of life which are of God is redemptive.[142]

Like creation, redemption brings wholeness and harmony out of chaos. We look for redemption not only through Christ but also through ourselves, seeing a redemptive force within our own lives. The Pauline living in Christ is a "refocusing of self-consciousness."[143] We need sensitivity and power, both of which are found in men and women.[144] It is not so much guilt that must be expiated as bondage from which we must be freed.[145] Sin is "the disruption of communion."[146] Redemption means the vanishing of sinful structures that cause the disruption of mutuality.[147] The life and death of Jesus does not bear a penal or sacrificial character but rather is "bound up with communication between persons."[148] If God does not suffer then he or she does not undergo the "profoundest experience of human love."

Grey sees redemption as God giving birth, for the passion of Jesus is compared to birth pangs (John 16:21-22).[149] Redemption is Rachel weeping for her children.[150] Grey seeks to renew the image of birthing with relation to redemption, but seemingly she does not connect it with the earth dying (winter) and rising (spring) or devote sufficient space to the resurrection, as Schillebeeckx does.

## *Conclusion*

We have sketched some ideas of redemption. They are contingent upon the images of God prevailing in society and church at the time of their development. We have seen on the whole a God who is severe and exacting, one who requires to be appeased or satisfied: redemption was partially conceived as a legal, economic, or sacrificial transaction. This was accompanied by a rather negative view of human nature. We discern a movement away from this, especially in liberation theology and feminism. In our contemporary world, however, we also see a desire to include the whole Trinity in a theory of redemption and to emphasize the community as well as the individual. We now turn to consider another side of God's nature and its effect on our ideas of redemption.[151]

# 2

# The *Pathos* of
# God the Father

IN THE LAST CHAPTER WE HAVE SEEN THAT MANY OF THE traditional models of redemption are not wholly compatible with contemporary thinking concerning God and salvation. One of their deficiencies is the portrayal of God mainly as judge and exacter, an honorific being standing somewhat aloof from humanity and, finally, effecting redemption through the agency of his Son whom he submits to degradation and abusive death. The remoteness of God became emphasized with the introduction into Christian theology of Greek philosophical ideas of the supreme being, which tended to isolate God as impassive, omnipotent, emotionless, wholly other. The weight of vicarious suffering was placed upon the humanity of the Son. One explanation for this "distortion" may be the loss of Semitic influence on early Christian thinking. Some Jewish-Christians must have withdrawn from the synagogue during the war between the Romans and the Jews (66–74 C.E.).[1] The fall of Jerusalem in 70 C.E. must have been followed by large emigrations to the diaspora. But the decisive separation between church and synagogue came during the second rebellion against Rome (132–135 C.E.), for many accepted its leader, Bar Cochba, as Messiah. Christians could not consent to this. Had Semitic influence continued in the church, perhaps we should have had a very different soteriology.

## *God's* Pathos

The suffering, or *pathos,* of God is certainly found within the Hebrew Scriptures. Here we meet a God who is empathetic with his people, on intimate terms with many of their leaders, involved in the nation's pain and joy, a constant helper of the unfortunate, e.g., Cain, Noah, Abraham, Hagar, Sarah, and Joseph. This is eminently clear in the exodus narrative and in God's concern for the Babylonian exiles in the sixth century B.C.E.

Here is a God who can laugh, weep, rejoice, mourn, show divine wrath,[2] and "repent"; who is designated "bridegroom," "healer," "Father," "Mother," as well as divine warrior, judge, and many other epithets.

### Heschel's Concept of the Pathos of God

In his classic study on the prophets, Abraham Heschel[3] has discussed with acumen and sensitivity the *pathos* of the God of Israel. It is the prophets who are in touch with and communicate to the people the very *pathos* of God, the divine intimacy with humanity and the world. There are several important observations to be made with reference to God's *pathos*. God is deeply affected by what happens in the world; this is not an irrational emotive response, but rather a purposeful, free act of God, wherein God knits together *pathos* and *ethos*. God is the God of justice. Therefore his or her *pathos* is ethical and personal.[4] God freely chooses to become involved in human history and has a stake in the destiny of the chosen people.[5] Heschel states:

> Never in history has man [*sic*] been taken as seriously as in prophetic thinking. Man is not only an image of God; he is a perpetual concern of God. The idea of *pathos* adds a new dimension to human existence. Whatever man does affects not only his own life, but also the life of God insofar as it is directed to man. The import of man raises him beyond the level of mere creature. He is consort, a partner, a factor in the life of God.[6]

*Pathos* is the bridge between God's nature, as wholly other and mysterious, and humanity. It is the meeting point of eternity and history, and it is through God's *pathos* that there is a lively encounter between God and humanity. This idea of the deliberate *pathos* of God for the world is closely associated with the covenant. The covenant relation is more than contract. It is an affectionate relationship between God and man and woman. So *pathos* represents the divine will.[7] Heschel[8] asks, "What hidden bond exists between the word of wrath and the word of compassion, between 'consuming fire' and 'everlasting love'?" *Pathos* is also one of the basic meanings of *ruaḥ*, Spirit. It is *pathos*.[9] The concept of God's ability to suffer broadens our idea of the image and likeness of God; human beings are a mirror that reflects both God's joy and God's pain, divine exaltation and divine humiliation. It is not only the humanity of Christ that suffers with regard to our redemption but the very being of God per se. The suffering is one of anguished love.

### Miles's Biography of God

I had completed this manuscript before the publication date (April 14, 1995) of Jack Miles's book, *God, A Biography*,[10] but I was able to add some remarks to my text. In a sprightly and captivating style Miles presents a *lit-*

*erary biography* of God culled from the Hebrew Scriptures. Miles feels that it is legitimate to attempt this, for through being in the image and likeness of God, we humans may attempt to gain some understanding of the divine nature and comportment as we seek to know others through biography. He avers, "After God has been understood in his multiplicity, in short, he needs to be imagined again in his riven and difficult unity."[11] Miles (28) claims that God made the world because he wanted humanity, wanted a self-image; for the God of Israel had no family, spouse, social life among other gods and goddesses as in other religions. Miles sees God, then, as a mixture of strength and weakness. God's covenant bond with Abraham is a fertility pact and a contractual relationship (243–245, *pace* Heschel), not personal and affective, although God does become a friend or benefactor of Abraham and his family, e.g., the women in the family and Joseph. Miles (67) calls this God's "domestication." Indeed, in the Hebrew Scriptures God does not engage in a "private life"; all his actions are oriented toward humankind. God has "no history, no genealogy, no past. . . ."[12] As he engages in war for his people, he is transformed into the divine warrior, a liberator, a lawgiver. But a crisis occurs for God in the defeat of his people by the Babylonians and subsequent exile. Has God failed? Miles asks what effect the defeat of the covenant partner had upon God per se. Through the prophets we see the agitation, the inner tensions of God.[13]

> Like a gifted and resourceful warrior-statesman, he labors under extreme duress to produce something from within himself that may be relevant to a crushing external crisis. . . . He who had no history at the start, now has a powerfully suggestive history. He must mine it aggressively, and he does.[14]

He calls the prophets to his assistance. They will demonstrate God's *pathos* to the people. Miles opines that it is through the text of Isaiah that we see God entering "most deeply and recklessly into himself, providing the most searching inventory of his own responses to the agony occasioned in his own life by the agony he[15] has inflicted on his chosen people."[16] God searches for new ways and finds them in teaching his people his uniqueness, insisting on mystery as a source of power and holiness. In a sense, the defeat of the people has shown God his own identity. He approaches his people in power but also most spectacularly in great tenderness;[17] he has a new awareness of the pain, doubts, and fears of mortals. Miles claims that the God of Israel has not really *loved* until this point; with the Exile he undergoes an emotional transformation. God also becomes more androgynous.[18] The covenant relationship reaches a new intensity. So Miles would see God growing closer to humanity through his or her *pathos* for the covenant partner. There is no doubt that the God of the Hebrew Scriptures is personal and relational:

. . . the total absence from the conclusion of the *Tanakh* of any impersonal alternative to the personal God is undeniable. The action right down to the last page of the collection begins with God or with human beings. There is no third alternative: no Fate, no Nature, no Cosmos, no Ground of All Being.[19]

And this is to God's advantage as well as ours. The way of humanity is shot through with the *pathos* of God. The way of the God of Israel lies in the "bundle of life" that she or he shares with the divine self-image, the chosen people.

In Heschel and Miles—to mention only two names—creation and redemption find their origin in the *pathos* of God. It is not the capricious *pathos* of the pagan gods and goddesses, but a consequence of God's freedom. The images of Yahweh as friend, lover, and parent convey this. Heschel contrasts the Stoic concept of *homo apatheticus*[20] with the Jewish concept of *homo sympatheticus* He speaks about the "bipolar theology of the covenant." It is the *ruaḥ* of Yahweh who inspires human beings with the *pathos* or empathy of God.

### Kuhn, the Rabbis, and the Pathos *of God*

The rabbis continue the study of the *pathos* of God. Kuhn's work[21] bears witness to the constant tradition of God's lamentation and grief in the Bible and rabbinic literature. God mourns over Adam's fall,[22] over Cain,[23] over the destruction of the world by the flood,[24] and so on. Indeed, God is inconsolable on three occasions in salvation history; the destruction of humanity in the flood, the drowning of the Egyptians (N.B.: not God's chosen people) in the Reed Sea, and the destruction of the first temple. God rejoices over those who leave Egypt but mourns over the Ephraimites who remain in Egypt.[25] God's grief is shown, too, on the occasion of the worship of the golden calf,[26] over the death of Aaron's sons, over the Israelites in the desert, and over the death of Moses. God is equally disconsolate over the destruction of the Second Temple and the exile, indeed, she or he is like a mother mourning over her daughter.[27] God's weeping over Israel is unceasing. It is expressed most dramatically in the mourning of the Shekinah over the loss of the temple.[28] Jerusalem, the beloved city, makes God and, indeed, all creation weep. God weeps also over the catastrophes suffered by the rabbis. He does not rejoice in the death of an evil person. He mourns over violent death. God's grief will continue in the eschatological age. The mourning of God may be inarticulate or a verbal lamentation; in silence, with bereavement rituals;[29] or with gestures of formal mourning.

### Goldberg, the Shekinah, and Pathos

Goldberg's work[30] comprises an excellent collection of texts from rabbinic sources on the Shekinah. The Shekinah is essentially the feminine aspect of God. Of particular interest to us are her wandering in the desert,[31] her withdrawal from the sanctuary[32] and the reasons for this,[33] the Shekinah in exile,[34] and her sufferings. She becomes, as it were, a slave with the Israelites, involved in the struggles of the community and of the individual, both in Egypt and the desert, and in their redemption.[35] In the second part of his book Goldberg speaks about the etymology of the word Shekinah, the varying concepts of her, and analogous terms for her, e.g., Holy Spirit, glory, warrior. He then addresses the concept of the Shekinah in past salvation history and in the time of the rabbis, and concludes with the eschatological aspect.

The theology of the Shekinah presumes a "self-differentiation" in God per se. In the Shekinah, God, as it were, cuts him or herself off from him or herself. The cause of this rift is God's passion for freedom. God gives humankind the freedom of dissent. Redemption is the repair of this rift. Further, the rabbinic and kabbalistic theology of the Shekinah describes the self-humiliation of God. In fact, there is a series of divine self-humiliations in creation, in the slavery in Egypt, and in exile. God accommodates him or herself to human frailty.

> The idea of the Shekinah includes these three aspects: the present *indwelling* of the Lord in Israel; the form assumed by the *condescension* of the Eternal One; and the *anticipations* of the glory of the One who is to come.[36]

God can be described as the "ransom" for Israel.[37] In this way the *glory of God* (the Shekinah) *is intimately linked with the suffering of God.*[38]

### *The* Pathos *of God and the Holocaust*

The importance of Shekinah theology for the contemporary world, and especially for an understanding of the Holocaust, is expounded in a recent book by Michael E. Lodahl, *Shekhinah Spirit.* Lodahl addresses anti-Judaic tendencies in Christianity, especially the question of their complicity in the Holocaust. He focuses on the Spirit as "a way of talking about God as 'near' or in active relationship to creation, and especially to humanity."[39] How can this Spirit be present in the concentration camps? He believes that we can come to a greater understanding of God and the problem of evil by a study of Holocaust theologians and thinkers. He selects three for his own study: Martin Buber, Arthur Cohen, and Emil Fackenheim.

The Spirit (*ruah*, Shekinah) is God's presence in the world. Humankind created in the image and likeness of God means humanity's awareness of and relationship to God's presence. It is a "dynamic, pneumatic giftedness."[40] But the *ruah* also has a dark and ambiguous character. In post-biblical Judaism this is expressed by the Shekinah, who is closely associated with the chosen people. It is the Shekinah who, as we have seen, is God's intimate presence and who accompanies Israel in times of crisis and distress—especially in exile and "God's exilic suffering *in relationship to, and together with Israel.*"[41] A phrase used by the rabbis is "the confinement of the Shekinah," (*tsimtsum ha-Shekhinah* which means the "concentration of God's presence in a particular place"[42]). God is in the world and is experienced as a lure towards wholeness and harmony, offering us new and surprising possibilities.[43] He is the "One Who Calls, ever beckoning creation to new and higher possibilities of complexity and harmony."[44] The Shekinah is *incognita* "quietly and subliminally alluring creation forward."[45] God calls human beings to be his "helpmates," and indeed to *mutual redemption*. Mutual redemption becomes especially important in kabbalistic Judaism.

Mystical Judaism elaborated the concept of the *Shekhinta b'Galuta*, the Shekinah in exile, and hence in the Kabbalah, "a hermeneutic of exile displaced the dominant rabbinic hermeneutic of certainty and divine power."[46] In this way the dark and ambiguous aspect of the Shekinah was revealed. Lodahl quotes Gershom Scholem: "[Most Kabbalists] have a strong sense of the reality of evil and the dark horror that is about everything living. They do not, like the philosophers, seek to evade its existence with the aid of a convenient formula; rather do they try to penetrate its depth."[47] This hermeneutic replaces the impassible transcendent deity with one who is dynamic, passable, complex, and relational. Active emanations (the *sefirot*) flow from this deity. The attributes of the deity are many, both male and female, and through these, human beings perceive God. "For the kabbalists, then, God's consciousness was an ever-expanding, ever-deepening interconnection of what Harold Bloom has called 'relational events.'"[48]

There is, then, an intermingling of human and divine, both sharing in tragedy as well as triumph. Human sin affects the divine life and causes a certain self-alienation in God. This is expressed through the myth of the exile of the Shekinah. The Shekinah becomes divorced from the other *sefirot*.[49] So Adam's sin is of cosmic proportions and it

> *inter-rupts* the relational flow within God and between God and creation. The Shekinah [*sic*], God's [feminine] presence, by Adam's sin is sundered from the sefirotic union and banished from the Garden, abandoned and vulnerable. Adam, also banished from the Garden, stumbles upon the Shekinah [*sic*] and together they go into exile.[50]

Hence the dark side (*sitra ahra*) of God is exposed and, as it were, separated from God's *ḥesed*; the divine love is spurned. This causes havoc in the world. The coming of the Messiah brings hope for a recovery of cosmic harmony.

Lodahl illustrates these theories from the teaching of Isaac Luria (1534–1572). The universe exists through the *tsimtsum* of God, that is, the "shrinkage" of God, as if he or she held back his or her breath (*ruaḥ*) and became *dyspnoeic.* God withdraws to give others freedom and integrity, and this "self-*di*vestment, a divestment of both full presence and absolute power," begins with the act of creation. God must withdraw to allow the other to "stand forth" in freedom and integrity.[51] All the cosmos is in exile (*galut*) and the sparks of the Shekinah are scattered abroad. God wanders between presence and absence; the metaphor "postponed presence" is given to this state. "God is 'captivated,' as it were, by God's own shattered, exilic world."[52] Yet his transcendence obtains. This state of affairs necessitates human and divine cooperation in the redemptive process. *Tikkun* (restoration) means the human response[53] that will "allow" God to repair the cosmic rift and to unite the Shekinah.

Lodahl sees the Holocaust as an "interruption *within* interruption."[54] The *shoah* (holocaust) is the Shekinah, maimed, raped, left for dead.[55] Although Buber does not fully discuss the exile of the Shekinah, the myth seems to have been for him a symbol of God's immanence and solidarity with those who suffer. She is

> the tragic lover wandering through a broken world, trying to find her way back to reunion and fulfillment. Buber's neo-Hasidic portrayal of God is of one who shares in the absurdities and horrors of our world.[56]

Human beings play their part in redemption by *kavvana,* devotion of the heart to God. It is love that causes both suffering and healing. Human sin causes the exile of God's glory; human love can help to restore it. Fackenheim finds in the absent presence of God the voice of command. In this he modifies the older concept of the absolute power of God. A command invites a response to *share* power. "It awaits the obedient response of the hearers, and so accords them a power of their own in the matter of effecting redemption."[57] His or her command at Auschwitz was to live. Arthur Cohen would say that the efficacy of God's speech depends upon the human response, "I will" (*hinneni*). Process theologians would speak of God's persuasive power, God as poet of the world, with tender patience leading it by his vision of truth, beauty, and goodness. This emphasizes God as a supremely relational being and redemption as a relational process, God co-opting the active response of humans. To quote Heschel again, God is unique "the circle, all-embracing and involved."

## The Pathos of God in Christian Thought

### The Early Church

While the targumists, the rabbis, and the Jewish mystics were elaborating the concept of the *pathos* of God and the theology of the suffering Shekinah, Christians, on the whole, turned away from their Jewish heritage and incorporated the Aristotelian and Platonic views of the distant and impassive deity into much of their theology. For the ancient Greek, "passion" was frightening, undignified, mysterious, probably demon-inspired, an experience where a person lost self-control. If *pathos* were unworthy of the human being, how much more unworthy of God, the Supreme Being. So for many philosophers, God was free from pain, pleasure, and emotion. For the Stoics and the Cynics the ideal person strove to attain complete freedom from all emotion. The goal of the Stoic sage was *apatheia*, but the goal of the prophets was *sympatheia*. For them true passion is equated with the Spirit (*ruah*) who inspires persons to great deeds performed with *pathos*.

One can see the early church struggling with this problem. Some early and important Christian writers affirm the possibility of God in relationship to the passion (*pathos*) of Christ. For instance, Clement of Alexandria (c. 150–215 C.E.) declared: "Believe, O man, in man and God: believe, O man in the living God that suffered and is worshiped" (*Protrepticus* 10.106.4). Ignatius of Antioch (c. 35–107 C.E.), when faced with persecution and martyrdom for his faith, prayed: "Permit me to be an imitator of the passion of my God" (*Letter to the Romans* 6.3). Similarly Tatian (c. 160 C.E., *Oration to the Greeks* 13.3) and Melito of Sardis (d. c. 90; *Frag.* 7) spoke of the suffering deity. Theopassianism[58] (the suffering of God) was adopted by certain Monophysites,[59] and it was said that Peter Fullo,[60] the Patriarch of Antioch, altered the Trisagion so that it read: "Holy God, Holy Mighty, Holy Immortal, thou who for our sakes was crucified (*ho staurōtheis di'hēmas*), have mercy on us."[61] This formula was quite widespread in the fifth century, and even the Emperor Justinian issued an edict in its favor. This occurred after the Council of Rome (382 C.E.) had declared in canon 166:

> If any one says that in the passion of the cross it is God himself who felt the pain and not the flesh and the soul which Christ, the Son of God had taken to Himself . . . he is mistaken (Council of Rome, 382, Canon 166).

Indeed, Patripassianism,[62] a Monarchian heresy propounded by Noetus,[63] which declared that God suffered, and Theopassianism,[64] which tended to confuse the two natures of Christ, were repudiated by the certain Christian writers. For example, Augustine argues: "The Father, indeed, suffered not, but the suffering of the Son was the work of the Father and the Son (*Sermon* 2.8)." So an increasing number of Christians, especially as theology was elaborated, postulated the impassibility of God. Those who objected to the suffering of God were often influenced by the Aristotelian concept of the "unmoved mover." Impassibility was predicated of God because suffering was thought to arise from the tension between desire and capacity. The compound nature of the body led to passions and infirmities, and change was thought to imply imperfection. God was considered self-sufficient, impassible, and without "emotion."

### Contemporary Thought

However, today we must ask whether the idea of the impassibility of God undermines the integrity of the incarnation.[65] Could a God of love remain untouched and uninvolved in the suffering of his or her creatures and creation? The incarnation gives us what appears to be a radically new insight into the being of God. Jüngel states:

> Revelation is that event in which the *being of God* itself comes to word. In revelation, therefore, we have to do with *one* internally-distinguished being of God. The *oneness* of this internally-distinguished being of God is grounded in the fact that revelation is "not another over against God" but "a reiteration of God." This reiteration denotes the fact that in God's taking form God is in his revelation his own double. God's taking form is thus not an *accidens* of God but an event: an *event* which presupposes a self-distinction in God, "something new in God, a self-distinction of God from himself, a being of God in a mode of existence . . ." in which he can also exist for us. . . .[66]

So the passion of Christ is a further expression of the *pathos* of God.

Jürgen Moltmann[67] addresses the question of the apathy or passibility of God. He speaks about the absolute subject in the concepts of nominalism and idealism:

> Impassible, immovable, united and self-sufficient, the deity confronts a moved, suffering and divided world that is never sufficient for itself. For the divine substance is the founder and sustainer of this world of transient phenomena; it abides eternally, and so cannot be subject to this world's destiny.[68]

If God does not suffer, then Christ's passion is only human tragedy, not divine, and God becomes "the cold, silent and unloved heavenly power. But that would be the end of the Christian faith."[69] But we can argue that God is not subject to the same kind of suffering as human beings. It must be different in scope and quality. God suffers because of the love that is "the superabundance and overflowing of his being."[70] Moltmann points out that Origen (*Commentary on the Letter of Paul to the Romans* 7.9) appears to be the first to recognize this.[71] But to predicate suffering of God, we must speak in trinitarian language; we must consider an "inner-trinitarian suffering."[72]

We cannot measure the psychological or spiritual dimension of the suffering of God in the crucifixion of Christ. Rather God's suffering is the *ek-static* suffering of God in the sufferings of humankind, not as a necessary co-distribution of suffering but as a free act of love.[73] God takes on our godforsakeness until the resurrection, when there will be the ultimate and final realization of presence-without-absence projecting toward the consummation of God's kingdom as the joyful, all-pervasive *ek-stasis* of God in communion with the whole of his creation.[74]

### Does the Suffering of God Precede the Incarnation?

Moltmann[75] turns to the work of Unamuno.[76] For Unamuno the *congoja* (anguish) of Christ shows his essential nature. This is portrayed in Unamuno's poem, "The Christ of Velázquez."[77] Unamuno explains his concept of the infinite sorrow of God. God "envelops our anguish with his immeasurable anguish, which knows no end."[78] Only through pain can we and God become compassionate, empathetic. This introduces again the concept of self-differentiation within the godhead and can be understood only in trinitarian terms. Sorrow is deeper than pain.[79] There can be no true happiness without sorrow. But it must not be a sorrow that lacks hope. It must be bound up inseparably with joyful exaltation of the resurrected Christ. Hope is the redeeming joy of God. We anticipate the consummation of our salvation "in the feast of God's eternal joy and in the dance of those who have been redeemed from sorrow."[80] Unamuno argues against the God of the rationalists, the *ens summum*, the *primum movens*. For Unamuno, one gains knowledge of God only by love and suffering. He states:

> Definition kills him [God], for to define is to impose boundaries, to limit—and it is impossible to define the absolutely indefinable. This God is lacking in inner amplitude; he does not form a society within himself. This lack was superseded by the vital revelation and belief in the Trinity, which makes God a society and even a family in Himself, and no longer a pure individual. . . . An isolated person ceases to be a person—for whom should he love?[81]

Unamuno[82] confesses that he believes in God as a friend, he feels the breath of his affection and his intangible hand. He has an inner sense of a special providence that guides his destiny, for a person can feel the universe calling out to him or her. For Unamuno, love and suffering are interwoven—God suffers when we suffer; God gives us God's love but expects love in return. Only one who suffers can be human. Only the God who suffers can be divine.[83] Suffering is the "substance of life," the "root of personality."[84] Fate is the "brotherhood of love and suffering."[85]

God's suffering is inescapably bound up with the divine gift of freedom to humankind. History is the tragedy of freedom, not of doom. This freedom is traced back to God's longing for humanity, the yearning of the lover (or friend) for the beloved. "This longing of God's [*sic*] is a movement in God himself, which leads him out of himself and brings him to his counterpart, his 'Other'—man [*sic*]."[86] Tragedy begins within the godhead, for "consistent monism must fall a victim to acosmism. . . ."[87] In this way it becomes impossible "to assert the tragic destiny of the Son of God and his expiatory death without at the same time admitting movement in the divine life."[88] But this does not predicate deficiency in God, rather, assuredly, creative fullness. One can call it the "thirst of God" (Julian of Norwich, *Revelations* 31). Moltmann comments further:

> The love of God for his Other must already be presupposed as a matter of course in the love of God for his Son. The creation of the world is nothing other than "a history of the divine love between God and his Other self." This means that God's love for the Son also potentially presupposes the Son's *incarnation*. The incarnation of God's Son is not an answer to sin. *It is the fulfillment of God's eternal longing to become man* [sic] *and to make of every man* [sic] *a god out of grace; an "Other" to participate in the divine life and return the divine love.*[89]

We cannot interpret all suffering as a punishment for sin, but rather it is the result of love and freedom. Only love explains innocent suffering. God's *pathos* precedes human sin—the "fall."

However, we must, for a moment, consider God's own freedom. Karl Barth declares: "He [God] could have remained satisfied with Himself and with the impassible glory and blessedness of His own inner life. But he did not do so. He elected man [sic] as a covenant-partner."[90] God chooses not to be self-sufficient. But this power of choice is not in the nature of lordship and power, rather it is a freedom that invites community and fellowship.

> Here "free" has the same etymological root as "FRIENDLY"; its cognates in meaning are "kind," "to be well-disposed," "to give pleasure." . . . This freedom consists of the mutual and common participation in life, and A COMMUNICATION IN WHICH THERE IS NEITHER LORDSHIP NOR SERVITUDE. In their reciprocal participation in life, people become free beyond the limitation of their own individuality. . . . His freedom is vulnerable love.[91]

Like a parent, God allows adult children choice and self-determination. But the *pathos* of God is not predicated on his or her nature but on God's relationship to humanity. In this way God shows God's love, which may be described as "the passionate self-communication of the good."[92] Love draws one out of oneself. God's love is trinitarian and in engendering the Son she or he shows the *love of like for like.* One must see the redemption as "*the feast of the divine joy.*"[93] I add, this is a feast to which host and guest have contributed in mutual love. The trinitarian communion is eucharistic in nature.

### Does the Suffering of God Precede Creation?

Rolt[94] argued that God suffers from eternity. James Hinton, commenting on the Johannine statement, "He who has seen me has seen the Father," says, "If God would show us Himself, He must show us Himself as a sufferer, as taking what we call pain and loss. These are His portion; from eternity He chose them. The life Christ shows us is the eternal life."[95] Molt-mann (32) adds: "Consequently Golgotha is the inescapable revelation of his nature in a world of evil and suffering." Love converts "brute force" into "vital energy."[96] God suffers what contradicts God's own nature, e.g., chaos at creation. Pain in the Trinity is transformed into glory. Moltmann dis-cusses the subject further in *The "Crucified" God*.[97] Here he argues that we must understand the crucifixion in the context of the relationship between God the Father and God the Son. This death both affects and "expresses God," it is a "statement about God himself [*sic*]."[98] Further, the divinity of Jesus is revealed in the cross and his humanity in his exaltation.[99] But God the Father also suffers, and God's suffering is the "infinite grief of love," which is just as important as the physical death. It demonstrates the empa-thy between the Father and the Son, their mutuality in will.[100]

> In the cross, Father and Son are most deeply separated in forsakenness, and at the same time are most inwardly one in their surrender. What proceeds from this event between Father and Son is the Spirit which justifies the godless, fills the forsaken with love and even brings the dead alive, since even the fact that they are dead cannot exclude them from this event of the cross; the death in God also includes them.[101]

This has a profound effect on our approach to salvation—the Spirit through abandonment reaches out to forsaken persons. God's self-humil-iation reaches its abyss in the crucifixion, and especially in the cry of aban-donment of Christ on the cross. Christ took upon himself all loneliness and rejection so that "all the godless and the godforsaken can experience communion with him [or her]."[102] Grief, suffering, and humiliation do not diminish the glory of God and the Shekinah but are its very core, as we shall see in the *pathos* according to John.

> Only if all disaster, forsakenness by God, absolute death, the infinite curse of damnation and sinking into nothingness is in God himself, is community with this God eternal salvation, infinite joy, indestructible election and divine life. The "bifurcation" in God must contain the whole uproar of history with-in itself.[103]

Love is an event, unconditioned and boundless.[104] God is the compan-ion, the co-sufferer. She or he offers new possibilities for humankind. Christ is more than a representative of humankind, he is a new creation, a new mode of existence.

### The Suffering of the Earth
We have reflected on the suffering of God and specifically related it to the suffering of humanity and to Christ's death on the cross. Some theolo-

gians, however, would elaborate this to include ecological tenets. Sallie McFague argues that we can speak metaphorically of the world as the body of God.[105] This is not to identify God per se as the world, just as we do not identify ourselves with our bodies. The world is the self-expression of God; as such it brings the deity into responsibility and vulnerability. God can be seen as willing to suffer with the world[106] because it, too, needs healing and restoration (cf. Rom. 8:18-25). I add that this is the very meaning of "compassion" ("suffer with"). McFague asserts: "It is a vision of salvation as wholeness, characterized not by the overcoming of differences, but by their acceptance and inclusion."[107] She also states:

> The world as God's body, then, may be seen as a way to remythologize the inclusive, suffering love of the cross of Jesus of Nazareth. In both instances (God's willingness to suffer and the crucifixion), God is at risk in human hands: just as once upon a time in a bygone mythology, human beings killed their God in the body of a man, so now we once again have that power, but, in a mythology more appropriate to our time, we would kill our God in the body of the world.[108]

God is intimately related to the world which she or he created, and God tends the world just as we care for our bodies (cf. Eph. 5:29). God is "in touch with all parts of the world through interior understanding."[109] God suffers with all those parts of creation. So the cross is not a once and for all event but is "present and permanent." It affects not only humanity but the whole of creation, as Paul says: "The creation itself will be set free from its bondage to decay, and obtain the glorious liberty of the children of God" (Rom. 8:21). On our part sin is "the refusal to be the eyes, the consciousness, of the cosmos."[110] *It is the failure to care for the world as a friend.* God also enjoys the world's happiness and ecstasy. And we, too, as with God's help we seek to redeem the earth, must hold firm the hope of the all encompassing event of the resurrection. Against this background we gain a deeper understanding of this mystery; it becomes a "worldly, present, inclusive reality."[111] Redemption is and will be a cosmic event.

## *Conclusions*

This chapter has suggested a deeper understanding of the complexity of the nature of God. It has presented a God who suffers with and anguishes over his or her people. We have seen that this is consonant with biblical and rabbinic tradition and appealing to the twentieth-century Christian. We have dealt at some length with the problems of holocaust and the "justification" of God with respect to this tragedy.[112] Much of our discussion could apply also, *mutatis mutandis,* to other cosmic catastrophes, e.g., Hiroshima. We have considered the Christian tradition and found that the suffering of God per se was accepted by many in the early church. We have remarked on God's self-humiliation in the crucifixion of Jesus. We turn now to an inquiry into the feminine aspect of the suffering or *pathos* of God.

# 3

# The *Pathos* of
# God the Mother

S AVE FOR THE RABBIS, THE TEXTS AND SCHOLARS THAT WE HAVE considered in the previous chapter implicitly associated the *pathos* of God
with the male/paternal model. We saw God's prowess, omnipotence, and
ire as well as his *angst,* his torment over his suffering people, his ecstatic
response both in anger and judgment and in tenderness. But we must ask
whether the image of God the Father is really adequate to describe the
deep *pathos* of God. The paternal model evokes the image of one whose
semen gushes forth from his body, who projects his empathy outwards,
"outside" his body. He must seek beyond himself for resources, nourishment, shelter, protection, and help for the fetus. He does not have the lux-
ury, privilege, the startling intimacy of feeling the created being within
him. He is not confronted with death before the imminence of the birth of
the child. No suckling nourishment exudes from him, and the child is fully
aware of this. In a sense the paternal model portrays one who largely loses
contact with the offspring before it has achieved independence. Perhaps
this is part of his suffering: there is a chasm between the object of his
*pathos* and himself. Surely, there is another model, one that complements
the male *pathos.* Now, therefore, we turn to another aspect of the *pathos* of
God, one less tumultuous, quieter, more delicate, and perhaps more self-
sacrificing—the maternal image. It is still God's *pathos* but in a more perspicacious sense.

## *The Image of Mother*

The mother image is one that shows the reception of life within her own
innermost being. The life force—physical, psychological, and spiritual—
enters the wet darkness of the uterus and unites with the ovum. In other
words, an unique act of creative communion takes place. The ovum wafts
through the mystery of darkness to be embedded within the very flesh of
the recipient. It is literally fed by the lifeblood of the mother, and there is

an ontological union of the mother and the child. In fact, three are present—the male element (the semen), the female element (ovum), and the Spirit, which is the lifeblood.

This is quite a spectacular image of the Trinity, the ecstasy of love meeting the nourishing immanence and abiding there with the vitality of the Spirit—flowing, communing, love-engendering within the creator herself. This Trinity, having gone forth in the ecstasy of love, abides in the mysterious darkness of the womb of the world, its presence growing, its vitality increasing until it shall burst forth upon the world of light. Conception is the image of the intercommunion between the three persons in the Trinity. In its dark world it is vulnerable. But the maternal aspect of the deity also illuminates the *pathos* of God, not only in conception but also in self-giving, immolating love. The woman and the maternal *pathos* of God must carry the child within her own person.[1] She provides protection like a walled city.[2] Her heart of flesh is one with the child. Love, warmth, and nourishment flow constantly between the two beings. The uterine walls and the amniotic fluid absorb the shock of blows and outward behavior or violence, perhaps even cushion against raucous noise. Within her own person and with her own personhood the mother cradles the one (or more!) who—according to some—is not yet accepted as a person according to the world's canon. The mother provides nourishment from her own body through the placenta. It is nourishment free of charge, already warm, digestible, medicinal, complete in every way. Mother and child are "face to face," isolated in the dark prison or crucible of the womb, the child often kicking, perhaps in protest! This could be the exilic, even holocaust, experience. When the pregnant woman has supplied all that is needful from her own flesh and blood, often at a cost to her own nutritional needs, she must face the life-and-death situation of delivery. Approximately one out of three women died in childbirth in antiquity. In this case the conception of a child often carried with it a death warrant for women. Yet because of her selflessness and the depth of her loving *pathos,* she faces the situation courageously. The mother gives birth in pain and writhing, in blood and water, in mortal fear and perennial hope. In many cultures this experience is called "giving light," *dar luz,* and so on. The new creature bursts into a realm of light, of change, of new relationships, of new fears, pains, and joys. It is a new existence and not without conflict.

And as if the mother's *pathos* were not sufficient, she must continue to rear the child. In hunger she must feed him or her from her own breast (not always pleasurably or painlessly); she must change the baby; provide him or her with warmth and comfort; train, protect, and educate him or her. She must play with the child (cf. Prov. 8:30-31). In other words she must place the baby's life before her own. She is his or her co-redeemer.

The devotion of mothers is celebrated worldwide. After all this care, she must grant the child the privilege of freedom and independence, even though the child may not make wise decisions and may fall into perilous circumstances.

Therefore, we do not compare God with a mother only in the point of giving birth to her child but also in all the sacrifice involved in rearing the child. We shall see that we may be able to approach both the *pathos* of God and the suffering of Christ from a feminine point of view. Both the Father in creation and the Son in his incarnation undergo birth pangs and give of their life substance to re-create humanity in a new mode of being. We turn now to the image of mother for God in the Scriptures.

## *The Hebrew Scriptures*

The Hebrew Scriptures have a selection of references to God as mother, wet nurse, and midwife.[3] These texts are eloquent and gain in importance once they are seen in context.

### *A Maternal View of Creation*

In Genesis 1:1 the Spirit (*ruah*, which is always feminine in gender in Hebrew), is likened to a bird brooding over chaos to transform it into creation and harmony. Augustine[4] says God "hovered" like a mother bird to give warmth to her young. Moreover, Alfonso Schökel[5] has shown how male and female mythical symbols of the deity still emerge from the texts of the Hebrew Scriptures. For example, the earth is seen as a mother who unites with the masculine heaven and generates the universe. He compares Isaiah 26:17 and Psalm 65:10-14 with Hesiod,[6] who presents God as a gardener[7] cooperating with the pregnant dew of the earth.[8] In the Hebrew text the dew is seminal and proceeds from the deity.[9] In Isaiah 26 the Lord gives new life to the dead and once more the earth is pregnant. Similar ideas occur in Deuteronomy 11:10-12 and Job 38:25-30, especially vv. 28-29:

> Has the rain a father;
> or who has begotten the drops of dew?
> Out of whose womb comes the ice,
> and who gives the hoarfrost its birth in the skies? . . .

Further Psalm 139:13, 15 portrays children as being formed in the earth and nourished at her fertile breast.[10] Schökel compares Song of Solomon 4:12, 15.[11] So the Hebrew Scriptures still suggest the masculine and feminine roles in creation. We may also compare Romans 8, where creation groans in travail awaiting redemption of humanity, which will liberate her.[12]

*Humanity Made in the Image and Likeness of God*

Genesis 1:27-28, states that God made humanity in the divine image and likeness, male and female. "Image" suggests "representation"[13] and "should not be understood as if the meaning were: not the same but only like. The Hebrew word does not carry this attenuating sense."[14] Humanity is in the image and likeness of God, that is, in the whole person, corporeally and spiritually.[15] The image of God implies partnership with God, the ability to enter into relationship with the divine. Humanity is to live in God's presence, to be the viceroy, attorney, and administrator of God's gifts.[16] Like the monarch in Egypt or Mesopotamia, humanity is the image of God: the phrases reflect the royal ideology. But one notices that the emphasis is on humanity as a whole, not only the male. There is also no exclusion of race, social status, or religion: all men and women reflect the image and likeness of God. Westermann observes (160):

> A consequence of this is that there can be no question of an "essence of man" [sic] apart from existence as two sexes. Humanity exists in community, as one beside the other, and there can only be anything like humanity and human relations where species exists in twos.

The neglected text of Sirach 17:1-18 might be called the third creation story. It speaks of humans (*anthropos*) in the image of God, although the English translation is misleading.

## *Female Redeemer*

### *God Portrayed as Mother Bird*

a. In the context of the first redemption, Exodus 19:4 speaks about God bearing Israel up on eagle wings. One obviously thinks of the female bird.[17]

b. The above text is elaborated in Deuteronomy 32:18-14: "like an eagle he [sic] stirs up his nest, over his young he flutters. He spreads his wings, he takes him [the young], he bears him up on his wings." This can refer only to the mother eagle. Compare also Psalm 17:8 and 63:8, which refer to God's protective wings.

### *God as Carrying a Child*

In Numbers 11:12-13 we read of Moses' remonstration with God, that not he (Moses) but God begot Israel and should carry them.[18]

### *God as Giving Birth*

a. Deuteronomy 32:18 has the maternal image of God in verse 18: "the Rock that begot you, . . . the God who gave you birth." "Begot" and "gave birth to" are maternal attributes.[19]

b. Isaiah 42:14[20] predicts that God's judgment (and theophany) shall be like the pangs of a woman in childbirth.[21]

> I have looked away, and kept silence,
> I have said nothing, holding myself in;
> But now I cry out like a woman in labor,
> gasping and panting.

Gruber[22] notes "how unusual is the phenomenon of a whole series of maternal expressions applied to the LORD in Isaiah 40–66." He finds four such references—Isaiah 42:14; 45:10; 49:15; 66:13—that is, at least one verse in each of the main sections of Second Isaiah. He observes with reference to Isaiah 42:14 that the prophet compares God to *both* a warrior *and* a woman giving birth within two verses (13–14). Both are specifically active, not passive, roles.[23] He also translates 14b: "I will scream like a woman in labor. I will inhale and I will exhale simultaneously. . . ." He observes[24] that the prophet describes the breathing techniques prescribed for the transition period of labor—in modern medicine according to Fernand Lamaze:[25] four to six short inhalations and then a quick exhalation through the mouth. But Gruber could have referred to texts in the ancient world, e.g., Soranus, who refers to retention of breath in order to assist labor.[26]

c. Another maternal reference is found in Isaiah 45:10: "Woe to him who asks a father, 'What are you begetting?' or a woman, 'What are you giving birth to?'" These last two texts occur in the context of God announcing the redemption of the chosen people from exile in Babylon through the hand of Cyrus. The prophet is describing a redeemer/mother. A number of images are used to express this coming salvation, but two are of interest to us. Verses 8 and 9a read:

> Let justice descend, O heavens, like dew from above,
> like the gentle rains let the skies drop it down.
> Let the earth open and salvation bud forth;
> let justice also spring up!
> I the Lord have created this.
> Woe to him who contends with his Maker. . .

The last line contains the antecedent to our verse. Thus here the Lord explicitly compares him or herself to a potter (v. 9), to a father (v. 10a), and to a mother (v. 10b). Verse 11 then confirms this interpretation by combining the two ideas of "maker" and "begetter" (male and female):

> Thus says the Lord,
> the Holy One of Israel, his maker:
> You question me about my children,
> or prescribe the work of my hands for me!

d. In Isaiah 49:15a again God compares him or herself to a mother:

> Can a mother forget her infant?
> Be without tenderness for the child of her womb?

Gruber thinks that the word "child" (Hebrew: 'ul) probably refers to a nursing infant, and he adds that this "may allude to the important role of nursing in establishing emotional 'bonding' between mother and child."[27] He also notes Gordis's[28] comment on the play on words in the second clause, which seems to indicate, "the special bond which should link mother and child by referring to the mother as raḥam 'woman,' a cognate of reḥem 'womb' and to the woman's progeny as ben-bitna 'child of her womb.'"[29] The emphasis in this text is on the fact that a woman at times may forget her child but that God will not, for God is the Mother of Israel. Stuhlmueller[30] observes that the walled city is pictured as a pregnant mother, her child safely within her womb as a city is safe within its walls.

e. The last verse in Second Isaiah[31] that refers to God as mother is: "I shall comfort you like a man whose mother comforts him, and you shall be comforted through Jerusalem" (66:13). The context of this statement from God is important. Sometimes there is a subtle shift from the image used for God and used for the people Israel; we shall find the same phenomenon in images used for Jesus and the church. The shift is important because it suggests the immanence of God within his or her people, the intimate union of the two and their partnership in suffering. This section of Isaiah begins thus:

> Before she comes to labor,
> she gives birth;
> Before the pains come upon her
> she safely delivers a male child.
> Who ever heard of such a thing,
> or saw the like?
> Can a country be brought forth in one day,
> or a nation be born in a single moment?
> Yet Zion is scarcely in labor
> when she gives birth to her children.
> Shall I bring a mother to the point of birth,
> and yet not let her child be born? says the Lord;
> Or shall I who allow her to conceive,
> yet close her womb? says your God. . . .

In this part of the text God appears to be either the procreator or the midwife.[32] Here redemption from exile is seen as childbirth—childbirth wholly reliant on God for safe delivery. However, there appears to be a subtle change in vv. 10-13. Now Jerusalem seems to be the mother (or wet nurse), the mother who has abundant breast milk for her children, who are carried in the mother's arms and fondled on her breast. Then v. 13 speaks of God as a mother comforting her son (a change of gender for Israel). The Targum adds a messianic note for v. 7 reads "as pains upon a woman in travail, her king will be revealed." It also omits the nursing image from v. 11.

f. We may also compare Micah 4:8-10:

> That you [Israel] are seized with pains
> like a woman in travail?
> Writhe in pain, grow faint,
> O daughter Zion,
> like a woman in travail . . .
> Therefore shall the Lord redeem you
> from the hand of your enemies.

Micah 5:2 refers to Zion giving birth to the One who is to come. Compare also Isaiah 54. Again, God is midwife.

g. Hosea 11:1-4 is most probably a maternal image, although a paternal or parental one is also possible. It shows God like a mother teaching her child to walk, taking her in her arms, drawing her "with human cords, with bands of love," fostering her, raising her to her cheek, and stooping down to feed her.

## God's Pathos *Towards the Infant Child*

Psalm 22:9-10 also uses maternal imagery, although not directly of God.[33] Mollenkott refers to Jesus' quotation of this psalm on the cross and observes:

> Since this Psalm . . . contains many harrowing details that well describe crucifixion, the midwife image takes on added poignancy here. We may imagine that in the hour of his own anguished "birth contractions" on the cross, Jesus tried to comfort himself by remembering that God had been the midwife drawing him out of the womb of his own mother.[34]

Jesus would hope that God in the role of midwife would help his present condition. Mollenkott also sees God playing the same role to assist creation in Romans 8:26-29 and Galatians 5:22.[35]

One notices that all the above texts have creation or redemption as their main theme; thus the authors show us a maternal aspect of the redeemer God. For our thesis, this is an excellent example of God's suffering as childbirth. We note also that the childbirth image occurs in two of the most crucial and painful times in Israel's history, the slavery in Egypt and the exile in Babylon. In these God serves both as mother and midwife. We may conclude, therefore, that the maternal redeemer figure is intimated in the major events of Israel's history. God's *pathos* is maternal as well as paternal.

## Wisdom Literature[36]

The clearest references, however, to the femininity of God are found in the wisdom literature. Proverbs 8 portrays feminine wisdom as the first begotten of God (v. 22) who was with him at creation (vv. 22-29). She was

God's craftswoman, and she is described as giving delight to God by her playing and her taking delight in humanity. The subsequent chapter presents her as a sage and teacher inviting students to her house where she prepares a banquet for them.[37] She is contrasted with Mistress Folly.[38]

### The Immanent Nature of Pathos

However, in the book of Sirach, Wisdom's prestige is greatly increased. She is part of the divine assembly (Sirach 1–7), she is an *ekstasis* from the mouth of the Most High. She is also a descending figure who freely[39] chooses Israel for her dwelling on earth. Again she invites humankind to receive nourishment from her. She is compared to luxurious vegetation[40] and flowing streams.[41] The Torah, with which she is often identified, is compared to the great rivers of Pishon, Tigris, Euphrates, Nile, and Gihon.[42] Wisdom is an even more exalted figure in the Wisdom of Solomon. In Wisdom 7:1–8:1 twenty-one (seven multiplied by three) attributes are predicated of her so that she becomes an aspect of the deity him or herself. Particularly noteworthy in this chapter are the description of her as "the aura of the might of God and a pure effusion,[43] of the glory of the Almighty" (v. 25), and "the refulgence of eternal light,[44] the spotless mirror of the power of God, the image[45] of his goodness" (v. 26).

### Wisdom as Goddess

Winston[46] has a full discussion of Wisdom 7:22b–8:1. He compares the twenty-one characteristics to the so-called *Mithras Liturgy* and the Zoroastrian *Ahuna Vairya*.[47] He also refers to the Stoic Cleanthes, who used twenty-six attributes of the deity and also the list of the heavenly sons found in the *Apocalypse of Abraham* 17.8–21, which in part parallels Sirach 7. Winston also refers to similar rabbinic texts.[48] Finally, he compares the Isis cult. Many cult names are predicated of this goddess, in fact, she is called *myrionymos* (of many names).[49] In an Oxyrhynchus papyrus[50] over twenty epithets are applied to her.[51] In his verse-by-verse commentary, Winston shows which epithets of wisdom are also attributed to other goddesses such as Demeter, Persephone, and Athene. Thus there is no doubt that wisdom was a goddess-redeemer figure for the author of the Wisdom of Solomon. Wisdom enters into holy souls and makes them friends of God and prophets.[52] Moreover, she is the redeemer of God's people, from the time of Adam through the rescue from Egypt.[53]

Corrington[54] has a succinct survey of the role of wisdom as instructor, as the source of life, as heavenly mediator, as descending to earth,[55] as incarnate in those who observe the Torah, as concerned with justice, and as savior.

Wisdom 7, however, may result from a "refinement" of the figure of

Lady Wisdom in the sapiential literature where she was most probably presented as a goddess in her own right. Lang[56] points out that Proverbs 8 portrays wisdom not only as a teacher, but also as a goddess who is judge of potentates and dwells in the presence of God.[57] Like the goddess Ishtar she "gives scepter, throne and royal power to every king."[58] The Egyptian goddesses Hathor, Isis, and Neith have a similar function. There could be a loving relationship between a sovereign and the goddess, just as there was between Solomon[59] and Lady Wisdom.[60] Wisdom was also present with God at creation, she was "brought forth by birth" before the foundation of the earth. She is the begotten of the Creator, and he cares for her like a nursemaid (Proverbs 8:30). Lang translates v. 30 as follows: "Wisdom is the child of the Creator. She is a noble ward, . . . the Creator cares for his ward like a nursemaid."[61] Again, we see God as a maternal figure. Eventually the divine status of wisdom was hidden and her place taken chiefly by the *Memra*, the Word of God, especially in the *targumim*, and as the Shekinah, the female aspect of God in rabbinic Judaism.

## Female Mother/Savior Figures in the Greco-Roman World

### Isis

In the Greco-Roman world contemporary with Jesus and the nascent church many goddesses[62] were regarded as savior figures. This is especially true of the Greek goddess Athene and the Egyptian goddess Isis,[63] who proved a great rival to Christianity. Corrington[64] quotes R. E. Witt:

> In her the believer could discern the warm affection of the bereaved wife, the tenderness of the mother suckling her baby, . . . the concern of the midwife for the safe delivery in childbirth, the sexual passion symbolized by the . . . erect phallus and by the legend that she had played the harlot for ten years at Tyre.[65]

Both cults were widespread.[66] There were also mortal women who played the role of redeemers, such as Iphigenia, whose death was redemptive and vicarious[67] (she pays the price for Helen's shame), and Lucretia, whose suicide freed the Roman Republic from the Tarquins.[68]

### New Testament

The New Testament has scant references to God or Jesus as mother.[69] The only maternal image used is the one given by Jesus (Matt. 23:37). He compares himself to a mother hen. Early Christian writers used this text to advantage. Augustine compares Christ becoming incarnate to the hen who becomes infirm like her children and protects them with her wings.[70] Jerome also uses this simile and says, "And will you now let us fly about at random with no mother near us? Will you leave us to dread the swoop of the hawk, and the shadow of each passing bird of prey?"[71]

## Gnosticism

Perhaps the earliest Christian texts that portray Jesus as mother are from the Nag Hammadi Library.[72] Elaine Pagels has given much attention to this in *The Gnostic Gospels*.[73] In chapter 3, "God the Father/God the Mother," she discusses the Gnostic texts that refer to God as mother.[74] In an extract cited by Hippolytus 5.6 we read: "From Thee, Father, and through Thee, Mother, the two immortal names, parents of the divine being, and though dweller in heaven, humanity, of the mighty name."[75] Valentinus describes the godhead as a dyad: "The divine can be imagined as a dyad; consisting, in one part, of the Ineffable, the Depth, the Primal Father; and, in the other, of Grace, Silence, the Womb and 'Mother of the All.'" Pagels points out that in his celebration of the Eucharist, Marcus, the magician, calls the wine "her blood." He offers the cup and prays that "grace may flow" into all the participants. Marcus described himself as "the *womb* and *the recipient* of silence." He received visions of the divine in female form.[76] Another Gnostic text explains the origin of the universe from a male and female;[77] the female is "a great Intelligence" that produces all things.[78] Some Gnostics thought of God as the "great male-female power."

In Gnostic writings the Holy Spirit is described as "Mother." John purportedly received a vision that informed him: ". . . I am the one who is [with you] always. I [am the Father], I am the Mother, I am the Son."[79] The author of the *Secret Book* describes the Spirit as follows: "She [is] . . . [the] image of the invisible, virginal, Spirit who is perfect. . . . She became the womb of everything for it is she who is prior to them all, the Mother-Father [*matropater*] . . . the first man, the holy Spirit, the thrice-male, the thrice-powerful, the thrice-named androgynous one, and the eternal aeon among the invisible ones, and the first to come forth" (*Ap. John* 4.31).[80] The *Gospel of the Hebrews* names the Spirit "Mother."[81] Hippolytus[82] reports that Simon Magus used the male/female imagery with regard to Paradise:

> Grant Paradise to be the womb; for Scripture teaches us that this is a true assumption when it says, "I am He that formed thee in thy mother's womb" [Isa. 44:2] . . . Moses . . . using allegory had declared Paradise to be the womb . . . and Eden, the placenta . . . (Hippolytus, *Refutation* 6.14).[83]

Another text, the *Trimorphic Protennoia,* speaks about the supreme power as androgynous: "I am androgynous. [I am Mother (and) I am] Father since [I copulate] with myself [and with those who love] me. . . I am the Womb [that gives shape] to the All. . . . [I am] Me[iroth]ea, the glory of the Mother."[84] The *Thunder, Perfect Mind* is more explicit: "I am the first and the last. I am the honored one and the scorned one. I am the whore, and the holy one. I am the wife and the virgin. I am [the mother] and the daughter. . . . I am she whose wedding is great, and I have not taken a husband. . . ."[85] So for the Gnostics the mother was the agent in creation, infusing the creator with her own vital energy and sharing her ideas with him, but he was ignorant even of his own mother.[86] These and other Gnostic texts may have been suppressed because many women were active in these so-called "heretical" groups. However, it should be pointed out that Sophia was not the mother goddess and did not rank in the highest echelons of the Gnostic hierarchy. Nevertheless, the Gnostics constituted a highly influential group in Christianity, and their approach to the deity as both mother and father was not necessarily offensive to all Christians.

### Odes of Solomon

A rich source for the maternal image of God is the *Odes of Solomon*.[87] Here we find a clear reference to divine lactation. Since the passage is significant, I quote in full:

> A cup of milk was offered to me,
> and I drank it in the sweetness of the Lord's kindness.
> The Son is the cup,
> and the Father is he who was milked;
> and the Holy Spirit is she who milked him;
> Because his breasts were full,
> and it was undesirable that his milk should be released without purpose.
> The Holy Spirit opened her bosom,
> and mixed the milk of the two breasts of the Father.[88]

Here it is God the Father who provides milk for the children. Again in *Ode* 35 we find: "And I was carried like a child by its mother; and he gave me milk, the dew of the Lord."[89]

## Early Christian Writers

Further, there is some evidence for femininity of the deity even in patristic texts, especially with reference to lactation. In the Middle Ages this constituted an effort to develop a more affective spirituality to counterbalance speculative theology.[90] Bradley explains that it was thought that, unlike angels, humanity could not eat the divine bread of the Father until Christ became incarnate and it became milk from his breast.[91] Thus Christ became both mother and slave. Mother was the most apt metaphor for the humanity assumed by Christ because "like the mother he suffers the birth pangs that signify salvation, and like the mother he becomes vulnerable in driving away the enemy that threatens the weak ones in Christ."[92] We have a brief reference in Irenaeus: "Those, therefore, who do not partake of Him, are neither nourished into life from the mother's breasts, nor do they enjoy that most limpid fountain which issues from the body of Christ. . . ."[93] Here the wound in Christ's side is associated with lactation. We shall discuss this below (pp. 128–35, 193–99). Clement of Alexandria, who cites the wisdom literature some two hundred times,[94] gives a full explication of divine lactation and closely associates it with the Eucharist (*vide infra*). His approach to the incarnation is similar:

> And God Himself is love; and out of love to us became feminine. In His ineffable essence He is Father; in His compassion to us He became Mother. The father by loving became feminine; and the great proof of this is He whom He begot of Himself; and fruit brought forth by love is love.[95]

According to Augustine, Christ, at his own volition, accepted maternal weakness and hence suffered in the passion, he was not reluctant to surrender divine glory.[96] The body of Christ feeds us, his wisdom is converted to milk.[97] We are to place our "egg of hope" under the divine wings.[98] Further the Christian must conceive and give birth to salvation for him or herself.[99] Augustine is explicit in his Tractate on John:

> But the whole church, that bindeth and looseth sins;[100] nor did the latter [i.e., John] alone drink at the fountain of the Lord's breast, to emit again in preaching, of the Word in the beginning, God with God, and those other sublime truths regarding the divinity of Christ, and the Trinity and Unity of the whole Godhead. . . .[101]

Augustine also says that God is both Father and Mother for believers, a Father in judging, ruling, building and a Mother in nourishing, suckling, and gathering the child to her.[102] Ambrose also speaks in birth imagery when referring to the Trinity: "the Father's womb is the spiritual womb of an inner sanctuary, from which the Son has proceeded just as from a generative womb."[103] In the same work he describes the Son nourishing us with his milk, and in his treatise on virgins, his carrying us in his womb, giving birth to us and suckling us.

The Syriac father Ephraem also uses maternal imagery in his hymns. See the work of Sebastian Brock (listed in bibliography). Albert the Great speaks of wisdom as our first mother, in whose womb we were carried and he also speaks of Christ suffering the hardship of childbirth.[104] He uses the lactation figure in the same work.[105] Bonaventure speaks of wisdom conceiving, enduring the pangs of childbirth, and giving birth.[106]

This tradition of the femininity of God and Christ did not lie unused. Caroline Walker Bynum[107] in her fascinating and meticulously documented book, has shown that the motherhood of Christ was not a creation by Julian of Norwich. Rather she was heiress to a long tradition.[108] Bynum shows that this tradition of Jesus as Mother, usually as nourishing mother, was popular among male spiritual writers during the Middle Ages. They used it especially to encourage a motherlike approach of superiors and prelates towards those under their charge. Illustrious names include: Bernard of Clairvaux (1153); Aelred of Rievaulx (1167); Guerric of Igny (c. 1157); Isaac of Stella (c. 1169); Adam of Perseigne (1221); Helinand of Froidmont (c. 1235); William of St. Thierry (c. 1148), a black Benedictine, Anselm of Canterbury (1109).[109] The whole of Bynum's article is well worth perusal. Women were also devoted to this image.[110] A climax in the theology of the motherhood of God and Jesus is found in the writings of the English anchoress, Julian of Norwich, especially in *Showings* 57–60.[111] For example, she says:

> How we are brought back by the motherhood of mercy and grace into our natural place, in which we were created by the motherhood of love, a mother's love which never leaves us. Our Mother in nature, our Mother in grace, because he [Jesus] wanted altogether to become our Mother in all things, made the foundation of his work most humbly and most mildly in the maiden's womb.[112]

She then expatiates on the virtues of motherhood—ready service, profound love, security, the bearing of pain and sometimes death, giving of her milk from her own body, as Jesus in the sacraments gives us "the precious food of true life." She opines that the property of motherhood is "love, wisdom and knowledge, and this is God." As the child matures, the mother's love does not diminish, but she allows the child to become independent.

## Conclusion

We see, therefore, that the maternity of God is not a modern idea of feminists but that the redeemer/mother has a long history beginning even before Christianity. It was predicated of all three persons of the Trinity. God per se endured the most acute birth pangs on the cross. To this we turn now.[113]

# 4

# Why Crucifixion?

IN CHAPTERS 2 AND 3 WE HAVE DISCUSSED THE *PATHOS* OF GOD and observed that contemporary theologians accept more and more readily the idea of the suffering of God per se. This becomes acutely patent in the incarnation, which is the enfleshment of both the joy and the anguish of God. However, a further question we must pose concerns the nature of the death penalty inflicted on the second person of the Trinity, Jesus. Why crucifixion? Why the most obscene penalty? And why did Luke pronounce that this was "according to the definite plan and foreknowledge of God" (Acts 2:23)?

The redemptive role of Jesus began with his conception by Mary, and his entire earthly ministry and his exaltation, not only his death, was redemptive in nature. Jesus must have been conscious of the grave risk that he ran by consorting with marginal and "criminal" people. They were his FRIENDS (Mark 11:19; Luke 7:34). His arrest and death were the consequence and culmination of his work for the underprivileged. He was condemned and executed because of friendship.[1] In the Markan predictions of his suffering and death,[2] Mark does not mention crucifixion specifically, but from his childhood experience he must have known that it was a possibility.[3] I surmise that Jesus was ready to undergo crucifixion in order to identify himself completely, undeniably, and dramatically with the most debased and detested people in his contemporary society. Crucifixion was a slave's penalty; it meant that Jesus united himself even with those who were not considered "persons." In addition to this, crucifixion for a Jew meant a curse, a spiritual excommunication from the chosen people and abandonment by God. This is why Jesus' cry of godforsakenness from the cross is so important to the first three Gospels (Mark 15:34 and parallels). How could God be alienated from God? It is the symbol of the sensation of total self-disintegration and degradation surely felt by Holocaust and Hiroshima victims. But it is also the drama of the rift in God per se (see pp. 27–28). Undergoing the penalty of crucifixion is the climax of Jesus' mission to the depersonalized. They have no voice, no recourse to justice. In the crucifixion the Word becomes voiceless, seemingly with no recourse even to the highest court of justice. It is the crucifixion of God, in an ineffable way. Jesus goes to "calamity's depths" for his friends, as it were, to dehumanization, de-deification. In order to understand this, we must look in more detail into the phenomenon of crucifixion. Here we shall be dealing not only with physical pain but with the whole gamut of excruciating suffering—physical, mental, and spiritual—of God, of man, and of woman. Although there are a number of important monographs on crucifixion,[4] I should like to highlight a few aspects pertinent to our inquiry.

Whereas all forms of capital punishment[5] involved pain and degradation, crucifixion, impalement, and *apotympanismos*[6] were purposely designed to combine the greatest possible physical pain with the greatest possible psychological, social, and spiritual abuse.[7] In some cultures it was believed that the total destruction of the body, left to the savagery and destruction of birds of prey and wild animals, was a security against ghost-haunting by the condemned. Once the body, especially the vital organs, were utterly consumed, the ghost was laid. Did the authorities who ordered Jesus' capital punishment wish to lay his ghost? If so, there is an element of humor in the resurrection.

Thus it is understandable that crucifixion was called *mors turpissima* (the most foul death); *infamis stipes* (infamous wood); *infelix lignum* (luckless stump); *maxima mala* (incomparable evil); *servitudinis extremum summumque supplicium* (the most disastrous and most extreme servile punishment).[8] Sociologically speaking, crucifixion was the greatest indignity a human person could undergo, hence Paul's realistic statement that the cross was a stumbling block (*skandalon*) to the Jews and folly (*mōria*) to the Greeks (1 Cor. 1:23).[9] Honor and shame were pivotal values in the Mediterranean world. Honor included: keeping one's good name; giving ripostes to challenges; keeping the honor of one's family, especially the chastity of one's wife; maintaining one's body in honor; possessing enough wealth to be almost self-sufficient; and having children, especially males.[10] Crucifixion[11] was designed to shame a person, or a group of persons, in all their human relationships—social, political, and even familial. This explains a great deal of the fear experienced by the disciples, fear not only of pain and death but also of repercussions on their kith and kin. Their involvement with Jesus after his arrest endangered both men and women and their family members.

Seneca, who appears to have seen many crucifixions, says:

> Can anyone be found who would prefer wasting away in pain, dying limb by limb, or letting out his life drop by drop, rather than expiring once for all? Can any man be found willing to be fastened to the accursed tree, long sickly,

already deformed, swelling with ugly tumors on chest and shoulders, and draw the breath of life amid long-drawn-out agony? I think he would have many excuses for dying even before mounting the cross.[12]

Yet, this was the lot which Jesus of Nazareth chose.

Whereas I shall deal with crucifixion in the Greco-Roman world in general, I shall have in mind particularly the crucifixion of the Jewish Jesus and the audience in the Greco-Roman world to whom the Gospel of John was preached.

## The Shame of the Cross[13]

I should like to go through the procedure of crucifixion step by step in order to explicate the unspeakable shame that the victims and his or her friends[14] underwent.

### Loss of Status[15]

The sentence of crucifixion (if there were any due process and sentence) deprived a person of his or her social status both locally and nationally. Shame on this score was even greater when it involved loss of superior rank, for example, membership in the Jewish priesthood, possession of Roman citizenship, or being in the status of free man or woman. By the verdict the victims were peremptorily and brutally expelled from their place in society, and their shame was displayed to the community at large. Moreover, at least in the Roman Empire, crucifixion was used chiefly as a punishment for slaves (or traitors). Many slaves entertained a realistic fear of crucifixion. Plautus frequently refers to this punishment in his comedies, e.g., Sceledrus, a slave of Pyrgopolynices, one of his characters, says: "I know the cross will be my tomb. There's where my ancestors rest—father, grandfather, great-grandfather, and great-great grandfather."[16] Even if this is hyperbole on the part of Sceledrus, nevertheless it is a witness to this deep-rooted anxiety. In *Mostellaria*, or *The Haunted House* (358–360), Tramio says: "I'll give two hundred pounds to the first man to charge my cross (*in crucem excucurrerit*) and take it—on condition his legs and arms are double-nailed, that is."[17]

We may, however, point out that the crimes for which a person was crucified in the Roman era were usually piracy, murder, false witness, high treason, rebellion, and sacrilege, crimes that brought great shame upon the victim and society. Thus strangers passing by a crucifixion site were likely to make a harsh judgment upon the victim(s). In this way the person lost his or her good name and was labeled as a criminal of the worst kind. "Gallowsbird" (*furcifer*) was a frequent appellation for lower-class slaves.[18]

It was a title of shame.[19] Perhaps the most trenchant objection to the loss of honor and freedom is found in Cicero's *Verrine Orations*, where Cicero accuses Verres of crucifying a Roman citizen. I quote at length:

> Does freedom, that precious thing, mean nothing? nor the proud privileges of a citizen of Rome? nor the law of Porcius, the laws of Sempronius? nor the tribunes' power, whose loss our people felt so deeply till now at last it has been restored to them? . . . You dared to crucify any living man who claimed to be a Roman citizen? . . . that citizenship whose glory is known throughout the world. . . .[20]

Cicero accuses Verres of declaring war "upon the whole principle of the rights of the Roman citizen body" and of placing Gavius's cross on the Pompeian road that overlooks the Straits.[21] He says:

> This place with its view of Italy was deliberately picked out by Verres, that his victim, as he died in pain and agony, might feel how yonder narrow channel *marked the frontier between the land of slavery and the land of freedom,* and that Italy might see her son, as he hung there, suffer the worst extreme of the tortures inflicted upon slaves . . . it was not Gavius, not one obscure man, whom you *nailed upon that cross of agony: it was the universal principle that Romans are free men.*[22]

Cicero's indignation arose from the fact that a Roman citizen had been demoted to the status of a slave by being crucified.

To the Jewish Jesus, his disciples, relatives, and community, this deprivation of status, name, and freedom struck at the root of their exodus theology. They believed that God per se had redeemed them from the servile state and had given them the status of prophets, priests, and sovereigns. When we add to these considerations the fact that Christians believed Jesus to be the Son of God, the offense is immeasurably aggravated. Yet we can understand God's acceptance of this humiliation in the light of the Shekinah mysticism. God embraces the dark horror, indeed, the "dehumanization" and "de-deification" of him or herself. Instead of requiring vengeance for his or her wounded honor, God submits to the most egregious dishonor.

### Scourging Preceding Crucifixion

Scourging was often a regular procedure before crucifixion. Needless to say it was grossly humiliating to the victim and family, especially in the case of a woman. First, the perpetrators stripped the person of his or her clothes. Whereas nudity[23] for the male was not a matter for censure among Greeks and Hellenists, it was so among the Jews[24] and many other cultures. Particularly blameworthy was the exposure of the genitals and buttocks[25] and, for a woman, the breasts. Neyrey observes that the penis was the symbol of a man's strength and superiority and that exposure by a third party meant a public loss of power and status.[26] Moreover, an erection or swelling of the male organ that occurred in crucifixion would be a further cause of jeering and mockery. Hengel quotes from *Catalepton* 2a18 (attributed to Virgil): *parata namque crux, cave, stat mentula* (beware, for the cross is ready and the penis erect).[27] With regard to a woman's nudity Jewish law showed some delicacy in that a woman's face was turned away from the crowd. Incontinence in a woman and defecation in a man exempted the accused from further stripes. Thus: "If [the scourged] committed a nuisance, whether with excreta or with urine, he is exempt (from the rest of the lashes, cf. Deut. 25:3). R. Judah says, "A man with excretion, and a woman with urine."[28] Incontinence would, of course, be a matter of shame to men and women. But the Jews may have been the only ones who practiced the above "clemency."

A number of passages in the Hebrew Scriptures condemn nudity (e.g., Exod. 20:26; 28:42; Isa. 47:3; Lev. 20:17) and this obtains also in the Christian Scriptures (e.g., Rev. 16:15 and 17:16). An eloquent witness to this is the stripping and scourging of Eleazar in 4 Maccabees 6:2-3.[29] Neyrey avers, "Nudity means the complete absence of boundaries; the body is accessible to any and every one, thus destroying its exclusivity as something 'set apart.'"[30] Moreover, clothing was intimately associated with one's position in society, one's status, and one's personality. Office, both religious and secular, was symbolized by special garments. Thus stripping of these was stripping of status and a deprivation of personhood. There is some debate whether the prisoner was stripped for the scourging and consequently, still naked, carried the shaft of cross through the town. But, even if the stripping of clothes were performed again at the execution site, there would still be exposure of the body for hours or even days. It is highly unlikely that the Jewish victims were allowed to retain a loincloth (nearly always depicted in portrayals of Jesus' crucifixion), although when the Jews themselves crucified their own people they may have extended this courtesy.[31] Earlier practice apparently allowed the head to be veiled before suspension on the luckless tree.[32]

*Carrying the Cross*

After the scourging the prisoner was compelled to carry the gibbet, the part on which she or he was to be crucified, to the site of the execution. Fulda[33] observes that in the early Roman tradition the *furca* was a wooden frame that was placed on the neck of the transgressor and then fastened to the arms. In this way the victim was driven through the town accompanied by ribald humor on the part of the crowd. I quote Plutarch at length for the interesting sociological details that this passages contains:

A certain man had handed over one of his slaves to other slaves with orders to scourge him through the forum, and then put him to death. While they were executing this commission and tormenting the poor wretch, whose pain and suffering made him writhe and twist himself horribly, the sacred procession in honor of Jupiter chanced to come up behind. Many of those who took part in it were, indeed, scandalized at the joyless sight and the unseemly contortions of the victim, but no one made any protest; they merely heaped abuse and curses on the head of the master who was inflicting such a cruel punishment. For in those days the Romans treated their slaves with great kindness, because they worked and even ate with them themselves, and were therefore more familiar and gentle with them. And it was a severe punishment for a slave who had committed a fault, if he was obliged to take the piece of wood with which they prop up the pole of a wagon, and carry it around through the neighborhood. For he who had been seen undergoing this punishment no longer had any credit in his own or neighboring households. And he was called "*furcifer*"; for what the Greeks call a prop, or support, is called *furca* by the Romans.[34]

Originally, therefore, the *furca* was designed as a punishment of shame and loss of status that was not necessarily followed by death. A slave was subject to the wishes and whims of his or her master or mistress.[35] Further degradation lay in the fact that the *furca* was used for cattle.[36] In other cases, especially in the city, the prisoner was attached to a crossbar and driven to a place outside the town. Whereas perhaps only a small number of people had witnessed his or her humiliation in scourging, the carrying of the *patibulum* or *furca* through the town would attract a large crowd of men, women, children, and stray animals. Hengel cites Plautus (*Carbonaria* frag. 2) who speaks of carrying the cross through the city and then being nailed to it (*patibulum ferat per urbem, deinde offigitur cruci*).[37] In Plautus (*Mostellaria* 1.1.54) Grumio says:

Oh, I bet the hangman will have you looking like a human sieve (*cribrum*), the way they'll prod you full of holes as they run you down the streets with your arms on a crossbar, (*ita te forabunt patibulatum per vias stimulis carnufices*) once the old man gets back!

The condemned often carried an inscription describing his crime; this appears to have been worn around the neck[38] and was a warning to others. Domitian caused such a placard to be worn by a man who had favored a Thracian gladiator; it bore the words, "A favorer of the Thracian who spoke impiously."[39] Suetonius also mentions a slave who was accused of theft. After his hands were cut off, he was forced to wear a placard proclaiming his crime to the guests.[40] This, of course, is an extreme and cruel form of "labeling" a deviant. On the theories of "labeling" see Malina and Neyrey.[41] At times the crime was published in a more ingenious and scurrilous way. Tacitus reports that the slave who had betrayed the Tarracines was crucified wearing his equestrian insignia: "The Tarracines, however, found comfort in the fact that the slave of Verginius Capito, who had betrayed them, was crucified wearing the very rings that he had received from Vitellius."[42] We might find a parallel to this in the passion according to John. John never reports that Jesus was stripped after being clothed in his regal garb (John 19:1-5).[43] Did he still wear the purple robe on the cross? If so, this was extreme mockery both of Jesus and the Jews.

### Site of Crucifixion

The site of crucifixion was usually a public area with plenty of thorough-fare. In Rome one such site was the *Campus Esquilinus*. Juvenal speaks of this hill as the place where the vulture hurried from the carcasses of animals to those of human beings that hung on the cross:

> The vulture hurries from dead cattle and dogs and gibbets to bring some of the carrion to her offspring . . . so when their progeny are of full age and soar up from the rest, hunger bids them swoop down upon that same prey which they first tasted when they broke the shell.[44]

Plutarch says that this was the place of execution for those condemned by the emperors.[45] Appian reports that after the defeat of Spartacus, the leader of the slave revolt in Sicily, six thousand prisoners were crucified on the *Via Appia* between Capua and Rome.[46] Severus crucified slaves "on the street which his slaves used most frequently on the way to the imperial palace."[47] Tacitus relates the story of Pedanius Secundus, who was murdered by a slave. All his household was put to death, and Tiberius was obliged to guard the whole length of the road along which the condemned were marched accompanied by detachments of soldiers.[48] In addition to the publicity of the site of execution, the Jews would find the very locus to be polluted in the deepest sense—through mingling of Gentile and Jew; shedding of blood and defiled matter, such as corpses and bones; and the presence of unclean animals and birds. It would be regarded as a haunt of demons and unclean spirits.[49] For the Jew, of course, the crucified person was in a state of complete ritual impurity. Fulda[50] mentions that at times the victim was required to carry a bell to warn people that an unclean person was approaching, but this may be a later practice.

### Fastening to the Cross

Generally people used the most available material as gibbets for executions. This might be rocks, trees, beams, or rafters; sometimes they left the upright beam in place. In Ezra a simple beam from the house is taken: "If any man violates this edict, a beam is to be taken from his house, and he is to be lifted up and impaled on it; and his house is to be reduced to rubble for this offense."[51] This, according to Fulda, was a Persian custom and had a macabre significance, for the victim was hung on part of his or her own property. We see a similar case in Esther 7:9, where a high gibbet is prepared for Haman at his own home. Fulda lists various kinds of material for crosses or gibbets.[52] Certainly there must have been a shortage of trees for these mass executions. In mythical literature Prometheus and the princess Andromeda are fastened to rocks. The victim was either nailed or bound to the gibbet. In *Letter* 14, Seneca speaks of other instruments of torture:

> Picture to yourself under this head the prison, the cross (*cruces*), the rack (*eculeos*), the hook, and the stake[53] which they drive straight through a man until it protrudes from his throat . . . and of all the other contrivances devised by cruelty, in addition to those which I have mentioned.[54]

As Hengel remarks, crucifixion was a punishment in which the caprice and sadism of the executioners were given full rein.[55] Seneca says:

> Yonder I see instruments of torture (*cruces*), not indeed of a single kind, but differently contrived by different peoples; some hang their victims with head towards the ground, some impale their private parts; others stretch out their arms on a fork-shaped gibbet (*patibulum*).[56]

Titus, who conducted the siege of Jerusalem in 66–70 C.E., allowed his soldiers this license when, according to Josephus, they crucified five hundred victims a day before Jerusalem.[57] The twisted and grotesque postures would cause the body to writhe and go into convulsions, possibly to the amusement of the onlookers.[58] This, of course, would be another cause of ignominy.

The height of the cross varied; sometimes the victim was hung with his or her feet on the ground and so was exposed to dogs, wolves, hyenas, and other wild animals. Catullus says that the black-throated raven devoured the sunken eyes; dogs, the intestines; and wolves, the remaining limbs (Catullus, *Epigrams* 107).[59] Martial (*On the Spectacles* 7) gives an even more graphic description of Prometheus's and Laureolus's crucified bodies undergoing this shame and torture. "To feed the ravens on the cross" was a synonym for hanging (Horace, *Epodes* 1.16.48). On the other hand, the cross could be made very high. Suetonius reports that Galba crucified a man for poisoning his ward, but when the man declared he was a Roman citizen, Galba, pretending to lighten his punishment by some consolation and honor, ordered a cross to be painted white and raised higher than the rest and the man to be transferred to that cross.[60]

### Lack of Burial

In many cultures burial was disallowed in the cases of crucifixion, impalement, and *apotympanismos*. However, the friends and relatives often stood near the cross waiting for the last breath so they could take the body for burial. Sometimes the friends would pay for a speedier death or for the cadaver.[61] In the light of this it is understandable that the women disciples and John stood near the cross of Jesus, and perhaps it is not insignificant that Joseph of Arimathea was a rich man (Matt. 27:57). He *may* have paid for Jesus' body.

To the person in the ancient world, lack of burial, or common burial with other criminals, was a source of deepest shame. Even a handful of earth over the remains, or at least covering up the bones,[62] was sufficient. Hiding the cadaver to avoid pollution in the eyes of the gods and goddesses was important for the gentiles, and avoidance of pollution of the earth for the Jews (Deut. 21:22-23). Burial also was an act of piety, and through it the departed were able to enter the other world.

In summary, for the male, crucifixion comprised loss of power, freedom, and status; severe abuse of almost every member of the body; profuse shedding of blood; public and unbridled mockery (violent psychological abuse); rejection by the peer group; execration of his name; nudity; and, of course, the final and irrevocable insult of death; and in many cases, lack of burial. Jesus' passion represented the exact opposite to the good or ideal life, a life of honor. Indeed, when Jesus bade his followers to take up their crosses and follow him, they may not have taken him literally, but rather in a metaphorical sense, as does Seneca.[63]

The incarnate God allowed himself to undergo the most obscene punishment inflicted in the ancient world. His intention was not to be a scapegoat or sacrificial victim but rather, a friend who would "go to calamity's depths" for his friends, including the most abused in the world. Today he might have allowed himself to be a victim of the Holocaust, of Hiroshima, of Nagasaki, of Bosnia, or of Rwanda. We shall discuss the topic of friendship in the next chapter.

## *Impalement and Crucifixion in Jewish Practice*[64]

I append a note on crucifixion among the Jews as our inquiry concerns the Jewish Jesus, who was handed over to Pilate to be crucified. The most important aspect of crucifixion for the Jew was that the person who was hung on the tree was cursed.

> If a man [*sic*] guilty of a capital offense is put to death and his corpse hung on a tree, it shall not remain on the tree overnight. You shall bury it the same day; otherwise, since God's curse rests on him who hangs on a tree, you will defile the land which the Lord, your God, is giving you as an inheritance (Deut. 21:22-23).

This act was implemented as a deterrent to other people. It could be performed after both hanging and strangulation. There was, however, no denial of burial rites. There is no hint here of hanging a living body on the tree. However, in the case of the king of Ai (Josh. 8:23-29) it is possible that they crucified him alive.[65] However, since the discovery of the Qumran scrolls and, more particularly, *4QpNahum* and the *Temple Scroll,* there is some evidence that certain Jews did practice crucifixion for specific crimes, mainly sorcery, blasphemy,[66] and giving one's country over to the enemy. In the *Temple Scroll,* Deuteronomy 21:22-23 reads as follows:

> If a man passes on information about his people and betrays his people to a foreign people and does evil to his people, then you shall hang him on the wood, so that he dies. On the strength of two witnesses or on the strength of three witnesses he shall be killed and they shall hang him on the wood. If a man has committed a capital offense and flees to the nations and curses his people, the Israelites, then you shall hang him on the wood, so that he dies. Yet they shall not let his corpse hang on the wood, but must bury it on the same day, for cursed by God and men are those who are hanged on the wood, and you shall not pollute the earth, which I give to you as an inheritance.[67]

Obviously here a living body is hung on the tree.[68] We may have further evidence of crucifixion in *4QpNahum/4Q169,* where the "Lion of Wrath" hung his political enemies "alive on the wood."

> [And chokes prey for its lionesses; and it fills] its caves [with prey] and its caves with victims (12a-b). Interpreted, this concerns the furious young lion [who executes revenge] on those who seek smooth things and hangs men alive . . . formerly in Israel. Because of a man hanged alive on [the] tree, He proclaims, "Behold I am against [you, says the Lord of Hosts]."

In all probability the text refers to Alexander Janneus, who ordered a mass crucifixion of Pharisees. Merino discusses this text and the *Temple Scroll* in detail.[69] Clines and Davies also refer to the Aramaic inscription found at En-Gedi (sixth century B.C.E.).[70] They quote the pertinent passage that conveys again the importance of shame felt before God and human beings for such a crime.[71]

However, the Qumran scrolls are not our only witness to Jewish crucifixion or impalement. Merino's article is an interesting and thorough treatment of the punishment of crucifixion in Jewish intertestamental literature. First he discusses the terminology and the distinction between impalement and crucifixion.[72] He points out that Philo appears to limit crucifixion to murderers, and that he has a free rendering of Deuteronomy 21:22-23.

> The lawgiver would, if he could, have sentenced them (murderers) to die times beyond number. But since this was impossible he ordained another penalty as an addition and ordered the manslayers to be crucified (*anaskolopizesthai*). Yet after giving this injunction he hastened to revert to his natural

humanity and shews mercy to those whose deeds were merciless when he says, "Let not the sun go down upon the crucified but let them be buried in the earth before sundown."[73]

*Anaskolopizein* could mean "hang" but "crucifixion" seems the better translation in view of two other texts from Philo. In *On Dreams*, he compares the mind to a crucified body: "Thus the mind stripped of the creations of its art will be found as it were a headless corpse, with severed neck, nailed like the crucified (*hoi anaskolopisthentes*) to the tree of helpless and poverty-stricken indiscipline (*On Dreams* 2.213).[74]

## The "Crucifixion" of Women in Antiquity[75]

We are accustomed to thinking about the crucifixion of males and to seeing a male figure on the cross. However, it is important to ask whether women also faced this punishment and disgrace. Did Jesus undergo a death that would show his empathy only, or chiefly, for men? Were the logia about bearing the cross,[76] which occur within the context of the three predictions of his own rejection and death, addressed only to men?

In general we may say that throughout history in secular and ecclesiastical practice, women have normally been subject to the same punishments, including the death penalty, as men, although they were rarely afforded all the privileges and responsibilities enjoyed by males. Greco-Roman law does not seem to have exempted women from any form of the death penalty, and this may be true for other parts of the world.

Nevertheless, the idea of conceiving a female figure on the cross is arousing the interest of Christians internationally. As mentioned briefly in chapter 1, in 1975 the artist Edwina Sandys broke with tradition by portraying in sculpture a bronze Christa, a naked[77] woman with outstretched arms on the cross. Michael J. Farrel described the furor the work provoked when it was shown in the Episcopal Cathedral of St. John the Divine in New York.[78] Some found the sculpture profoundly moving, but others were exercised that the incarnate crucified God be portrayed as a woman. Some men and women saw Christa as symbolic of the many ways in which woman has been metaphorically crucified throughout the ages.

Yet Sandys was not the only artist to portray a Christa on the cross. In 1977 Arthur Boyd, an Australian artist, won the Blake prize for his picture of a (pregnant)[79] woman on the cross; behind her is the bare Australian countryside in which the trees are cruciform.[80] He said that he wished to portray the suffering of women as well as men. An African artist also sculptured a crucifix on which the figure was both male and female and showed a child being born from her side—surely symbolic of the church born through the blood and water from the wounded side of Christ (John 19:34).[81] On May 10, 1986, in Toronto, Canada, the sculpture of a woman on the cross by the artist Almuth Lutkenaus-Lackey was officially present-ed to Emmanuel College, a theological college of The United Church of Canada. Much discussion and controversy ensued. This is recorded in some detail in the book on the subject by Doris Jean Dyke.[82] This author also mentions *Christine on the Cross*, a two-foot sculpture by James M. Murphy. This was exhibited in St. James Chapel at Union Theological Sem-inary, New York, in 1984. I have not seen a representation of this, but apparently her legs are spread and nailed on the lowered crossbar and her arms pulled up and nailed above her head to the vertical bar. The artist said:

> Last Easter my sketch in soft clay took the shape of a woman. I realized there-by that the world's rejection and hatred of women culminates in crucifying a female Christ.[83]

There is also a crucified woman in clay from Latin American. She is depict-ed with the daily instruments of a woman's suffering, the hoe, machete, and so forth. Barbara Listenik from Florida also offers an interesting portrayal of a woman on a cross. We may also compare the description of the portrait of the crucified mother in Chaim Potok's *My Name is Asher Lev*.

Thus it would seem that the subject of the theology of the crucifixion of women is well under discussion. However, I am not aware that anyone has approached the question of women's crucifixion from an historic point of view. In this chapter[84] I have tried to document evidence for the "crucifix-ion" of women in the ancient world. I have entitled my section the "cruci-fixion" of women, but I should like to use "crucifixion" in a more generic sense as in the rest of this work.[85] I wish to focus on those capital punish-ments in antiquity that involved rendering the body of the victim immo-bile in order to produce a protracted death, lasting one to ten days or longer. I remind the reader that this type of capital punishment was designed to produce: (a) the maximum amount of physical pain; (b) the utmost extremity of shame; (c) in some cases, to offer propitiation to the gods and goddesses; and (d) often, to prevent the victim's ghost from trou-bling his or her executioners and their accomplices. The latter was thought to be avoided by entirely destroying the body by exposure to birds and ani-mals of prey or by impaling the vital organs, such as, the heart, liver, or intestines.[86] A crucified woman would incur far, far greater shame than even a male victim. Again, I am dealing only with cases where living per-sons were affixed to crosses. A full investigation of the Christian sources does not lie within my purview.

Naturally, we should not expect to find as many references to the cruci-fixion of women as to those of men. Women, save in exceptional cases, e.g., the Spartans;[87] Boudicca; and Semíranis, queen of Babylon, did not fight in armies, practice piracy, actively join in military forces during revolutions, or constitute an armed power threat to male leaders. These carried with them the danger of punishment by crucifixion. After a defeat, women and children were normally sold into slavery. Nevertheless, we can produce the following evidence for the crucifixion of women.

### Babylonian and Assyrian Sources[88]

Crucifixion (impalement) is found in the *Code of Hammurabi*. The punishment for breaking through a wall in a house was death followed by impalement. Impalement after death reflects the crime: he pierced the wall, so his body is pierced.[89] But another even grosser punishment is inflicted upon an adulterous woman who instigated the death of her husband for the sake of her lover. In *Code of Hammurabi* 153 we read: "If a woman has procured the death of her husband on account of another man, they shall impale that woman."[90] Further, both Babylonian and Assyrian law demand impalement for a woman who procures an abortion. Driver and Miles[91] note that the Babylonian phrase is "they shall put her on a stake," but the Assyrian law has "they shall set her up on pieces of wood." Driver and Miles continue: "The substitution of a plural noun suggests crucifixion on crossed pieces of wood, which further agrees with the use of the derived Syriac verb meaning 'set up, erected' for 'crucified' (Syr.: *zqap*)." She is also denied burial:[92] the woman suffers the same punishment of death as she inflicted on her infant.[93] This appears to be implementing the *lex talionis* (law of retaliation).

### Jewish Sources

A fairly clear reference to crucifixion of women during the persecution by Antiochus Epiphanes is found in 1 Maccabees: "Women who had had their children circumcised were put to death, in keeping with the decree, with their babies hung from their necks; their families (*tous oikous*) also and those who had circumcised them were killed" (1 Macc. 1:60-61).[94] Goldstein[95] assumes that both parents were crucified and this is supported by Josephus's account of the incident:

> Indeed, they were whipped, their bodies mutilated, and while still alive and breathing, they were crucified, while their wives and the sons whom they had circumcised in despite of the king's wishes were strangled (*apēgchon*), the children being made to hang from the necks of their crucified parents (*tōn anestauromenōn goneōn*).[96]

The motif of shame is important here: not only do the parents suffer the public shame of crucifixion but a mockery is made of the very mark of the covenant, namely, circumcision (cf. Gen. 17). Josephus[97] also refers to the crucifixion of brigands and those of the common people who were their complices (*kai tōn epi koinōnia phōrathentōn dēmotōn, hous ekolasen, apeiron ti plēthos ēn*). These may have included women. He also relates the story of Florus's cruelty in Jerusalem.[98] On this occasion Florus extracted seventeen talents from the Temple treasury. Jews passed round a collection box for him! He responded to the insult by attacking Jerusalem. He asked that the ring leaders of the collection should be handed over to him.[99] Upon their pleading for the "culprits" he ordered his soldiers to sack the "upper market,"[100] but the soldiers went into every house and many of the citizens were handed over to Florus for scourging and crucifixion:

> Many of the peaceable citizens were arrested and brought before Florus, who had them first scourged and then crucified (*anestaurōsen*). The total number of that day's victims, including women and children (*ho de sumpas tōn ekeinēs apolomenōn tēs hēmeras arithmos sun gunaixin kai teknois, oude gar nēpiōn apeschonto*), amounted to about three thousand six hundred.[101]

### The Case of Ida

Another interesting case appears in Josephus (*Jewish Antiquities* 18.65-80). In the reign of Tiberius there was a certain noble Roman matron, Paulina. One Mundus fell in love with her, and because she refused to be bribed for sexual favors he accepted the help of a freedwoman, Ida, in order to attain his desire. She arranged with the priests of Isis to go and inform Paulina that the god, Anubis, was exceedingly pleased with her and requested that she dine with him and then share his bed. Paulina, after securing the approval of her husband, went to the temple. As would be expected, Mundus took the place of Anubis. A short while afterwards Mundus met Paulina and mockingly pointed out that he had succeeded in his desire. The case was brought before the Emperor. Josephus reports as follows: "When Tiberius had fully informed himself . . . he crucified both them and Ida, for the hellish thing was her doing and it was she who had contrived the whole plot against the lady's (Paulina's) honor."[102] One wonders whether all the priests of Isis were male. It is noticeable that Mundus was merely penalized with exile. His offense was less because he was moved by male sexual passion.[103] From a sociological point of view, crucifixion in this case is inflicted on a woman for both sacrilege and depriving a Roman husband of his honor. Josephus calls the incident *praxeis aischunōn ouk apēllagmenai* (deeds of a scandalous nature); he speaks of the daring deed of the priests of Isis (*tou tōn Isiakōn tolmēmatos*); he describes Ida as expert in every kind of evil (*pantoiōn idris kakōn*); and, in summing up, refers to the scheming of the priests as *hubrismena* (wanton violence).

### Eighty Alleged Witches at Askalon

The *Babylonian Talmud, Tractate Sanhedrin* 43b has a discussion on hanging after stoning. The sages maintain that this is only for the blasphemer and idolater:

> A man is hanged with his face towards the spectators, but a woman with her face towards the gallows: this is the view of R. Eliezer. But the sages say: a man is hanged, but not a woman. Whereupon R. Eliezar said to them: But did not Simeon b. Shetah hang women at Ashkelon? They retorted: [on that occasion] he hanged eighty women, not withstanding that two [malefactors] must not be tried on the same day.[104]

This apparently refers to the death of eighty witches by one of the most outstanding Rabbis of the first century. The note in the English Talmud reads:

> Witchcraft among Jewish women prevailed at that time to an alarming extent, and in order to prevent a combined effort on the part of their relations to rescue the culprits, he had to execute all of them at once. He hanged them, then, to prevent such practices and to avoid rescue, but his action is no precedent, and in itself was actually illegal, as the Sages pointed out.[105]

*Sanhedrin* 46a explains that more severe punishment was required by circumstances of the times. Simeon's eighty women may refer to exposure after death but could also mean hanging while they were alive, which would prove a great deterrent to magic and witchcraft.[106] There is not, however, enough evidence to form a decision on this point.

Hengel[107] has a full discussion of this text in his monograph.[108] Hengel argues that "Askalon" could be taken in a metaphorical sense and that the "women" could refer to men who conducted themselves in an effeminate way.[109] He concludes that the incident does not refer to women's crucifixion but to the period when the Pharisees gained power under Alexandra and took vengeance on their foes.[110] I cannot wholly concur with Hengel over this, and I think that his position might have been different if more examples of the crucifixion of women had been available to him.[111]

## Greco-Roman Literature

I now turn to some examples from Greco-Roman literature.

### Tacitus: The Case of Pedanius Secundus

According to ancient Roman law, if a slave murdered his master, all the slaves of the household should suffer the same punishment, in case they were accomplices in the deed, and because they represented a continual threat of danger to their masters or mistresses. Tacitus relates the case of Pedanius Secundus, who was murdered by a slave: his household, which included four hundred slaves, was crucified.[112] Tacitus says that the people objected to the mass destruction of all Pedanius Secundus's slaves, especially on account of the lack of discrimination, "with regard to number, age, sex, and, even more, their undoubted innocence."[113] Nevertheless, according to Tacitus, all were executed; women, old slaves, children without distinction were sent to the cross. As mentioned earlier, Tiberius was obliged to line "the whole length of the road, by which the condemned were being marched to punishment, with detachment of soldiers."[114]

### Apuleius: Four Modes of Punishment for a Young Girl

The African writer Apuleius was born in Madaura towards the beginning of the second century C.E., and later he resided in Carthage, which was his home base for itinerant sophism. In his novel *Golden Ass,* or *Metamorphoses,* he recounts an interesting tale. The ass reports that thieves brought in a young maiden, probably a gentlewoman, whom they intended to keep as a hostage until her parents paid the price.[115] They left her in charge of an old woman who told her fables to assuage her grief.[116] The ass tried to rescue the maiden but the thieves caught him and threatened him with death. They then discussed the fate of the maiden. They had already secured her with chains (*puellaque statim distenta vinculis*) but they suggested four capital punishments: (a) burning alive; (b) being thrown to the beasts; (c) hanging on a gibbet (*tertius patibulo suffigi*); (d) flaying alive with tortures.[117] One man suggested a more cruel way. He asserted that he did not agree to beasts, crosses, fire, or torture (*feras nec cruces nec ignes nec tormenta*), rather the ass should be killed and the maiden be sewn up in the carcass and thus undergo all the forms of punishment together—wild beasts, fire by scorching in the sun, the agony of the cross (*patibuli cruciatum*), and being eaten by vultures and dogs (32).

Apuleius and Lucian, who also reports the tale, probably draw from a common source. I realize that my reference here occurs in fictitious material, but the modes of punishment are those that were implemented in real life, and the importance of this story does not lie in its romance but in the listing of punishments, including crucifixion, that are assumed to be appropriate for women as well as men.

### Petronius: The Case of the Widow of the Crucified Man

Another interesting case occurs in the satirical novel of Petronius.[118] This particular tale[119] is set in Ephesus and is told by one Eumolpus.[120] Petronius remarks that "he was not thinking of old tragedies or names notorious in history, but of an affair which happened in his lifetime." A widow followed her husband's corpse into the vault to mourn beside him. It so happened that some thieves were crucified near the vault where the widow mourned. A soldier, who was keeping his station and guarding the bodies of the crucified so that none of the relatives would take them for burial, went down to comfort the widow and encourage her to take sustenance and then made sexual advances toward her. During his absence from the crucifixion site one of the bodies was stolen. The soldier realized that this would endanger his life, but the widow came to the rescue and permitted her husband's cadaver to be put on the cross. Petronius continues:

> The sailors received this tale with a laugh; . . . But there was no laugh from Lichas: he shook his head angrily and said: "if the governor of the province had been a just man, he should have put the dead husband back in the tomb, and hung the woman on the cross."[121]

It would appear then that the widow's sin was sacrilege because she disinterred her former husband. The story has an explicit anti-feminist motif (*Satyricon* 110) and is told to show that the most devoted wife can succumb to the advances of a stranger.

### Aristophanes: Lysistrata

A further example is found in Aristophanes' *Lysistrata* 679:

> Shall we let these willful women,
> O my brothers, do the same?
> Rather first their necks we'll rivet
> tightly to the pillory frame (*es tetrēmenon xulon*).[122]

This is probably a case of *apotympanismos* (see bibliography for the monograph by Kerampoullos).

We turn now from fictitious to more historic material.

### Justinus: The Case of Agathocles and his Concubines

Justinus reports in *Epitome of the Philippic History*[123] another incident of the crucifixion of women, namely, the concubines of Agathocles. The context was the hostilities between Antiochus, king of Syria, and Ptolemy of Egypt. Ptolemy opposed Antiochus, but was content with retrieving the cities that were lost, and subsequently he became involved in a dissolute life with the illicit mistresses of Agathocles. The latter began to rule the state, and no one was less powerful than the king himself. However, when matters became known to the populace, they killed Agathocles, and out of revenge for the death of Eurydice, the king's wife, crucified the women. In the punishment of these women there seems to be expiation for the dishonor of the king of the kingdom.[124]

### Dio Cassius: The Cases Concerning Nero and Buduica

Dio Cassius was a close relative of the orator Dio Chrysostom and a native of Bithynia. His father was a Roman senator and served in Cilicia and Dalmatia. The date of his birth seems to have been between 155 and 164 C.E.. He himself became a member of the senate. Dio Cassius may be, therefore, an important authority with regard to our subject. He recounts two cases of female impalement or crucifixion.

a. Dio Cassius (*Roman History* 62.13.3) reports that Nero fastened naked boys and *girls* to stakes, covered them with the hides of animals, and then satisfied his brutal lust upon them. Repulsive as this case of child abuse and sadism may be, Dio Cassius recounts an even worse incident that may be dated to about 61 C.E.

b. He describes a horrendous incident in which Buduica, the war-like queen of the Britons, after delivering a powerful harangue to her troops, led her army against the Romans. She sacked and plundered two Roman cities, and most dreadful atrocities were inflicted upon the captives. I quote:

> The worst and most bestial atrocity committed by their captors was the following. They hung up naked the noblest and most distinguished women and then cut off their breasts and sewed them to their mouths, in order to make the victims appear to be eating them; afterwards they impaled the women on sharp skewers run lengthwise through the entire body. All this they did to the accompaniment of sacrifices, banquets and wanton behavior, not only in all their other sacred places, but particularly in the grove of Andate. This was their name for Victory, and they regarded her with most exceptional reverence.[125]

It is interesting that the torture, involving crucifixion and impalement (presumably after death), is associated with religious rites. In this case human sacrifice is seen as pleasing to the gods and goddesses, either in expiation or in thanksgiving. We are not without examples in Scripture.

### Diodorus Siculus

Diodorus Siculus, as his name shows, was from Sicily and seems to have begun his writing about 56 B.C.E. There are five incidents that are of interest to us.

a. In book 2 of *The History*, Diodorus relates the events in Asia beginning with the time of the Assyrians. He describes how Ninus, the king of the Assyrians, defeated Pharnus, the king of Media. "And himself, being taken captive along with his seven sons and wife, was crucified."[126] Both verbs are in the singular but appear to refer to the king and his family. Therefore, I do not think that we can state with certainty that the spouse and children were actually crucified, but the text is tolerant of different interpretations. If the conqueror intended to exterminate the race and their postmortem influence, then we have a motive for the crucifixion of the women and children.

b. Also in book 2 we find a sequel to this story. Diodorus recounts in considerable detail aspects of the life of Semíramis, whom King Ninus married. She was a woman of surprising ability and succeeded to the throne on the death of her husband. According to Diodorus, she founded Babylon, made the hanging gardens, and waged campaigns against Egypt, Ethiopia, and India. He reports that the king of the Indians, Stabrobates, wrote a letter to her accusing Semíramis of being an aggressor and strumpet and calling the gods to witness that he would crucify her when he gained the victory.[127] The motif behind this threat may have been the shaming of a woman who had dared to take upon herself the role of a man, especially in war and leadership. Semíramis usurped the military prerogatives of males.

c. In book 18, Diodorus Siculus discusses the disturbances in the armies after the death of Alexander and how Perdiccas rose to power. The latter, after defeating King Ariarathes, took the king and his supporters captive. Dio concludes this portion, "Now the king and all his relatives Perdiccas tortured and impaled."[128] In this case, as in the incident of Pharnus above, the motive is important. If the conqueror(s) intended the extermination of the race, then the children and women must have been killed, preferably by crucifixion so that their ghosts or their descendants did not wreak vengeance on their enemies.

d. Speaking of the year 206 B.C.E. Diodorus reports that the Carthaginians after the Libyan War had crucified members of the Numidian tribe of the Micatani, "women and children included, and crucified all whom they captured."[129]

e. In Book 35 Diodorus reports an incident in Sicily. Bandits killed a father and his son. The grandson, Zibelmius, exacted vengeance where he could. His action is described thus: "On the most trivial provocation he tore men (some) limb from limb, or crucified them or burned them alive. He slaughtered children before the eyes of their parents or in a parent's arms."[130] He also tells us that Cratesipolis, a woman leader, crucified about thirty captives.[131] Vengeance was not confined to males.

### Ammianus Marcellinus

We can find another allusion to the crucifixion of women in Ammianus Marcellinus (b. 330 C.E. in Syrian Antoch). He describes how one Aginotius was condemned and hoisted up (*sublimis raptus occiditur*), and his woman accomplice condemned to the same fate (*pari sententia Anepsia interfecta*), although this case may be either hanging or crucifixion (Ammianus Marcellinus, *The History* 28.1.56).

Our evidence for crucifixion of women is not at all prolific, but the references above extend over a considerable portion of time, from the *Code of Hammurabi* to the time of Constantine. Geographically we have found references in Assyria, Babylonia, Palestine, Rome, Britain, Greece, and India. We have found no statement that women were not crucified. We might venture to suggest, therefore, that the crucifixion of women was not unprecedented in the Greco-Roman world. We now turn to mythical texts.

## Mythical References

### Pseudo-Plutarch

There are two curious mythological references to the crucifixion of women in Pseudo-Plutarch *Concerning Rivers*.[132] This work discusses the etiology of the names of rivers and mountains. It is dated after the second century C.E.

a. The author tells us that Chrysippa fell in love with a relative called Hydaspes. At dead of night and with the help of a nurse (servant) she attained her desire. But the king, learning of these matters, ordered the nurse to be buried alive, and then, having crucified the daughter, he was overwhelmed with grief and threw himself into the river. Hence the river was called Hydaspes.

b. In the same chapter we also read of some local virgins who lived unchastely and were crucified and flung into the river while a hymn was sung to Venus.[133] Curiously the Latin translation omits the reference to crucifixion.

These references are interesting because both have a reference to Venus. The first would seem to suggest that Chrysippa's unlawful love was related by the wrath of Venus and also that the punishment of both the nurse and the girl may be expiatory sacrifices offered to atone for unnatural love or incest, which might have incurred a more severe punishment. In the second text, we are obviously dealing with a case of sacrilege; the fact that a song is sung to Venus as the punishment is being implemented may suggest that the human sacrifice was offered to appease the goddess.

### Prometheus and Andromeda

a. Hengel, in his informative book on crucifixion, discusses the "crucifixion" of Prometheus, or perhaps more accurately the *apotympanismos* of Prometheus.[134] Prometheus, the god who procured fire for mortals, was fastened to the Caucasian rock with nails and chains (or hoops of iron). This myth was immortalized in Aeschylus's play *Prometheus Bound* and satirized in Lucian's treatises *Zeus Catechized* and *Prometheus*. But a similar tale was told about a feminine figure, princess Andromeda. Hengel gives less attention to her, although she was fastened to a rock like Prometheus.[135] But the "crucified" maiden appears to have been of interest in the ancient world. Euripides wrote a play called *Andromeda*,[136] which seems to have influenced Aristophanes in the *Thesmophoriazusae*, a work that centers on women celebrating the festivals of Demeter and Persephone, the givers and guardians of the home. They wish to put Euripides on trial for his scathing remarks about women. Euripides persuades his friend Mnesilochus to dress up as a woman and defend him. However, the ruse is discovered and Mnesilochus suffers the fate of *Apotympanismos*, although he is rescued in time so that he does not die. But the play makes obvious references to Andromeda, so that Euripides' friend's suffering is but an echo of hers. Thus Andromeda may have been to women what Prometheus is to men. Both are crucified mythical figures who brought blessings to humankind.

Andromeda is not a goddess, but her "exaltation" to the heavens is referred to in Manilius's *Astronomy*.[137] He sees Andromeda in the zodiacal sign of Virgo.[138] Manilius describes how nature, even the breeze, empathized with her. Perseus, her rescuer, arrives and calls the chains happy to "clasp such limbs." So he won a place in heaven for Andromeda.[139] Noticeable in the Manilius passage are the ideas of vicarious sacrifice, propitiation of the gods and goddesses,[140] and the details referring to *apotympanismos* and crucifixion.

b. Another interesting reference to Andromeda occurs in Achilles Tatius. He describes a sculpture erected in Pelusium. It was a double picture painted by Evanthes that portrayed both Andromeda and Prometheus. They were both in chains and secured to a rock, and both were tortured by monsters—Andromeda by the sea beast and Prometheus by the bird. They both had deliverers—for Andromeda, Perseus and for Prometheus, Heracles. Both deliverers were Argives.[141] Andromeda rested in a hollow in the rock. She wore a look of both fear and beauty even though her arms were pinioned above her head.[142] Evanthes had depicted the beast just rising out of the water and Perseus descending to help the maiden. Achilles Tatian tells us that rocks and iron formed the bonds of Prometheus. He is writhing in agony but, like Andromeda, wears a look of both fear and hope.

Evanthes' sculpture would suggest that some people saw Andromeda as a parallel to Prometheus. This material is complex but it does suggest an apotropaic and sacrificial[143] approach to the crucifixion of a woman, albeit one found in myth rather than history.

## Conclusions

A summary of the cases of the crucifixion of women described above renders the following result. There are twenty-two cases, and they fall into the following categories: one as a punishment for violating the rights of a husband; six as a penalty for sacrilege; two in propitiation to the gods and goddesses; one was a case of child abuse; two were meted out for the practice of sorcery; seven were perpetrated in order to exterminate a race (or kinship group) and, implicitly, to prevent vengeance by descendants or haunting by ghosts; three appear to have been due to wanton cruelty; and one was a punishment for abortion.

In the light of the above comments one may ask whether crucifixion of men and women was merely cruelty or sadism. Was there a religious or anthropological explanation for this form of execution? Some solution toward this can be found in Keramopoullos's book on *Apotympanismos.* Keramopoullos discusses the apotropaic use of nails used in crucifixion to warn off the evil eye, diseases, and the powers of enemies.[144] He suggests that this may help us to understand the early Christian veneration for the wounds of Christ. We have already referred to his remarks about destroying the vital organs to prevent vengeance by enemies or ghosts.

My conclusion must, indeed, be tentative, but I should like to make two points. First, that many women in the ancient world must have felt the threat of crucifixion, and this was actually realized in the case of the Christian slavewoman Blandina, who was impaled and obliged to face the beasts.[145]

Blandina was hung on a post (*epi zulou*)[146] and exposed as bait for the wild animals that were let loose on her. She seemed to hang there in the form of a cross, and by her fervent prayer she aroused intense enthusiasm in those who were undergoing their ordeal, for in their torment with their physical eyes they saw in the person of their sister him who was crucified for them, that he might convince all who believe in him that all who suffer for Christ's glory will have eternal fellowship in the living God (*Martyrs of Lyons*).[147]

Thus the *logion* to take up one's cross and follow Christ applied to women as well as men. In the light of this we may see Mary and the other women disciples in the New Testament in a new light—as women of wisdom, outstanding courage, and commitment; for they, too, might have faced the possibility of crucifixion. Second, the fascinating myth of Andromeda would have enabled women in the Greco-Roman world to see the possibility of the crucified female agent of redemption. The contemporary figure of the Christa would have caused them no *admiratio.*

Salvati speaks about the autocommunication of God in Jesus Christ: *autocom-municazione salvifica e rivelante di Dio raggiunse il suo vertice assoluto con Gesò di Nazaret* (59).

Jesus is the essential epiphany of God, the sacrament of encounter with God. It is the Fourth Gospel that brings this revelation to a climax (59). The humanity of Jesus becomes the sacrament of the divinity. He is the history of God and the God of history, the living narrative of the Father; his human life in each thought, emotion, comportment, and action is like an extended narrative of God (60). However, we understand this only through the cross and resurrection. To lack a deep appreciation of the shame of the cross for men and women is to lack appreciation of the paternal and maternal anguish of God.

# 5
# The *Pathos*
# of Friendship[1]

W E HAVE LOOKED AT THE SUFFERING GOD—the *pathos* of the masculine
aspect and the *pathos* of the feminine aspect—and we have suggested
that through the incarnation of the Son and his fateful death we catch a
glimpse of the highest expression of divine *pathos*. Our task now is to seek an
image or model that will accommodate the intensity of this *pathos* and that
will not be exclusive with regard to gender, race, or social status.

I should like to propose the model of friendship in the deepest sense of
the word. The friend comes to rescue a friend and enables him or her to
realize the totality of their potential. This model would complement God
seen as Father or Mother guiding children, patron patronizing clients,
shepherd leading sheep, or the warrior God "getting himself glory" (Exod.
15). After a discussion of friendship in general in the second part of this
book, I shall focus particularly on the Gospel of John.[2] Here the amicable,
covenantal relationship with God is manifested far more brilliantly than in
the other Gospels or the Pauline epistles. To some extent I shall be expand-
ing Grey's ideas of mutuality and communion, and Zizioulas's and
LaCugna's concept of ecstasy.[3]

## *Characteristics of Friendship*

I am not alone in selecting this image of God. Sallie McFague[4] discusses this
model briefly.[5] She notes the characteristics of friendship. They include the
following: (1) Friendship rises from no necessity.[6] It is the *most free* of all
human relationships,[7] for it is not bound by biological ties or by duties, nor
by function or office;[8] it is the consequence of purposeful and creative
choice and desire. Aristotle says that even one who possessed all goods
would not wish to live without friends (*Nichomachean Ethics* 8.1.1155a). He
does not say "cannot" live without friends. In the light of our earlier discussion of the *pathos* of God, this characteristic is peculiarly appropriate. God

freely enters into an affectionate and emotive relationship with the chosen people (*pace* Miles). Therefore, friendship can comprise the very essence of the theology of divine election.[9] (2) Friendship is based on (mutual) attraction but is combined with a profound respect and disinterested love for the unique characteristics of the other. (3) Friendship involves joy, sorrow, and trust. It is the joy of being in each other's presence, the love that follows the beloved even in grief and catastrophe. (4) Friendship as bonding is sometimes termed "mating of souls." This is the quality of *ḥesed*/covenant relationship. In the words of Daniel Day Williams,[10] love (friendship) is "spirit seeking the enjoyment of freedom in communion with the other."[11] For this reason, many of the mystics speak about enjoying the friendship of God; so also visions of paradise "reflect the qualities of deep friendship: the dance of the saved circling God in mutual attraction and joy."[12] We may compare the Greek word *perichōrēsis* from *perichoreuō* (dance around), often predicated of the Trinity.[13] (5) Montaigne[14] avers that a friendship relationship is *superior to marital relationship*. Therefore the image of God as friend is in many senses better than God as spouse or parent. Friendship involves a wider social circle and more shared interests. This is not, however, to deny that husband and wife may also be friends in a profound sense. (6) Friendship rejoices in community, especially in meals together, where need and pleasure are combined. Indeed, *com-pan-ion* means one who shares one's bread. We may compare the meal with God in Exodus 24:9-11, Proverbs 7, and the theology of the Eucharist. Most religions engage in sacred meals. (7) Friendship forms strong bonds, and betrayal of a friend ranks as the most dastardly of deeds. McFague[15] points out that Dante reserves the inner circle of hell for betrayers, e.g., Judas, Brutus, and Cassius. (8) Finally, friendships, according to McFague, are found *more frequently among women* than men.

These points will enable us to see friendship as a deeply "*complex and even mysterious*" phenomenon,[16] both mundane and celestial. In Proverbs 8:31, Wisdom delights to play with the children of human beings, and in Wisdom 7 she enters holy souls and makes them friends of God and prophets. All these characteristics can be predicated of divine as well as human friendship. They are consonant with our contemporary models of God and of our contemporary trinitarian theology.

## *Definition of Friendship*

We might define friendship as the bonding of two (or more) parties by free choice in a reciprocal relationship.[17] This is pertinent both to human and divine bonding. McFague, however, notes that there are three paradoxes in a friendly relationship: ". . . in a free relationship, a bonding occurs; in a relationship of two, an inclusive element is implied; in a relationship supposedly for children and angels, adult characteristics are required."[18] So a free relationship carries with it a hidden, huge, necessary, and unstinting responsibility.[19] It is one that may necessitate death for the loved one. Friends also have common concerns and interests beyond their affection for one another. Friendship is no passing entertainment or ephemeral pleasure but something of supreme importance—a vision, a project, a goal *in* life and *after* life.

If we see friendship in such a light we can predicate the same friendship in the covenantal love of God for his or her people. Bounded by no necessity, of his or her own deliberate volition God creates and nourishes humankind in a covenant bond more intimate than that of marriage.[20] The divine artist discovers a lure toward that which she or he has created and is prepared to remain united to the creation in joy and in sorrow. God's goal is the salvation of humanity and restoration of the earth. God's covenant friendship begins with the particular, exclusive love of Israel, but gradually expands to be also inclusive, since its common vision may embrace many persons from diverse backgrounds (*pace* Aristotle). Particular love prepares one for inclusive love.[21] Status and gender are irrelevant to friendship (cf. the inclusive love of Jesus for all ranks). So friendship appears to be the most inclusive of our relationships. Moreover, as McFague opines,[22] we can build a friendship not only with humans, but with animals and inanimate objects, a friendship with the earth.[23] Moreover, friends are adults in that they are responsible for others and for the earth, and they enjoy interdependence in the church, which is the body of Christ, and in the earth, which has been designated the body of God.[24] *Friends are images of God* by imitating the divine friendship within the Trinity and for human beings and the earth. For the Jew and Christian, friendship must be understood as covenant solidarity with one another and with God. Further, it is also seen within the very mystery of the Trinity.[25] McFague states that too often emphasis on relationships within the Trinity negates the essential doctrine, namely, that "God, as intrinsically relational, is, as are we, the *imago dei* interrelational with other forms of life."[26] She quotes from Brian Wren:

> One function of trinitarian theology is to express and guard the truth that God is not a Oneness of uniformity, self-absorption, or isolation. . . . If we, with all our multifaceted relationships, are made in God's image and likeness, *it follows that the creative God-head is, contains, and moves in, an incredible richness and reciprocity, in which all our varieties of relationship find their source.*[27]

McFague defines salvation: "Salvation is the reunification—the healing and liberation—of the torn, alienated, enslaved body of the world through the revelation of the depths of divine love for the world which gives us the power both to work actively for reunification and to suffer with the victims of estrangement."[28] Pentecost means God's free, permanent presence with us.[29]

Further, Ruth Page[30] states that God is not a tradesperson or problem solver on whom we call in an emergency. Rather the divine presence is with us in our ambiguity and suffering, bringing a different status to the creature. In the divine-human relationship lies the re-configuring of all relationships with creation, according to God's will and possibility.[31] She quotes Alastair Campbell: ". . . the heart of friendship is a *way of being*, not any particular activity."[32] She finds, therefore, the epithet "companion" for God better than parent, overseer, and so on. God wields power, but it is the power of attraction.[33] God can be seen as the lure for "creative advance into novelty."[34] It is a warm relationship without distinction of class, race, gender, or color. God is seen in this role in the exodus tradition, in the incarnation, and in the sending of the Spirit.[35]

## Friendship in the Greco-Roman World[36]

Did the Greco-Roman world provide a fertile soil for the early Christian writers to develop this kind of friendship in relationship to God and within the primitive communities?[37] I believe that it would be safe to assert that in antiquity friendship was regarded as the royal highway to the fullness of the happy life or, as we would say, authentic living.[38] It was certainly a favorite *topos* in philosophical circles and in drama.[39] The importance of the *topos* of friendship for the early Christian communities was the sense it gave of shared fellowship, communion, and equality, and the fact that it could be predicated of God as well as humanity. As such it had an academic and practical influence.

### The Pythagorean Life[40]

Important for the concept of friendship in the ancient world is the Pythagorean life. Pythagoras (fifth century B.C.E.) founded a community and taught the ideals of temperance, courage, and friendship.[41] Friendship was especially important for the Pythagoreans because it not only united human beings[42] but also made possible communion between the divine and the human, and the human and the animal world;[43] we might say it was an integrative and unifying force. Pythagoras himself was a sage and, as such, mediated between the gods, goddesses, and humanity. With regard to community life, Pythagoras elaborated the principle that "friends have all things in common."[44] He described the basic principle of justice: "All should approximate as nearly as possible in their attitudes to having one body and one soul in which all have the same experience, and should call that which is mine and that which belongs to another by the same name. . . ."[45]

One might compare the church as the body of Christ and the community of goods in the Jerusalem communities (e.g., Acts 4:32-37[46] and 1 Cor. 12–14). Pythagoras demonstrated the importance of "fellow-feeling" (*oikeiōsis*) and the obliteration of estrangement (*allotriōsis*) and contempt (*kataphronēsis tou koinou genous*). He also advocated bringing human beings into a friendly relationship with animals, and he decried killing them for food.[47] Indeed, he asked, if we are to be friends with animals, how much more with fellow human beings?[48] He also taught non-violence against one who had wronged an individual.[49] Iamblichus addresses the subject of friendship (*philia*) directly.[50] The passage[51] is worth quoting at length:

> Friendship of all with all (*philian de diaphanestata pantōn pros hapantas*), Pythagoras taught in the clearest manner; of gods with human beings through piety and scientific worship; of doctrines with one another, and generally, of the soul with the body, and of the rational part of the soul with all forms of the irrational through philosophy and contemplation in accord with this, of human beings with one another; of citizens through sound observance of law and of those of another race through correct inquiry into natural laws, of a husband with a wife or children, brothers and relatives, through an unperverted spirit of community; in short, friendship of all with all, and furthermore, with certain irrational animals through justice and natural union and affability; and friendship of the mortal body with itself, by reconciliation and conciliation of the opposite powers concealed in it, accomplished through health and a way of life conducive to this and temperance conducive to this, in imitation of the efficient functioning of the cosmic elements.
>
> For all these instances taken together, then, there is one and the same word, that of "friendship," of which, by common consent, Pythagoras was the discoverer and legislator, and he taught such an admirable friendship to his friends (*chrōmenois*), that even now many say of those who are unusually well-disposed to one another that they belong to the Pythagoreans.[52]

This is certainly a comprehensive understanding of friendship, and wholly consonant with a Christian soteriology.[53]

Pizzolato[54] explains "friendship" in this context as a unitive relationship between two entities. Friendship between human beings is grounded in *eusebeia*; between body and soul, in philosophy and contemplation; between fellow citizens by observance of the laws; with strangers on a recognition of their common humanity; between individuals and their families, a natural community; between humans and animals on justice and common nature.[55] All this is founded on humanity's atunement to the rhythm of the cosmos.[56] A certain anonymous Pythagorean defined "friendship" as "a musical harmony (equality)." Indeed, for the Pythagoreans friendship spanned many generations.[57] It is understandable that the Pythagoreans were said to be persons united in an intense friendship.

Pythagoras taught that in order to maintain friendship of any kind, one must remove competition and rivalry.[58] Reproof must be couched in gracious and benevolent words. Trust (*pistein*) is an absolutely essential element in friendship.[59] Falsehood mars the core of friendship. Friendships must be carefully chosen and be "definite and established."[60] Relationships should not be broken except for "great and incorrigible vice."[61] Iamblichus relates the story of Phintias and Damon.[62] In his conclusion Iamblichus explicates friendship with God.[63]

> Much more wonderful than these, however, were what they established about partnership in divine goods, and about unity of intellect and the divine soul. For they often encouraged one another not to disperse the god within themselves. At any rate, all their zeal for friendship, both in words and deeds, aimed at *some kind of mingling (theokrasia) and union with God, and at communion with intellect and with the divine soul.* For no one could find anything better, either in words spoken or in ways of life practiced, than this kind of friendship. For I think that all the goods of friendship are embraced by it. Hence, having included all excellences of Pythagorean friendship in this summation, as it were, we need say no more about it.[64]

Pythagoras also taught that we should do friendly deeds even for those whom we have never met according to the belief that "good men (*spoudaioi andres*), even dwelling in earth's farthest parts, are friends to one another even before they have become acquainted and conversant."[65] *Philos* became a technical term for a member of a close community. We may compare the Christian use of "brother" ("sister"). The Pythagoreans considered friendship as the epitome of all virtues.[66] Much of this Pythagorean thought was adopted by the Stoics, and in all likelihood by the early Christian communities.[67]

### Socrates' and Plato's Teaching on Friendship

In the age of Socrates, the concept of friendship oscillated between the archaic tradition[68] and the distinctly personal.[69] According to Herodotus it found its implementation in hospitality and in political alliance. We find a similar use in Thucydides, though he also has a more philosophical, ethical approach, and relates friendship to justice and virtue. With Socrates,[70] friendship is definitely focused on the human and psychological plane. He considers friendship the most precious of all possessions, the greatest blessing that a person can possess.[71] A friend shows generosity and courage in supplying every need of his friend.[72] There are some friends for whom one would sacrifice everything.[73] The qualities in a friend for which he seeks are: hospitality, humanitarianism, self-control with regard to pleasure, justice, and eagerness to help his benefactors.[74]

Plato's[75] *Lysis*[76] comprises a discussion on friendship and love, mainly on a human level. Pizzolato emphasizes the importance of the *Lysis*.[77] While it is generally accepted that the *Lysis* is our first sample of a specific reflection on the theme of this *topos*, he does question this premise. He states that Plato does not give an actual definition of friendship. Plato says that persons are only friends when they are alike in goodness, for just as the body craves what is beneficial for it, friendship craves the good. The *Lysis* shows that friendship is superior to love because it guarantees better the interpersonal characteristics of stability and faithfulness.[78] Indeed, the poets, Plato continues, state that it is God who makes people friends by drawing them to each other.[79] For example, Homer says: "Yea, ever like and like together God doth draw. . . ."[80] God makes them acquainted (*poiei gnorismon*). The sages also assert that a person is attracted to one who is similar to her or himself.[81] Socrates concludes that two friends belong to each other because there is a natural bond, and:

> In the case where one person desires another . . . or loves him, he would never be desiring or loving or befriending him, unless he somehow belonged to his beloved either in soul or in some disposition, demeanor or cast of soul. . . . [W]hat belongs to us by nature has been shown to be something we needs must befriend. . . . Then the genuine, not the pretended, lover must be befriended by his favorite.[82]

A confidence grows up in friendship, whereby one trusts a friend in the areas in which she or he is competent.[83] Such a friendship will perdure even when evils have passed away. A friend would never do any good or harm to the other that he would not do to himself.[84] An important aspect of Plato's argument, however, is that the beloved is not always a friend of the lover: "Then people must often be loved by their enemies, and hated by their friends and be friends to their enemies and enemies to their friends."[85] In this case affection is not reciprocal. It is not always true that opposites are attracted to each other, e.g., the just person to the unjust (Plato *Lysis* 216B).[86] There is, however, some grain of beauty in the other, and the beautiful is friendly (Plato *Lysis* 216C). "For we say that, in the soul and the body and everywhere just that which is neither good nor bad, but has the presence of the bad, is thereby friend of the good" (Plato *Lysis* 218B). So there is always the hope of reconciliation. A friend is a friend for the sake of a friend, that is, the original, veritable friend.[87] True friendship belongs to the noetic world. One can ask, then, "Is not this the nature of the good—to be loved because of the bad by us who are midway[88] between the bad and the good, whereas separately and for its own sake it is of no use?"[89] A friend can supply a need as a doctor can supply a patient with health. But the friendship remains when the evil has been eradicated. Wickedness is alien to humankind, but goodness naturally belongs to it.[90]

Platonic friendship can also be a civic virtue. Plato's *Alcibiades* identifies *philia* and *homonoia* (concord).[91] *Philia-homonoia* in Plato are the direct result of justice. The state must be above all *amico di se stesso*.[92] Hence flourish, too, the virtues of prudence and temperance.[93]

## *Christian Application*

In the light of that which we have noted above, we may now ask whether the Incarnation can be seen as an act of friendship. Here we shall consider the life of Jesus in general as it is found in the New Testament, later we shall turn specifically to the Gospel of John. We shall also see that Philo interprets the covenants in Genesis and Exodus in terms of friendship. (1) If it is goodness that attracts one person to another in friendship, then we may see the grounds for friendship between God and humanity. For God created humanity in the divine image and likeness, and declared all creation "very good." Persons are attracted to those with similar characteristics. As Dawe[94] states, there is an innate attraction of godhood for humanity and vice versa. They are not a polarity but complementarity. "Image and likeness" are the basis of divine-human friendship. (2) As in classical thought it is the deity who draws humanity to God's self and creates interpersonal relationships. (3) Friends belong to each other. As we shall see in John's Gospel, God sees humanity as "his own." This is seen not only in creation but through salvation history, especially in the covenant bond.[95] (4) A friend must be conscious of a friend's existence. This is won by living together, preferably in a similar social milieu. This is the whole heart of the incarnation, God's coming to dwell in the flesh with humanity, to live together, to converse, to communicate thoughts, to make *koinōnia* so that humanity is, as it were, a second self to God. In Christian terms the confidence that grows between friends is faith in God and Jesus and the inspiration of the Spirit. Indeed the Spirit is the mingling of two selves or spirits. Jesus comes not as a patron to clients, but as a friend. (5) As Plato avers, however, the friendship may not be reciprocal, and there may even be bad characteristics in the object of one's devotion. But God incarnate in Christ reaches out to humanity—even though it may be an enemy of God, faithless to the covenant. God sees that there is always good in the worst sinner. This is why we find Jesus befriending marginal or sinful people and confronting the self-righteous. (6) Plato explains that the wicked "are never like even to their own selves, being so ill-balanced and unsteady; and when a thing is unlike itself and variable it can hardly become like or friend to anything."[96] Thus the wicked never enter into true friendship, either with good or bad people. But for the Christian, this is the purpose of redemption, namely, to develop human potential through godly grace, and to enable men and women to be themselves in God, bonded by God's purifying Spirit. It is vital to "win over" the enemy. (7) We may add to this our general consideration of friendship (see pp. 73–76). God works under no necessity: absolutely freely, she or he chooses humankind, is prepared to join in joy and sorrow, and is the Spirit who seeks the "enjoyment of freedom in communion with the other."[97]

## *Friendship in the* Symposium[98]

We must ask another pertinent question: Is there a specially feminine aspect to Platonic friendship? Indeed, there seems to be. Interestingly enough, the teaching about love[99] as friendship that Socrates (Plato) expounds in the *Symposium* is alleged to be that of a woman, the prophetess from Mantua named Diotima.[100] It is, therefore, not surprising that very feminine imagery (e.g., conceiving, giving birth, the role of the midwife) is used to express divine love and divine activity, and the attraction of human beings for this love. The *Symposium* lifts love and friendship into a new dimension. Plato, reporting Diotima's teaching, states that the guiding principle in life is Love[101] and that love inspires us with the noblest valors.[102] For Plato, Love is a god,[103] indeed, "the most venerable and valuable of gods" who has sovereign power to provide all virtue and happiness to humankind, whether living or deceased.[104] The lover, who is thus filled with a god (*entheos*), is nearer to divinity than the beloved. But Love is not always noble, only when she "impels us to love in a noble manner."[105] This noble love is the Love that belongs to the heavenly goddess, heavenly per se and precious both in public and private life. The lover and the beloved should have an equal zeal for the pursuit of virtue. Eryximachus, one of the fellow guests, states:

> Thus Love, conceived as a single whole, exerts a wide, a strong, nay, in short, a complete power: but that which is consummated for a good purpose, temperately and justly, both here on earth and in heaven above, wields the mightiest power of all and provides us with perfect bliss; so that we are able to consort with one another and have friendship also with the gods who are above us.[106]

After this it is Socrates who delivers his own speech, the inspiration for which he attributes to Diotima. He states that, whereas deities and humans do not normally mingle, yet the spiritual person is able to have intercourse and converse with the gods, and the gods with humans, whether awake or through dreams.[107] He cites the craftpersons, spiritual people—among whom are poets.[108] Love yearns to possess the everlasting good,[109] and it is this eagerness and exertion of those who pursue the good that is called Love. This pursuit of love brings about a begetting in the soul,[110] a "begetting of a beautiful thing by means of both the body and the soul."[111] People can be pregnant both in body and in soul, but this spiritual begetting is "an immortal element in the creature that is mortal; and it cannot occur in the discordant." The ugly (*aischrōn*, "shameful") is not in harmony with the divine.[112] Thus Love is the begetting of the beautiful. With regard to this pregnancy of the soul, Diotima taught that there are those who are still more pregnant in their souls than in their bodies. They conceive and bring forth all that is proper for the soul, such as prudence and virtue in general. Included among those begetters are all the poets and craftspersons who are styled "inventors."[113] Below we shall discuss the text of John 3:1-15 in the light of this text. Neumann summarizes Diotima's thesis:

> The salient point is that pregnancy does not come about by the agency of an external begetter or male element, since it is innate. Although pregnancy is inborn, the means of relieving it are external. Those things in which or through which mortals can give birth are beautiful. Beauty is defined as that which makes possible the transition from pregnancy to childbirth. . . . [114] Taking this beauty in hand, he fathers in his [the beauty's] soul the things which have been on his mind for a long time (209C1–3). Once having given birth to the beauties of virtue in the other's soul, he joins his beloved in rearing their offspring (290C4). Their bond of togetherness (*koinōnia*) and friendship through their "children" is more secure than physical bonds, since the fruits of their intercourse are lovelier and more immortal (209C5–7). Thus the one pregnant in soul generates the fairest part of wisdom in an attractive soul.[115]

He concludes that *erōs* (love) is principally creative, not contemplative.[116] Friend shares with friend all that is nurtured and begotten, "so that men [*sic*] in this condition enjoy a far fuller community with each other than that which comes with children, and a far surer friendship, since the children of their union are fairer and more deathless."[117] First the lover sees the physical beauty of the beloved, and then she or he sees the beauty of the soul, which is much more valuable, even though there may be only a little grace in that soul. He will love and care for it and seek to augment the little grace and the improvement of the young.[118] Such a spiritual person sees the whole province of beauty and escapes from the slavery of the single instance. Then he comes to the "final vision of beauty which exists for ever in the singularity of its form, absolutely independent." All beauties participate in this.[119] In this way she or he may contemplate the divine beauty in its unique form. "So when he has begotten a true virtue and has reared it up, he is destined to win the friendship of heaven (*theophilei*); he, above all men, is immortal."[120] When a person has begotten virtue in her or himself, she or he plays midwife to others to enable them to beget.

## *Christian Application*

(1) One notes the preponderance of love in the New Testament and especially in the Gospel of John.[121] The Christian might agree with Plato's declaration that love is divine,[122] if she or he regards God as love, and the communication of that love as the Holy Spirit. The Holy Spirit does, indeed,
provide all virtue and happiness for humankind, especially with her
fruits.[123] (2) Love, for the Christian, is not a desire for ignoble things but
only for that which is noble.[124] It is this love that is our communion with
God, the bridge between earth and heaven. (3) It is the incarnation, however, that distinguishes Platonic love from that of the Gospels, especially
Johannine thought. In Christianity, body and soul participate in the life of
God. There is no dichotomy between divine and human; the noetic world
and the sensible world are one. Christ is the incarnate *pathos* of God, uniting the noetic and the sensible world. (4) Love does possess the everlasting
good. It is the pursuit of this that brings about begetting. It is faith and love
in Jesus that leads to the rebirth in baptism that is couched in Hellenistic
terms, similar to ideas in the *Symposium.* In Jesus' words to Nicodemus he
speaks about begetting by the Spirit and the things above.[125] Jesus shares all
that was nurtured and begotten in the heavenly sphere with his earthly
brothers and sisters. (5) Jesus did, indeed, see the beauty of the human
soul even though it might be obscured by sin, and he did nurture "the
bloom" in any likely soul. Jesus does bring us to the friendship of heaven
and immortality, or, more accurately, everlasting life for the entire person.
(6) Above all, true friendship requires that one should be willing to lay
down one's life for a friend. Plato avers that only those in love will be prepared to die for others: this applies to women as well as men; he gives the
example of Alcestis.[126] The gods give special honor to those who do such
deeds. Indeed, sometimes they send up their souls from Hades, e.g.,
Achilles who was prepared to die for (*huperapothanein*) Patroclus.[127] The
*Phaedo,* which comprises Socrates' pre-mortem speech,[128] declares that
philosophers ought to be ready and willing to die, and that the wise person
will not be reluctant to leave the service that the gods have laid upon
them.[129] The souls of the good enter the realm of the pure, everlasting,
immortal, and changeless, but the unjust go into the bodies of wild preda-
tory animals and birds. The philosopher must prepare his or her soul for
the other world by educating and nurturing it so that she or he can take
these things with her. The soul who has lived purely and justly on this
earth will find gods as leaders and companions (*xynemporōn*) in the other
world.[130]

Jesus certainly fulfills this ideal of friendship. In all four Gospels he predicts his voluntary and dire suffering and death. In John's Gospel, Jesus speaks about his followers already enjoying eternal life, and Jesus does indeed impart heavenly knowledge to them. They see the Father in him.[131]

## Aristotle[132]

Aristotle divided friendship into three classes: friendship based on utility,[133] friendship based on pleasure,[134] and friendship based on virtue.[135] We shall be concerned principally with friendship based on virtue.[136]

In the teaching of Aristotle we find a more practical discussion of friendship than we found in Plato. However, this does not preclude the higher form(s) of friendship that focus on the absolute, and, indeed, Aristotle would have been acquainted with Platonic teaching. Aristotle sees friendship as an essential interpersonal relationship leading to the goal of moral life—happiness.[137] A human being needs friends because she or he is a social and political animal.[138] Justice belongs to the very nature of friendship,[139] and friendship produces *homonoia* (concord). Thus, friendship has an impressive social aspect. Aristotle defines[140] a friend as follows:

> A friend is defined as (a) one who wishes, and promotes by action, the real or apparent good of another for that other's sake; or (b) one who wishes the existence and preservation of his friend for the friend's sake. Others say that a friend is (c) one who frequents another's society, and (d) who desires the same things as he does, or (e) one who shares his friend's joys and sorrows.[141]

Aristotle emphasizes action rather than desire in friendship.[142] A happy person needs virtuous friends.[143] A person, however, must be conscious of the friend's existence, and this is attained by living together, conversing, communicating thoughts. Friends should have everything in common, for friendship is a "partnership" (*koinōnia*), and a friend becomes a second self.[144] Friends have one soul[145] between them.[146] Liking is an emotion, but friendship a fixed disposition acquired through choice.[147] Yet antiquity as a rule, including Aristotle, would find it difficult to imagine the highest form of friendship between a man and a woman.[148]

Aristotle addresses the subject of friendship especially in Books 8 and 9 of the *Nichomachean Ethics*. Like Plato, he discusses whether likeness or opposites bring people together and whether only good people can be friends.[149] In speaking of the friendship based on virtue, Aristotle says that we measure benefits by the intention of the benefactor.[150] In unequal friendships there is mutual benefit, but the benefit that the donor receives is a larger share of honor, and that which the needy receives is the larger share of gain.[151] Sometimes it proves impossible to bestow sufficient honor on a benefactor in an unequal friendship, but one can only comport one-self according to one's abilities. This is not dissimilar to the love that children show to their parents, for we love what is good and what is superior to ourselves. Similarly, we love God for the divine goodness and for qualities that we do not possess. A benefactor is friendly towards a recipient even if the affection is not reciprocal.[152] Affection is an active principle and is found in the more active party in the relationship.[153] Love arises when the benefactor loves at great cost (e.g., a mother for a child). Yet, ideally, there should be reciprocity of affection. The perfect form of friendship is between the good.[154] A friend loves another simply for his or her sake, and not accidentally. The absolutely good is the object of his or her affections.[155] These friendships require time (*chronou*) and intimacy (*synethēias*). It is characteristic of friends that they seek each other's company (*hōs to suzēn*). Further, they may have common property, according to the saying, "Friends' goods are common property" (*en koinōnia gar hē philia*).[156] However, the good person also likes his own company, for his mind is stored with good things to recall.[157] Aristotle also taught that: "in loving their friend they love their own good, for the good man in becoming dear to another becomes that other's good by affording him pleasure; for there is a saying, 'Amity is equality,' and this is most fully realized in the friendships of the good."[158] Moreover, one feels toward a friend as one feels toward oneself, ". . . very intense friendship resembles self-regard."[159] Indeed, it is necessary to have a friend in order to know oneself.[160] Happiness does not lie in self-sufficiency.[161] Affection is more than goodwill (9.5.2), rather goodwill is the beginning of friendship, affection its fruit. Friendship gives more affection than it receives; hence, if there is mutual love (*philophilon*), the friendship endures. Mere concord is not the essence of true friendship. Those who are equal in station must love each other equally. But Aristotle also asks whether we are bound to love a person who was good when we formed a friendship with him or her but who later becomes a wicked person. He says that we should break off the friendship only when our friend becomes "incurably bad."[162] A friend shares the pleasures of his friend and, most importantly, this includes divine and teleological pleasures:

> Surely their partnership will be pre-eminently in things included in the end. Hence we should study together, and feast together—not on the pleasures of food and necessary pleasures (for such partnerships do not seem to be real social intercourse but mere enjoyment), but each really wishes to share in his friends the End that he is capable of attaining, or failing this, men choose most of all to benefit their friends and to be benefited by them (Aristotle, *Eudemian Ethics* 7.12.14.1245b).

Aristotle reaches a climax when he states that a person's conduct is guided by the interests of his or her friends and she or he is prepared to sacrifice wealth, power, and a long life for nobility of conduct. He concludes: "And this is doubtless the case with those who give their lives for others; (*hyperapothneskein*) thus they choose great nobility for themselves" (*Nichomachaean Ethics* 8.9). Below we shall be looking at further examples of those who give up their lives for others.[163]

## *Christian Application*

As Christians we can see how powerfully this teaching about friendship speaks to the essence of the incarnation. Jesus comes as the redeemer who wishes, and actively promotes, the existence, preservation, and good of humanity for its own sake, not for his own glory.[164] This he accomplishes on two levels: in this world with his healing and teaching mission; and on the heavenly level when through his life, death, resurrection, and exaltation he promotes eternal good and everlasting life for those who believe in him. In his earthly life he frequents the company of persons from every level of society, and is prepared to enter fully into their joys and *angst*: this is particularly manifest in the nature of the death that he chooses. In the Eucharist under the dynamic symbol of blood, which is life, he imparts his "soul" to his believers.

Friendship as a bond in society is manifested in Jesus' bringing to full realization the covenant initiated by God in the Hebrew Scriptures.[165] One could describe the bond between Jesus and humanity as an unequal friendship, perhaps even patron and client, but this is to miss the very point of the incarnation; namely, that Jesus made himself equal to us and took on the role of servant (Phil. 2:6-11). However, this is not to deny that God is our superior and should receive the honor. God's grace is ineffable, incalculable, and incomparable, but the incarnation means that Jesus put this aside to create an equal friendship. And this friend, whether God or Christ, bestows his graces and gifts even on the ungrateful, even when no affection arises in the recipient. Yet ideally God and Jesus wish this affection to be present. To this end Jesus directed his teaching and sent the Spirit as the bond of unity between God and humanity, and among all humanity. Jesus strives for that form of friendship that is perfect, where both parties are good and there is mutual affection.

Jesus is the friend who shares the pleasures of others, but these are not merely the pleasures of social conviviality as at Cana (John 2:1-12). He imparts to them a sharing in the divine nature itself. In accordance with the last quotation from Aristotle, the end is the focus of Christ's teaching; it is a teleological teaching where the human person can attain his or her full dignity in this world and the next. Jesus' last statement on friendship is his fateful death, a voluntary death that would hardly be found in a patron-client relationship.

## *Epicurus*[166]

With the advent of Hellenization, the concept of "friendship" changed. There was an emphasis not so much on the "friendship" of the body of citizens but on the *philoi* of the monarch. It became a friendship between patron and client that always ran the risk of adulation and insincerity. Yet there arose also personal friendships, and these are reflected in Middle Comedy. We find the title *synapothnēskontes*, indicating people bound together by an agreement to die together. In the New Comedy of Menander youths are joined together as *synepheboi* The theater provides an important insight into friendship, for we see the philosophical tenets set against the social background.[167]

The Epicurean community of friends is explicable against the background of the loss of friendship mentioned above. It is not a political friendship in any way. In the Epicurean philosophy, which minimizes the role of the gods, the human person is face to face with his or her problems, and must overcome pain and seek happiness without divine assistance, although perfect friendship may lead to intercourse with the divine. The life of wisdom is the true way to liberty. So interpersonal relationships became of utmost importance.[168] Although Epicurus sought the highest quality of friendship, he did not despise the friendship of utility. Friendship is a way to "salvation," liberation, and tranquility. Friendship gives hope for the future.[169] The Epicurean garden, and their cosmic liturgical celebrations, both solidified friendship.[170] The Epicureans also commemorated their deceased friends.[171]

Fiore[172] points out that Epicurus[173] suggests that a friend can effect a change in a person, and this can lead to a community of those living with pleasure.[174] This was true of most of the philosophical "schools," for the teacher was seen as the friend of the disciple. For example, Xenophon shows pupils living in close association with Socrates.[175] Fiore also observes that:

> Epicurus regularized and institutionalized the free *hetaira* of the Socratic association, with periodic meetings, mutual but not forced sharing of goods, commemorative banquets to reinforce free sharing, a hierarchy of succession to serve as depositories of his doctrine and continuators of his beneficence.[176]

O'Connor demonstrates that there was a public recitation of tales about heroes, e.g., "the story of Epicurus' tranquility in his final hours in the face of great bodily pain, that might be read to the assembled community."[177] Similarly the Gospels and the epistles must have been read to the early Christian communities[178] and the narrative of the passion and resurrection of the hero Jesus read and interpreted.

## Christian Application

Through the characteristics of universalism and equality (of both men and women), of plenitude of wisdom and affection, and through the idea of immortality, the Epicurean friendship communities seem very close to the early Christian ones. Jesus has a similar relationship to his disciples. Epicurus believed that true love is divine and that through this the human person approached the deity. The early Christians, like the Epicureans, engaged in rituals, meals, anniversaries, and communal studies that developed into full liturgical and sacramental celebrations.

## Stoic Friendship

The constituency of Stoicism is more complex than that of Epicureanism. Stoicism falls into three periods, Old, Middle, and New Stoicism. We have few original sources for this philosophy. We know of two specific works on friendship, one by Cleanthes[179] and one of Chrysippus.[180] The Stoics deemed friendship a necessity for those on the way to wisdom. Friendship begins with love of self,[181] then widens by concentric circles until it embraces the whole world.[182] This is the result of realizing one's common humanity, and of the practice of *oikeiōsis* (fellow-feeling). One unites oneself in *philia* with the rest of the human race.[183] This explains the propriety of love of self: in order to love others one must love oneself.[184] Perfect friendship, however, is not possible with every person, for some may not be seeking moral perfection (i.e., the *phauloi*, in distinction from the *sophoi*). Indeed, there are diverse kinds of friendship, almost a social classification of it.[185] Only the wise and virtuous person attains perfect friendship, but the Stoics are interested not only in the wise person, but also in the people who are "on the way," whom they might encourage and inspire.[186] Stoic philosophy in its various forms penetrated the Greco-Roman world at large. It also influenced Christianity and offered a *modus vivendi* for the individual and community, especially the martyrs.

## Friendship in the Roman World

One finds the *topos* of friendship in the Roman world more frequently in political than philosophical discourse. It tended, therefore, to be less idealistic and more practical, and often referred to the relationship between patron and client, which could be called a friendship of utility.[187] A similar relationship obtained between Rome and her allies who were bound by a *foedus,* or contract, that sanctified the friendship.[188] Those allied to Rome were called *amici et socii populi Romani.* We may compare the phrase "friend of Caesar."[189] Friendship often led to hospitality, sometimes on a large scale.[190]

### Cicero

Cicero wrote both as a statesman and as a philosopher. He was probably greatly influenced by Stoicism. One of the most famous treatises on friendship is Cicero's *On Friendship.* I shall comment only briefly on his work here, as I shall be using much of his material in the subsequent chapters. Cicero complements many of Aristotle's *dicta* concerning friendship. He states that friendship is according to nature,[191] and as nature is immutable, so true friendships are eternal (9.32).[192] He sees the essence of friendship as " the complete agreement in policy, in pursuits and in opinions."[193] He distinguishes "kinship" and "friendship," in that goodwill is always present in friendship but not always present in blood relationships. He opines that in friendship we seem to behold "a sort of lamp of uprightness and virtue." This virtue attracts us even if the person is absent; indeed, we could even see it in an enemy. Love is strengthened by kindly service that enables it to grow into intimacy.[194] Fiore[195] underlines the importance of *benevolentia* for Cicero. For him friendship was not only the "reasoned relationship" of the Stoic philosopher but rather its "resting place," its source and energizer.[196] Fiore, citing Dugas,[197] opines that there is a "reciprocal penetration of spirits" that grows into a psychological *suzēn* (living together) and complements the physical aspect of friendship. Friendship raises one's vision to things that are "lofty, noble and divine."[198] Cicero avers:

> For when men have conceived a longing for this virtue they bend towards it and move closer to it, so that, by familiar association with him whom they have begun to love, they may enjoy his character, equal him in affection, become readier to serve than to demand his favors, and to vie with him in a rivalry of virtue.[199]

The above quotation, *mutatis mutandis,* almost perfectly describes the Christian attitude towards Christ.

## Christian Application

We can certainly say that the friendship that Jesus offers is immutable and eternal. To some extent we could say that the friendship that Jesus pursues seeks for agreement but not uniformity in policy, in pursuits, or in opinions. The idea of the "penetration of spirits" could find its implementation in Jesus' bestowal of the Spirit (see especially John 20:19-23). The Spirit, like friendship for Cicero, becomes the source and energizer of the Christian community. In the Farewell Discourses Jesus speaks about mutual indwelling (John 14:20). Jesus' presence, both pre- and post-resurrection does effect a change in a person and his followers living together in a community characterized by the joy of the Spirit even in the midst of suffering.[200] We mention again that Culpepper has compared the Johannine school to (other) philosophical schools.[201]

## Friendship in the Jewish World and Christian Antiquity

Judaism and Christianity shared beliefs about creation, salvation, and about the human being's relationship to God, and both were influenced by the philosophy of the Greco-Roman world. I shall focus on Philo as our most important extant model for examining the *topos* of friendship in Judaism and as a vital link between Hellenism and Judaism.[202]

Christianity and Judaism took an approach similar to the Pythagoreans, Epicureans, and Stoics, in that both regarded all humans as equal and recognized the possibility of every class of person to draw near to God. This presents a different concept from that of Aristotle. But in the Hebrew Scriptures this is enhanced by the concept of a God who loves humanity disinterestedly and forms a ritual contract of friendship with them through the covenant. This is notably different from the concept of human autonomy (self-subsistence) that is found in philosophies such as the Epicurean.[203]

### Friendship in Philo[204]

In Philo, we find an important link between the philosophical schools and Judaism, and eventually also Christianity, because so many early Christian writers are deeply influenced by Philo. Philo describes God as the lover, or friend, of human beings.[205] God is also "parent."[206] Further, Philo is explicit about friendship for God on the part of human beings. He says: "This is the most noble definition of deathless life, to be possessed by a love of God and a friendship for God with which flesh and body have no concern."[207] Again, when discoursing on Genesis 28:21, Philo represents Jacob's thoughts as follows:

> He (God) shall no longer exhibit towards me the masterfulness that characterizes the rule of an autocrat, but the readiness to bless that marks the power that is in every way kindly, and bent on the welfare of men [*sic*]. He shall do away with the fear we feel before Him as Master, and implant in the soul the loyalty and affection that goes out to him as Benefactor.[208]

In the next paragraph of this treatise, Philo describes God as continuously kind, bountiful; the giver of good things and the "strong bulwark of cheerfulness of spirit." We enjoy freedom from danger when we have rested our confidence in a sovereign who is not urged by the greatness of his dominion to inflict injuries on his subjects, but whose love for humankind makes it his delight to supply what is lacking to each one.[209] In teaching on the freedom of the good person, Philo says that, if he has a friend in God, he has perfect felicity, for God does not overlook the "rights of friendship."[210] Moreover, Philo's sense of "friendship," and the community consequent on it, is intrinsically bound up with Israelite monotheism and monolatry. He confesses that the Hebrews' strength does not lie in numbers, but rather in their "unanimity and mutual attachment." He continues: "And the highest and greatest source of this unanimity is their creed of a single God, through which, as from a fountain, they feel a love for each other, uniting them in an indissoluble bond."[211] Further Philo avers that even blood relatives should be cast aside if they repudiate God and monotheism, and others who are not blood relatives be accepted, for they "will receive in exchange kinships of greater dignity and sanctity."[212]

### Philo on Abraham[213]

Philo makes a clear statement that Abraham and his family placed friendship (fictive kinship) with God above blood kinship.[214] Their departure from Mesopotamia was an act of piety. He observes: "the stronger attraction of piety which leads him to endure separation from his most familiar and *dearest friends who form*, as it were, *a single whole with himself.*"[215] In his discussion of the *akedah* (the binding of Isaac, Gen. 22) Philo inquires whether Abraham's motive for the sacrifice of his son was prompted by (a) custom, (b) ambition for honor, or (c) fear (*On Abraham* 188). He describes Abraham's love for Isaac: "His feeling of affection for him was necessarily on the same high level of truth, higher even than the chaste forms of love and also the much talked of ties of friendship."[216] Nevertheless, Abraham put aside kinship affection and was prepared to perform an ineffable action, "since his whole weight is thrown into the scale on the side of acceptability with God (*pros to theophilēs*). His conduct in it is practically unique (*exaireton*)."[217] Thus the most affectionate father, acting as priest, began the sacrificial rite of the best of sons.[218] So the *akedah* is seen as an act of friendship towards God, an act that transcends kinship affection.[219]

### Philo and Moses

The theme of friendship recurs and reaches a certain climax when Philo expounds upon the life of Moses. In discussing the revelation of God's name in Midian, Philo says that a person who is confident of the "divine comradeship" (*theias symmachias*) has no cowardly fear. He avers that to incorporeal souls who worship God "it is likely that He should reveal Himself as He is, conversing with them as friend with friends" (*dialegomenōn hōs philōn philais*).[220] This is obviously based on the biblical observation that Moses spoke to God face to face as to a friend,[221] but Philo applies this to other friends of God. Philo has a lengthy section on Moses and philanthropy (practicing love for human beings). Of particular interest are the following points: Moses administered the Torah in such a way as to incite and train "all his subjects to fellowship" (*koinōnia*).[222] In speaking of the Book of the Covenant (Exod. 21–23) Philo also states that Moses commanded the people to love not only their nation, but "incomers," whom they should love not only as friends and kinsfolk but even as themselves.[223] Philo says of the immigrants that they "have demonstrated a disposition of friendship with God (*theophilēs ēthos*) which above all leads to friendship and kindred relationship (*eis philian kai oikeiotēta*)."[224] They become dearest friends (*philtatous*) and closest kinsfolk (*syngenestatous*). Thus Philo is significant for our theme in that he makes a clear association between friendship and the covenant and, implicitly, redemption. In summing up our examination of friendship in the Greco-Roman world we will quote Rader:[225]

> [N]ot only was Plato influenced by their system, but in some sense Pythagoras' maxims upon friendship formed the ultimate inspiration of the public school and the residential university. There is no doubt that the Pythagorean Order attained lasting significance by providing an organizational model for later philosophic schools. The Academy, the Lyceum, the Stoic School, and the Epicurean Garden followed the Pythagorean experiment in basing their internal structure on the maxims of friendship. The members of these schools were known as *philoi* or "friends."

Our discussion of friendship in the Greco-Roman world may lead us to assume that the early Christian communities must have been influenced by this phenomenon and sought to implement many of its principles in their daily life. We must turn to the Fourth Gospel to inquire whether this was true in the Johannine community.

# 6

# The *Pathos* of
# Wise Men and Women

I N OUR DISCUSSION OF FRIENDSHIP WE HAVE INDICATED that this quality
extends beyond person-to-person relationships. One can develop
friendship not only with the deity but with oneself, with animals, with
nature; indeed, there can be a kind of cosmic friendship. Here we need to
consider briefly how the sages maintained this friendship, especially with
themselves and amid traumatic circumstances. This should cast light on
the comportment of Jesus during his ministry, passion, and death. Chapter 4 portrayed the utter degradation concomitant with condemnation to
crucifixion. In this chapter I wish to inquire whether there was an attempt
to triumph over suffering and dishonor in the ancient world. Did any of
the contemporaries of the early church manage to turn the shame of suffering and death, especially crucifixion, into glory? I think that we may
find an answer in some of the principles of the philosophical schools. In
the second part of this book we shall see that John goes beyond their tenets
in showing Jesus not only overcoming the worst shame and death but overcoming it *as God* and in full hope of the resurrection and exaltation. He
will enrich the theme of "glory" that so interested many philosophers and
the New Testament writers.

Mark and Matthew portray the acute agony of Jesus in the garden when
he appears to cringe with fear before his impending death. Mark's descrip-
tive words *ekthambeisthai kai adēmonein* (Mark 14:33) are, perhaps, collo-
quially, but most aptly, translated as saying that Jesus "came to pieces at
the seams." On the other hand, the portrayal of Jesus in the Garden in the
Lukan[1] and Johannine text is one of poise, authority, and strength. Jesus is
the true martyr, accepting his fate with tranquillity of soul.[2] In the Johannine text he is also the majestic Jesus, the monarch, but not of this world. I
have addressed the latter point in a paper read in Spain[3] and will discuss it
in my last chapter. Now I wish to reflect on men and women who tri-
umphed over their fate and were seen as honorable or glorious[4] by their

contemporaries. Like the Epicureans they did, indeed, achieve friendship with the Divine, with human beings, of soul with body, with citizens, with families, with animals and nature.[5]

## *Philosophical Background*

What caused Luke and John to redact the text of the passion narrative in so vivid and "contrary" a fashion? I think that the answer lies in the nature of their audience. John speaks to the Greco-Roman world in Asia Minor, many of whose inhabitants would see only shame, embarrassment, and folly in the cross.[6] Certain more enlightened, philosophical minds, however, were quite well prepared to accept a Cynic or Stoic philosophy that could see that infamy might lead to honor. I am not saying that for Luke[7] and John, Jesus' passion is merely a Cynic or Stoic phenomenon; rather, for the readers or hearers, a Cynic or Stoic background might lead them to a greater understanding of Jesus' death and resurrection. It might enable those who were horrified by the crucifixion to discern even in its outward dastardly form a role model that, by the grace of God, they might seek to imitate. Culpepper has discussed the philosophical schools as a background to the Johannine school.[8] Indeed, scholars have found a number of affinities between Stoicism and Christianity.[9] Moreau avers that Stoicism defined right and justice and, in a complementary manner, Christianity taught and developed charity.[10] He also points out that Zeno, the founder of Stoicism, was a Phoenician and, therefore, a semitic Greek. He taught a spirit of universalism and cosmopolitanism. He advocated equanimity and freedom from ambition and from the fear of the deities, addressing these teachings to a group of his friends. He believed in a power that governed the world—universal reason.[11] These concepts do not militate against Lukan and Johannine theology.

### *The Concept of Glory (Honor)*

I begin with a very brief overview of the concept of "glory" (*doxa*) in the Greco-Roman world.[12] *Dokeō* (*doxa*) and its cognates often signify "good standing" or "good reputation," so Kittel: "In this sense, *doxa*, with the Homeric *kléos* and later *timē*, achieves central significance for the Greeks. Supreme and ideal worth is summed up in the term. A man's [*sic*] worth is measured by his repute."[13]

In addition to this, *doxa* in the New Testament often has the sense of "divine mode of being." This meaning gains greater importance in the Gospel of John; hence, the passion and resurrection comprise the book of glory. Here Jesus reveals the "divine mode of being" in a novel way. The question before us is, How can the disgrace of the cross be both "glory" and a "divine mode of being"? I look for two themes in the philosophical milieu contemporary with the final redaction of Luke's and John's Gospels: (1) the wise person or philosopher who can bear pain, insult, and death with equanimity; (2) the wise person who is the true and only monarch (this will be discussed below). I pay attention especially to Cynic[14] and Stoic[15] philosophy and to one passage from Plato's *Republic.* Although my discussion of John's Gospel is in part 2, I shall make a few anticipatory references to this work.

We need spend little time on the more secular use of doxa as "opinion," "good standing," or "reputation."[16] In the LXX, *doxa* translates a number of Hebrew words including *kabod* (the glory of God) and *hesed* (the loving faithfulness of God). In the New Testament the dominant use is "radiance" and "glory," the "majesty" of God and the "being" of God. It is used for that which is "intrinsically impressive in the being of God."[17] This meaning obtains in much of the pseudepigraphal literature. In the *Targumim, kabod* is used for God's mode of being and is associated very closely with the Shekinah. At the "fall" (Gen. 3) humanity dimmed the divine radiance and failed to imitate the divine mode of being. Redemption and salvation include regaining this. Those who are saved will participate in the glory of God.

There is, however, one important aspect which we must not overlook. In John, glory, suffering, and shame are fused. We see this in the Farewell Discourses. Thus the glory of God and Jesus is not the glorious majesty of an impassible, immutable God but the glory of God in his or her *pathos.* It is the same glory as that of the Shekinah who goes into exile with her people, the tortured Shekinah present even in the concentration camps of World War II and at Hiroshima. This, in a sense, means that we can restore the title "sovereign" to God, not a sovereignty of impassive omnipotence, but a sovereignty of "omnipoignancy" and "omnidecorum." Glory is the full exposition of the *hesed* of God, and this *hesed* often involves suffering.[18] For the moment we turn to the secular models of persons seeking to live honorable lives and win glory.

## Cynic[19] *and* Stoic[20] *Tenets*

### Stoic Goals in Life[21]

The Stoic has four main goals:[22] (a) to arrive at the full realization of the truth; (b) to attain greatness of soul by the exercise of courage and the accomplishment of noble deeds; (c) to maintain self-preservation and independence, and to exercise justice that enables one to be of service to others and to contribute to the common good;[23] and (d) to sustain order or decorum.[24]

*Quest for Truth.* The Stoic sought for truth and reasonableness in theory and in practice. For example, Epictetus, after criticizing the lifestyle of hedonists, addresses his readers as "you eager followers of the truth (*zēlōta tēs alētheias*), and of Socrates and of Diogenes. . . ."[25] A fragment ascribed to Epictetus and Stoic in tone, if not Epictetic in style, reads:

> The truth is something immortal and eternal, and does not present us with a beauty that withers from the passage of time, nor a freedom of speech which can be taken away by justice, but it presents us with what is just and lawful, distinguishing the unlawful therefrom, and refuting it.[26]

Similarly Cicero asserts that the quest for truth is peculiar to human beings and urges that they pursue it passionately and refuse to submit their minds save to a teacher of truth.[27]

John's Gospel attempts—and succeeds—in portraying Jesus as the wise person who seeks after truth even in the face of suffering and ridicule. We may remark the importance of *alētheia* (twenty-four references) and *alēthēs* (thirteen references) in the Gospel of John.[28] John's Jesus is portrayed as one who constantly seeks to reveal the truth[29] and who asserts that the truth makes one free.[30] Particularly important are Jesus' declaration of himself as the way, the truth, and the life (John 14:6); his discussion of the Spirit of truth (John 14:17; 15:26; 16:13); the characterization of himself as the monarch who witnesses to the truth (John 18:37); and also Pilate's cogent and stark question: "What is truth?" (18:37-38). This insouciant inquiry, "What is truth?" is representative of the *kosmos* that is indifferent to the truth, indeed, even scorns it. But it is also the question that the entire Gospel asks the reader. John represents to the Cynic and Stoic world a role model that far exceeds even Heracles (Hercules),[31] Socrates,[32] and Cato.

*Attainment of Greatness of Soul.* Seneca describes the kingdom of the soul as follows:

> The soul itself is manifold, and is likened to a State, in which all is well if the governing part have wisdom and benevolence proportionate to its power, and if the lower parts are content to fulfill their respective duties; but if the balance of the State is upset, all becomes disorder and misery. Lastly, this kingdom is itself a part of the greater whole, namely the Cosmopolis or universal State. . . . He [the King] has a kingdom in his own mind and soul and heart. Let him be content to find his happiness in rightly administering it.[33]

It seems to the present writer that this philosophical principle is a good background to the Johannine idea of Jesus' kingdom, especially as seen in Jesus' words to Pilate: "You say that I am a king. For this was I born . . . to bear witness to the truth" (John 18:37). The Cynic or Stoic reading the Gospel of John would see Jesus as an individual with health of soul, meaning that his soul possesses "true tone" (*eutonia*). They would also see in Jesus the invincible person who is able to answer a challenge, whether it be verbal or physical. Epictetus, when asked who was the invincible person, replied, "he whom nothing that is outside the sphere of his moral purpose can dismay."[34] Similarly Plutarch, asking how one was to defend oneself against an enemy, proposed the reply, "by proving yourself good and honorable."[35]

While the Johannine Jesus does portray greatness of soul throughout the Gospel (indeed, sometimes to the point of appearing quite truculent!), it is in the passion that his greatness of soul is most brilliantly portrayed, especially against the sociological and anthropological background of the shame and obscenity of crucifixion that we have traced above. The foot-washing is followed by Jesus' magnanimity to his betrayer, Judas, in giving him the "morsel" (John 13:26-27). It is precisely at this moment when all is "night" that Jesus enters into his glory, the glory that illuminates the world through greatness of soul (John 13:30-31). The Farewell Discourses are Jesus' testament, just as the *Phaedo* describes Socrates' testament. Both of them are the last words of persons who have chosen to follow the bidding of the deity through pain, insult, and death—for Jesus, even crucifixion. The last prayer (John 17) brings all this to a climax.

*Self-Preservation, Freedom, and Independence.* The Stoics believed that one had the freedom of choice in spite of fate, for freedom was the ability to determine one's own actions and disposition.[36] For the Stoic, only the wise person was truly free. The freedom of the wise was harmony with nature and with the will of the gods and goddesses.[37] Seneca says, "We have been born under a monarchy; to obey God is freedom."[38] He counsels his reader:

> To avoid fighting against the inevitable and providentially ordered flow of events is the negative freedom of the man whose plans are never frustrated and whose apparent hardships are never unforeseen. . . . But the smooth flow of life is possible and this is the freedom which the wise man alone enjoys. It is the inevitable result of a complete consistency with himself and with the will of Zeus.[39]

The Stoics also developed the idea of *oikeiōsis* (orientation), making something one's own. This involved affection.[40]

The Johannine Jesus exhibits a remarkable independence, particularly for one who lived in a dyadic society[41] where culture and economics tended to make individuals or groups depend upon others. According to John, Jesus challenged the religious authorities especially through their spokespersons, the Pharisees and Sadducees. He also challenged convention and status. But most importantly, he declared that he had the power to lay down his life and take it up: no one took it from him (John 10:15-18).[42] John 13–17 also shows Jesus' independence from the world, and his exercise of true justice in contrast to worldly justice ("when the [Spirit] comes, it will convict the world of sin, of righteousness, and judgment" [cf. John 16:8]). Jesus' life and death are seen as a service to the community, in that it leads all to the possibility of witnessing to the truth and participating in new and eternal life. Neyrey comments that John 10:17-18 does not have a soteriological element, but John 10:11-15 has: his life is laid down for the good of others.[43] Neyrey points out that when Jesus says that no one takes his life from him, he makes "a remarkable claim found nowhere else in the New Testament."[44] Further, as Jesus' death is according to the will of the Father, it is no accident; it is not a "shameful thing."[45] Jesus shows plainly that no person has control over his life and death but God per se: this is a superhuman claim. Jesus' death is not that of a victim. Jesus' death is the return to the Father. It

> is no mere turning of the tables or vindication of the rejected, motifs that stand behind the apologetic remarks that his death was ironically glory-in-shame and exaltation-in-humiliation. Death becomes the occasion to resume his true existence with God in glory.[46]

In a sense, one could say that the highest form of self-preservation is found in Jesus' confidence in his own resurrection and the eternal life wrought through the Spirit. As Neyrey avers, Jesus claims an absolute authority over death.

*Decorum (To prēpon).*[47] The Stoic thought that a person who possessed the *logos*[48] could show divine qualities when she or he was "a living being, happy, immortal and benevolent towards men."[49] These qualities could be exhibited even in adverse conditions. For example, Epictetus asserted that the forlorn person is the one without help and exposed to those who wish to injure him. "For it is not the sight of a human being as such which puts an end to our forlorn condition, *but the sight of a faithful, and unassuming, and helpful human being.*"[50]

The decorum of Jesus is shown in the garden, where he takes the initiative, offers himself freely, and asks for security for his disciples (John 18:2-11). It is seen in the dignity of his bearing during the interrogation by the Jews, even when the servant slaps his face (John 18:22), and in his extraordinary self-confidence and fearlessness in his interviews with Pilate (John 18:33-38 and 19:10-11). It reaches its peculiar glory in the care he takes for his mother and John (John 19:2-27) and in the final cry of triumph, "It is consummated" (John 19:30), that replaces Mark and Matthew's cry of despair.[51]

## Stoic Teaching on the Equality of All Humanity

One can also see some affinities between Stoic teaching and John's Gospel in four other areas. Most of the Stoics taught that all persons were equal.[52] Contrary to many in the Greco-Roman world, they taught that slaves were human and, therefore, that their masters and mistresses should treat them with respect. The Stoics did not strive to abolish the system of slavery but to mitigate it. However, it was a debated question whether one should go to the point of dining with one's slaves. Writing to Lucilius, Seneca begins *Letter* 47 with the following imaginary dialogue:

> I am glad to learn . . . that you live on friendly terms with your slaves. This befits a sensible and well-educated man like yourself. "They are slaves," people declare. Nay, rather they are men. "Slaves!" No, comrades. "Slaves!" No, they are *unpretentious friends.* "Slaves," they are our fellow-slaves, if one reflects that Fortune has equal rights over slaves and freemen alike.[53]

Seneca continues by arguing that in early times the Romans did dine with their slaves and they became their friends: "They spoke at the feast, but kept silence during torture."[54] He means that they did so to protect their masters, whereas in his day slaves, out of fear of punishment, kept silence during the feast but spoke about the master among themselves and under torture. The Stoics' basic argument was that each person had within him or her the divine *logos*; this meant that all shared a common nature. Therefore, slavery and sexual inequality are *contra naturam.* In these tenets they were influenced by the Cynics.[55] As Moreau asserts, Stoicism could be adopted by all classes, from the slave Epictetus to the emperor Marcus Aurelius.[56]

I do not think that it is difficult to see the bearing of this on the footwashing pericope in John's Gospel. John alone portrays Jesus washing the feet of the disciples at the Last Supper. Much has been written on the sacramental background to this pericope (which seems to be the fusion of two traditions) and also the exemplar of humility in the master's washing the disciples' feet. But I think that we can go further if we glance at a possible Stoic background to this scene. I am not suggesting that John knew, read, and used the writings of the Stoics (although that is not outside the bounds of possibility) but rather that he absorbed the philosophical views of his cultural environment and could make Jesus a role model to which men and women of the philosophical schools could look, over and beyond the role models of Heracles and Cato. Heracles cleans the stables, Jesus washes feet, both perform menial tasks. Jesus engages not only in a servile task but in one that expresses a service of friendship that does not expect reciprocity. This idea is fully developed by Schneider:[57]

Jesus, acting out of that salvific mission, so loved his own in the world that he laid down his life for them (10:17-18; 13:1). Jesus' self-gift was not, in John's perspective, the master's redemption of unworthy slaves, but an act of friendship. . . .[58]

We note that Jesus states that he does not call the disciples "servants" anymore but friends (John 15:15). This is close to Laelius's definition of friendship: Friendship is in fact nothing other than "a community of views [*consensio*] on all matters human and divine, together with goodwill and affection. . . ."[59] Friendship is "gratuitous, spontaneous, and freely willed,"[60] but friends may not be true sages. The disciples still had to travel towards this goal. Moreover, the present writer believes that the footwashing is an integral part of the whole Johannine passion; indeed, it might be called Jesus' "keynote" action for a prelude to his bloody torture and death. By this very act Jesus unequivocally identifies himself with the most downtrodden and jested in the Greco-Roman world. The footwashing is his initial step towards this destiny; and the crucifixion, the action that clinches it. Both are acts of friendship. No one has greater love than the one who lays down his or her life for a friend. So in John's Gospel we interpret Jesus' death as an act of friendship and solidarity with the abused, a supreme act of friendship that welds together the human and the divine. It is prefigured in the footwashing.

### The Stoic Concept of Fate[61]

In all four Gospels Jesus speaks of his death as inevitable, as the design of the Father. The Stoic reader of the Gospel of John might see in Jesus the wise person who accommodates himself or herself to fate. The wise person is under the law of fate but exercises his free will and offers a self-sacrifice. Inwood[62] quotes Aulus Gellius, who gives Chrysippus's definition of fate:

> "Fate," he says, "is an eternal and inevitable series and chain of things, rolling and intertwining itself throughout eternal and regular sequences out of which it is assembled and joined together." I have cited the very words of Chrysippus, as far as memory allowed, so that if anyone should think that my translation itself is obscure, he might compare his own words . . . "a natural arrangement of all things from eternity, following on each other and moving among each other, such an entwinement being inevitable."[63]

Such a tenet would not be disconsonant with Johannine thought. The Stoic must not only resign himself or herself to fate but accept it enthusiastically, not only as something inevitable but as something reasonable.[64] Similarly, in John's Gospel, Jesus is fully attentive to the Father's will and emerges as a hero through meeting his fate courageously. The Johannine Jesus is fully aware of the betrayal by Judas, yet he accepts it as a true Stoic would.

### *Stoic* Apatheia

Another Cynic-Stoic virtue was *apatheia,* control of the emotions, especially in times of crisis. The wise person attempted to free himself or herself from the dominance of the passions—pleasure, fear, pain, and desire—but this disposition was not a "state of *anaisthēsis* in which the subject feels nothing at all."[65] The Stoics taught that bad emotions arise from false judgment:

> Since the passions arise entirely from intellectual error, they are within the jurisdiction of reason, for reason possesses the capacity to make correct judgments about moral values and thus to substitute virtue for vice. The Logos can do this if it so chooses. By a single massive act of will it can alter its moral stance. Stoic ethics is as much an ethics of will as it is an ethics of reason.[66]

Seneca says that the wise person can receive neither injury nor insult.[67] In the light of the above quotation, the Johannine Jesus appears as a Stoic in the garden, in contrast to the picture portrayed by Mark and Matthew. When he is arrested, he is like the Stoic who counted the vicissitudes of life as irrelevant matters (*adiaphora*).[68]

### *Replacing Folly with Wisdom*[69]

The ancient Stoa endeavored to replace folly with wisdom.[70] The individual must consider: his solidarity with human nature and the duties incumbent on him; his own talents, gifts, and social status; and his goal, which is to discover "what he can make of himself using his free will."[71] Epictetus[72] taught that, although some things may be included in the category of *adiaphora* (indifferent matters), suffering is a good that develops moral character.[73] Seneca agrees with this.[74] For Cicero also, pain is not an evil, although it does cause suffering. He brings forward the example of Heracles.[75]

> Rather, the doctrine of *apatheia* recognizes the existence of pain, takes its measure, and triumphs over it through reason, which enables man to understand the place of suffering in a wider moral or cosmic context, as the Stoic example of Heracles (Hercules) makes clear.[76]

For John, Jesus is the incarnate Logos who does, indeed, triumph over the darkness of evil, including torture, and whose suffering has a cosmic significance.

### *The Stoic Attitude Toward Death*[77]

The Stoics often discussed death and its attendant fears. For example, Seneca—a man who had certainly suffered many vicissitudes, especially under Nero—saw death as a good. Under certain circumstances (the rule of a tyrant, old age, insanity, terminal disease) suicide was justified.[78] Marcus Aurelius was also interested in death but did not discuss suicide as much as did Seneca. "According to Marcus, the chief task of philosophy and the chief virtue that one can acquire is to unshackle oneself from the fear of death."[79] Marcus thought one should struggle against pessimism and inactivity. Cicero asked whether pain and death were evils. He decided that, if the soul were immortal, then death was not evil.[80] Epictetus averred:

> Only let me not give up my life irrationally, only let me not give up my life faintheartedly, or from some casual pretext. . . . But if God gives the signal the wise will obey him.[81]

One might also consider the following statements of Epictetus: "Mere death is not, in fact, glorious; but a brave death is glorious."[82] "All these things (sickness, pain, poverty, exile, death) are in themselves neither honorable nor glorious; but any one of them that virtue has visited and touched is made honorable and glorious by virtue. . . ." "Death is honorable when related to that which is honorable; by this I mean virtue and a soul that despises the worst hardships." "[H]ow can brave endurance of death be anything else than glorious, and fit to rank among the greatest accomplishments of the human mind?"[83] Although there is no linguistic affinity, one might compare Seneca's concept of a noble death as a "great accomplishment" (*magna res*) with Jesus' cry on the cross, "It is consummated."[84]

The fact that the Johannine passion is the "book of glory" might suggest that it has some affinity to the Stoic idea of glory in death, although it is a far richer concept than this. Moreover, the Johannine Jesus seems relatively fearless before death and speaks of it as "going to the Father." His entire ministry prepares him for his "hour" when he will suffer and be resurrected. His death is just as much part of his glory as his resurrection. Thus I suggest that the redactors of John's Gospel sought to portray Jesus to his Greco-Roman educated audience[85] as a role model far surpassing even Heracles (Hercules), Socrates, Cato, Heraclitus, Ulysses, Diogenes the Cynic, Zeno, and Cleanthes, the examples so often proffered by the philosophers.

## *Plato's Just One Impaled*

Finally we must touch on an exceedingly interesting passage that occurs in Plato's *Republic.* This is mentioned by Hengel, and Benz[86] devotes a monograph to it. I quote in full.

> What they (those who commend injustice above justice) will say is this: that such being his disposition the just man will have to endure the lash, the rack,

chains, the branding-iron in his eyes, and finally, after every extremity of suf-fering, he will be crucified (*anaschinduleuthēsetai*, literally, impaled), and so will learn his lesson that not to be but to seem just is what we ought to desire.[87]

His point is that true justice is practiced when, though the just person is just, in outward appearance and circumstance she or he does not appear so, as in the case of a crucified person, that is, he has no "counterfeit decorum."[88] Epictetus said, "Only the irrational is unendurable.... Even hanging (*apanx-asthai*) is endurable."[89] The Stoic would find in Jesus "the imperturbable calm which the wise man should possess under all circumstances."[90]

Thus I submit that John spoke to the philosophical ideals of his audi-ence. He adapts these in his retelling of the passion of Jesus. Although these ideals have no direct or explicit reference to crucifixion per se, they do provide an interpretative framework within which the Christians of the Johannine school might operate and make an appeal. Jesus seeks greatness of soul in life and in death. John will show this in Jesus' dying for his friends.

## *Note on the Female Sage*[91]

It is important to realize that, although we have less information about the female sage or wise woman, such persons did exist. Rivkah Harris has dis-cussed the female sage in Mesopotamian literature.[92] She describes the female scribe and the goddesses, e.g., Seshat, patroness of writing in Egypt, who were attested as scribes. She mentions Enheduanna, the high priestess of the moon god among the Sumerians, who describes her creative work under the symbol of childbirth (p. 8). She refers also the Ninshatapada in the old Babylonian dynasty of Uruk, who "stands in a long tradition of princely women of Sumer who enriched Sumerian literature with their creative talents" (citing Hallo). She also mentions the female sages of Egypt, especially Hatshepsut, Tiy, and Nefertiti (p. 15).

Claudia V. Camp has studied the female sage in ancient Israel.[93] She argues that the woman Wisdom's figure in Proverbs, Wisdom, and Sir-ach arose from the social milieu of actual wise women.[94] She concludes that these women were able to address theological and, often, political questions and that the wisdom theology that we find in the sapiential books is not wholly academic but theological and "daily-life wisdom."[95]

More pertinent, however, to our subject is the role of women philoso-phers.

## Women Philosophers

In the seventeenth century, a period of interest in learned women and the background to Molière's *Femmes Savantes*, Gilles Ménage published a Latin work on women philosophers in antiquity. He claimed to have discovered sixty-five such women. This interesting work has been translated by Beatrice H. Zedler.[96] She lists the learned contemporary women apparently known to Ménage.[97] Ménage also attended various literary salons.[98] Ménage dedicated his book to Madame Anne Lefebvre Dacier. Ménage divides the women philosophers according to schools and/or sects, although in chapter 1 he does describe women philosophers who belong to no particular sect. Of the Stoic women philosophers Ménage says:

> I have found no woman in the books of the Ancients who professed the Stoic philosophy. But since Apollonius the Stoic, according to Photius in the *Bibliotheca*, wrote a book on women philosophers, it is probable that there were some. But I think it is true that among these, not one woman who professed the Stoic philosophy was outstanding, inasmuch as *apathy*, which the Stoics professed, is rarely found in women.[99]

However, he does mention Porcia (d. 42 B.C.E.), daughter of Cato, wife of Brutus, whom Plutarch (*Life of Brutus*) calls a philosopher, with Arria her daughter (d. 42 C.E.), Arria her granddaughter (fl. 66 C.E.), and Fannia (d. c. 108 C.E.). He says:

> There is a firm opinion that Arria, wife of Caecina Paetus, and Arria, his daughter, wife of Thrasea, and Fannia, daughter of Thrasea and wife of Helvidius, were Stoic philosophers in fact, although not by profession.[100]

Arria stabbed herself to commit suicide and then handed the dagger to her husband who had been involved in political conspiracy. It is also said that her daughter Arria was willing to kill herself for the sake of others. Fannia followed her husband into exile twice.[101] Ménage lists twenty-one Pythagorean women philosophers.

Jouette M. Bassler[102] has argued that of all women, widows may have been much freer to play an active part in society.[103] She also mentions women who were members of or attended philosophical schools. This phenomenon prevailed when in "the centuries immediately preceding the advent of Christianity, a gradual liberation of women occurred in the Greco-Roman world."[104] The Neo-Pythagoreans admitted women adherents.[105] Harrison, cited by Kathleen Wider,[106] says that "under Pythagoras we have clear indications of a revival . . . of matriarchal conditions, and with it a realization of the appeal of women to the spirit as well as to the flesh." Pythagoras is believed to have acquired some of his wisdom from his mother, and in addition Diogenes Laertius says that he drew on the wisdom of a priestess of Delphi, one Themistoclea. Pythagoras committed his writing to the care of his daughter, Damo, when he died.[107] Iamblichus lists twenty-six women disciples.[108] Wider refers to John Toland (1726) who says that the women disciples of this philosopher were so numerous that Philochorus of Athens filled an entire book with them. In theory the Stoics adopted the philosophy of the equality of all human beings, but there is little evidence that they accepted women as candidates. The Epicureans, however, did include women from various social levels and even allowed them to hold the presidency.[109] The Cynics also attracted women disciples.[110] Both Plutarch[111] and the Stoic Musonius Rufus[112] encouraged women to study philosophy, but also insisted on their subordinate state. Wider[113] gives a good survey of women philosophers from the preclassical period to the fifth century C.E. She states that we know that women were members of the Pythagorean school in the fifth to sixth centuries. These include:

• Theano, thought to be the wife of Pythagoras; she was renowned for her elegant learning.

• Myia, Damo, and Arignote, probably the daughters of Theano and Pythagoras; Damo bequeathed the writings of Pythagoras to her own daughter.[114] She wrote on the mystery cult of Demeter.

• Perictione, fifth century B.C.E.

• Melissa, dates unknown.

• Phintys, perhaps third century.

In the Classical period we have:

• Aspasia (470–410 B.C.E.), was *hetaira* of Pericles, the ruler of Athens, was intellectually very active, and knew many of the leading thinkers of Athens. Plutarch speaks of her "rare political wisdom."[115] She was also a friend of Socrates.

• Diotima (fl. 468 B.C.E.), from whom Socrates obtained much wisdom.

In the Hellenistic period we can name:

• Arete, head of the Cyrenaic school of philosophy after her father Aristippus died in 350.[116] Her son was called Metrodidaktos (mother-taught).

• Hipparchia (c. 328 B.C.E.), sister of the Cynic Metrocles. She married Crates and adopted his Cynic lifestyle; Diogenes also reports that she said to Theodorus, "Do I appear to you to have come to a wrong decision, if I devote that time to philosophy, which I otherwise should have spent at the loom?" He adds "These and many other sayings are reported of this female philosopher."[117]

• Pamphile, disciple of Theophrastus, director of the Lycaeum after Aristotle.

• Leontion (Lioness), who was a member of the Epicurean school.

Apparently she wrote a book refuting Theophrastus.[118] Diogenes Laertius also lists the following women among Plato's disciples: Lastheneia of Mantinea and Axiothea of Phlius. Diogenes also mentions Mammarion, Hedia, Erotion, and Nikdion.[119]

The Stoic school countenanced some women adherents. These included Argeia, Theognis, Aremisia, and Pantaleia, all daughters of the Stoic Diodorus Cronus (c. 315–284). All these were mentioned as logicians in Plato's *Menexenus*, which purports to be a funeral oration composed by the woman philosopher, Aspasia.[120]

• Hypatia.[121] She was born about 370 c.e. in Alexandria, the daughter of the mathematician and astronomer, Theon, who was director of the museum. She studied in Alexandria and perhaps in Athens.[122] She is said to have surpassed her father in astronomy.[123] Damasicius states:

> Her noble fervor led her to the other branches of philosophy. She took the mantle of philosophy and wandered through the city, lecturing to whomever would listen, in public address, on the philosophy of Plato and Aristotle or other philosophers. . . . She was righteous and demure and remained a maiden during her whole life. And she was also very pretty and had a fine figure.[124]

Socrates Scholasticus, in his *Ecclesiastical History*, asserts that Hypatia was an internationally known teacher and philosopher, and even a public figure, who applied philosophy in political settings.[125] Hypatia was director of the Neo-Platonic school in Alexandria. She was highly skilled as a rhetorician and teacher. One of her students was the famous Synesius. She was, unfortunately, murdered by rival factions in the city, one of which was Christian.[126]

Thus we might propose that, just as women could have experienced crucifixion, so also they might have learned a philosophical approach to suffering and death that would have prepared them for Christian teaching and martyrdom. They would follow in the footsteps of the Jewish matriarchs and heroines such as Sarah,[127] Rachel, Rebecca, Deborah, Jael, Judith, Esther, and the mother of the Maccabean martyrs (2 Macc. 7:20-23). They were prepared to die for their families, friends, religion, and country.

Anticipating our discussion of John's Gospel we should also refer to Schneider's article on the Johannine women.[128] She finds that they are presented positively and that they have an intimate relationship with Jesus. They are very individual in character, bold in their speech, and energetic in Jesus' cause.[129] They are unconventional in the roles that they play.[130] They appear at public functions (weddings and funerals). Only two are represented as wives or mothers. They are real women; they engage in theological dialogue, proclaim the Gospel, and serve at the table of the Lord. They relate directly to Jesus, not through the mediation of males. They do not seem to have a stereotyped place in society.[131] This suggests that women played a lively part in the Johannine community and that the author of the Gospel was "someone who had a remarkably rich and nuanced understanding of feminine religious experience."[132] Against the philosophical background described above, these Johannine women would not surprise the readers of the Gospel.[133]

# PART 2

# 7

# Friendship in
# the Gospel of John

THE SECOND PART OF THIS BOOK IS DEVOTED TO the Gospel of John. We have two questions before us: (1) Does John see redemption as an act of friendship? and (2) Does he include a feminine aspect in his approach to redemption?

## *Friendship in the Gospels*

### The Synoptics

In the Synoptic Gospels, *philos*[1] does not occur frequently. It is absent in Mark. Luke has a reference to the friends of the centurion (Luke 7:6), to the friend begging bread at midnight, and to the disciples who are called "friends" by Jesus (Luke 12:4). *Philoi* occurs twice in the teaching about table etiquette (Luke 12:10, 12), once each in the parables of the lost sheep (Luke 15:6), of the lost coin (Luke 15:9), and of the prodigal son (Luke 15:29)—they are the words of the elder son. Luke also mentions friends of the mammon of unrighteousness (Luke 16:9) and friends handing over Christians in times of persecution (Luke 21:16). On the whole, *philos* is found in rather negative contexts in Luke. *Philos* is found only once in Matthew. It is on the occasion when he reports the criticism against Jesus, namely, that he is a *philos* of tax collectors and sinners (cf. Matt. 11:19; cf. Luke 7:34, which also uses *philos*). This reference is significant. It is because of the *friendship* Jesus keeps that he provokes opposition and eventually death at the hands of his opponents. He recognizes no boundaries in friendship, disregards ritual purity, and is ready to embrace sinners as well as saints.[2]

The verb *phileō* is also used mainly in negative contexts. Matthew uses *phileō* of the Pharisees who love honor (Matt. 6:5; cf. Luke 20:46), of loving kin more than fictive kinship in him (Matt. 10:37), of loving the first couches at feasts (Matt. 23:6), and of Judas's kiss of betrayal (Matt. 26:48; Mark 14:44; Luke 22:47).

*Friendship in John*

In contrast to the above, John[3] has *philos* six times: the *philos* of the bridegroom (John 3:29); Jesus' *philos*, Lazarus (John 11:11); the important statement about surrendering one's life for one's friends (John 10:11); and the solemn nomination of the disciples as *philoi* (John 15:13, 14, 15). He also mentions "friend of Caesar" (John 19:12). His use of *phileō*, however, is still more interesting. It is used of the Father loving the Son (John 5:20); of Jesus loving his friend, Lazarus (John 11:3, 36); of the one who loves his life but will lose it (John 12:25); and, finally, of the *kosmos* who loves "its own." The Father loves the disciples because they have loved Jesus (John 16:27). There are also five references to the disciple whom Jesus loved (John 20:2) and, finally, in what appears to be an appendix to John's Gospel, Jesus' discourse about *phileō* and *agapaō* with Peter (John 21).

The New Testament is distinctive in that it does not use *erōs* but rather *agapē*. Nygren's classical work[4] gives a full discussion of the pertinent texts. He demonstrates the difference between *erōs* and *agapē* in the following way:[5]

• *Erōs* is acquisitive and longing.

• *Erōs* is the human way to God.

• *Erōs* is human effort: it assumes that the human's salvation is his own work.

• *Erōs* is egocentric love, a form of self-assertion but of the highest, noblest, sublimest kind.

• *Erōs* seeks to gain its life, a life divine, immortalized.

• *Erōs* is the will to get and possess that depends on want and need.

• *Erōs* is primarily *human* love; God is the *object* of *erōs*. Even when it is attributed to God, *erōs* is patterned on human love.

• *Erōs* is determined by the quality, the beauty, and the worth of its object; it is not spontaneous but "evoked," "motivated."

• *Agapē* loves and *creates value in its* object.

• *Agapē* is God's way to man [*sic*].

• *Agapē* is sacrificial giving.

• *Agapē* is unselfish love, it "seeketh not its own"; it gives itself away.

• *Agapē* lives the life of God, therefore it dares to "lose it."

• *Agapē* is freedom in giving, which depends on wealth and plenty.

• *Agapē* is primarily *God's* love; God *is agapē*. Even when it is attributed to man, *agapē* is patterned on divine love.

• *Agapē* is sovereign in relation to its object and is directed to both "the evil and the good"; it is spontaneous, "overflowing"; "unmotivated."

But I think that Nygren has failed to see the "supernatural" aspect of *erōs*. Whereas *erōs* may begin with preferential, particularistic love, it rises above this until it participates in the ideal beauty and becomes a universal love (cf. Plato's *Symposium*). As Meilaender[6] states:

> *Erōs* without gratification means for the lovers a shared life in the pursuit of wisdom. When *erōs* is sublimated, the lovers are able to recognize its character as sign and call and enabled to move beyond it toward that to which it points. In this way *erōs* leads to philosophy; lover and beloved now share in the love of wisdom. Indeed, friendship at its best consists in such a shared love of wisdom, for Plato philia is the end result of sublimated *erōs*.[7]

*Pathos* comprises both *agapē* and *erōs*, for it certainly does not lack the passionate dimension.

Having very briefly seen the use of *philos* and *phileō* in the text of John, we can now look to the Gospel for themes similar to those found in the philosophy of friendship in the classical works and the Hebrew Scriptures. It is wise to seek clusters of words with similar meanings rather than to rely on only one specific word.[8] For example, a certain quality of love is necessary for friendship, a love that differs from, for instance, a love for gain or prestige. Further, beyond the actual word *philia* we shall seek the qualities that form the essence of friendship and attempt to find these within the text of John's Gospel. As we have seen above from our discussion of classical sources on friendship, important in this respect are: immanence; mutuality; relationship; generosity; hospitality; and courage, especially in the face of torture or death—and the virtues especially pertinent to the covenant—love and faithfulness (*hesed*).

The readers and hearers of John's Gospel would have known the current discussions on friendship and, if they were Jews, would also have had an ineffable appreciation of the Hebrew covenant and, as we saw in Philo, they would have been able to apply Greek teaching about friendship to their Jewish-Christian beliefs. They would see Moses, who spoke to God face to face, like a friend, as a charismatic leader who bonded them in friendship to God and to their fellow human beings. Like Philo, they might have known the *Logos* as a manifestation of the deity, almost a hypostasis. Thus, those who accepted Christ would be able to see him as the fulfillment of the covenant and as the climax of philosophical teaching on friendship.

### Friendship with God

Over and above friendship with human beings, Hellenistic Jews and Christians would have seen friendship with God as the ultimate goal of life. We may compare the *Sentences of Sextus*: "The goal of piety is friendship with God, further the acme of piety is friendship with God."[9] They may have known the teaching of the Neo-Pythagoreans, who speak about friendship with the deities. They could have embraced the Epicurean belief in two kinds of friendship, "the one the highest possible, such as the gods enjoy (*hoia peri tōn theōn*), which cannot be augmented, the other admitting addition and subtraction of pleasure."[10] For Plato, love is divine, and the mind and soul of the human being yearn for unity with her.[11] It must be noted, however, that Plato tends to disregard the body; thus a new situa-tion faces Christians who believe in the goodness of the body and its resur-rection, rather than only the immortality of the soul. We might add that where the body exists, emotive power (*erōs*) will also obtain.

With the incarnation we have God's supreme act of friendship. THE INCARNATION IS THE REIFICATION OF THE *PATHOS* OF GOD. It links deity and humanity in a new mode of intimacy in which God shares God's nature with the beloved. Here there is "descent" to the level of the beloved, intimate relationship, mutuality, immanence, co-suffering, and empathy.[12] All these we saw to be qualities of friendship as conceived in the Greco-Roman world. Now we must trace them in the Gospel of John.

## *The Prologue*[13]

The Prologue is like an overture which introduces all the major themes of the *opus*.[14] It presents us with another model of creation/redemption. This takes the form of the concept of the descending and ascending redeemer figure found in Hellenistic Judaism. Bultmann[15] and others proposed a Gnostic influence on John. On the other hand, Talbert[16] has argued convincingly for a non-Gnostic background to this concept. He cites pertinent texts in the Mediterranean world.[17] He compares the wis-dom myth in Jewish literature.[18] He notes that some of these descent-ascent texts speak about the Angel of the Lord:[19] this angel is often iden-tified with Yahweh. Talbert discusses analogous activities attributed to archangels.[20] He concludes:

> A myth of a heavenly redeemer who descended and ascended in the course of his or her saving work existed in pre-Christian Judaism and alongside first- and second-century Christianity. It existed in a multiplicity of forms. . . . In its extreme form the diverse traditions had run together so that the communities conceived of one redeemer who was many-named.[21]

Then Talbert supports his thesis with numerous examples from early Christian literature.[22] He examines the Pauline corpus and Hebrews.[23] Finally he focuses on the Fourth Gospel where he finds this pattern in the Prologue, and *passim* in such phrases as "coming from the Father" and "returning." His thesis would argue for a nonexpiatory, nonsacrificial aspect of redemption. This redeemer is the friend who descends in order to immerse herself or himself in the "uproar" of life and history and then to ascend to sublimate humanity. She or he will transform brute oppressive forces and bestial cruelty into divine energy and glory.

Yet perhaps the most influential article is that of Meeks.[24] He notes the difference between the Gnostic myths and John:

> Perhaps the most important difference, which Bultmann did not fail to notice, is the fact that in gnostic myths most comparable with the Johannine pattern, the redeemer's descent and ascent parallel the fate and hope of the human essence (soul, pneuma, seed, or the like), while in the Fourth Gospel there is no such *analogia entis* between redeemer and redeemed.[25]

In contrast to the Gnostic myths in the Gospel, the redeemer does not report what he has seen and heard, only that he is to be identified as the revealer.[26] The "descent" is not described, merely presumed.[27] We find no commissioning, no bestowal of armor, no warning of dangers of journey, and so on, and the "*motif belongs exclusively to discourse, not to narrative.*"[28] In Meeks's words, Jesus comes as "the Stranger *par excellence.*" The redeemer figure is a relational, friendly figure. She or he comes to reconcile humanity and God. "Ascend/descend" first occurs in John 1:51 (the conversation with Nathanael), which we will discuss below. For now we turn to the background of the Prologue.

### The Logos (Word)

One needs more than the myth of the descending and ascending revealer figure to understand the Prologue; it is interwoven with allusions to the Hebrew Scriptures, the LXX, rabbinic texts, and classical philosophy. Essentially it is Greek thought clothed in Hebraic dress, or vice versa.

We have argued that communion and mutuality within the deity and God's self-differentiation are important for understanding divine *pathos* and redemption as a trinitarian event. The Prologue strikes a binitarian[29] aspect of God. There is self-differentiation in God: God and the Logos, just as we have God and Wisdom in the Old Testament and God and the Shekinah in Rabbinic literature. The Logos is truly divine and is present at creation. Between the begetter and the begotten there is not only relationship and mutuality but also ontological union. Through the begotten the life of the deity overflows into the human realm and becomes light for humanity; it is to this light that John the Baptist bears witness(v. 7). This light flows into the world (*erchomenon eis ton kosmon*), that is, it is the *ekstasis* of the deity. The Logos is the expression of God's purpose in creating, preserving, and redeeming the world.[30] The Logos is "in the beginning." This is not a temporal phrase—one cannot predicate history or time of the Godhead—rather it implies that "God's plan is an eternal expression of his being."[31] The Logos is the outpouring of God's super-abundant love on humanity. As such, she or he is friend and mediator. She or he is the embodiment of covenantal *ḥesed*. It is this *ḥesed* that redeems.[32] It is shared, profound communion between God and humanity. The Logos comes unto his own (*oi idioi*). *Oi idioi* means those who belong to one another in a special sense. In mysticism and Gnosticism these are the elect or favored ones. They are also comrades in battle, compatriots, colleagues, relatives, worshipers of the same god or goddess. So the Logos comes to his special friends. But the world does not recognize him. This statement presupposes God's awful and perilous gift of freewill, and the bipolar nature of the covenant and redemption. God in freedom chose God's people; they in freedom "dischoose" God's manifestation of God's self, that is, they give no human response to God's movement towards redemption, his or her offer of divine hospitality. Nevertheless, on those who do offer him hospitality he confers the power to be sons and daughters of God (vv. 12-13). In other words, God brings to pass an amelioration of relationship so that humanity attains an intimate and filial relationship with (and in) the Godhead.[33] It is with these verses (1:12-13) that we have the first of the birth images that are so important, even if expressed in a cryptic way, in the Johannine Gospel.[34] John 1:12-13 is the keynote to the entire Gospel. Redemption is fecund; it brings a new mode of relationship.

In 1:14, John emphatically announces the incarnation of the Logos. We note that he uses *sarx* (flesh), not *soma* (body), probably to suggest weakness and vulnerability but also to emphasize human potential. The Logos becomes immanent among us, just as the true friend in classical literature shares the joys and pains of the beloved, irrespective of a response in him or her. It is the incarnation, the immanence, and the covenant of grace and truth that comprise the *doxa* of the only Son of the Father. That is, the deity assumes another mode of existence. This grace and truth flow over to humankind, "grace for grace." The Logos comes to make God visible and completes the covenant initiated through the agency of Moses. He comes from the Father's "bosom" or "lap" (*kolpon*) (v. 18). This is certainly a term of endearment that can also be used in the feminine sense of the "womb."[35] The metaphor expresses rest, protection, revivification, security, *refrigarium* (refreshment), all of which we associate with a mother's womb. *Kolpon* (v. 18) is sometimes found in a meal context and, if this were implied here, it would form an *inclusio* with the Beloved Disciple resting on the bosom of Jesus at the Last Supper (John 13:23). It is a concept of some consequence, because it begins the Johannine theme of paternal/maternal image of God. It is this Logos coming from the "womb" of God who brings a new mode of existence to humankind through another kind of birthing.

### The Prologue and the Memra *(Aramaic: Word)*

The Hebrew Scriptures were translated into Aramaic, in which the feminine noun *Memra* (word) is equivalent to the Greek masculine *Logos*. Thus in the *Targumim*,[36] which were recited in the synagogue and *midrashim*[37] used for teaching purposes, the feminine word *Memra* was used. We may compare the feminine *sophia* (wisdom). Evans compares the Prologue with this targumic and midrashic material.[38] The *Memra* was in the beginning, and she was with God; she also participated in creation; she brings life, truth, and light; people (e.g., Abraham) pray in the name of the *Memra;* and the *Memra* is associated with the Glory of God. We find the phrase "the Word of my glory." Dalman, Díez Macho, and McNamara see "glory" in the *Targumim* as the background of *doxa* in John.[39] The *Memra* is also said to rest in the bosom of the Holy One (*Aboth Rabbi Nathan* # 31; cf. *Genesis Rabbah* 8.2).[40] For scholars who disagree with the comparison between the *Memra* and John's Logos, see Evans,[41] but the Neofiti Targum was unavailable to these earlier scholars.[42] The feminine *Memra* stands, then, as friend and mediator with God and humanity like the Logos and wisdom. From this background we can see self-differentiation in God in Jewish terms. Speaking to a Hellenistic audience, however, John may have preferred to begin with the Greek masculine *Logos*.

### The Prologue and the Old Testament

The Prologue shows the influence of various Old Testament texts. Craig A. Evans sees three main ones: Genesis 1–2, Exodus 33–34, and Sirach 24.[43] Of particular interest to us is the statement that Moses asks to see God's glory but cannot enjoy the full vision (Exod. 33:18-23),[44] but the Prologue claims, "We beheld God's glory." God told Moses that no one had seen his face (Exod. 33:20, cf. 23), but the Prologue declares that the only begotten Son has seen God;[45] Moses' fleeting vision of God can be contrasted with the Son's existence with God from the beginning."[46] The Logos dwelling with humanity complements the presence of God in the tabernacle (Exod. 20–40). As C. R. Koester says, "tabernacle imagery is uniquely able to portray the person of Jesus as the locus of God's Word and Glory among humankind."[47] We notice the importance of the temple imagery in John, e.g., John 2:19-22, and recall that the cleansing of the temple is reported in John 2:13-22, rather than just prior to Jesus' passion, as it is in the Synoptic Gospels. Jesus is the new temple. Both Moses and Jesus are sent from God, that is, each bears the office of *shaliach* (formally appointed messenger).[48] So, using Old Testament texts, John shows the fulfillment of Sinai covenant in Jesus.

## The Prologue and Wisdom

As well as reflecting the Aramaic feminine *Memra,* the Prologue echoes the theme of *Sophia* (Lady Wisdom). For example, parallels with Sirach 24 include: Wisdom/Logos's origin from the Most High; Wisdom/Logos's role in creation; their preexistence and dwelling (immanence) with God; the lack of recognition of Wisdom/Logos; and the association with light and glory. Further parallel wisdom themes are found in Wisdom 9:4 (wisdom was with God); wisdom's role in creation (Wisd. 7:22; 9:2); God's begetting wisdom (Prov. 8:25); wisdom as the *emanation of God's glory* (Wisd. 7:22, 25); her descent and ascent (Prov. 30:4); wisdom dwelling with all flesh (Sirach 1:10; cf. Bar. 3:37); and wisdom as redeemer (Wisd. 9:18).[49] In fact, it has been noted by a number of scholars that the author of the Prologue has taken the attributes of feminine wisdom and transferred them to the masculine Logos. A precedent for this is found in the sapiential books, for wisdom is identified with the Word in Wisdom 18:15, when she rescues the Israelites by killing the firstborn of the Egyptians.[50] Scholars ask whether this is a hymn to wisdom or to the incarnate Word.[51] John reveals Christ as wisdom incarnate who makes holy souls friends of God (cf. Wisd. 7:27).

## Wisdom Christology

The Wisdom Christology of John is the subject of a recent monograph by Martin Scott.[52] He seeks to relate this to the role of women in the Fourth Gospel, for women are prominent "at crucial *christological* points in the unfolding of the drama of the Fourth Gospel."[53] He argues for a "*thoroughgoing* Sophia (wisdom) Christology" in the Gospel of John and he questions the "mysterious disappearance of the Logos after John 1.1-18": this is rarely discussed.[54] Scott examines the role of the goddess in the ancient world, particularly with regard to fertility, the sacred marriage,[55] and as goddess of love. In these capacities she is associated with the cosmic (celestial) bodies. She represents the epitome of beauty, nurture, and sexual appeal. The feminine figure of Sophia emerged in Judaism despite patriarchy and monotheism, and shows features similar to the goddesses. She pronounces judgment, gives life, teaches, nurtures, and thus would appear to be taking over the role of the prophets of Yahweh. Yahweh "begat" (*qnh*) her, and she plays an active part in creation. In Proverbs 9 she plays hostess to men and women.[56] She represents God's universal sovereignty.[57] In Sirach 24 she is shown as the embodiment of the Torah. In Wisdom she is creator, redeemer, and revealer (e.g., 9:18); the people are saved by Wisdom (*kai tē sophia esōthēsan*). Johnson[58] states that she "brought about the decisive revelatory and liberating events of the people of Israel."[59]

Scott sees in wisdom *a fully developed expression of Yahweh in female terms*: this occurs before the completion of the New Testament.[60] He finds that by the time of the New Testament, *Logos* and *Wisdom* were practically synonymous.[61] He observes parallels to wisdom theology in nearly every verse of the Prologue (see above), wisdom/Logos was preexistent, cocreator, giver of life and light.[62] He concludes that "the Logos in the Prologue is none other than Sophia."[63] Thus the Prologue presents us with a fully developed but occult female redemptive figure: occult because she is called *Logos* (masculine).

### Wisdom in the Rest of the Gospel

Scott then turns to the theme of Wisdom in the rest of the Gospel.[64] She is also the way and truth (Prov. 3:17; 8:32; 8:34). She is symbolized by the vine (Sirach 24:17-19). She descends from heaven (Wisd. 9; Sirach 24:3-17). She is on intimate terms with God, for whom she has filial love (Prov. 8:30-31; Wisd. 8:3-4). Both Wisdom and Jesus call God "Father" (Wisd. 2:13, 16; 14:3; Sirach 23:4; 51:10). She is also revealer (Wisd. 7:17-27). Jesus and Wisdom are both teachers and have disciples (cf. Sirach 4:14 with John 14:21). The notion of "abiding" is predicated of both (John 15 and Wisd. 7:27). Both Jesus and Wisdom are rejected by their "own" (1 Enoch 42:1-3 and 4 Ezra 5:9-11).

Johnson states:

> If the deity of Christ is the deity of wisdom incarnate, then to recognize the deity of Christ is to recognize that in Christ God manifested herself, her power as Creator, her love as Savior, in a full and final way. The gender particularity of Jesus does not reveal that God must be imaged exclusively as male. In Jesus Christ we encounter the mystery of God who is neither male nor female, but who is the source of both and Creator of both in the divine image can in turn be imaged as either. Through wisdom Christology we see that their saving power and love are poured forth in the world through this crucified human being—a coincidence of opposites in every dimension.[65]

Scott accounts for the disappearance of the Logos in the rest of the Gospel, because after the Prologue, John wishes to show Jesus as Sophia in action. He then demonstrates this by an examination of the wedding feast at Cana,[66] the Samaritan woman,[67] the women at Bethany,[68] and the women at the cross.[69]

Of greatest interest to us, however, is that Wisdom passes into holy souls and makes them *friends* of God and prophets (Wisd. 7:27). Wisdom, like the Logos, is the friend of humanity and as such redeems humankind. Again we have a feminine aspect of the Prologue.

### The Prologue and Hellenistic Judaism

Tobin[70] and other scholars[71] have argued for a Hellenistic background to the Prologue as well as to Jewish wisdom speculation. *Logos* has a long history. Our extant sources include Aristobolus, who shows the Logos serving in a cosmological role.[72] A full exposition of the Logos is found, as we have seen, in Philo, who is influenced both by Stoicism and Middle Platonism. For Philo the Logos is the principle through which (whom) God created the world;[73] he uses the same phrase as the Prologue, that is, *dia tou logou* (through the word), thus suggesting an intermediate figure.[74] For Philo the Logos was a guide for humanity *"whom he addresses as 'friends.'"*[75] Philo also sees believers becoming children of the Logos and then of God.[76] The Prologue and Philo elaborate the account of the creation of light and darkness, for the Logos is "the invisible and intelligible light" (*to aoraton kai noeton phōs*). Further, a similar idea of the conflict between light and darkness is found in the Prologue and Philo. We may find also a similarity, but not identity, of thought about the concept of life. In John the Logos is life. In Philo, life comes from breath (or the spirit): "The one [incorporeal essence of breath] he [Moses] entitles the 'breath' (*pneuma*) of God, because breath is most life-giving (*zōtikotaton*), and of life (*zoē*) God is the cause" (*On the Creation* 30).[77] The Logos is also described as the "eldest son,"[78] that is, he has a "special relationship of filiation" with God; the Logos is the firstborn and Son of God.[79] The Word is "placed nearest, with no intervening distance, to the only truly existent One,"[80] and he was God.[81] He assisted in creation[82] and was the light shining in the darkness.[83] God's Word is "the human being after his image,"[84] for only the Logos is like God.[85] God did not reveal his face even to Moses[86] but has revealed himself or herself to us.

But Philo's Logos did not become a human being. In fact the Logos is sometimes called an angel.[87] However, he is a mediator between God and humanity and brings friendship and concord, which is the cause of *koinōnia* and peace.[88] The Logos is also advocate, compare the Johannine Paraclete.[89] Both Wisdom and Logos are agents of redemption. The Logos has many names, including firstborn, Word, beginning, name of God, man after his (God's) image.[90] For Philo, also, the Logos is seen in the figure of the heavenly man.[91]

Thus the Hellenistic background could enable us to see the rich background of the concept of Logos, one who brings humanity into friendship with God.

## Summary

With this type of background, the Johannine community might have interpreted the Prologue of John's Gospel somewhat in the following way. God in the Hebrew Scriptures had formed a ritualized friendship[92] with the chosen people. Now the Logos himself[93] freely elects[94] to come to his own. "His own" is already a kinship and/or friendship term. As Godhood has an innate attraction for humanhood, so the deity in the Logos comes to dwell among "his own" (like attracting like). But the "beloved" does not always accept him (John 1:11); that is, there is not necessarily mutual affection. However, for the time being, God may conduct himself or herself as gracious helper in the greatest sense of the word. The Logos comes to share all things, human and divine, with his friends (an Epicurean principle). He comes to be conscious of their existence and to promote their good (Platonic and Aristotelian principles). He comes to share in their joy, for instance, at the wedding at Cana, and their sorrow, as at the death of Lazarus. He bears good will (*benevolentia*) to all, even his enemies, and he is prepared to go, like Isaac, to "calamity's depths" and even to surrender his life for his friends. Thereby he will effect a change in them that will lead them to become sons and daughters of God (John 1:12-13). As incarnate Wisdom, he comes to make people "friends of God and prophets" (Wisd. 7:27). In the Book of Glory (John 13–20), *agapē* in friendship is the scarlet thread that runs through the narrative. The mission of the Logos might be accommodated to two *dicta* of Cicero. He says that the sages especially value friendship, "for they *incarnate the force of the soul and its autonomy*, and they are drawn into friendship relations with each other by the good of their characters";[95] and, "nor is it easy to find men *who will go down to calamity's depths for a friend.*"[96]

Seen from the point of view of the Hebrew Scriptures and Hellenistic Judaism, the incarnate Logos comes to befriend the chosen through a renewal of the covenant *hesed* (vv. 16-18); *hesed* and *emeth* and *charis* come through the Logos. As the great Hebrew leader, Moses, spoke to God as a friend face to face and became a mediator of God's revelation, so the Logos comes from the bosom of God to "exegete" (interpret) the Father (v. 18). In seeing him, the disciples look upon the face of the Father (John 14:9).

## Jesus and the Disciples

John shows the historic Jesus gathering his disciples immediately after the witness given by the Baptist (John 1:19-34). Surprisingly, in John the initiative for discipleship appears to be with the disciples, not the teacher. This is different from the Synoptic Gospels and may denote the *freedom of choice* to respond to God's invitation to redemption.[97] This makes Jesus' "school" similar to the Pythagorean, Socratic, and Epicurean circles,[98] where disciples come of their own volition. One notices the emphasis on *menein* (abide), which will become so important in the Farewell Discourses and also on *akolouthein* (to follow). The disciples must share daily life with Jesus (the friend). The climax of the gathering of the disciples is found in Philip's call of Nathanael (John 1:43-51). Meeks[99] notes that the concept of ascending and descending first occurs in this context. He observes that it depends on a midrash on Genesis 28:12. I add that *Targum Neofiti* reads:

| *Targum Pseudo-Jonathan* | *Neofiti* |
| --- | --- |
| He had a dream, and behold, a ladder was fixed in the earth with its top reaching towards the heavens. And behold, the *two* angels *who had gone to Sodom and who had been banished from their apartment because they had revealed the secrets of the Lord of the world, went about when they were banished until the time that Jacob went forth from his father's house. Then, as an act of kindness they accompanied him to Bethel, and on that day* they ascended *to the heavens on high, and said, "Come and see Jacob the pious, whose image is fixed in the Throne of Glory, and whom you have desired to see." Then the rest of the holy* angels of *the Lord* came down *to look at him.* And, behold, *the Glory of* the Lord stood beside him and said *to him. . . .*[100] | And he dreamed, and behold, a ladder was fixed on the earth and its head reached *to the height of* the heavens; and behold, the angels *that had accompanied him from the house of his father* ascended *to bear good tidings to the angels on high, saying: Come and see the pious man* (Jacob) *whose image is engraved in the throne of Glory, whom you desired to see.* And behold, the angels *from before the Lord* ascended and descended *and observed him.*[101] |

In both texts, when Jacob awakens from sleep he declares that the "glory of the Shekinah" dwells in the place. It could be that in our text Nathanael knew the context of Jesus' statement and its association with the glorious presence of God. Meeks agrees with Eduard Schwarz that this pericope has the "form of a solemn prophecy which, because of its place at the beginning of the book, demands some fulfillment in the subsequent narrative."[102] It introduces the title "son of humanity" and also the concept of descent and ascent, and is much more than a symbol of the union between earthly and heavenly things. The meaning is clarified by the passion and resurrection.

## Feminine Texts in the Book of Signs
### John 1:12-13

> But to all who received him, who believed in his name, he gave power to become children of God; who were born, not of blood nor of the will of the flesh nor of the will of man, but of God.

We have noted the skillful blending of male and female aspects in the Prologue. We must now examine specific texts within the Gospel to see whether they hold special attraction for women readers. In the Prologue we noted that John 1:12-13 strikes the keynote of rebirth. It is made pointedly feminine by the inclusion of the phrase "not by the will of the male" (v. 12: *andros*). Over the course of centuries these verses have been the subject of lively discussion, because manuscript tradition witnesses to the use of both the singular ("of him who was born") and the plural ("children of God, who were born"). It is helpful to see both alternatives in two modern translations.

> But to all who received him, who believed in his name, he gave power to become children of God, who were born, not of blood nor of the will of the flesh nor of the will of man, but of God (RSV).

This would apply, therefore, to believers who are reborn through belief in Jesus and baptism. The alternative reading is seen in the Jerusalem Bible:

> But to all who did accept him he gave power to become children of God, to all who believe in the name of him who was born not out of human stock or the urge of the flesh or will of man but of God himself.

This text, would refer, therefore, to Jesus' (virginal) conception and/or his birth from Mary.

However most, but certainly not all, exegetes accept the plural reading.[103] The present writer feels that the plural is more consonant with the theology of the Gospel. It introduces the idea of rebirth and it uses feminine imagery that will be significant in understanding other pertinent texts. With the notion of rebirth we are led directly into this subject in John 3.

### Nicodemus[104] *Comes by Night*[105] *(John 3:1-21)*

Nicodemus is a symbol of official Judaism.[106] However, the plural pronouns in v. 7, and perhaps v. 11, show that John is also addressing the readers who would include women. To Nicodemus, Jesus shows himself as the revealer. The passage resumes some of the themes that we have already seen in the Prologue: life, begetting, light and darkness, witness. The main theme of this pericope, however, is that redemption/salvation, first expressed in kingdom language and then in the idea of birth from above and by water and the Spirit. "See the Kingdom of God" appears in v. 3, but v. 5 employs the more traditional saying "to enter the kingdom."[107] With v. 3 we may compare Wisdom 10:10, where wisdom *showed* Jacob "the kingdom of God and gave him knowledge of holy things." Meeks observes that Nicodemus and Jesus belong to two different worlds.[108] We note that Nicodemus is a teacher and that the Johannine Jesus expects him to know about being born from above. Why should he know? He could have surmised this from Scripture.[109] We must, however, remember the Gospel's implied audience. Nicodemus could have known about mystical begetting if he were acquainted with the Socratic metaphor of begetting from the world of forms and being spiritually begotten (by a teacher), which occurs in the speech by Socrates who uses the teaching of Diotima, the priestess.[110] Diotima taught Socrates about pregnancy of the soul when the soul gives birth to prudence and all virtues.

> So when a man's soul is so far divine that it is made pregnant with these from his youth, and on attaining manhood immediately desires to bring forth and beget, he, too, I imagine, goes about seeking the beautiful object whereon he may do his begetting . . . and if he chances also on a soul that is fair and noble and well-endowed, he gladly cherishes the two combined in one. . . . For I hold that by contact with the fair one and by consorting with him he bears and brings forth his long-felt conception . . . men [*sic*] in this condition enjoy a far fuller community with each other than that which comes with children, and a *far surer friendship*, since the children of their union are fairer and more deathless (italics mine).

The Johannine text occurs against the background of Jesus gathering his disciples and beginning his teaching ministry, like Socrates, he is "midwife" assisting birth in his followers. Diotima speaks of a "right and regular ascent" to the beautiful itself.[111] The wise person goes from height to height as upon a ladder[112] and then sees the essence of beauty. We have a clear notion of ascent, although not a verbal affinity, in John.[113] Those who befriend (or belong to) the son of humanity will be begotten unto eternal life. This is possible because God so loved (*agapaō*) the world that he sent his own begotten Son to save humankind (John 3:16). It is at this point that John uses *hupsōthēnai* (lifting up) again to denote both the manner of his death and his exaltation. We recognize in this "lifting up" the passion and death that will draw all people (John 12:32, again in the context of "lifting up"). The idea of surrendering one's life (implicit in "lifting up") for friends is not absent from the *Symposium*:

> For a man in love would surely choose to have all the rest of the host rather than his favorite see him forsaking his station or flinging away his arms; sooner than this, he would prefer to die many deaths: while, as for leaving his favorite in the lurch, or not succoring him in his peril, no man is such a craven that Love's own influence cannot inspire him with a valor that makes him equal to the bravest born; and without doubt what Homer calls a "fury inspired" by a god in certain heroes is the affect produced on lovers by Love's peculiar power.[114]

Furthermore, only such as are in love will consent to die for others; not only men will do it, but women too.[115] It is this love unto death that provides the possibility of begetting. The love of the Father and the Son is this valor "equal to the bravest born." Verses 33-36 speak of the reciprocal love of God and the Son, and that the Son may "befriend," give everlasting life to, the believer.

The birth metaphor is brought out even more clearly if we agree with B. Witherington III.[116] He suggests that the "water" mentioned in John 3:5 could refer to baptism but that it is more likely to refer to the amniotic fluid, the breaking of the waters at birth, and/or the semen fluid. He refers to the symbol of a "cistern" or a "fountain of water," used of women. He compares a number of examples from the Hebrew Scriptures, e.g., Proverbs 5:15-18, where the male semen—called "streams" or "water"— are not to be dispersed outside the home; and the wife is called "your own cistern [well]" and "your fountain"; Song of Solomon 4:12-15, where the bride-to-be is designated as "locked-up pool," "sealed fountain," "well of living water," or "fountain gushing out," i.e., the rupture of the amniotic membrane. He also cites other Jewish texts[117] and ancient Near Eastern literature. M. H. Pope[118] quotes from a pertinent Sumerian text: "My mother is rain from heaven, water for the finest seed. . . . An irrigation ditch carrying luxuriant waters to the garden plot."[119] He states:

> Stol[120] has demonstrated that the Hebrew verb *HYL* (*halum* in Akkadian), usually translated "to give birth," literally means or denotes the rupturing of the amniotic sack or membrane. If the saying in John 3:5-6 was originally given in Aramaic or Hebrew, then this may prove to be a very significant piece of information.

Witherington argues that *gennaō* (v. 4) in the passive means to give birth rather than beget. His conclusions are: (a) *anōthen* "(from above, from the beginning)" should be taken as "again" or "(birth) anew"; (b) if the waters are the amniotic fluid, then there is no necessity to argue that the "water" is a secondary addition;[121] (c) he terminates his article by elucidating 1 John 3:5, where the waters could also refer to physical birth, "in which case we may say (in the light of 1:1 and 4:2 which help to prepare for these verses) that the three that testify are the Incarnation, the Death, and the Holy Spirit. These three are also major themes in the Fourth Gospel."[122]

The Nicodemus text, therefore, portrays entry into the kingdom through the realistic image of birth. It takes up and elaborates the logion in the Synoptic Gospels, where Jesus states that only those who become like children can enter the kingdom. For a comparison between the Synoptics and John on this concept, see B. Lindars.[123] He explains that "to become like children" (Matt. 18:3)[124] does not signify being childlike but being in a similar situation to children.[125] Lindars translates *anōthen* as "from above," a euphemism for "from God."[126] He compares John 1:13; 3:6, 13, 27, and 31. If John had meant *anōthen* to mean "again," probably he would have used *deuteron*, as in v. 4. It points forward to Jesus' use of *tekna* (children) in John 13–16. Birth is not repeated, but a new kind of birth *brings us into the kingdom of Jesus.*

### Rebirth and the Ascent Texts

One of the most important recent articles on this pericope is by William C. Grese.[127] First he addresses the lack of continuity between John 3:1-12 and vv. 14-21. Using the insights of Odeberg[128] and Meeks,[129] Grese argues that the language of the ascension in v. 13 is related to being born from above in v. 3: it should be understood against the background of a heavenly journey. The assertion of John that only the son of humanity has ascended may be a polemic against the stories of ascents and *merkabah* (throne) visions.[130] Grese argues that the passage 3:1-21 is akin to a manual for heavenly journeys and instructs outsiders how they can enter the Johannine community. But this journey leads to faith in the incarnate Jesus rather than a *merkabah* vision. Grese then outlines descriptions of heavenly journeys that are often similar to the journey that souls make after death. But this journey (in John 3) precedes death.[131] These heavenly journeys have diverse objectives, but the goal of the journey under discussion is to acquire revelation. He compares the Mithras liturgy in which the goal is also revelation: "I may gaze upon the immortal beginning with the immortal spirit . . . with the immortal water . . . with the most steadfast air . . . that I *may be born again in thought.*"[132] In these heavenly journeys, regeneration is sometimes demanded prior to the ascent.[133] In our text, a student and teacher are in dialogue; the latter maintains that rebirth is a necessary prerequisite to the ascent. This follows the principle that "like can only be known by like, only those who are 'born from above' are able to make the heavenly journey, to enter into the kingdom."[134] The student, however, fails to understand, just like Nicodemus.[135] In our pericope Jesus speaks about rebirth through baptism (vv. 3-6), and then the evangelist shows him baptizing candidates (v. 22).[136] John 3:14-21 shows the heavenly mysteries have been seen by the one who has been in the heavenly realms. These mysteries include the lifting up (in the sense of crucifixion and ascension) of the son of humanity and his role as eschatological judge. This is the greatest revelation. The judgment is already taking place (John 3:17).

> The heavenly journey set before Nicodemus is not a trip through the heavens to see God, but through the enigmas and riddles that surround the heavenly revelation made available through Jesus.[137]

Nicodemus is destined to see the revelation of God's love in the crucifixion and exaltation of Jesus (cf. John 19:38-42). John 3:14-21 draws together all the major themes of the Gospel.[138] In the Farewell Discourses, John will show Jesus setting out on the return journey to the Father and once again he uses the simile of a woman's parturition (John 16:21). Thus this important dialogue speaks to the experience of every mother. She would understand the amniotic fluid breaking forth from the womb of the Christian community and producing new life—children (*tekna*) born of God.[139]

In this chapter we have tried to show how the incarnation and redemption can be seen as an act of friendship par excellence on the part of the Triune God. In his Prologue John blends the theology of the feminine aspect of God, wisdom, the *Memra,* and the Shekinah with the theology of the Logos, thereby weaving together friendship and motherhood themes. We concluded by indicating that the historic Christ, the Logos, and incarnate Wisdom began to gather together his school of friends. The prerequisite for belonging to this school was spiritual begetting. His full amicable relationship with the disciples, men and women,[140] will be expounded in more detail in the Farewell Discourses, but for the moment we turn to further feminine-oriented texts in John's Gospel.

## *Wisdom's Feast (John 6)*

### *Wisdom as Hostess and Nourisher*

In this section we consider *pathos* as compassion and nourishment. We think especially of the woman who feeds her baby either as a fetus within the womb or, when born, at her breasts. The whole of John 6 is a text con-

cerning nourishment. John reports the sign of the feeding of the five thousand[141] and the walking on the water (vv. 16-21). The discourse on the
bread of life follows these two signs (6:22-71) and is interpreted, to some
extent, in their light.[142] In this portion of my work I do not intend to
expound a detailed or comprehensive exegesis of John 6; rather I am interested in the feminine approach. This, however, is not the only interpretation; the text is polyvalent and speaks on a number of levels.

John 6 is impregnated with sapiential themes that would suggest a feminine-oriented text. It has clear echoes of Wisdom as hostess and nourisher; indeed, the very topic of bread introduces a feminine note, for women
sowed, reaped, ground, kneaded, baked, and served bread.[143] Jesus, like
Wisdom and like nearly all mothers in antiquity, prepares and distributes
the meal of bread and fish. K.-G. Sandelin makes an excellent contribution
to the understanding of this aspect of wisdom in his book *Wisdom as
Nourisher*. He begins with Proverbs 9:1-6, where wisdom prepares her
banquet. He[144] notes that those who issue the invitation on behalf of wisdom are women, probably wisdom teachers, and that, although it is singular to have women messengers in the Old Testament, this is attested in the
Ugaritic texts.[145] He sees wisdom's banquet as a meal in a dwelling house,
that is, a home, not a sanctuary.[146] It is on the occasion of consecrating the
house.[147] Lang elaborates this aspect and adduces parallel descriptions of
building similar to wisdom's house with seven pillars in which there were
the national celebrations and lavish banquets, and expands the image of
"house."[148] He discusses the image of dining and states, "learning is as
receptive a process as eating."[149] The loaves scene suggests table fellowship:
Lang asks, "Is not being wisdom's guest like being a god's guest in a temple, partaking of that god's table?"[150] Wisdom offers food for a long life.
Sandelin adds the dimension of wisdom as a nourishing mother, nourishing with spiritual food, as seen especially in Sirach 14:20–15:10.[151] The
most important verses for our perusal are:

> And she will meet him like a mother
> and she will receive him like the woman[152] of his youth.
> And she will feed him with the bread of insight
> and will give him the waters of understanding to drink.
> (Sir. 15:2-3)

Sandelin notes the affinity between the mother figure of Wisdom in this
passage and the Old Testament references to God as mother.[153] The food
that Wisdom offers is the "bread of insight" and the drink, "waters of
understanding" (cf. Isa. 49:10). The bread of Wisdom implicitly refers to
the manna in the wilderness (Exod. 16:32 and Deut. 8:16). *So Wisdom
functions like the Savior God*, who gave bread from heaven and water from

the rock. In other words, Wisdom and Jesus resemble the redeemer God, who nourished those whom she or he had liberated on their journey to the promised land. Now, however, the nourishment is not a material substance. Indeed, Wisdom is more than a mother who gives physical food. Sandelin concludes that in this passage (Sir. 14:20–15:10) we have Wisdom as a female figure representing God in the temple in Jerusalem. She instructs those who repair to the temple. Again, as in Proverbs, Wisdom acts as a nourisher, even as Yahweh did in the Exodus salvation history.[154] Another text showing Wisdom in a cult setting is Sirach 24, where God gives her authority to settle in Jerusalem (v. 10 f.). Here she is a fruit-bearing tree, as is seen by the comparison with an olive, a palm, and a vine. The fruit of the trees is Wisdom.[155] Yet those who partake of her fruits will still hunger and thirst (vv. 21-22). Sandelin then turns to Wisdom as nourisher in the Hellenistic-Judaic tradition. This representation of Wisdom is especially prominent in Philo. For Philo, Wisdom also is hostess and nourisher.[156] She offers "the sweet water of discourse," enabling people to reach the stage of spiritual intoxication. Philo's language is reminiscent of Plato's *Phaedrus* and of the mystery cults. The sustenance that Wisdom offers is "most divine."[157] It is "heavenly nourishment"[158] and is compared to manna.[159] Wisdom is also the tree of life that gives power to life.[160] Philo describes the tree of life as "virtue in the most comprehensive sense."[161] The nourishment gives immortality to the soul,[162] as the tree of life offers immortality.[163] Philo also identifies the miraculous rock[164] with the manna, and in interpreting Exodus 16:15,[165] it is clear that he "sees the manna, the bread from heaven, as being the same thing as the Word of God,"[166] the heavenly nourishment of the soul.[167] Philo also treats Wisdom as mother in his allegorization of Sarah.[168] He, like John, merges the figures of the Word (Logos) and Wisdom. Further, Philo makes Wisdom's feast into a "cultic drama of cosmic proportions."[169]

In the light of these Wisdom texts we can see that both Wisdom and Jesus are seen as nourishers; both are the bread (of life) and "living water." So Jesus, identifying himself with the provider of the bread of life, presents himself as Lady Wisdom. This would be easily recognized by Palestinian and diaspora Jews. Furthermore, in Sirach 24, Wisdom not only offers nourishment, but she speaks of "those who *eat her*" (*hoi esthiontes me*), just as Jesus speaks about himself as nourishment (cf. John 6:51 and 57). In *The Worse Attacks the Better* 115–118, Philo identifies Wisdom with the manna, therefore the line between Wisdom as nourisher and Wisdom as nourishment is a slender one. Likewise, Jesus indicates that he is the manna from heaven.[170] Sandelin concludes that John uses Wisdom theology as his model in the bread of life discourse. Jesus descends from heaven by the will of the Father; he comes to save; he gives life; he is both nourisher and nourishment. Once again (as in the Prologue) John has admirably blended male and female figures. Jesus is wholly in concert with nourishing Lady Wisdom.

However, there are important differences between John and Wisdom. Wisdom's return to heaven is not part of her saving mission: she is not incarnate; Wisdom theology has not a full eucharistic doctrine, and Wisdom does not explicitly identify herself with the bread *of life*. Sandelin contrasts John 6:35 and Sirach 24:21:

| | |
|---|---|
| Those who eat me will still hunger and those who drink me will still thirst. (Sirach 24:20)[171] | I am the bread of life the one comes to me will not hunger and the one who believes in me will not thirst. (John 6:35) |

Sandelin[172] observes that there are three kinds of bread that cannot give eternal life: the bread given to the 5,000 (and 4,000), the manna, and the law. Thus the nourishment offered by Jesus is different from that offered by Moses. The disciples of Jesus, unlike those of Wisdom, are not unsatisfied; Jesus gives them himself in his teaching and in the Eucharist, which meets all their religious longings.[173]

### The Eucharistic Discourse (John 6:51-71)

Jesus offended his fellow Jews by insisting that the believer must eat his flesh and drink his blood, and many withdrew from him at this point (John 6:51-59). This would seem understandable. Not only does the suggestion appear repugnant to the Jews, who do not imbibe even animal blood, but the text generally could be patient of an abhorrent cannibalistic interpretation.[174] In the times of the early church, Christians were accused of killing and eating babies.

However, if we are to follow the wisdom motif and see her as both nourisher and nourishment, we can take a feminist approach to John 6:51-59. According to Sirach 14:2-3, wisdom is like a mother and like the woman of one's youth, i.e., one's nursing mother. Philo also[175] describes wisdom as a nursing mother. In this text, the image of the rock is blended with that of mother.

> He (Moses) uses the word "rock'"to express the solid and indestructible wisdom of God, which feeds and nurses and rears to sturdiness all who yearn after imperishable sustenance. For this divine wisdom has appeared as mother of all that are in the world, affording to her offspring, as soon as they are born, the nourishment which they require from her own (*ex heautēs*, literally "from herself, in her own body") breasts.[176]

But Jesus speaks about the believer *drinking his blood* and masticating his flesh (vv. 51-57). One must ask whether there is a correspondence between lactation and drinking blood.[177] We may answer in the affirmative. According to ancient and medieval physiology, breast milk was thought to be processed blood.[178] The loving mother, like the pelican[179] to whom Christ is compared, feeds the infant with her own blood. This concept is found in both Jewish and classical sources.[180] Kottek quotes *Niddah* 9a which reads:

> According to the view of R. Meir the menstrual blood is decomposed and turns into milk while according to the view of R. Jose, R. Judah and R. Simeon the woman's limbs are disjointed and her natural vigor does not return before the lapse of twenty-four months. So it was also taught: The menstrual blood is decomposed and turns into milk; so R. Meir. R. Jose states; Her limbs are disjointed and her natural strength does not return before twenty-four months.

The notes to the *Soncino Talmud* on *Niddah* 9a state that the menstrual blood changes into milk for the child, but if the child dies it turns back into menstrual blood.[181] Kottek says that R. Meir's opinion was similar to Aristotle's and Galen's theories, and to those pertaining throughout the Middle Ages. It was even believed that there was a direct arterial connection between the womb and the breasts.[182] I add that we find a similar text in *Bek* 6b:

> The blood [during the nursing period] is disturbed [decomposed] and turns into milk; and since it is an anomaly (blood is normally prohibited), therefore even from an unclean animal the milk should be permitted. . . . This would indeed hold good according to him who says that the blood [during the nursing period] is disturbed [decomposed] and turns into milk. But according to him who says [that the reason why there is no menstruation period while nursing is] because her limbs become disjointed (on account of the labor of childbirth) and she does not become normal in herself for twenty-four months, what can you reply? It is still necessary. I might have been inclined to assume, that since there is nothing which proceeds from a living being which the Divine Law permits and yet milk which is similar to a part from a living animal [is permitted], therefore even from an unclean animal the milk should be permitted . . . *and a land flowing with milk and honey.* Now if milk were not permitted, would Scripture commend the country to us with something which is not fit to be eaten? Or, if you prefer, I may deduce it from here; *Come ye buy and eat, yea, come buy wine and milk without money and without price.*[183]

I wish to thank Professor James Vanderkam for translating an article in modern Hebrew for me.[184] Here Kottek mentions nursing males (*Shabbat* 53; *Mak* 6.7; and *Meg Esther* 1053). The material provides an interesting, though uncertain, background to the idea of Jesus' breast-feeding.

Rancour-Laferriere mentions abuse with regard to the Eucharist; Epiphanius reports those perpetrated by the Gnostic sect of the Phibionites who offer male semen and menstrual blood at the Eucharist.[185] Epiphanius wishes to "cause in every way a horror in those who hear about their shameful practices."

Breast milk and blood continued to be associated. Bynum[186] states that in medieval legends, such as the tale of the lactation of St. Bernard, and in devotions, e.g., to the Sacred Heart, "milk and blood are often interchangeable, as are Christ's breasts and the wound in his side."[187] Isidore of Seville (seventh century) explains as follows:

> *Lac* (milk) derives its name from its color, because it is a white liquor, for the Greeks call white *leukos* and its nature is changed from blood; for after the birth whatever blood has not yet been spent in the nourishing of the womb flows by a natural passage to the breasts, and whitening by their virtue, receive the quality of milk.[188]

Bartholomew of England states that "while the fetus exists in the womb it is nourished on blood, but at birth nature sends that blood to the breasts to be changed into milk."[189] Breast milk fed not only the body but also affected the character of the child, particularly as the nursing mother built emotional ties with the baby. As plants draw strength from their roots, so the infant draws strength from the breasts of the mother. Soranus, the ancient gynecologist, gives much emphasis to the importance of breast milk and the qualities that one must seek in a wet nurse and the quality of milk, because of its effect on character.[190]

Moreover, we have earlier evidence for divine lactation even in "orthodox" texts.[191] We have a brief reference in Irenaeus.

> But the Spirit is truth. Those, therefore, who do not partake of Him, are neither nourished into life from the mother's breasts, nor do they enjoy that most limpid fountain which issues from the body of Christ. . . .[192]

The antecedent seems to be the Spirit but passes on to Christ. However, it is Clement of Alexandria who gives a full exposition of this interpretation of John 6. He links lactation with the Eucharist. In *The Instructor* 1.6, discussing Galatians 4, where Paul says, "I have fed you with milk in Christ," Clement identifies the Word with the milk: "by the Word, the milk of Christ, instilling into you spiritual nutriment." So he opines that the Word is figuratively represented as milk. He refers to Homer who speaks of righteous men as "milkfed" (*Iliad* 13.6, but this refers to drinking mare's milk). He then explains that adults do not suckle but "drink" the symbol of "perfect appropriation," and he accommodates this to John 6, "For my blood . . . is true drink" (John 6:55). He then explains that those who are given "meat" to eat are given the same substance as milk, although under another form. Again he accommodates it to the eucharistic text, "Eat ye my flesh, and drink my blood." He explains the ancient physiology:

> For the blood is found to be an original product in man, and some have consequently ventured to call it the substance of the soul. And this blood, transmuted by a natural process of assimilation in the pregnancy of the mother, through the sympathy of the parental affection, effloresces and grows old, in order that there may be no fear for the child. Blood, too, is the moister part of flesh, being a kind of liquid flesh; and milk is the sweeter and finer part of blood. For whether it be the blood supplied to the fetus, and sent through the navel of the mother, or whether it be the menses themselves shut out from their proper passage, and by natural diffusion, bidden by the all-nourishing and creating of God, proceed to the already swelling breasts, and by the heat of the spirits transmuted . . . that is formed into food desirable for the babe, that which is changed is the blood. For of all the members, the breasts have the most sympathy with the womb. . . .

Here there is some association between milk, blood, and flesh. Thus the blood is changed to milk, and the spirit discharged from the neighboring arteries being mixed with it, the substance of the blood, still remaining pure, it becomes white by being agitated like a wave; and by an interruption such as this is changed by frothing it. This is not dissimilar to the sea. Yet still the essence is supplied by the blood. So, he argues, the "blood of the Word has been also exhibited as milk." Further he states that the breasts after childbirth cease to look in the direction of the husband but incline to assist the child in suckling. Clement avers that all this is from God who generates and regenerates. Clement then compares the manna. He says that nurses call the first milk "manna." The church nurses her children with holy milk, that is, the Word. The milk is Christ:

> For the milk was this child fair and comely, that Body of Christ which nourishes by the Word the young brood which the Lord Himself BROUGHT FORTH IN THROES OF THE FLESH, WHICH THE LORD HIMSELF SWATHED IN HIS PRECIOUS BLOOD. . . . The Word is all to the child, both father and mother, and tutor and nurse. "Eat my flesh . . . and drink my blood." Such is the suitable food which the Lord ministers, and He offers His flesh and pours forth His blood, and nothing is wanting for the children's growth. . . . The blood points out to us the Word, for as rich blood the Word has been infused into life; and the union of both is the Spirit and the Word. The food—that is, the Lord Jesus—that is, the Word of God, the Spirit made flesh, the heavenly flesh sanctified. The nutriment is the milk of the Father, by which alone we infants are nourished. The Word Himself, then, the beloved One, and our nourisher, hath shed his own blood for us, to save humanity; and by Him, we believing on God, flee to the Word, "the care-soothing" breast of the Father. And He alone, as is befitting, supplies us children with the milk of love, and those only are truly blessed who suck this breast (translation *Ante Nicene Fathers*).

Augustine[193] also speaks in a similar, though not identical, way in his explanation of the Psalms.[194]

Ambrose has a similar interpretation, by a strange "twist" of thought claiming Christ as the Virgin:

> He is, then, the Virgin who bare us, Who fed us with her own milk, of whom we read: "How great things has the virgin of Jerusalem done! The teats shall not fail from the rock, nor snow from Lebanon, nor the water which is borne by the strong wind" [cf. Jer. 18:13]. Who is this virgin that is watered with the streams of the Trinity, from whose rock waters flow, whose teats fail not, and whose honey is poured forth? Now, according to the Apostle, the rock is Christ. Therefore, from Christ the teats fail not, nor brightness from God, nor the river from the Spirit. This is the Trinity which waters the church, the Father, Christ and the Spirit."[195]

John Chrysostom also associated Christ as mother and the Eucharist.[196]

It would seem, therefore, that there may be a maternal interpretation of participating in Christ's body and blood in the Eucharist. Whereas we can make no definite statement about the New Testament text, yet the tradition about Jesus as the nourishing mother is strong from early patristic times and continues in the Middle Ages.[197] We can, however, ask whether there was any similar belief about breast-feeding in non-Christian religions contemporary with the primitive church. Was there any culture or ritual that would have been familiar to the Johannine audience?

## The Milk of Salvation in Non-Christian Sources

In her article "The Milk of Salvation,"[198] Gail Paterson Corrington examines symbols of salvation that would have been congenial to women (and men) in antiquity. She observes that one of the most popular savior figures in the Greco-Roman world was that of the divine mother, the goddess Isis, whose cult, beginning in Egypt, spread throughout the Mediterranean. She was the protector and savior of both men and women, but particularly women during crisis periods in their lives, adolescence, marriage, conception, and birth. But the most common portrayal of Isis is that of Isis Lactans, where the goddess is seated on a throne and nursing her son Horus. This image has been found outside Egypt from the eighth century B.C.E. but is particularly prevalent in the first to fourth centuries C.E. in Egypt, Asia Minor (the probable home of the Johannine writings), Gaul, and pre-Roman Spain. She takes on the role of the Greek nursing deity, the *kourotrophos.*[199] The *kourotrophos* is the nursing mother used for *Gē* (Earth) and figuratively for Hellas Ithaca[200] and also for a variety of Greek goddesses.[201] Price shows the importance of this cult vis-à-vis the emphasis on the family and child rearing in antiquity.[202] She distinguishes it clearly from fertility cults per se.[203] She also observes its importance in oriental cultures.[204] The literary sources are scanty, but archaeological finds are abundant.[205] According to V. Tran tam Tinh the importance of these cults lies in the belief that "milk from the divine breast gives life, longevity, salvation, and divinity." This belief exists "in the mentality of the populations of the Delta from the earliest, and manifests itself in the official imagery of the Pharaohs."[206] The divine power of the pharaoh is derived from the milk of the goddess. Of interest, too, is the idea that the infant king is breast-fed three times, at birth, at enthronement, and at his rebirth as Horus revived from the dead.[207] The divine milk is thought to have both protective and reviving power. Symbolic rebirth of the king took place in "birth-houses" (*mammisis*). One ritual formula reads:

> Milk of Isis (milk?) of Hesat [another name for Isis]! Enter into the belly of the Lord of the Double Land, the child! Purify him, protect him from all evil.[208]

Even the Roman emperors Augustus and Tiberius sent offerings to Isis Lactans.[209] Thus Isis's milk is life, healing, and victory over death. Isis became one of the focuses of the Greco-Roman mystery religions, the female savior (*sospitatrix*) and mother (*matrix*). Popular belief ascribed to her the "power to turn mortals into Heroes and give them spiritual qualities with her divine nursing."[210] Breast milk is the "medicine of immortality." Price states: "The sacramental act of nursing, symbolic of divine adoption, protection, or initiation as a means of divinity, is found in the Eleusinian, Orphic, and later Sabazian mysteries."[211]

All this tradition is not unrelated to biblical studies. Kloppenborg opines that the twenty-one attributes of Lady Wisdom in Wisdom 7:22–8:1 belong originally to Isis, although Wisdom 7 takes a cosmic, rather than maternal, view of Isis.[212] In fact, nursing is now seen as symbolic of bestowing wisdom and experience, rather than in its natural setting. This means that it can be applied to males as well as females.[213] Again, we find examples in Philo. He speaks of Wisdom as "mother" and "nurse."[214] In *On the Migration of Abraham* 24.13, God is presented as nurse and source of wisdom: "For he is the one who nourishes and nurses (*tropheus kai tithenos*) wise deeds, words, and thoughts."[215] The Cynic philosophers also saw themselves as "nurses."[216] We find the same idea in Paul.[217]

While we cannot find any direct verbal affinity between the New Testament texts and the "milk of salvation," we must confess that similar ideas are found in Paul, Peter, and the Epistle to the Hebrews (5:12-13).

Like newborn infants, long for the pure milk of reason (*to logimon adōlon gala*), so that in it you may grow up to salvation, since "you have tasted that the Lord is good" (1 Pet. 2:2).[218]

There remains the possibility of its influence on John.

## Lactation and Roman Charity

De Cueleneer[219] has an interesting article on the legends of adult women (usually virgins) breast-feeding relatives who are in dire need, e.g., dying in prison. His material comes from art and from literature. The most ancient literary source is from Valerius Maximus to the emperor Tiberius in 31 C.E.[220] Valerius Maximus's works became popular in the Middle Ages. There seem to have been two legends, one Roman (a mother nourished by her daughter) and one Greek (the father Myco by his daughter Pero).[221] Pliny tells us that a plebeian woman succored her mother who was in prison.[222] He speaks about the act as one of filial piety "with which the rest could not compare." As consequence of this act the mother was released, she and her daughter were both maintained for life, and a temple was consecrated in honor of the Filial Affection (*Pietas*, the personification of affection between members of the same family). The story is modified by Sextus Pomponius Festus (fourth century), who speaks about the father being breast-fed; C. Jolius Solinus (third century) also says that it was the father. Hyginus *Fab* 254, (before 207 C.E.) names the daughter "Xantippe."[223] The Egyptian Nonnus[224] reports an analogous story, but the heroes are Tektaphos, a general of the king Deriades, and Heriea. In spite of the differences, the legend obtains and the main points are the same. The legend is curious but persistent and attests to extremes of familial affection. It may suggest the belief in the potency of a woman's milk and witness to the honor attributed to the nursing mother or wet nurse. The filial act is usually rewarded by a quasi-redemptive act of release from prison for the captive and maintenance for life for the "redeemer" and prisoner. But perhaps this legend and the imagined male lactation would also enable people to overcome the baby image, rather than adult image, which is not entirely compatible with the modern stress on the mature, responsible Christian.

## Conclusions

Thus we see a feminine aspect of redemption through the redeemer God, who not only rescues his people from Egypt and Babylon but who is also their nourisher, feeding his children from his breasts. It would not, there-

fore, be surprising if Jesus saw himself in a similar role. He undergoes crucifixion as the labor pangs and then cares for the child, especially through
the image of breast-feeding. Therefore, it might be one approach to the
eucharistic discourse to see the eating of Christ's flesh and the drinking of
his blood as a maternal image, his blood becoming breast milk and nourishing the growing child. But there is also an affective aspect of breast-
feeding: the mother feeds, plays, sings, and teaches the child, always with a
constant love.[225] Therefore, for John, like the prophet Isaiah, God as mother is one of the most potent images in his society.

### A Note on John 7:37-39

I add a note on the curious text of John 7:37-39.

> On the last day of the feast, Jesus stood up and proclaimed, "If any one thirst,
> let him come to me and drink. He who believes in me, as the scripture has
> said, 'Out of his heart shall flow rivers of living water.'" Now this he said about
> the Spirit, which those who believed in him were to receive; for as yet the Spir-
> it had not been given, because Jesus was not yet glorified.

This is punctuated differently in some manuscripts and the translation
accordingly is either:

| | |
|---|---|
| If any one thirst, let him come to me and drink. | If any one thirst, let him come to me; |
| He who believes in me, as the Scripture has said, | and let him drink who believes in me. |
| "streams of living water shall flow from within him [the believer]."[226] | As the Scripture has said, |
| | "streams of living water shall flow from within him [Christ]."[227] |

Cortéz[228] observes the parallel between these verses and John 4:13-14, the
dialogue with the Samaritan woman, especially in the words, ". . . for the
water that I shall give him will become *within him* a spring of water always
welling up to eternal life" (John 4:14).[229] Cortéz[230] concludes that the reading which makes the believer the source of the flowing water is prefer-
able.[231] The phrase "she or he who believes" is found seven times in John's
Gospel.[232] Zane C. Hodges[233] remarks on the connotations of the opening
phrase "on the last great day of the feast." He avers that Tabernacles was
the first of Israel's feasts, and this is significant. He thinks that this points
to the day of resurrection and the gift of the Spirit of which Ezekiel's temple is a fit image (Ezek. 47). It is strange that he does not refer to the Johannine Pentecost.[234] However, it is curious that no one appears to have associated the text with Lady Wisdom as Mother, from whose breasts we

receive abundant nourishment, especially in Sirach 14:20–15:10 (see our discussion above). This would explain the reference to *koilia* (abdomen) and *kardia* (heart). Again this seems to be a feminine image. *Koilia* can mean "womb," and we have seen that breast milk is thought to originate in the uterus. The natural origin of nourishment from the body is the breasts of a woman. Jesus here presents himself as Mother Wisdom and indicates that the believer may also nourish others in a similar way. At least one should recognize the possibility of seeing John 7:38-39 as a feminine text that complements the eucharistic text in John 6.

M. Miguens[235] has pursued a detailed study of this text, especially with regard to the Hebrew Scripture background,[236] the LXX,[237] and the Qumran texts.[238] He finds a strong wisdom tradition behind the text. Wisdom is the source of the spring of water, but the texts also compare her disciples to springs, canals, aqueducts, wells, rivers, and the sea. It is a symbol of teaching flowing from Wisdom, the sage, or the community. The *pesher* on Habakkuk gives the symbol an eschatological tonality.[239] He concedes that in the sapiential literature, the symbol of water coming from the *vientre* of the sage is normal; the abdomen of the teacher is compared to a vessel. This explains the presence of *koilia* (abdomen) in the text. The water symbolizes the Spirit. He quotes Job 32:18: "I am full of words, the spirit within me (*pneuma tēs gastrōs*) constrains me." He concludes that Christ presents himself (and perhaps the believer) as wisdom, who invites people to drink of his doctrine. We may also compare Philo who mentions waters from *koilia* (cf. *Gig* 24): when wisdom is shared it does not diminish in quantity, and often gains in quality.

## Summary

In this chapter we have suggested a Greek and Semitic idea of friendship woven into the fabric of the Prologue, which sets the tone for the entire Gospel. It is the friendship of the Father and Son who seek a symbiosis with humanity. For this purpose John uses sapiential material and the myth of the descending and ascending redeemer. Participation in Christ's ascent is possible through being born from above. This theme of birth is continued in the dialogue with Nicodemus, which uses symbolism from physical birth. But the feminine image emerges clearly in John 6 and 7, where Jesus reflects Wisdom as a breast-feeding mother. The Eucharist in John 6 can be understood as breast-feeding by Christ, incarnate Wisdom. John 7 may also reflect this image in the waters that flow from Christ's and/or the Christian's *koilia* (abdomen, womb) or *kardia* (heart). The image of breast-feeding would be well known in the Greco-Roman world, especially in the cult of the goddess Isis.[241]

# 8

# The Footwashing

O UR GOAL IN THIS AND THE FOLLOWING CHAPTER is to examine the Farewell Discourses (John 13–17) from the aspect of friendship, motherhood, and redemption. We follow that incarnate God who, as friend, prepares to lay his life down for his friends—the supreme act of friendship. But we shall see that he not only shows forth the glory of the *pathos* of God as Father but also as Mother. First, however, it is necessary to place the Farewell Discourses within their context. The book of glory is preceded by the raising of Lazarus (John 11), which provokes some of the Jewish leaders to seek Jesus' (John 11:45-57) and Lazarus's life (John 12:10). This confirms the close association between death and resurrection.[1] John follows this with Mary anointing Jesus' feet (John 12:1-8), which forms an *inclusio* not only with Jesus' washing the disciples' feet in John 13 but also with the anointing of Jesus prior to his burial (John 19:38-42):[2] we notice the extravagance in each case. We also note the role of Judas in the anointing scene and in the Last Supper (John 13:2, 18). But perhaps the most important point is that both in Mary's anointing of Jesus, and in his post-mortem anointing, the intimation is that he is sovereign. The sovereignty of Jesus is given remarkable emphasis in this Gospel. It is thrown into high relief in the triumphal entry into Jerusalem (John 12:12-18), where the people publicly proclaim that Jesus is sovereign. Farmer[3] points out that only John mentions *palm* branches (John 12:13) and that the Maccabean coins bore the image of a palm and were inscribed with the words "for the redemption of Israel." Similar coins were found during the two revolts of 66–74 and 132–135 c.e. Palms were used both by Judas Maccabeus on the occasion of the rededication of the Temple (2 Macc. 10:1-9) and by Simon Maccabee when he cleansed the citadel (1 Macc. 13:52).[4] Important, too, is John's insertion that his disciples understood the meaning of the triumphal entry after Jesus was glorified (*edoxasthē*). This strikes the note of glory that is so emphatic in the succeeding chapters. John alone mentions Lazarus and the effect of his resurrection on the crowd (John 12:17-19). Another significant detail in chapter 12 is the reference to the Greeks. The chain of communication—Philip, Andrew, Jesus—reminds us of the gathering of the disciples in John 1. But around this rather obscure reference are clustered theological points of great import: (a) the arrival of Jesus' hour and his glorification (vv. 23, 27-28, 41, John suggests that his glory was seen by Isaiah); (b) the third reference to Jesus being "lifted up" (vv. 32-34); (c) the esoteric title "Son of Humanity" on the lips of the crowd (v. 34);[5] (d) the reference to death and resurrection under the symbol of wheat (vv. 24-25); (e) the emphasis on the disciples following Jesus even to death; and (f) the role of the Father and Jesus' union with him (vv. 26, 44-45, 49-50). The Greeks may represent the preaching of the Gospel beyond Judaism, but they also indicate the Hellenistic culture of John's audience. In John 12:32, Jesus says: "I, when I am lifted up, will draw (*helkusō*) all human beings to myself." Figuratively the verb is used of the pull on one's inner life. Jeremiah 38:3 reads: "The Lord appeared to him from afar, saying, I have loved thee with an everlasting love: therefore have I drawn (*heilkusa*) you with compassion." Song of Solomon 1:3-4 has ". . . therefore do the young maidens love you. They have drawn (*heilkusan*) you. . . ." Maccabees 15:11 reads: ". . . although all the many promptings of maternal love pulled the mother toward the bond of affection for them (the children). . . ."[6] See also Plato *Phaedrus* 238A regarding a pull towards pleasure, and Porphyry, who says, "Only virtue elevates (*heklei*) the soul up."[7] Muñoz[8] refers to Odeberg,[9] who says that this term, "is idiomatic in rabbinic literature for expressing religious experience."[10] It is "going to calamity's depths" on the cross that will draw all peoples to Jesus. The "drawing" is love agapetic and erotic, such as a bosom friend or a mother shows. In this text, then, salvation is effected purely by love, not by expiation.

Forestell[11] has argued cogently that John's Gospel does not have a sacrificial view of the death of Jesus.[12] Forestell says: "The present study undertakes to show that the properly Johannine theology of salvation does not consider the death of Jesus to be a vicarious and expiatory sacrifice for sin."[13] He opts for the originality of John's thought and considers also the Hellenistic influence on it, although he thinks that Jewish Palestinian influence is more likely than Philonic. The death of Jesus was the necessary condition for communicating life to humanity. The litany of messianic titles in John 1 means that Jesus is the contact between heaven and earth. We must see this throughout the public ministry of Jesus. Jesus is greater than Abraham (8:52-53), than Jacob (4:12), and than Moses (5:46; 6:32-35); John claims that he is sinless (John 8:46, cf. 7:18, 18:38, 19:4, 6). But the most solemn proclamation is the statement, "Before Abraham was, I am" (John 8:58); that is, Jesus is preexistent. Jesus' works are a manifesta-

tion of a "unique relationship between Jesus and the Father."[14] Faith for
John is a comprehension of heavenly things (*epourania*) and a vision of
the Father.[15] Jesus' origin as the Word points to "an origin from God
much more intimate than the mission of a prophet."[16] This is clear from
the *ego eimi* declarations. Forestell claims that: "In the fourth gospel the
passion of Jesus is never referred to as something humiliating or degrad-
ing . . . the vocabulary of redemption and expiation is completely absent
from the gospel."[17] Instead of "death," John speaks about "elevation,"
"glorification," "return to the Father," and "ascent." Remission of sin is
mentioned only in John 20:23, and blood does not appear to be atoning
blood. Salvation for John is the manifestation of the presence and power
of God and God's glory. Jesus' glory belongs to his preexistent state. For
John, then, the cross is the "visible sign of the exaltation and glorification
of the Son of Man in the presence of God." The offering of Jesus' life is
his self-devotion as the shepherd. The high priest's statement about one
dying for the people (John 11:50-52) is concerned "with the universal
and unifying efficacy of Jesus' death" (cf. 12:32). Forestell would agree
with F. Mussner that *zōe aiōnios* (eternal life) is John's all-embracing
concept of salvation which expresses all "that the God-sent 'savior of the
world' brings to men [*sic*]." Forestell notes the importance of friendship.
"Friendship, however, presupposes a community of life based on mutual
knowledge one of the other. . . . The knowledge of friendship, however, is
also an affective and intuitive knowledge which manifests itself in love
one for the other"—even to laying down one's life.[18] It is this last point of
Forestell's that I wish to elaborate.

## Footwashing and Hospitality

### An Act of Friendly Service (John 13,19; cf. Luke 12:37)[20]

The footwashing is definitely a *semeion* (revelatory sign) and, like the other
*semeia*, it manifests Jesus' glory (cf. John 2:11). Jesus speaks about the
Father giving all things into his hands (John 13:3). Richter[21] observes that
this authority or commission is the power to effect the salvation of
humanity. He sees the crucifixion not as a contradiction to Jesus' messiahship but rather as an integral part of his messianic commission. The
cross is the climax, the crowning and perfection of his messianic work.[22]
But in this verse we also see Jesus' free acceptance of the responsibility;
and in 3b, the descent/ascent motif. There is nothing about vicarious suffering or sacrificial offering, nor is there a scapegoat theory.[23]

In John 13:1 the evangelist says: "having loved his own (*tous idious*) he
loved them to perfection."[24] The *eis telos* (to perfection) forms an *inclusio*
with *tetelestai* (it is consummated or perfected) in John 19:30. R. M. Ball[25]

discusses patristic interpretations of John 13:1. He notes especially the aorist *agapēsen,* which seems to refer to an act of love prior to the passion, and he sees this in the institution of the Eucharist.[26] Although the Johannine Last Supper is not a Passover meal, it is closely associated with the Passover. Origen and others, however, think that the morsel given to Judas was the eucharistic bread.[27] Whereas the present writer hesitates to accept this interpretation, she thinks that Ball makes an interesting comparison with Luke 12:50: "how I am constrained until it [my baptism] is accomplished."[28] Thus Ball would think that we have an implicit reference to the Eucharist in John 13. But even apart from the Eucharist, the meal context is important. Like the Epicurean or (Neo-)Pythagorean meals,[29] it is the natural setting for expressions of friendship, sympotic discourse, and a farewell speech.[30] More importantly it makes the betrayal of Judas Iscariot as a guest and intimate friend the height of horrendous behavior.

The symbolism of the footwashing has been variously interpreted, e.g., purification of believers, baptism for remission of sin, the Eucharist, an act of humiliation that the disciples should imitate, Jesus' submission to death, his offer to the disciples of a share in his own "personality," and his destiny[31] and an act of eschatological[32] hospitality.[33]

### Jesus Girds Himself

Jesus' removal of his clothes and the girding with a towel are of interest. They are symbolic of a change of status from master to slave. Etan Levine[34] interprets the towel with which Jesus girds himself as symbolic of the wrestling belt. He says: "To recapture the full sense of Jesus girding on the towel during the *pedilavium* it is necessary to realize the wide currency of the girding on the wrestling-belt as a symbol in diplomatic, nationalistic, juridical and spiritual Old Testament discourse."[35] Although he provides a great deal of interesting material from the ancient Near East, the Hebrew and Christian Scriptures, the present writer is not quite convinced by his thesis. Perhaps more suitable parallels are: (a) Jesus' warning to Peter that another will "gird" him and take him where he does not wish to go. The redactor explains that this refers to the death by which *he* was to *glorify* God (John 21:18-19); (b) Acts 21:11, where Agabus takes Paul's girdle and binds his own feet and hands to symbolize Paul's impending arrest; (c) the symbolism may be close to the girdle figure in Jeremiah 13. The *Targum* reads: "For just as a girdle clings to a man's loins, so I *brought near* to *my service* all the house of Israel and all *those of* the house of Judah, says the Lord, to become *before* me a people and a name and praise and dignity; but they would not *listen*" (Jer. 13:11).[36] In Jeremiah this is a prophetic sign or symbolic action, as, indeed, it seems to be in John 13. In Jeremiah, the loincloth symbolizes the people of Israel, and the prophet represents God per se. The context in Jeremiah is his repudiation of the alliances with Mesopotamia, which he views as a *betrayal of the covenant.* This symbolism could be accommodated to the Johannine text but only with some difficulty.

### The Washing of the Feet as an Act of Friendship

Sandra Schneiders[37] sees the washing of the feet not only as an act of humiliation but *essentially* as an act or service of friendship.[38] She discusses different types of service and their goals which often involve manipulation and self-interest, and concludes that the service of a friend is the highest form of service. This would involve no manipulation or power play and seek no reward or compensation. The friendship consists in going to "calamity's depths" for one's friends.[39] The footwashing is a "parable" of this. Jesus, of his own volition, surrenders his life, not in the glory of battle as the heroes of the *Iliad* or the *Odyssey* but on the wood of shame, so that he might be conscious of the mode of existence of the most humiliated and jested of humankind, the slaves and "personless." So the prelude to the passion is a slavelike but essentially friendly service. Jesus wishes to share in all circumstances of humankind. We might compare Lucian's *Toxaris* (*friendship*) for other role models, e.g., the story of Demetrios of Sunium and Antiphilos of Alopece, where unforeseen circumstances bring Demetrios into prison. His friend, Antiphilos, wishing to share his whole suffering, actually joins him in prison and performs the most menial tasks for him.[40]

### Footwashing Creating a Bond or Covenant of Friendship

I agree with W. von Rohden[41] that is it essential to recall not only that Jesus was teacher but also that at the Last Supper he was the host (*Tischheer*) with all its attendant duties and authority. This makes it all the more unusual that he should wash his disciples' feet. Rohden sees the episode of the woman anointing Jesus' feet (John 12:1-8)[42] as a mirror image of Jesus' action of footwashing at the Last Supper. Elisabeth Schüssler Fiorenza takes a similar approach:[43]

> She (the anointing woman) anticipates Jesus' command to wash the feet of each other as a sign for the *agapē* praxis of true discipleship. Both stories—the messianic confession of Martha and the anointing of Jesus' feet by Mary— point to the death and resurrection of Jesus, to his hour of glorification.

She sees Mary as a true disciple and a minister whom John contrasts with Judas the betrayer. Rohden observes that in antiquity footwashing not only showed honor to the guest but offered him (her) acceptance into the house community. The climax of the domestic fellowship is the ᵗable fellowship of the covenant of friendship. When Jesus says to Peter, "If I do not wash you, you have no part in me," then with this he offers him a covenant ultimatum: friend or foe—"a disciple, whom I chose, or a hostile stranger, who repudiates me and whom I repudiate." Are the twelve disciples the first fruit of a friendship world of God; through Jesus' footwashing will they be drawn over from the impending covenant of strangers, from disloyalty and hostility into a purified covenant bond of friendship?[44]

Hultgren[45] develops the hospitality theme and compares the *Testament of Abraham* 3, where Abraham, as host, washes the feet of his guest. It is Isaac who fetches the water but the patriarch who washes Michael's feet. Michael's tears fall into the water and become precious stones. Hultgren also refers to the novelette *Joseph and Aseneth* 7.1 and especially 20.1-5 where this act of hospitality creates a bond between the two parties, Joseph and Aseneth. The bride's words when Joseph objects to her washing his feet are:

> . . . because you are my Lord from now on, and I (am) your maidservant. . . . For your feet are my feet, and your hands my hands, and your soul my soul, and your feet another (woman) will never wash. And she urged him and washed his feet. And Joseph looked at her hands, they were like hands of life and her fingers fine like (the) fingers of a fast-writing scribe.[46]

Hultgren takes the symbolism further and sees this washing as Jesus "receiving his disciples into the place to which he is going, the very house of the Father" (14:2).[47] In this case, God the Father is the rich host who receives them. As Son, Jesus can both offer hospitality on behalf of his Father and also share his inheritance. We may compare Peter who can have no part (*meros*) in Jesus unless he is washed.[48]

### Ritualized Friendship (Xenia)

At this point it is appropriate to make some reference to "ritualized friendship." Does the Johannine Last Supper bear any resemblance to such a practice? Herman,[49] in his seminal work on this subject, defines this association as follows: "a bond of solidarity between individuals originating from separate social units."[50] The disciples would represent a variety of social statuses, although all seem to have been Jews; they certainly differed in status from Jesus. Herman classifies three groups of "friends": (a) *xenos, idioxenos, doryxenos*; (b) *philos, hetairos, epitēdeios, anankaios,* and *oikeios*; (c) *syngenēs, euergetēs*.[51] Excluded from the bond were any persons who would have a financial interest, e.g., merchants, soldiers, employers.[52] In these groups there was friendship, trust, and mutual aid. "The *xenos*-dyad was an outsider with respect to his partner's group. In the extant sources, no two people with the same group identity are ever referred to as *xenoi*."[53] The majority of ritualized friends came from the upper class.[54] This friendship obtained after death and was passed on through a number of generations. Herman regards the *xenoi* as more than friends but less than kin.[55] They exhibited the outward form of affection (e.g., in greetings) but did not necessarily have the inward disposition of affection.[56] Sometimes they received kinship appellations, e.g., father, son, or brother. However, Aristotle says that *xenia* is the firmest of *philiae*, seeing that "they have no common object for which they dispute with one another as fellow-citizens do."[57] Herman relates many vivid stories about these friendships and comes to the conclusion that behind them must lie a stylized etiquette, ceremonies, technical language, and ritualistic devices.[58] He continues: "Two peculiar features of this code of conduct are worth pointing out: its being constrained by moral, rather than institutional, sanctions; and its transcending political as well as cultural barriers."[59] Isocrates, speaking about the panhellenic festivals, also addresses this subject. He says that certain participants made a truce, settled their quarrels, met together in one place and offered their prayers and sacrifices in common. They recalled their kinship (*syngeneia*) that existed among them, and renewed their good will, "reviving old *xenai* and establishing new ones."[60] Some of these features can be compared to the early Christian communities. Herman[61] deduces the following procedures from the texts that he discusses: (a) There was a renunciation of hostilities and violence;[62] we may compare Jesus' new commandment that the disciples love one another (John 13:34-35). (b) Often a mediator was employed; in the Farewell Discourses the Paraclete plays this role. (c) There were greetings, and the right hand of fellowship (*dexia*) was extended (cf. Gal. 2:9). The ritual handshake was impregnated with the character of the donor; it nullified aggression and created a lasting bond.[63] (d) *Spondai* (libations) were offered. Jesus' fellowship bond occurs during a solemn departure meal. (e) Sometimes an oath was sworn. (f) *Pista* or *pisteis* (exchange of gifts) occurred; these could be articles of nugatory value but they were highly symbolic.[64] We may compare the morsel offered to Judas. (g) There was a bringing together of the parties (*synistani*, which is a technical term/title). In the Farewell Discourses Jesus unites his "own" and the Father. (h) Good deeds or favors were performed. The *best favor was to save the party's life*. Thus a sacred bond was established and the benefactor placed the beneficiary in a status of indebtedness. Herman remarks that

> Abstract concepts, personal attributes and concrete objects are thus conceived of as somehow sharing of common substance. For, in the world of ritualized friendship, as in the world of Odysseus,[65] "every quality or state had to be translated into some specific symbol, honor into trophy, friendship into treasure, marriage into gifts of cattle."[66]

Herman also has an interesting discussion of *symbola*. A *symbolon* was an object that could be made of almost any durable material (bone, iron, etc.). It was in two parts and indented. Each party took a part, and when they met to renew the bond of friendship or wished to prove it, they fitted the halves of the *symbolon* together, the jagged edges dovetailing. Herman also has a discussion of "blood brothers." Tegnaeus,[67] too, has studied blood covenant in antiquity and with special reference to Africa. Jesus ,then, in the capacity of the Father's *shaliach* (messenger), establishes friendship with the disciples in a manner similar to but not identical with ritual friendship in the ancient world.

### Footwashing and Ascent-Descent Theories

George G. Nicol[68] sees the *mandatum* as the pattern of descent and ascent that was taken up in John 1 and 3. He compares Philippians 2:6-11 and sees John 13:3-12 as an "important transitional stage in the gospel." John may have structured his work around five elements: (a) Christological statement (John 1); (b) description of descent (John 1:14, 2:1–12:50); (c) exposition of humiliation in terms of servant Christology (John 13:1-12a); (d) revelation (John 13:12b–16:33); (e) ascent and glorification (John 17:18-20). In this case the footwashing that stands at the beginning of the book of glory implements or reifies the themes of the Prologue.

## False and True Guest Friends

### Judas

Against this hospitality background we must see the role models of Judas, the betrayer, and the beloved disciple, true guest-friend. Judas is not only a disciple but also a table companion. Both were present on the occasion of the anointing by Mary. The horror of Judas's violation of hospitality is illumined by a text from Aeschines:

> And you twice put to torture with your own hand and moved to punish with death the same man in whose house you had been entertained at Oreus. The man with whom at the same table you had eaten and drunken and poured libations, the man with whom you had clasped hands in token of friendship and hospitality, that man you put to death. When I convicted you of this in the presence of all Athens, and charged you with being the murderer of your host, you did not deny the impious crime, but gave an answer that called forth a cry of protest from the citizens and all the foreigners who were standing about the assembly. For you said that you held the city's salt as of more importance than the table of your foreign host.[69]

The enormity of Judas's betrayal is emphasized by the fact that Jesus gave Judas the mysterious morsel (v. 26). No cogent explanation has been given of this. There is, however, a curious injunction in the Neo-Pythagorean

*Akousmata,*[70] which *might* or *might not* throw light on this. Here amid discussion on friends we find an unusual counsel: "Do not break bread (*arton mē katagnuein*)." One interpretation of this is that it is an injunction not to dissolve friendships "stressing the importance of the duration of friendships."[71] Diogenes Laertius continues, ". . . for once friends used to meet over one loaf, as the barbarians do even to this day; and you should not divide bread which brings them together; some give as the explanation of this that it has reference to the judgment of the dead in Hades, others that bread makes cowards in war, others, again that it is from it what the whole world begins."[72] With the giving of the morsel does Jesus dissolve the friendship with Judas? In the garden scene in John there is no mention of a kiss as there is in Luke 22:47-48; Mark 14:44-45; Matt. 26:49-50, and Jesus does not address Judas as *hetaire.*

The seriousness of Judas's offense is brought out in v. 20 after the quotation from Psalm 41:9. Anthropologically, one sent as an agent of another is to be treated precisely the same as the sender. Here, the agent Jesus is as the sender (God); they are identified. Thus the deed of Judas was directed not only against Jesus but also against God per se. Judas is the faithless friend of Jesus and of the Father.

### The Beloved Disciple

The beloved disciple (v. 23) seems to be directly juxtaposed with the betrayer in order to bring the contrast into higher relief. He (or she) is the ideal of the faithful friend.

The beloved disciple appears for the first time in John 13:23. Eller[73] does not believe that he is to be identified with John, the son of Zebedee, who is never mentioned in John's Gospel.[74] He states that John 11:1–12:19 (from the raising of Lazarus to the triumphal entry) is "the pivotal passage of the Writer's finely constructed Gospel." In the pericope about Lazarus' death, his sisters refer to him as "he whom you (Jesus) love" (v. 3). This affection of Jesus for Martha, Mary, and Lazarus is mentioned again in vv. 5 and 36. Lazarus is called "friend" in v. 11. Jesus weeps at his death. Eller surmises that all these references to affection may be a subtle allusion to the beloved disciple.[75] He suggests that Lazarus was one of the Jewish intelligentsia, like Nathanael, Nicodemus, and Joseph of Arimathea; Lazarus may have assisted in the burial arrangements for Jesus.[76] He would be one of the educated, open-minded Jewish leaders. Further, Bethany, where they met, is only two miles from Jerusalem. We learn, too, that Jewish leaders came to comfort Mary and Martha. They, too, declare how much Jesus loved Lazarus. Lazarus and other believing Jewish academics are a sign that one can become a follower of Jesus without renouncing one's Jewish faith. The resurrection of Lazarus challenged the faith of the Jews; many believed but some did not (John 11:45-46). Lazarus was also present at the supper where Mary anointed Jesus.[77] John seems to indicate that a crowd or group of other Jewish leaders attended the supper (John 12:9): they came to see Lazarus raised from the dead. After this both Jesus and Lazarus faced death threats. At the triumphal entry into Jerusalem, although Lazarus is not mentioned, a number of Jewish witnesses to his resurrection join the exultant crowd; they were with Jesus when he performed the miracle (John 12:17-18). Thus the resurrection of Lazarus triggers off both hostility and allegiance vis-à-vis Jesus. Eller opines that Lazarus stands as the "disciple-pivot around whom the Gospel is organized."[78] The two great role models for male discipleship in the Fourth Gospel are Lazarus and the beloved disciple. They never appear in the same scene. But from John 13, the beloved disciple appears and from this point "is in every major scene" to the end of the Gospel. He is often paired with Mary (Magdalene), who may be his sister (see below). Thus Eller's findings are as follows: (a) Lazarus (= the beloved disciple) may have been the guest of honor at the Last Supper; (b) he is in the high priest's court (18:12-27) and seems to have some close relationship with him. Probably his status as scholar and teacher afforded him privileges that may not have been available to Galilean fishers; (c) Lazarus *qua* beloved disciple stands at the foot of the cross. He may be with his sister, Mary; (d) he is associated with the burial of Jesus; (e) Peter speaking to Christ on the sea shore (John 21) fears for the beloved disciple (v. 20), and Jesus assures him that all will be well if he perseveres in teaching the message of Christ. If the beloved disciple is Lazarus, then Peter's question about his death seems more pertinent.[79] Will one who has been raised from the dead die again? (f) verses 31-35. At this meal Jesus gives the love commandment, by which he means reciprocal love: see especially vv. 34-35. This is even more ironic because it occurs just after the betrayer leaves.[80] The disciples are to follow Jesus' example, if not in the literal washing of feet, then in the humility and communion aspect.[81] The poignancy is increased when in vv. 36-38 Peter offers the supreme act of friendship, namely, to surrender his life for Jesus. This he fails to implement. But the beloved disciple stands at the foot of the cross also probably risking death.[82] Further, Segovia sees the washing as an integral part of the "hour," and it must be seen from the point of view of *relationship*.[83] Refusal to be washed would dissolve the relationship.[84] It is followed by special instructions to the disciples. It is Jesus' last act before he bids his disciples farewell. It offers the disciples a permanent union with Jesus, but it cannot be understood until the glorification takes place.

Robertson[85] sees the washing as the universal baptism that Christ will undergo in his crucifixion and which is sufficient for redemption. It is the Johannine equivalent to Mark 10:32-45, namely: Jesus' third prediction of his death; his refusal to grant the request of James and John to sit at his right hand of his glory—although they may share his baptism; and Jesus' final emphatic statement that all must be servants, slaves of all; and that the son of humanity came not to be served but to serve and give his life as a ransom (Mark 10:45).[86] The disciples can only participate in Christ if they are prepared to face suffering and death, that is, the baptism of suffering. Robertson also compares Luke 22:27 (the dispute about greatness), which he suggests "might have been specifically written as commentary on the footwashing. Luke's narrative contains other echoes of Johannine themes."[87] So the disciples also will lay down their lives for their friends.[88]

## Conclusions

The footwashing, therefore, stands in a strategic position at the beginning of the book of glory. Jesus is about to exhibit the greatest act of friendship, i.e., to lay down his life for his friends. But this solemn and scandalous action in which Jesus adopts the status of a Gentile slave or a woman— both of whom could wash feet—is pregnant with meaning. It is an act of unsolicited, disinterested service of a friend to friends. It creates or deepens the bond of friendship and reciprocal respect. It is a concrete sign of Jesus' future destiny. But it is more than this. John's Gospel, far more explicitly than the Synoptics, attributes divine status to Jesus.[89] The Father had sent him to choose us in and from this world unto divine friendship.[90] It is God who washes the disciples' feet,[91] a dramatic sign of the imminent self-humiliation of God that will lead to crucifixion. This is God's self-humiliation.[92] He cleanses his people in preparation for salvation, as Moses commanded purification of the Israelites before the covenant on Sinai and as Ezekiel predicted (Ezek. 36:25, cf. 16:9). Rohden points out the importance of the Spirit in connection with the footwashing. The Spirit perfects the cleansing and recreation which the Logos began. In the new commandment to love one another, Jesus asks for the same *Freundesliebe* (friendship love) as he himself offered to the disciples. This commandment is the new decalogue. Through footwashing Jesus and God show their *pathos* for slaves and women. Against this background the betrayal of Judas is seen as an egregious breach of table fellowship, a poignant insult to a host who offers to his friends such lavish and generous hospitality on both earthly and heavenly dimensions.

# 9

# The Farewell
# Discourses[1]

IN THE PROLOGUE, WE SAW A BINITARIAN EXPOSITION OF the Godhead, the begetter and the begotten (Logos/wisdom). This encouraged us to seek ideas of redemption expressed in terms of relationship and friendship, the Logos (redeemer) descending as mediator and friend between God and humanity. The Farewell Discourses carry us far beyond this point. In them we see an *incipient, although implicit*, trinitarian[2] theology. We are invited to contemplate the inner life and communion of the deity, within whose life is found all that is essential for the basis of divine friendship extending to humanity. We shall look particularly at ecstasy, mutuality, immanence, doxology, freedom, and *koinōnia*. The Trinitarian friendship is no mere template for us to imitate. Rather we find the Godhead extending hospitality to believers, so that as a community abiding in God they share the very life of the deity. They are one and many, even as the Trinity is one and many. In John's thought there is no immovable mover, impassible, impassionate, and self-sufficient; rather there is a deity who reaches beyond her or himself in an ecstasy of love and sharing for humanity and the universe. And, as the triune deity within itself has communion, union, and interdependence, so does the *koinōnia* of the faithful. Salvation is no individualistic affair but takes place within a community of believers, a conventicle of the Spirit,[3] displaying love, immanence, freedom, mutuality, and ecstasy in concert with the Trinity. This means that they are related in the highest form of friendship. It is, indeed, in these Johannine discourses that friendship becomes the climactic point, the approximate center of the entire section (John 15:11-17).

## Modern Trinitarian Theology and the Farewell Discourses

I wish now to take some examples of modern theologies of the Trinity that focus on the ecstasy, mutuality, doxology, freedom, and intimacy of the triune persons, and then to attempt to express them in Johannine language. My intention is not a comprehensive study of the Trinity, but the translation of Johannine language into some contemporary theological thought about the Trinity.

*Ecstasy*

Ecstasy is a going beyond oneself. In mysticism, one leaves oneself and becomes united to God with intense desire. No pain is too great to swerve the lover from this union. But God also has ecstasy. God, by the overflowing of divine love and longing for relationship with the creatures she or he has made, experiences ecstasy, going beyond his or her being in a selfless longing for the other. God experiences *erōs* as well as *agapē*. As LaCugna states:

> When personhood is ultimate, then *Erōs* can be thought of as arising out of plenitude not need, because it is out of fullness not emptiness that the lover wishes to give himself or herself to another.[4]

Ecstasy is self-diffusive love. This is seen through the mutual outgoing love of the persons of the Trinity within themselves and by God's outgoing to humanity. God's ecstasy and fecundity shows first through the begetting of the Son and the procession of the Spirit, and then in creation and redemption. An ecstatic view of God and of his or her going forth from self (*ekstasis*) and then returning, is seen in John 13:1, where Jesus identifies his "hour" with his return from this world to the Father. Thus as the book of signs begins with Jesus (the Son) leaving (*ecstasis*) the bosom of the Father, the book of glory recounts his return. John does not speak of Jesus' demise, only the passing from this world (this mode of existence) to return to the Father. In fact, in John's Gospel, unlike the three predictions in the Synoptic Gospels, Jesus himself never speaks of his death or dying but rather of being "lifted up" and returning to the Father.[5] The community's understanding of God is that of the descending and ascending redeemer. God creates a covenant relationship with humanity. But it is a covenant of friendship,[6] as we saw in our discussion of the footwashing. E. A. Johnson sees Sophia-God as a "Trinity of friendship." She quotes Simone Weil:

> Pure friendship is an image of the original and perfect friendship that belongs to the Trinity, and is the very essence of God. . . . So too does the image of three women friends circling around together in the bonds of unbreakable friendship. In threefold "personal" distinctiveness Holy wisdom embraces the world with befriending power as unreachable Abyss, as self-expressive Word that joins history in the flesh, as overflowing Spirit that seeks out the darkest, deadest places to quicken them to new life. The eternal friendship that is the triune mystery of Sophia opens to encompass the whole broken world through awakening friends of God to the praxis of compassion and freedom.[7]

Friendship, as we have seen from Plato, is expressed in the terms of birth and procreation. In fact, in Plato we see the employment of *erōs* in the role of divine begetting, when the soul is raised to the world of forms. The Holy Spirit is the ecstasy of God: to be caught up in her is to be caught up in the ecstasy of God. In John, the ecstasy of God is his or her over-flowing love that transcends its being. In the Farewell Discourses we do not have the word "ecstasy" or its cognates. We do, however, have the constant theme of Jesus proceeding from the Father and returning to him—and then returning to collect his disciples. It is almost a circular movement, like that of the *perichorēsis* (circular dance). The phrases that imply *eksta-sis* are: John 13:1, *metabē ek tou kosmou pros ton patera* (pass from this world and go to the Father); John 13:3b, *apo theou exēlthen kai pros ton theon hupagei* (I proceeded from God and return to him or her; N. B., the prefix "*ex-*"); John 14:28, *Hupagō kai erchōmai pros hymas* (I go away and will come to you), *poreuomai pros ton patera* (I go to the Father); John 16:27-28, *para [tou] theou exēlthon. exēlthon para tou patros . . . palin aphiēmi ton kosmon kai poreumai pros ton patera* (I came from God, from the Father and . . . go to the Father); and John 17:11 (cf. 17:13), *Kagō pros se erchomai, pater hagie* (I come to you, Holy Father).

In other words, Jesus is speaking about the ecstasy, the descent of the Son of God and the ascent of the son of humanity (cf. John 1:51; 3:13). As divine being, he is the ecstasy of God, descending to humanity; as human and unit-ed to humanity, he is the ecstasy of the human friends of God who respond to God's call and who ascend with him to God. That is, we see a bipolar aspect of redemption, divine and human ecstasy in the descending and ascending redeemer and the community. Jesus is the revealer-redeemer who comes to mediate and effect this. In the Farewell Discourses this descent and ascent is given a "trinitarian" perspective. The son of humanity implements a mutual bond between God and humanity and lifts up the ecstatic (redeemed) humanity in his death and exaltation.[8] In addition, we have the five Paraclete sayings and references to the Spirit of truth, that is, the third person of the Trinity. The Spirit has a tandem relationship with Jesus and complements his ministry. Jesus addresses the disciples as *tekna*, children (cf. John 1:12-13). This is a "disciple" nomenclature, a term of endearment, but also filial address, and is consonant with the birth imagery. Jesus begets children for God (cf. John 1:12-13). The begetting of Jesus, his incarnation, and mission can be seen in terms of *ekstasis* (cf. *exerchomai*), which leads to a *perichōrēsis* of mutual interdependence[9] within the God-head, which through Jesus and the Spirit enrapture humanity to God. Redemption is communal ecstasy—or, as Zizioulas expresses it, beings, community members, who break through the boundaries in a movement of communion, who transcend themselves to communion with others.

*Relationship and Mutuality*

LaCugna[10] among others has also approached the question of the being of God in terms of relationship and mutuality. She observes that Greek medieval theology "related the trinitarian persons to a region far beyond our capacity to experience or understand."[11] But modern theology has tended to banish the *deus absconditus* (hidden God) and to link the doctrine of the Trinity closely to the doctrine of redemption. It emphasizes God's immanence in the world. There are reciprocal relationships and an intercommunion between the persons of the Trinity, but it is Jesus himself who gives these historic validity. In him, the immanent Trinity and the economic Trinity are fused. According to Rahner, the hypostatic union reveals not only God with us but God with God.[12] LaCugna quotes Kasper as pertinent to this point: "[I]n the economic self-communication *the intra-trinitarian self-communication is present in the world in a new way*, namely, under the veil of historical words, signs and actions, and ultimately in the figure of the man Jesus of Nazareth."[13] This is peculiarly patent in the Farewell Discourses. Jesus clearly states his union and mutuality with God under the title "the One who sent me" and the ontological link between himself, God, and the one whom Jesus sends (John 13:19-20), that is, the self-sharing of God through sending his Son and self-sharing of humanity commissioned and enabled by the Son. The next verse (v. 21) speaks about Jesus' being deeply troubled over the expected betrayal by Judas. This is also related to the one who sent him; it is the suffering passion of God, the infinite sorrow of a betrayed God described so eloquently by Unamuno.[14] Knowledge and love are interdependent. When a person comes to the knowledge[15] of God in Jesus, mutuality in love is established. As LaCugna says: "The biblical and pre-Nicene sense of the economy is the one dynamic movement of God (Father) outward, a personal self-sharing by which God is forever bending toward God's 'other'" (cf. Eph. 1:3-14).[16] This outward urge of God embraces the whole plan of creation and redemption to its full consummation in the communion of all with God. The creation of the world is the result of a personal, intentional act.[17] One may say precisely the same about redemption. La Cugna quotes MacMurray: "*An 'immanent' trinitarian theology of God is nothing more than a theology of the economy of salvation.*"[18] The mystery of God, however, is not wholly comprehended even in the divine immanence. Immanence, that is, abiding, is one of the dominant features of the Farewell Discourses. The life of the triune God is our life.[19] The doctrine of the Trinity is "the life of communion and indwelling, God in us, we in God, all of us in each other. This is the '*perichōrēsis*', the mutual interdependence that Jesus speaks of in the Gospel of John" (17:20-21).[20] But the economy of salvation is as ineffable as the mystery of God per se. Trinitarian theology is essentially a theology of relationship, God within God, God to humanity, humanity to God, humanity to humanity, and humanity to the universe. All of this we have in John: immanence fused with economy, self-communication with the deity, mutual love, and the role of the Spirit. Immanence is predicated not only of the Father and the Son but also of the Paraclete (14:6, 17).

The Father and the Son will come to the believer and abide with him or her; those who remain in Jesus will bear much fruit; abiding means mutual love.[21] The mutuality of the Father and the Son, and of the Son and the community, is difficult to separate from "abiding" or immanence, but the note of mutuality[22] is struck at the beginning of the discourses. John 13:20 assures the believer that anyone who accepts another accepts Jesus: *amēn amēn legō humin, ho lambanōn an tina pempsō eme lambanei, ho de eme lambonōn lambanei ton pempsanta me* ("Truly, truly, I say to you, he who receives any one who I send receives me; and he who receives me receives him who sent me"). The reciprocal nature of the relationship is underlined by the repetition of the same verbs, *lambanō* (receive) and *pempō* (send). The Father, Son, and believer have a mutual relationship and yet remain as individuals. In John 13:31-35, the son of humanity and the Father also participate in the same glorification process. But this glory seems intimately bound up with the love[23] that is Jesus' "new commandment" to the disciples; it is the love that he has shown to them and which they are to show to each other. It is spoken in the context of Jesus' supreme love in dying for his friends (vv. 33-34). It is love unto death that makes the reciprocal relationship possible, a love which Peter appears to offer but not to implement (vv. 36-38). In 14:1 we see another aspect of the mutuality: to have faith in God is also to have faith in Jesus, a faith that drives away *angst.* The mutuality between Father and Son is also shown in that access to the Father is only through the Son, who is the way, the truth, and the life (14:6-7). This statement of Jesus is brought to an emphatic conclusion by his declaration that to have seen him is to have seen the Father, for the Son abides (is immanent) in the Father and the Father in the Son (v. 9). In v. 10 the simple *en* (in) is replaced by *ho de patēr en emoi menōn* (the Father who dwells in me). In 14:19, the disciples will share the transformed life of Christ, and they will recognize the dwelling of Jesus in the Father, themselves in Jesus, and Jesus in themselves. Mutuality is on a triple level. This will lead to love on a triple level: the person who loves Jesus will be loved by the Father, and Jesus will love him or her and manifest himself (14:21). The love of Jesus and the keeping of his word will lead to the Father and the Son taking up their abode (*monēn*) in him or her, that is, lasting immanence (v. 23).

In 15:9-10, love flows reciprocally between the Father, the Son, and the believer; in 15:12 the disciples are told to love with a love identical to Jesus' love (cf. 16:27). Then comes Jesus' solemn assurance that he no longer regards them as servants but as friends, and that he will show them the greatest love by laying own his life for them.[24] The Father remains with the Son when all forsake him (16:32). Further, Jesus speaks about the love of "his own" (13:1; cf. John 1:11), love which is the foundation of mutuality, intimacy, and relationship. He loves them *eis telos*, to the end or perfectly. This must refer to the divine love that Jesus transmits from the Father. "It is the eternal, sacrificial (in the sense of sacred) love of God."[25]

### The Role of Freedom

Within this economy of creation and redemption, a central issue is freedom. Freedom eradicates fear, compulsion, domination, violence, insensitivity to another's approach and another's happiness. Freedom is essential to personhood and to friendship, not only to the human person but the divine. "God's being originates in love, ecstasis, self-diffusion, and fecundity."[26] However, all of this is of God's own volition. Jesus himself is the perfection of personhood. As a person is basically relational, Jesus is the sole source of our communion with God and of unity within humanity and the universe (cf. the Christology of Colossians and Ephesians). The self must be a person related to others and to the cosmos.[27] "Mutuality is the hallmark of personal identity and exists even in relationships of apparent inequality."[28] LaCugna summarizes MacMurray's definition of a person: "A person is a heterocentric, inclusive, free, relational agent."[29] Hence, I add, we see the importance of Jesus' empathetic statement that he has the freedom to lay down his life and take it up (John 10:18).

> True being comes only from the free person, from the person who loves freely—that is, who freely affirms his being, his identity, by means of an event of communion with other persons. Being, existence, is thus the event of persons in communion.[30]

Jesus in John's Gospel, in contrast with the Synoptics, emphasizes his foreknowledge and his commission by the Father (John 13:3) and also his freedom of choice. Jesus allows freedom to Judas and to Peter and freely accepts his own ignominious death. In the light of the above quotation we can state unequivocally that in the Farewell Discourses we behold an "event of communion." We affirm that only the free person can be a friend.[31]

> Community exists for the sake of friendship and presupposes relationships built on love. Friendship results from persons who are free, who do not relate out of fear of the other or fear of self. Family is the original human community and the norm of all forms of community. The family is established not by force or consent, nor by a duty, but by love. What distinguishes a community from a society is that a community is a group of persons united in a common life who actually form "fellowship" with each other.[32]

Most importantly for our purpose, we find genuine friendship with the Trinity[33] and, thanks to Jesus' new commandment, with each other. Friendship spells freedom, mutuality, common interests and joys, responsibility, co-suffering, hospitality—all these are found in the triune God. Adult friendship enables friends to increase their unique gifts. Johnson maintains: "Jesus-Sophia is the incarnation of divine friendship, hosting meals of inclusive table community and being hospitable to people of all kinds. . . ."[34] Jesus called his disciples "friends." Johnson suggests that they also may have used the term "friend" for Jesus. In a community, each cares for the other while respecting free will and individuality.[35] Religion becomes the celebration of the communal life of free persons. MacMurray describes God as:

> . . . a person Other who stands in the same mutual relation to every member of the community. Without the idea of such a universal and person Other it is impossible to represent the unity of a community of persons, each in personal fellowship with all the others. In its full development, the idea of a universal personal Other is the idea of God.[36]

Freedom and responsibility are also apparent in the Farewell Discourses. The Father places everything in the hands of the Son, and the Son willingly accepts this responsibility; in 13:18 and 15:16, Jesus speaks about his own choice of the disciples; in 13:22; Jesus seems to feel free to love the beloved disciple in a unique way (13:23-24; cf. 17:2, 6).

### Community (Koinōnia)

Zizioulas[37] sees the church as a person and every Christian as an ecclesial being. A person is an "open and ekstatic reality, referred to others for his or her existence." She or he is a "being which in its ekstasis breaks through these boundaries in a movement of communion." The person transcends him or herself to communion with others. But it is love which effects communion with others. The Christian finds freedom in conformity to the image of God in which she or he is made. God transcends him or herself, and begets the Son, and "brings forth" the Spirit. God's *ekstasis* is without limit. For Zizioulas, salvation would mean that *erōs* and the body cease to be the bearers of necessity, individualism, and death. Since *erōs* and the body are indispensable elements of being human, salvation cannot mean flight from the body. The body takes part in the *imago Dei*, God has assumed a body in Christ, and it is the *body* that is raised on the last day. Salvation means that *erōs* and the body are transformed into a new mode of existence that allows the person to transcend ontological necessity, to be free in love, to be a genuine event of communion. Zizioulas calls this the "ecclesial *hypostasis*" (sometimes also "sacramental" or "eucharistic" *hypostasis*).[38] This is the meaning of the love commandment in John. Now one is not only to love one's neighbor as one's self but to love as Jesus loved us. This is a love that transcends self. It is baptism that brings about this self-transcendence, this new relationship, this erotic expression. Rebirth in baptism allows one to enter the *koinōnia* through participating in the passion, death, and resurrection of Jesus, in other words, in *his threefold ecstasis, incarnation, death, and exaltation, condensed in John's phrase "lifting up"* (John 3:14; 8:28; 12:32-34). The resurrection of Jesus is necessary for our own resurrection, which is a transcendence of our mortal, destined nature. "The eternal survival of the person as a unique, unrepeatable and free 'hypostasis,' as loving and being loved, constitutes the quintessence of salvation."[39] Sin is fractured relationship, distortion of the image of God. Only love can heal and bind this:

> The Biological *hypostasis* is destined to remain an individual, divided from others, oriented to death, whereas *the person newly constituted in Christ is inclusive and catholic, eucharistic, eschatological, ascetic, eternal, and communal.* The deified person, conformed to the person of Christ, is an authentic expression of ecstasis toward communion, and thus an icon of God's own mystery of communion, which originates with the Father and subsists in Christ and the Spirit.[40]

Within this *koinōnia* there must be equality and mutuality. This, of course, includes the equality of man and woman as in Genesis 1:27-28. But, we repeat, this *koinōnia* is divine in nature, plurality in unity, and unity in plurality, as in the Trinity.

### Doxology, the Divine Mode of Being

Another concept that interests trinitarian theologians is that of glory. In the Farewell Discourses, Jesus also speaks about mutual glorification or doxology. John 13:31-32 runs thus: "Now is the Son of man glorified, and in him God is glorified. . . ." This is the doxology closely associated with suffering and lament, and it involves not only the Son but the Father. Thus it indicates that God suffers with (in) Jesus. There is mutuality of mission. On the cross there is no cry of abandonment, for God is within the crucified one. Hardy and Ford[41] observe that doxology "has a logic of its own: the logic of overflow, freedom, and generosity."[42] Doxology does not exclude pain or sorrow,[43] as we see from all the Gospels. It is the suffering glory of the Shekinah. Lamentation[44] is one aspect of doxology, it is a call to realize the covenant bond once again, it is a love-longing that communion (salvation) be re-established. The Christian seeks to glimpse the glory of God and through this to be changed. Glory is reflected in the image of God (cf. Sirach 17). Doxology is a calling upon the name (or character) of God and an opening to God's purpose. We may compare John 14:13, 25;

15:16; 16:23, the petitions in the name of Jesus. "Doxology is a remembrance (*anamnesis*) of the past, lifting up (*sursum*) of the present, and anticipation (*prolepsis*) of our future with God."[45] This is the work of the Spirit. The path to glory is God's own companionship through the process of salvation history, including the coming of and to Jesus. It is leaving oneself. It is the opening of oneself to the Spirit. When we encounter God's glory we are changed by it. Moltmann also associates salvation and doxology:

> There is no experience of salvation without the expression of that experience in thanks, praise and joy. . . . Only doxology releases the experience of salvation for a full experience of that salvation. In grateful, wondering and adoring perception, the triune God is not made man's object. . . . It is rather that the perceiving person participates in what he perceives, being transformed into the thing perceived through his wondering perception. . . . The "economic Trinity" is the object of kerygmatic and practical theology; the "immanent Trinity" the content of doxological theology.[46]

There is no need to remind readers that John 13–20 is called the book of glory, that is, the book that reveals a new aspect the divine mode of being, of God's *pathos*. This can be understood only as mutual glory of the Father and Son (John 8:54; 12:28, the Father glorifying the Son, and 13:31-32; 14:13; 17:1-10, mutual glory and their co-suffering). The book of glory resumes the theme of the Prologue (v. 14), of the first miracle, the wedding at Cana (2:11), and the last earthly miracle, the raising of Lazarus (11:4); all are orientated towards revealing God's glory. In our present text we have a dramatization of that glory, which is entirely distinct from earthly glory or honor. John contrasts true and false glory implicitly in 5:41, 44, and explicitly in 7:18; 17:5, 22, 24. It is important for the disciples to see and discern this meaning of glory. The disciples are to ask anything in Jesus' name, and he will do it, but within this very act the Father is glorified in the Son, that is, there is mutual glorification ("that the Father be glorified in the Son," John 14:13). The community can also promote the glorification of the Father by bearing much fruit ("in this is the Father glorified that you bear much fruit, and so prove to be my disciples," 15:8). The Spirit of Truth will teach the disciples and she or he will glorify Jesus ("he will glorify me," 16:14). So glory is the experience of the realization of salvation, and salvation is threefold in the Trinity.

The theme of mutual glory and glorification is particularly impressive in John 17, where the Father and the Son share the same glory: in 17:1, "glorify your Son so that the Son may glorify you." Jesus speaks about glorifying God on earth (v. 4a) and also prays that he may enjoy his preexistent glory (v. 5) "and now, Father, do you glorify me in your own presence with the glory which I had with you before the world was made" 17:5). In this chapter, Jesus also glories in what belongs to the Father (v. 10) and speaks about giving his disciples his glory. This glory will be the source of the unity of the disciples as it is within the Trinity ("The glory which you have given me I have given to them, that they may be one even as we are one," v. 23). He also prays that they may see his preexistent glory ("to behold my glory . . . before the foundation of the world," v. 24).

E. A. Johnson also opines that the primary objective of the doxologies is soteriological; they announce human liberation and cosmic reconciliation. An "economic" theory of the Trinity signifies redemption, God lavishing on the world the riches of her grace.[47] Further she states:

> Redemption, for example, belongs to the history of God: the Father hands over his Son, who in obedience undergoes the cross; in the abandonment of the cross both suffer loss in different ways; their mutual love in grief releases the Spirit upon the godless world. *The cross is a trinitarian event* opening up a path for the suffering of the world to enter the very being of God, there to be redeemed finally in the eschatological victory of divine life. This approach through saving history is crystallized in the programmatic statement (of Moltmann): "Any one who talks of the trinity talks of the cross of Jesus, and does not speculate in heavenly riddles."[48]

The Trinity is the highest example for the human ideal.[49] It indicates a community without rank, the matrix of discipleship of equals. A "threefold *koinōnia*" is the very essence of the Trinity.[50] Of supreme importance to Jesus is the community of loving disciples. He emphasizes several times his new commandment of loving each other as he has loved them (13:34, even unto death). The character of the community is determined by their theology of the *erōs* of God.

### The Promise of the Spirit

It is John's emphasis on the Spirit that completes the trinitarian aspect of the Farewell Discourses. The Spirit is the bond of friendship between God and redeemed humanity. Just as we saw that within human intimate friendship persons were one soul, there was an interpenetration of spirits, so now Jesus teaches the disciples about the very ontological link between humanity and divinity. The five Paraclete sayings[51] present an incipient trinitarian view, although Jesus speaks of "another Paraclete," suggesting that he is the first Paraclete (14:16). The five sayings are a preparation for Jesus' donation of the Spirit in John 19:30 and 20:22-23. They are solemn prophetic pronouncements. The Spirit is the *ekstasis* of the Father. She proceeds (*ekporeuetai)* from the godhead (15:26) and through Jesus through the birth pangs of the cross. She is also described as "sent" by Jesus (John 16:13-15). George Johnson[52] notes the figurative speech in passages about the Spirit, "spirit like water is cleansing agent (1:33); spirit like breath is a vital element (20:22); spirit as teaching, guiding, defending is a divine power (John 14–16). Unifying them all is surely the concept of a *Christlike power* that is finally in the control of God, the heavenly Father" (31–32).

The first Paraclete saying, John 14:16-17, speaks of the Spirit as immanent in the community. The Paraclete comes as counselor (one of the meanings of Paraclete) to lead the disciples into all truth and to dwell in them. This is close to the concept of wisdom in the sapiential literature, where wisdom as counselor/teacher/friend leads her disciples to truth. Jesus speaks about another Paraclete, so that Paraclete comes as an *alter Christus* (another Christ), it would seem, in his capacity of wisdom incarnate. The Paraclete is the possession of the *koinōnia*, and not of the world in general. The second Paraclete saying, John 14:26, again represents the Spirit as revealer and teacher. Again she comes as an *alter Christus*. In the third Paraclete saying, John 15:26-27, the Spirit comes as witness, and witness is a major theme in the Gospel. Here the Spirit appears in a quasi-legal context. However, the fourth Paraclete passage, John 16:7-11,[53] is of great importance. Here we see the Paraclete in the capacity of judge of the world. She will convict it with regard to sin, Jesus' concept of sin rather than sin according to the Mosaic law; to righteousness, Christ is proven righteous although judged a blasphemer; and to judgment, Christ is judge although he was judged by Pilate and unbelievers. The fifth Paraclete saying, John 16:12-15, identifies the Paraclete with the godhead. She will be one with the Father and the Son in her teaching, she will announce the future and will participate in the intra-Trinitarian glorification. But the second Paraclete cannot come until Jesus withdraws (16:7b). The other Paraclete will afford the disciples permanent divine immanence (14:16). The Paraclete is a mutual gift from both Jesus and the Father (14:16; 15:26; 16:7b). She, like the Logos, is an *ekstasis* from the Father (v. 26). The Father sends the Paraclete in the name or character of the Son (14:26), and this Paraclete will reveal the full knowledge of Jesus' teaching to the disciples (cf. 16:13). She will also come as judge (16:8-11).

In 17:12, Jesus assures the Father that he has guarded and preserved all whom the Father gave him (except Iscariot). There is a tandem relationship between Jesus and the disciples: as the Father commissioned him, so he commissions his own. In 17:21-23 he prays that the community will be one even as the Trinity is one; this unity will be a witness to the world. He also prays that they may abide in the same place as he, and behold his glory. He requests that the love of the Father that dwelt in him may dwell also in the disciples. Love is the Spirit.

Of communion within the Trinity, Elizabeth Johnson writes:

Jointly, inseparably, mutually the three persons dwell within each other and exercise powerful activity. . . . When trinitarian language is thus pondered as a whole, it is clear that the fundamental attempt of the doctrine is to secure an understanding of God as profound relational communion.[54]

The Christian community also must be a profoundly relational community. In 14:15 Jesus states the condition for receiving the Spirit, namely, the observance of his commandments; the new commandment is love of one another. This represents the act of voluntary response on the part of the disciples; it is their acceptance of the new covenant, the bipolar aspect.[55] Within the Spirit, John states the fundamental basis of immanence and mutuality. The Spirit comes from the Father through the intercession of Jesus; that is, there is another *ekstasis* of God, another witness to intercommunion and a reciprocity. The Spirit herself is also an intercessor.[56] The immanence produced will be perduring. The world has not fertile soil upon which to receive the Spirit, for a faith confession is necessary. John 14:18 adds another dimension, a filial or familiar *agapē* on Jesus' part, for he will not leave the disciples orphans. Verse 19 seems to point to the resurrection period; a little while and Jesus will not be seen, then he will be seen. The clause "because I live and you yourselves will live" indicates a new mode of existence for the community. John 14:20 explains this new mode of existence: human existence will be woven into divine existence; Jesus in his Father, the disciples in him, and Jesus in the disciples. This (v. 21) produces mutual love and a revelation of Jesus to the disciples. To Judas's question about the cause of Jesus' manifesting himself to them but not to the world, Jesus answers that the sole reason lies in LOVE (vv. 21, 23) and IMMANENCE. (v. 23, the word *monēn*). In vv. 25-26 we see the Spirit as the true and legitimate successor of Jesus. There is no hierarchical succession. She, too, is sent by the Father and is the chief source of revelation. There follows the promise of *shalom* (peace), which is salvation per se, but not in this worldly sense (v. 27), for the prince of the world has no power over Jesus. Both the peace and the Spirit look forward to the greeting of the resurrected Christ and his bestowal of the Spirit (John 20). Peace is also an important element in covenant making. The Spirit is the vital bond within the Trinity and between God and the community. Moltmann, speaking about God's *pathos* before the incarnation, says that as God's accommodations or self-humiliations are "accommodations of eternal love, they are at the same time already *anticipations* of the universal indwelling of God's eternal glory."[57]

Next, Jesus speaks about the hatred of the world. The difference between the world and Jesus is a matter love and hatred. The world loves its own (*to idion ephilei*). Then he repeats his explanation about the Spirit coming from (*exporeuomai*) God. The work of the Spirit is to confront the world with regard to sin, righteousness, and judgment. Sin is a broken (or never begun) relationship to Jesus; the failure of righteousness is confronted because they failed to recognize the relationship or mutuality of the Father, and about judgment, because the prince of this world, not Jesus, is defeated.

Unamuno speaks about redeeming the joy of God and the consummation of this in the "feast of God's eternal joy."[58] God's freedom is "undivided joy in the good. . . . We understand true freedom as self-communication of the good."[59] This kind of freedom belongs to community. "Free" is etymologically close to "friendly" and thus:

> This freedom consists of the mutual and common participation in life, and a communication in which there is neither lordship nor servitude. In their reciprocal participation in life, people become free beyond the limitation of their own individuality.[60]

All this is possible through the Spirit. It is at this point that Jesus commences his journey back to the Father. He travels alone, without human companionship. But God is with him (v. 32). He goes as a victor to conquer the world.

## Feminine Texts in the Farewell Discourses

There are three themes in the Farewell Discourses that speak especially to women: the vine (John 15:1-17), the image of childbirth (John 16:21), and the five Paraclete sayings.

## The Vine

### Symbol of Immanence

In John 15 we find the key concepts of abiding, immanence, and friendship. The vine is the symbol of these three. It is the symbol of those who are ontologically joined to Christ and God, whom God may, indeed, prune, but only to bring forth more fruit. Thus *koinōnia* is the friendship lifestyle of the heterocentric person who seeks what is beneficial to others. We note also the element of joy that this union brings to Jesus and to the disciples (John 15:11).[61]

Sandvik[62] has inquired whether the symbol of the vine is associated with the "fruit of the vine" in Mark 14:25.[63] He thinks, with Lohmeyer and Sahlin, that there may be an association to the temple here. According to Josephus, the Herodian Temple was adorned with vines on the portals.[64] Sandvik also finds traces of this symbolism in *Sukka* 49a, where Isaiah 5[65] is explained along these lines.[66] At Qumran the symbols of the temple (building) and planting are combined.[67] So the disciples are bidden to abide in Jesus as temple and vine. The early Christians would associate this with the Eucharist. A striking parallel is found in John 6:56 and 15:4, both refer to "abiding."[68] The throwing away of the unfruitful branches may refer to unworthy participants of the Eucharist.[69] The stark words of John 15:6 may reflect the *anathēmata*. Dodd[70] observes that the idea of God as vinedresser or gardener mourning the world, humankind, and the individual soul would be familiar to a Hellenistic audience. He suggests the indirect influence of Plato's theory of forms. Thus the true vine is ". . . that which makes a vine a vine, at once its inner essence, and the transcendental real existence which abides while all concrete vines grow and decay."[71] The vine is the last of the "I am" sayings. Carson sees a close association between the simile of the vine and 15:9-16 (mutual divine love).[72] He opines that the latter is a commentary on the former.[73] The central theme of both is fruitfulness, especially fruitfulness in prayer. Further, both sections exhibit a change in the perspective of salvation history: (a) the new covenant commandment to love others as Jesus loves his own (John 13:34-35 and 15:12) complements the requirements of the Mosaic covenant; and (b) Jesus raises the disciples from the status of servants (a term familiar to devotees of the Mosaic law) to friends. The image of the vine is a brilliant image for expressing mutual indwelling; the sap of life and growth pulses through the stem of the vine to the branches and their fruits. The image of pruning, as expressive of cleansing, is also persuasive. Carson does not think that John is transforming material from sources behind the Synoptic Gospels.[74] He disagrees with Bauckham,[75] who tries to discover an authentic parable of Jesus in this text.[76]

All commentators on this chapter point out that the vine is a common symbol for Israel, the covenant people.[77] It is used of the remnant in Isaiah 11:1, 10, and is applied both to the people and the Messianic king.[78] It is usually the unfaithful Israel who is symbolized by the vine. The vine and the cup appear commonly in Jewish art, ceramics, coins such as the Maccabean, tombs, ossuaries, and lamps. A clear example is found in Dura Europos.[79] The vine and wine seem to have been associated with the concept of immortality.

However, most scholars have failed to point out that the vine is a feminine image and that Israel herself is usually regarded as feminine in her relationship to God. The Greek noun *ampelos* is feminine. Furthermore, the vine is a symbol of a faithful and fruitful wife:

> Your wife shall be as a fruitful vine
> in the recesses of your home;
> Your children like olive plants
> around your table (Ps. 128:3).

Further, wisdom herself is compared to exotic trees and plants, including the vine, "meant to evoke in the reader or listener a feeling of pleasure and a desire for wisdom"[80] (Sirach 24:19ff.). She produces "fruits fair and rich" (v. 17b).[81] In Sirach 24:17 we read: "Like a vine I caused loveliness to bud and my blossoms became glorious and abundant fruit." Features that are common to this description and John 15 are vine, branches, and fruitfulness. In both texts the first person singular is used. In Sirach 24 there is also a reference to Israel and to immanence. Wisdom dwells in the midst of her people (24:1f., 7f., 10ff.). Jesus as the incarnate wisdom dwells amidst his people. Schnackenberg states: "Wisdom undoubtedly introduces a distinctive note into the exhortatory discourse addressed to the disciples and promising them a rich yield of fruit" (cf. Sirach 4:11-16).[82] For Philo, wisdom is the vine that the spies took when reconnoitering the promised land; it is the symbol of "noble living."[83] But a more interesting reference is found in *On Dreams* 2.190:

> We have explained one kind of vine (*ampelos*), that which is the property of gladness, and the potent drink which it gives, undiluted wise counsel (*akratos euboulia*). . . .

So "Philo presents the idea of wisdom giving her instruction through the metaphor of the vine offering its wine."[84] The vine is then another image of Sophia-God.[85]

Further, as Bauckham[86] has demonstrated, the vine in *Acts of Thomas* has become a cosmic symbol sending its shoots into the deep, its tendrils to the heavens. The vine is the eschatological people of God. It has become the world-tree. Baukham finds an affinity with *1 QH* 6.15-16 ,which is based on Ezekiel 31:3-9 and Daniel 5:7-9. This text describes the eschatological Israel, although here we have no reference to the vine per se.[87] Moreover, the *Acts of Thomas* 144.19-36 says that the grapevine spreads out and dominates all other foliage, and

> It alone inherits (*klēronomein*)[88] the land in which it grows and it dominates every place it shaded. . . . and it is bountiful for its master, and it pleases him even more, for he would have suffered great pain on account of these plants until he uprooted them. But the grapevine alone removed them and choked them, and they died and became like the land.[89]

We find another text in 2 Baruch 36-37, where the messianic kingdom is symbolized by a vine and a fountain that uproots a forest of trees. In 3 Baruch (Greek) 4.8, the vine is identified with the tree of knowledge; and in *Apocalypse of Abraham* 23.5f., the fruit of the trees of Eden was a vine (cf. 1 Enoch 32.4ff.). In Christian literature (*Didache* 9.2) Jesus is referred to as the "vine of David." The symbol of the vineyard is found in Herma:

the owner is God and the servant is Jesus. Here it is the servant who uproots all the weeds.[90] Moreover, the Mandaean literature makes use of the vine image,[91] e.g., "I (Hibil) am a gentle vine; I was planted (created) from the place of glorious splendor" (*Ginza* 301.11-14).[92] In these documents the redeemer represents the soul or the individual person. "We are a vine, the vine of life, a tree on which there is no lie, the tree of praise, from the odor of which each man receives life."[93] Here the vine is obviously the tree of life. Borig[94] observes that the image of the celestial vine was in the mind of the author.[95] Even in the Hebrew Scriptures (Ezek. 17:6-8) the image is transferred to the king (Zedekiah), although the word "Messiah" is not used in this context. Thus we see the interplay of the anointed one as vine and the people as vine.[96]

Most of these texts are later than John 15, but they show the potential of and suggest an ambiance for the image. It is intended to convey to us mutuality (of spousal relationships), immanence, femininity, and fecundity. Borig[97] opines that purification (John 15:3) is based on the acceptance of and fidelity to the *kerygma*; "purity" denotes a grace-filled quality given to the disciples. It is important that Jesus as the genuine vine, the true Israel, identifies himself so intimately with the branches, that is, with the Christian community. The image has the potential to become cosmic in scope and may be linked to the idea of the tree of life. Borig[98] states that John 15 speaks of an *ampelos tēs zoēs* in the sense of the vine of life. He finds the vine to be a genuine creation of John, of which examples cannot be found in history of religion parallels.[99] The vine as the tree of life prefigures the resurrection.

For the theological aspect of the vine, see Borig.[100] "To remain in" is a typically, although not exclusively, Johannine term and denotes a love relationship. The image of the grape vine does not introduce the idea of immanence but is used to deepen the concept and to emphasize that without the immanence or abiding, no fruit can be produced. It does not, however, apply to the individual but to the community, which must abide in Christ.[101] Whoever abides in Christ will have life. Borig himself does not think that this refers to the tree of life but rather to the enduring life of the community with the glorified Christ and through him with God.[102] This brings the graces of salvation. True relationship with the Son is salvation in the deepest sense. Borig[103] observes that this immanence endures without a break, whereas the categories "descent" and "ascent" suggest a break or distancing. He finds that this applies especially in the case of John 17:21-24[104] and in Jesus' remarks about the "little while" (John 14:18; 16:16-24).

*Entry into Immanence*

Borig asks how one enters into immanence.[105] The first answer to this question comes from John 3:1-21, the pericope concerning Nicodemus. This text does not speak of either immanence or life directly, but the act of baptism is the beginning of life. Similarly immanence is mentioned directly in John 6:56, "Who eats my flesh and blood abides in me and I in him or her." Participation in the Eucharist promises life and immanence. Birth through baptism is a community experience; so also is the Eucharist. The community aspect given here finds expression in baptism and the Eucharist and corresponds to image of the vine. There is a deepening of the immanence with the reception of the Spirit.[106] The Spirit is the principle of life and of revelation. Borig also emphasizes the importance of the role of faith.[107] The Logos gives the believers (faithful ones) the power to become children of God (John 1:12). Jesus' opponents do not have this faith and so they lack immanence (John 5:38). Immanence originates in God, whereas faith is more a human disposition (6:44). Immanence goes beyond faith. In immanence is the fullness of eschatological salvation, which creates for the disciples an eschatological existence.

*The Essence and Perfection of Immanence*

This is gained through knowledge and love, e.g., John 17:3.[108] We can see the images of the shepherd and the vine as symbolizing first knowledge and then indwelling. Reciprocal love deepens the expression of immanence.[109] The climax of Johannine statements about love is found in 15:9-13. Immanence is salvation, to be committed to the community of brethren with the Son; this is to be accepted as such into the divine love community as its prototype and foundation.[110] Obedience to the commandments is essential for immanence. As Jesus fulfilled his Father's commands, so the disciples are bidden to implement his; this is love. This obedience may involve risk of death, the loving surrender of one's life. Joy is a characteristic of this salvation. The consequence of immanence is loving the community of salvation with those who believe.

*The Fruit-Bearing Vine*

Fruit bearing is mentioned seven times. There are, in the main, two interpretations of this simile. Either it refers to the mission work of the disciples or to their moral-religious caliber; the latter is more acceptable. For Borig,[111] "fruit bearing" is obviously keeping of the commandments. This is certainly consonant with the meaning of fruit bearing in the Old Testament (Isa. 27:2ff.). To the unfruitful Israel will come the fruit bearing vine, the One who is come.

### The Friendship Statement

We have observed above scholars who have suggested that friendships of parity appear to be more common among women then men. It is, therefore, not surprising that as the climax to this important feminine discussion about immanence comes Jesus' declaration that he makes the disciples friends instead of servants (John 15:13-17). The declaration is a natural outcome of immanence, for a friend is one soul with a friend; there is interpenetration of spirits. So Jesus in this new covenant pronounces the disciples friends, not servants, friends with full knowledge of the purposes and actions of the other. It is a friendship of freedom, for Jesus has chosen them deliberately, and through him they have perfect access to God (v. 16).[112] Jesus clarifies the friendship relationship in 15:16. This is not based on equal rights but on Jesus' choice of the disciples. He calls them to his own friendship. Borig[113] states that the fruitful vine in the Old Testament is the keeping of the covenant, unity in covenant. Correspondingly, if the disciples keep the commandments of the Son, they remain in the salvific love-immanence with the Son (v. 10). In John, the main point is the new covenant people, its essential structure, and its basic commandments. The true vine is the Son, and he is the fulfillment of the prophetic promises for the eschatological salvation community of God.[114] The Son is the new people of God. The church comprises both the Son and the disciples. Jesus as vine is the church, the place where the Father effects salvation through the Son and brings his brethren into glory. We may compare Psalm 80:7-8 and 14-18, where the vine is identified with the son of humanity (vv. 18, also perhaps 16). The ecclesial community is vine branches and wife. We notice also how the vine complements the bread of life discourse, although not all scholars would take a eucharistic interpretation of the vine.

## The Birth Image (John 16:16-24)

We have referred to the birth pangs of God in the Hebrew Scriptures. The most explicit text is Isaiah 42:14:

> The Lord *is revealed to do prodigies* (*gbwr*) . . . Like *pangs upon* a woman in travail *my judgment will be revealed upon them, they* will *be devastated* and *come to an end* together (LXX: I have endured like a travailing (woman), *ekarterēsa hōs hē tiktousa*).

We have noted the birth image in the Prologue (John 1:12-13), in Jesus' conversation with Nicodemus (John 3:1-20), in the suggested nursing image in the bread of life discourse (John 6), and in Jesus' proclamation on the Feast of Tabernacles (John 7:37-39). Now we see a birth image in Jesus' *mashal* of the pregnant woman who has pain during childbirth but joy after the birth of her child (John 16:21). It is correct to say that Jesus explicitly applies this image to the disciples who will have grief over Jesus' departure but who will rejoice when he returns. Nevertheless it would appear legitimate to accommodate this also to Jesus' own sufferings for three reasons: (a) the context of the saying is within Jesus' prediction of his suffering, death, and resurrection; (b) the suffering of the disciples is nearly always seen to be identified with the sufferings of Jesus, especially in the Farewell Discourses; (c) the explicit reference to the "hour" must be interpreted against the other sayings about the "hour" in John's Gospel: all of them refer to Jesus' passion, death, and exaltation.[115]

We know that the birth image was applied to God in anguish over his people and also that the period of tribulation preceding the coming of the Messiah was described as the "birth pangs" of the Messiah. Here it is not the Messiah per se who suffers the pangs but the people, the earth, and perhaps the cosmos. A fine example comes from the Hymn Scroll from Qumran. In column 3 we read:

> And I was in distress,
> As a woman in travail brings forth her first child;
> For her birth pangs wrench,
> And sharp pain, upon her birth canal
> (or, with her birth throes),
> To cause writhing in the crucible of the pregnant one.
> For sons have come to the deathly birth canal,
> And she who is pregnant with a man is distressed by her pains;
> For through deathly contractions she brings forth a male child,
> And through infernal pains, there bursts forth from the crucible of the pregnant one,
> A Wonderful Counselor with his might,
> And a man is delivered from the birth canal by the pregnant one
> (1 QH 3:7-18 [or 7-11]).[116]

Holm-Nielson,[117] in discussing this section, observes that the two themes of birth and death are interwoven. "The unifying idea is that the moment of birth itself, with its agony, is identical with death."[118] He remarks the interpretation of Chamberlain, who reads the text in the sense of God letting the pregnant woman's firstborn come forth (cf. Isa. 9:5). This view is also espoused by B. Otzen, who thinks that the text describes (figuratively) God assisting the community through its afflictions,[119] that is, as midwife. The same metaphor is found in the pseudepigraphal literature. In 2 Esdras 4.42 the birth is eschatological; 1 Enoch 62.4-5 refers to the pains of eschatological epoch; and 1 Enoch 62.5 and 69.29 apply it directly to the Messiah. The figure expresses the idea of suffering producing a new era, an era of salvation: both the Messiah and the community are seen to be in the throes of childbirth. In John's Gospel, there is frequently an oscillation between Jesus and the believer/community.

Brownlee gives attention to the affinity between the suffering servant of the Lord in Isaiah and the Teacher of Righteousness. He sees in the Qumran hymn the birth of the Messiah from the community. For it would appear from the Old Testament texts, which lie behind this text, that the mother is corporate, Zion, or Israel.[120] However, one must note the first person singular, which has led Baumgarten and Mansoor[121] to opine that the writer speaks about his personal affliction.[122] Brownlee argues that the author must have felt that through his suffering in concert with the community, the Messiah would be born. The hymn seems to suggest that the Teacher of Righteousness is to be identified with the pregnant one.[123] The motif of refining is used in reference to the teacher in *1 QH* 5.15f. Brownlee then brings into consideration *1 QH* 11.10ff., where the purification is not for a prophetic office "but to share in the glories of the eternal society of holy men [*sic*] and holy angels."[124] Brownlee suggests that the text refers to "man [*sic*] in his weakness and unregenerate state and his exaltation to the eternal society—an action most likely ascribed to God."[125] The prophet or teacher must be refined to bring redemption to (God's) people. Here is an arresting parallel to the theology of Jesus' passion. Indeed, Brownlee avers that John's Gospel portrays Jesus as a *geber* (warrior). In John 14:30, he overcomes the prince of this world. But the anticipated joy will be preceded by pain (John 16:21f.). Like Isaiah, he links the idea of the warrior and the suffering mother (see above p. 41). Brownlee states:

> It is clear from this that John has intended more than a mere illustration of sorrow giving way to joy, that he believed that through Christ's death and resurrection an *anthrōpos* will truly be born into the world![126]

Brownlee comments on the use of "crucible" for the woman's uterus. He compares to the *Rule of the Community* (*Manual of Discipline*), where the purifying of the people is spoken of as a "refining" by the Holy Spirit.

Nancy Klenk Hill[127] has examined this Johannine pericope in her article "Woman as Savior" and suggests that one can see Jesus going to his passion like a woman approaching childbirth. She makes a parallel between childbirth as an excruciating experience, carrying with it the possibility of death but giving birth to a new generation, with Jesus' painful death, which did the same, although his birth and offspring are spiritual. She sees Jesus in John's Gospel as preparing the disciples for his death through the image of childbirth. She observes that Jesus speaks to the disciples in figures:

The figure repeated three times, "a little while, and you will see me no more; again a little while, and you will see me," is a chiasmus,[128] figuring the very form of Jesus' crucifixion. By their questions the disciples force the figure into the forefront of consciousness. . . .

In his explication Jesus uses another chiasmus, "you will weep and lament, but the world will rejoice; you will be sorrowful, but your sorrow will be turned into joy." The concluding, fourth element of the figure is an astonishing prediction, incomprehensible to the unseeing disciples prior to the resurrection.[129]

She sees the metaphor as a formally arranged, third, different chiasmus. When the disciples remain silent, Jesus encourages them to make petitions in his name. Hill compares this request to that made of Ahaz by the Lord (Isa. 7:10-14). The Lord sends him a sign, the birth of a child, Immanuel. The disciples then understand and declare that he no longer speaks in figures but plainly. She then refers to Isaiah 26:16-18, where the prophet likens Israel's suffering to childbirth. So for Hill, Jesus "reveals to us in his very person that union of female and male that the Old Testament figure brings forth as an image of God."[130] In contrast to St. Augustine, who portrays Jesus as a bridegroom going to consummate his marriage (*Homily* 108), "He came to the marriage bed of the cross, and there, in mounting it, He consummated his marriage. . . ." Hill points out that Jesus' attitude towards his sufferings and death were passive, like a woman, rather than active like a man. She quotes Theophan the Recluse: "Unless we suffer like a woman in travail, we shall not succeed in bringing to birth the spirit of salvation in the ground of our heart."[131] While Hill's article is not an exegetical one, it certainly provides food for thought.

We can say, therefore, that the image of the woman in childbirth is a weighty one. It portrays the passion of Jesus, either from his point of view or the disciples', as a birthing event. This theme is adopted by some of the early Christian writers, as we saw in our discussion of John 6 and shall see in our last chapter. We shall resume this theme later when we look at the piercing of Jesus' side (John 19:34): 16:16-24 foreshadows this.

## Conclusions

So the Farewell Discourses are a prelude of the trinitarian aspect of the passion and exaltation of Jesus. They enable us to see the extension of the friendship and motherhood of the Trinity into the human abyss of the passion. Both images give a hint of the resurrection, for the ontological union between the Trinity and humanity can bring to birth only life, not death.

# 10
# Sovereignty, Friendship, and Motherhood

## Christ's *Pathos* according to John

IT IS THROUGH THE WHOLE PROFUNDITY OF THE JOHANNINE "trinitarian" theology that we must approach the death and resurrection of Jesus. He and the Father are one, thus God per se faces his passion. However, first we need to measure that passion beside the valor of the heroes and heroines, Christians and others in antiquity. How does Christ differ from Socrates, Heracles (Hercules), Alcestis, or the mother of the Maccabean martyrs?

In chapter 4, I have discussed the ineffable shame associated with crucifixion, impalement, and *apotympanismos*. After this I attempted to show that it was possible to bear that shame with equanimity so that it could become a source of honor: this was similar to the aspirations of the Cynics and the Stoics. The wise person or philosopher bears pain, insult, and death with serenity. She or he is the only true sovereign. I concluded that the Johannine Jesus fulfilled the Platonic and Cynic-Stoic ideals and could provide John's Hellenistic audience with a role model superior to Heracles, Cleanthes, and other heroes and heroines.[1] When we combine these ideals with the theme of friendship, however, we find that the greatest feat and the truest love is found in a glorious death for the sake of one's friend(s). Jesus concurs with this when he says that the Good Shepherd lays down his life for the sheep, and that there is no greater love than to die for one's friends (cf. John 10:11 and 15:13). He solemnly designates the disciples as such friends (John 15:12-17).

### Going to Calamity's Depths for a Friend

#### Greco-Roman Examples
Dying for one's friend is a not infrequent *topos* in classical literature. We have mentioned it is what Homer calls a "fury inspired" by a deity that is found in certain heroes and heroines and is also the effect produced on lovers by Love's peculiar power (*Symposium* 179A).[2] Plato avers that "Only

such as are in love will consent to die for others; not merely men will do it, but women, too" (*Symposium* 179B). He, like other classical writers, cites the example of Alcestis, daughter of Pelias (*Iliad* 10.482, 15.262). I quote this interesting paragraph at length:

> Sufficient witness is borne to this statement before the people of Greece by Alcestis, daughter of Pelias, who alone was willing to die for her husband, though he had both father and mother. So high did her love exalt her over them in kindness, that they were proved alien to their son and but nominal relations; and when she achieved this deed, it was judged so noble by the gods as well as men that, although among all the many doers of noble deeds they are few and soon counted to whom the gods have granted the privilege of having their souls sent up again from Hades, hers they thus restored in admiration of her act. In this manner even the gods give special honor to zeal and courage in concerns of love.[3]

Further, Plato disparages Orpheus for wishing to enter Hades alive. Then he takes the examples of Achilles and Hector and describes how, on account of their friendship, they were sent to the Isles of the Blest. In the case of Achilles he "bravely chose to go and rescue his lover Patroclus, avenged him, and sought death not merely in his behalf but in haste to be joined with him whom death had taken."[4] He also cites the example of Codrus, a legendary king of Athens, who exposed his life for the sake of his "kingdom of children" (*huper tēs basileias tōn paidōn*). The deities give such people "distinguished honor" (*Symposium* 208D). All these heroes and heroines won a "deathless memory for valor."[5] Seneca also speaks about death for a friend: "For what purpose, then, do I make a man my friend? In order to have someone for whom I may die, whom I may follow into exile, against whose death I may stake my own life, and pay the pledge, too."[6] Epictetus speaks in a similar way: "If, then, it becomes necessary for me to risk my life for my friend, and if it becomes my duty even to die for him, where do I find beyond that any occasion to employ divination?"[7]

Hengel[8] has an important section on atoning deaths and dying for city, family, and friends. He cites Euripides' *Alcestis, Phoenician Women,* and *The Children of Hercules*; Plato's *Symposium;* and the innumerable deaths in battle. He points out that, according to Cicero, "*Honestumne sit pro patria mori*" was a rhetorical exercise and that dying for the city was included in philosophical catalogues of duties.

Another well-known work on friendship is Lucian's *Toxaris,* or *Friend-ship*,[9] which takes the form of a dialogue between two speakers who compete in telling stories about friends. He describes some of the classical models of friends who shared the acute suffering of comrades or even went to the point of dying for them.[10] He cites the friendship of Orestes and Pylades:

As friends they, surely, had proved themselves the best in the world, and had established precedents for everyone else in regard to the way in which friends should share all their fortunes.[11]

Each was ready to die for his friend, "counting it nothing to die if he saves his friend and intercepts with his own body the stroke that is being directed at the other."[12] Lucian also cites the friendship of Achilles and Patroclus, of Theseus and Peirithous.[13] Mnesippus, Toxaris's companion in the dialogue, tells of Agathocles of Samos and Deinias. The latter lived a dissolute life and lost his property and honor. But Agathocles paid his debts. Then Deinias committed a double murder for which he was exiled. Agathocles went with him (the only one of his friends who did so), provided for his daily necessities, and stayed with him when he was dying. He remained in the country of exile in order not to desert his friend even after his death. Then Mnesippus tells of Euthydicus of Chalcis and his friend Damon. When Damon fell overboard on a sea voyage in stormy weather, Euthudicus jumped into the water to save him. Then he relates the story of the three friends, Eudamidas and Aretaeus of Corinth and Charixenus of Sicyon. Before dying Eudamidas bequeathed his aged mother to Aretaeus and his daughter to Charixenus, for he knew that a friend would care for his needful family (cf. John 19:26-27). There was a reciprocal friendship between the three. The fourth tale concerns Zenothemis of Massilia, who had a severely handicapped wife. When Menecrates lost his property, his friend Zenthemis married his disfigured daughter in order to provide protection for her, but he received many graces from her. The fifth story is of Demetrius of Sunium, whose friend Antiphukus was imprisoned under appalling conditions (Lucian, *Toxaris,* or *Friendship* 29–30). Demetrius went to the prison, tended him in every way, and even engaged in manual labor to support them both. After a time, for security measures, the prison no longer allowed visitors, but Demetrius of his own volition accused himself of the same crime as Antiphilus and was condemned to prison with him. The prison guard allowed them to be chained next to each other, and thus Demetrius could still minister to his friend. At this point Toxaris begins his tales. He proceeds to speak about "blood and battle and deaths for the sake of friends."[14] He speaks about friendship among the Scythians and states the care with which friends are chosen:

And when a man has been singled out and is at last a friend, there ensue formal compacts and the most solemn of oaths that we will not only live with one another but die.[15]

He then describes the blood covenant: they cut their fingers, let the blood drip into a cup and drank the cup together. He begins with the story of Dandamis and Amizoces (*Toxaris,* 39–42). Three days after they made their blood friendship, the Sauromatae attacked their country. As Amizoces was being dragged off as a prisoner, he cried out to Dandamis. At the demand of the enemy Dandamis allowed his eyes to be cut out in exchange for the rescue of his friend. Amizoces put out his own eyes so that he could share the suffering of his friend. He tells another story of Belitta and his friend Basthes, who was attacked by a lion. His friend leapt upon the lion to save him, but all three died and were buried near each other. His third story is that of Macentes, Lonchates, and Arsacomas.[16] He sued for the daughter of the king of Bosphorus, and upon being asked about his wealth and property he declared: "I own no wagons or herds, but I have two noble friends, such as no other Scythian has." He was rejected because of his poverty. Upon returning to his friends he related the incident and his deep distress, not only about the rejection but the insult to his two friends. He said:

"And I think that you also have been equally injured, for a third of the disgrace belonged to each of us, since we live in the understanding that from the time when we came together we have been but as one man, distressed by the same things, pleased by the same things." "Not only that," Lonchates added, "but each of us is completely disgraced in your suffering such treatment."[17]

The three made an arrangement for rectifying the situation, and when Macentes returned with the bride, Mazaea, he declined the gratitude of Arsacomas saying:

To express gratitude to me for what I have done in this is just as if my left hand should be grateful to my right for ministering to it when it had been wounded and taking care of it fondly while it was weak. So with us—it would be ridiculous if, after having fused ourselves together long ago and united, as far as we could into a single person, we should continue to think it a great thing if this or that part of us has done something useful in behalf of the whole body; for it was working on its own behalf as a part of the whole organism to which the good was being done."[18]

After this a great battle ensues with the Alans and Sauromatae. Arsacomas rescues his two friends[19] at the grave risk of his life. Toxaris then relates the story of himself and his friend, Sisinnes.[20] When they found themselves robbed and destitute, his friend Sisinnes took part in a gladiatorial show to gain enough money for them. He won, although he was badly wounded. Lucian follows this with the story of Abauchas, who on the occasion of a fire decided to save his friend, Gyndanes, rather than his wife and children.[21]

When they have finished these stories they make a formal friendship: For the union of two or three friends is like the pictures of Geryon that artists exhibit—a man with six hands and three heads. Indeed, to my mind Geryon was three persons acting together in all things, as is right if they are really friends.

Mnesippus, however, suggests that they do not make a blood covenant, their promises are the surety.[22] I have devoted some time to these romances, for they may have been some of those that schoolboys learned in the classroom and repeated in their rhetoric, and therefore would have been well known in Hellenistic culture.

Thus as well as the *ars moriendi*, the art of dying,[23] a death as noble as the life one had lived,[24] one prepared for death as an athlete prepares for a contest[25] and a warrior for a battle.[26] The model death was that of Socrates.[27] Seneca (*Letter* 24.6–7) says that Cato fortified himself before his suicide with reading the *Phaedo*, and Philostratus says that Dio comforted himself with the same.[28] Socrates accepted his death at the will of the deity. He did not feel the necessity to justify himself.[29] Further, he desired to show himself utterly submissive to the laws of his country. In *Phaedo* 99A he states that it is "better and nobler to endure any penalty the city may inflict rather than to escape and run away."[30] Greek heroes and heroines also gave their lives for noble causes. Euripides[31] from his intense patriotic love composed unforgettable scenes of women and men who gave their lives for others. His Alcestis is the most "intensely personal example of what one student of Euripides has called his 'Verherrlichung der freiwilligen Hingabe des Lebens'"[32] (the glorification of the free surrender of [one's] life).

### The Jewish Tradition

Within the Jewish tradition, the author of 4 Maccabees takes a similar philosophical approach. H. Anderson[33] avers that the author had firsthand knowledge of Platonic ideas and also of contemporary Stoicism. He shows that the four cardinal virtues are embedded in the Torah. Eleazar, the elderly martyr, in contrast to his portrayal in 2 Maccabees, is represented as a philosopher, although he does not adopt all Stoic tenets. Anderson[34] finds his philosophy summed up in the phrase *ho eusebēs logismos* (the reasonable devotion), which enables the martyrs to endure for the faith (cf. 2 Macc. 1:1). Eleazer, the elderly Maccabean, espouses the doctrine of the afterlife. Further, he believes in the expiatory and vicarious nature of martyrdom, e.g., 6:28: "Make my blood their purification and take my life as a ransom for theirs" (cf. 2 Macc. 7:37).[35] An even more explicit statement comes in 4 Maccabees 17:20-22.

> These, (the martyrs) then, having consecrated themselves for the sake of God, are now honored not only with this distinction but also by the fact that through them our enemies did not prevail against our nation, and the tyrant was punished and our land purified, since they became, as it were, a ransom for the sin of our nation. Through the blood of these righteous ones and through the propitiation of their death the divine providence rescued Israel. . . .

Williams[36] observes that 4 Maccabees may have been composed for the commemoration of the Maccabean martyrs (under Judas Maccabeus). This would explain the strong rhetorical style that he calls "barely restrained encomium": the author uses the form of philosophical discourse.[37] Under these circumstances, Williams questions whether we can attribute to 4 Maccabees a doctrine of expiatory death, although the death of the martyrs does appear to effect purification of the land.[38] Further, he opines that Old Testament texts are not sufficient to account for the idea of the human blood of martyrs effecting expiation. He remarks that the style and vocabulary of 4 Maccabees shows that the author is a master of the Greek language and also familiar with Platonic and Stoic ideas.[39] The style reflects influence from the Cynic-Stoic diatribes. Williams thinks that the example of Socrates inspired the author's picture of Eleazar's death and that generally the Greek idea of the glorious death influenced 4 Maccabees.[40] Williams supplies evidence that some Hellenistic Jews did attend the theater as, indeed, Philo did. Our author could, therefore, be influenced by the great tragic figures of Greek drama: *Prometheus Bound* by Aeschylus; *Iphigeneia in Aulis*, *The Children of Hercules*, and *Phoenician Women* by Euripides. Death for the sake of others was often described in religio-sacrifical language.[41]

Anderson states that the author's importance lies in the fact that his work

> . . . affords us a singularly valuable specimen of the way in which a hellenistic Jew of the Diaspora can draw upon Greek philosophical thoughts and modes of expression in the formation of an essentially religious message of enduring elegance and validity.[42]

We have been arguing for a similar, not necessarily identical, influence on the Gospel of John.

Within the Hebrew Scriptures we learn of the suffering of the righteous, wise persons in the wisdom tradition (Wisd. Sol. 1:16–6:21). Their suffering is caused by the persecution of the wicked, but their souls remain safe in God's hand. Their trials are a test permitted by God, but God will reward them with fruitfulness instead of sterility. Indeed, an early death is a sign of God's solicitude, and they will be vindicated at the final judgment.[43] We have another catalogue of martyrs and/or confessors (men and women—they are all Jewish) in Hebrews 11. The author intends this list to be a eulogy on the virtue of faith, which in the next chapter (12:1-3) he sees in Jesus, the pioneer of our faith.[44] All these martyrs inspired by wisdom die as special friends of God (cf. Wisd. 7:27-28).

### The Consequence of the Noble Death

Williams[45] discusses the idea of *ho ponos agathon* (good hardship) among the Greek philosophers. Many believed that all suffering produced some good: ". . . suffering is a *doxa*[46] against which one fights by submitting to it, by declaring it paradoxically to be a good, *Ponos, penia, adoxia*, etc., which in the eyes of the world are evil, all have the epithet *agathon* in Cynic propaganda."[47] Williams cites the example of Antisthenes' *Ajax* and *Odysseus*, where Odysseus is seen as the humble and suffering kingly figure.[48] Such sufferings might involve torture and death, as in the examples of Zeno of Elea and Anaxarchus.[49] One turns evil into good when suffering is accepted and one's greatness of soul increases.

Seeley cites Seneca's *Letter 24: On Despising Death*, where he mentions Rutilius, Metellus, Socrates, Mucius, Cato, and Scipio. However, Rutilius and Metellus suffered exile, not death, and Cato and Scipio took their own lives. Their reason was twofold: to return to the gods and to avoid earthly tribulation.[50] Therefore, none of these are really parallel to the death of Jesus. A closer case is that of Regulus, to whom Seneca makes reference in *On Providence* 3.9. Regulus promised to return to Carthage as a captive when he had delivered a message to Rome. He did so and was tortured to death. The moral is shown in his integrity in the face of extreme suffering. Seeley says these deaths were vicarious,[51] but, he asks, precisely how was Jesus' death vicarious? Seeley does not see it as a cultic death, like the suffering servant of Isaiah or Abraham's offering of Isaac. The mode of Christ's death for him is *mimetic*. The reenactment of Jesus' death is performed in baptism (cf. Romans 6). Seeley concludes:

> He (Paul) used a notion available to anyone who breathed the intellectual atmosphere of the Hellenistic Kingdoms and the early Roman Empire. This was the Noble Death. It seems to have come to Paul quite naturally and to have been at hand for him to employ after his own fashion.[52]

We may ask, then, how does the death of Jesus differ for John from the deaths of heroes? It would seem that some of the Greco-Roman philosophers go beyond the notion of the mimetic nature of the noble death. For example, Seneca (*On Providence* 3.9) tries to answer the question why misfortunes befall good persons? He maintains that the consequence of such misfortunes is *friendship between good persons and the gods and goddesses*.

> Friendship, do I say? Nay, rather there is a tie of relationship and a likeness, since, in truth, a good man differs from God in the element of time only; for he is God's pupil, his imitator, and true offspring, whom his all-glorious parent, being no mild taskmaster of virtues, rears, as strict fathers do, with much severity.[53]

Thom quotes a similar paragraph from the *Pythagorean Way of Life*.[54] It is from Iamblichus's own hand:

> The stories told above are beautiful and fitting examples of friendship. Much more wonderful than these, however, are the things they taught concerning participation in the divine goods and concerning unanimity of mind and concerning the divine soul (*to peri tēs theias psychēs par'autois aphōristhenta*). For they often exhorted one another not to tear apart the god in them. Thus the whole effort of their friendship both in words and deeds was aimed at a mingling with God, at a union with God and a participation in the mind and the divine soul (240).[55]

John, too, would view the death of Jesus in a different dimension from the glorious death of heroes and heroines in Greco-Roman literature. It can only be seen in the light of the whole Gospel, and especially the Good Shepherd teachings and the Farewell Discourses. These show that Jesus dies (1) as a sovereign and (2) as God. He dies to attract humanity and unite it to God. This is effected by divine love. But we iterate that this was not implemented through an expiatory death. Williams[56] examines the New Testament texts that appear to speak of Jesus' death as expiatory but comes to the conclusion that Isaiah 53 is the only text in the Old Testament in which the idea of expiatory suffering is found, and that it is not until the Epistle to the Hebrews and 1 Peter that we find a clear allusion to that theme in the New Testament. Bultmann would see Jesus' death in John subsumed under the concept of revelation; it is an act or event of revelation. Forestell elaborates upon this idea.[57] G. Richter[58] argues for two series of texts: in the first the death of Jesus is given a Christological-soteriological interpretation, and in the second (from the redactor) the death is paraenetic, a deed of love that should be emulated. Ernst Käsemann[59] emphasizes the glory of Jesus that overshadows his public ministry and his passion. Jesus is the one in whom eternal life and resurrection are personified.[60] He states that the passion appears only at the very end. It looks almost like a postscript, but "his solution was to press the features of Christ's victory upon the passion story."[61]

His former student Appold[62] also sees the death of Jesus as "departure," but this departure is interpreted wholly in the light of the identity of Jesus as the exalted one. Ulrich B. Müller[63] also emphasizes "re-ascent" as the goal of Jesus' ministry. The death of Jesus is important for John, but it is overshadowed by the glorification. Nicholson[64] views the death of Jesus as departure, and argues that it is closely interwoven with the descent-ascent schema and is not "concerned with issues of ontology, but rather speaks about a *movement* and a *relationship* that persists throughout that movement."[65] He interprets the *hupsoō* (lifting up) sayings[66] in the light of the descent-ascent motif: these sayings include a reference to the crucifixion.[67] Nicholson interprets John 3:3 as a Christological statement: Jesus, as the believer will be, is born from above (cf. 18:37), but the text (like 3:5) is multivalent; it refers first to Jesus and then to the believer.[68] John wished his readers to understand that the crucifixion of Jesus was "not an ignominious death but a return to glory."[69]

## *Regal Glory as* Pathos

In the early part of this book, we have decried God as feudalistic Lord and divine warrior. Is there anyway in which we can "salvage" the sovereignty of God? Are omnipotence, remoteness, and power necessary attributes to the regal state? What was the thinking of the ancient world on this point? In this last section I wish to address the passion of John from the point of view of sovereignty, glory, and exaltation. John's Gospel must be read against the background of the philosophy of sovereignty in the ancient world and also the Roman imperial power, which wielded authority over Asia Minor, thought to be the origin of John's Gospel.

### *Jesus as Friendly Sovereign*

It is well known that John presents the passion of Jesus as the ceremony of the consecration of a monarch. This has been demonstrated by Blank,[70] Dauer,[71] Meeks,[72] Boismard,[73] De La Potterie,[74] and other scholars. Indeed, it forms the framework of the entire passion according to John. It comprises: (1) the anointing by Mary (John 12:1-8); (2) the entry into Jerusalem (John 12:12-19); (3) the crowning and homage of a king (John 19:1-3); (4) the proclamation (John 19:4-5); (5) the acclamation (John 19:6-7); (6) the enthronement on the *bēma*, judgment seat (John 19:13-16); (7) the naming (John 19:19-22); (8) the regal burial with abundance of spices (John 19:38-42).

I wish, however, to make three further reflections. First, it is not always noted that the anointing at Bethany (John 12:1-8) forms an *inclusio* with the anointing in the tomb (John 19:38-42). Indeed, John 12:1-43 is the prologue to the whole passion. Second, it has not been explicitly noted that the whole discussion of "glory" and "lifting up," and the blindness of the Jews in John 12:20-43, is prefaced by the request of the *Greeks* to see Jesus. Third, if Jesus' words in John 12 are addressed to Greeks and his Gospel audience is Hellenistic, we need to study the ideals of sovereignty among the Greeks in order to understand what John's readership brought to their hearing of his message.[75]

### Hellenistic Monarchy

In his discussion of Hellenistic monarchy, Walbank[76] observes that the fifth-century Greeks had experienced sovereignty in the form of tyranny but that it was the successors of Alexander the Great who became sovereigns in the true meaning of the word. Thus, in one sense, Hellenistic monarchy was a new political form in the fourth century B.C.E.[77] It was not derived through family descent but rather won through personal achievements.[78] We may compare the *Letter of Aristeas* 289, which clearly states that some men of common origins with their experience of misfortune and their share of poverty make better monarchs than hereditary ones, though even they may become tyrants (*Letter of Aristeas* 289). "In practice, the monarch maintained his or her realm not only by the support of the army but also, and not least, through the *charisma* surrounding his or her[79] person, which rendered him a formidable opponent to any rebel."[80] Walbank continues:

> A factor in the creation of this belief in a divinely favored personality with an overwhelming claim to men's loyalty may well have been the impression produced by the frequent repetition of such cult titles as "Savior" and "Benefactor" which marked the king out from ordinary men.[81]

John's audience may well have looked for such a sovereign in Jesus, a person of common origin but with powerful charismata.

### The Ideal Sovereign

Discussion of the characteristics of the ideal king existed long before the monarchies of Alexander's successors. As is well known, Plato thought the ideal constitution was one comprised of philosopher kings (*Republic* 499B-C), although in the *Statesman* (294A) he argues that a wise monarch is better.[82] In the *Laws* (4.711-712A) he avers that if one should find a person with a "divine passion for self-control and justice," one should surrender the city to him.[83] Further, a number of treatises appear to have been devoted to the theme of sovereignty. Walbank lists *On Kingship* by Aristotle; one by Theophrastus; others by Demetrius of Phalerum, Zeno, Cleanthes, Sphaerus, Persaeus, and Epicurus, but few are extant. Among those that do survive, we may mention Xenophon's panegyric on Agesilaus of Sparta and Isocrates' on King Euagoras of Cyprus. Isocrates also discusses the qualities of a monarch in *To Nicocles* and *Nicocles (or the Cyprians)*. Walbank (78) also refers to the three pseudo-Pythagorean treatises preserved in Stobaeus.[84] Strangely this scholar does not discuss fully the four discourses *On Kingship* by Dio

Chrysostom (see below). Dio Chrysostom lived c. 40–120 C.E. He was exiled under Domitian and traveled widely until restored to favor under Trajan. He wrote four discourses on kingship.[85] He was greatly influenced by Homer and Plato. At first he was opposed to philosophy but later was converted to Stoicism. Important for us is the fact that he was teaching and writing during the time of the formation of the Christian Scriptures. We also may mention Aristeas (*Letter of Aristeas*, second to third century B.C.E.). The section 180–294 of the *Letter* revolves around the virtues of monarchs. The host-king asks various guests questions about the characteristics of the ideal king. One of his questions is, "What is the definition of kingship?" The reply was, "Real self-mastery, not being carried away by wealth and glamour, nor having as a result, overweening or unworthy ambitions . . ." (211). Another guest replied that the "highest form of sovereignty" was control of one's impulses (222).[86] Walbank avers "Clearly, then, monarchy had a strong appeal to philosophers and thinkers at this time."[87] We may compare again the *Letter of Aristeas*,[88] where another guest describes how a monarch should use his time: "Time should be spent on reading and on the accounts of travels, which have been written and dedicated to thrones for the permanent betterment of mankind. This indeed you do, thereby winning glory beyond the reach of others, with God fulfilling your plans." He should also invite learned people to his banquets (286). It is important to note that the monarch and his kingdom resemble God and the universe: he is commander, overseer of justice and of the cult, and mediator between God and humanity.[89] In the light of these findings, it should cause us no *admiratio* that John chose as his theme for the book of glory the sovereignty of Christ, a sovereignty bonded to the monarchy of God and to be shared with humankind.

### The Debate about Glory

Of interest also to us is the theme of glory, which characterizes the second part of John's Gospel. Glory in the book of signs (John 1–12) is associated with the miracles but in John 13–20 with suffering. Here again we might find that this *topos* is pertinent to a first-century C.E. audience in Asia Minor or in the Roman Empire at large. Glory, or honor, was a puissant force in the ancient world (see the works of Malina, Neyrey,[90] and others) and was particularly relevant to ruler. Even more pertinent to our study, however, is the fact that some of the treatises on sovereignty take the form of fictitious dialogues between philosophers and monarchs. We also find fictitious anecdotes relating encounters between philosophers and kings. Walbank lists Cineas and Pyrrhus,[91] Bion and Antigonus Gonatas,[92] and Sphaerus and Ptolemy IV.[93] These enable us to examine the disposition and values associated with the ideal ruler.

An illustrative example from the first century C.E. is the work of Dio Chrysostom. P. Jones gives a good background to this philosopher and discusses his four discourse treatises on kingship.[94] He notes that these treatises are placed at the beginning of the collection of his work. "As this position implies, late antiquity considered them Dio's masterpieces, and they influenced Julian, Themistius, Synesius, and others."[95] What is of interest to us is that Dio addresses his teaching on kingship to an emperor, Trajan, who was reigning during the period when much of the New Testament, including the Gospel of John, was written or redacted. Dio is familiar with Rome and with Asia Minor. Although Trajan is not actually mentioned in Dio's treatises on monarchy, his presence is felt. Indeed, some of Dio's teaching may have been delivered in the presence of the emperor. Jones quotes Rostovtzeff who asserts that, "They [the treaties] are not only a registration of existing facts, but, first and foremost, an exposition of eternal norms which must be accepted or rejected by Trajan."[96] Trajan appears to have yearned for "glory,"[97] and Dio wished to communicate to him the essence of true glory. Dio also contrasts the ideal king (and implicitly Trajan) with Domitian, whom he regarded as a tyrant.

It is the fourth treatise, *On Kingship* (*Discourses* 4),[98] in which the present writer is most interested, especially the parts dealing with Alexander as a "slave of glory." There was an increased interest in Alexander with the establishment of the Roman Empire, and Trajan seems to have taken Alexander as a role model. Dio apparently wrote eight books on the virtues of Alexander.[99] Nevertheless, Höistad argues for the existence of a hostile tradition towards Alexander among the Cynics, who saw him as a man driven by ambition, aspiring even to immortality and divinity.[100] He cites a papyrus that shows Alexander mocking philosophers.[101] The antithesis seems to go back to the third century and is to be found in the Cynic-Stoic traditions.[102]

Thus about the time that Dio Chrysostom was exhorting Trajan to accept the Cynic Diogenes, not Alexander, as his model, John the Evangelist holds up Jesus as the model monarch to his audience, a monarch who turns the concept of glory and honor topsy turvy. For John, Jesus is the true sovereign and Pilate is the tyrant. We note the catalogue of vices of the tyrant and virtues of the philosopher king in Greco-Roman works.[103]

B.A. Mastin[104] has argued for the influence of the imperial cult behind Thomas's confession, "My Lord and my God" (John 20:28). He thinks that this is a Christian confessional formula catalyzed by Domitian's claim to be "Lord and God" (354).[105] According to Mastin, Domitian did claim divine honors, and his statues and images "filled the whole world."[106] After giving further evidence for the cult of Domitian, Mastin observes that there were distinctive developments in the imperial cult in Asia Minor, especially Ephesus. He quotes Dio Cassius:

Caesar . . . gave permission for the dedication of sacred precincts in Ephesus
and in Nicaea to Rome and to Caesar, his father, whom he named the hero
Julius. . . . He commanded that the Romans resident in these cities should pay
honor to these two divinities. . . .[107]

Mastin also compares the theme of sovereignty in John's Gospel to an
incident reported by Hegesippus (Eusebius, *HE* III, 20:4, 5). He says that
one of Jesus' brothers was arraigned and questioned by Domitian about
Jesus' kingdom, and he explained that it was neither "worldly nor earthly,
but heavenly and angelic." It would come at the end of the age, and everyone would be judged according to their merit. Although the incident may
not be historical, the reply placed in the mouth of the martyr (confessor) is
of interest. Certainly Jesus' conversation with Pilate in John's Gospel, and
the reaction of the crowd, would point to a rivalry between Christ and
Caesar. Mastin sees John 20:28 as the climax of the Gospel.[108] Thomas's
confession can be seen as a "rebuttal of the claims made on behalf of the
Emperor by the Imperial Cult,"[109] it is a "counterblast to the official, state
theology."[110]

### Sovereignty in the Gospel of John

The theology of sovereignty is carefully prepared throughout the Gospel.
The motif of kingship appears early in the book of signs in John 1:50, the
affirmation of Nathanael, and seems to form an *inclusio* with the theme of
sovereignty at the beginning of the book of glory, the entry into
Jerusalem.[111] The same theme occurs in John 6:15 after the multiplication
of loaves: the people wish to make Jesus king, but he eludes them (only
John records this detail) because their ideal of a sovereign is not acceptable
to him. Jesus' idea of a monarch is closer to the Cynic-Stoic tradition and
to the *Letter of Aristeas*. When one of the guests in this work is asked how
the king's accomplishments will last, one guest replies: "If his accomplishments by his actions are great and glorious, so that those who see them
show forbearance because of their beauty; and if he does not neglect a single one of those who carry out such works. . . ."[112] Asked what possession
was most important the guest replied, "The love and affection of his subjects," which produces a bond of unity.[113] These qualities we can, indeed,
find in the Farewell Discourses of John.

## Jesus as Friendly Monarch

Monarchy within the passion can only be understood against the background of John 10, the ideal shepherd. "Shepherd" is a synonym for
"ruler" and thus the discourse could be called "the ideal sovereign."[114] It

complements the philosophic treatment of the ideal monarch discussed above. It also introduces the theme of "his own," which occurs in the Farewell Discourses as well and, of course, the theme of laying down one's life (John 10:11). Over and above the general use of "shepherd" as a synonym for "monarch," we have a long tradition of this metaphor or simile from the age of Homer to the time of Dio Chrysostom and beyond.[115] Homer calls the king the "shepherd of his people." He should care not only for the good people but also the bad subjects. The shepherd who lives with his sheep cares for his flock better than one who does not. The shepherd's business is simply to oversee, guard, and protect flocks, not to slaughter them. He is savior and benefactor. The kindly and humane king is the one who is loved. Höistad comments on the strength of king and the weakness of tyrant.[116] He summarizes his findings about the ideal king thus far: "a king with pronounced individual-ethical qualities, with simple, uncomplicated social functions illustrated by the herdsman comparison, by the father figure and by the Homeric figures of a different kind." We have testimony of the features of sovereignty also from the Roman statesman and philosopher Seneca. Writing to the tyrant Nero, Seneca speaks about mercy gracing a prince, of real power being "potent for benefit," that a king should be a *friend* to his people, a king is greatest when he calls his power in check, and he concludes that "to save life by flocks and universally, this is a godlike use of power (*haec divina potentia est gregatim ac publice servare*)."[117] The Good Shepherd in John 10 implements all these requirements, but goes beyond them in that he is willing to lay down his life for the sheep. The discourse foreshadows the passion.

### Jesus and Pilate

Passing from the discourse on the Good Shepherd (sovereign) to the passion we find that, as soon as Jesus is delivered to Pilate, the word "sovereign" rings repeatedly in our ears: in 18:33, Pilate's question, "Are you king of the Jews?"; in 18:37-39, Pilate's further question about the royal status of Jesus, and his reply that he was born (begotten) a king and for this came into the world; in 18:39, Pilate's question to the Jews, "Do you wish me to release the king of the Jews for you?" We may compare also the homage of the soldiers as they cry, "Hail, king of the Jews!" (John 19:3); the Jews' assertion that everyone who makes himself king opposes Caesar (19:12); Pilate's taunt, "Behold, your king!" and "Shall I crucify your king?" (19:14, 15); the Jews' cry that they have no king but Caesar (19:15); and finally the title on the cross (or around Jesus' neck), "the king of the Jews" in three languages (19:19-21), and his burial in regal state with superabundant spices (19:38-42).

But above all it is the dialogues between Pilate and Jesus (John 18:33-38 and 19:9-11 (12-16) that reveal Jesus as the ideal sovereign. In John 18:33-38 we find Jesus' statement that his kingdom is not of this world and that his followers do not fight to deliver him. Some indirect light may be cast on this from our sources on monarchy. Turning again to the *Letter of Aristeas* we find that there are similar sentiments expressed by some of the guests; for example, that administration is best when it imitates the goodness of God and uses patience and leniency in punishment; that the ruler should show just judgment and humility; that he should rely upon God rather than troops in war and that he should acknowledge God's sovereign power; that he should forewarn his descendants of the dangers of fame and wealth. Here also Dio Chrysostom has reflections that cast an indirect light on Jesus' words. In the *First Discourse*, he asserts the following points about the ideal king: (a) He receives his office from Zeus; he is Zeus-nurtured and "like Zeus in counsel." He should reverence the gods and goddesses. No evil person can be king.[118] Jesus claims a unique relationship to God, and the Jews accuse him of this (John 19:7). (b) He expects and embraces toil and anxiety on account of his people.[119] (c) He does not accept the title "master" even from his slaves, for he is monarch for his people's sake, not his own.[120] We may compare Jesus' washing his disciples' feet and also his words in John 15:14-15. (d) Just as the sun cannot be the source of darkness, so the sovereign must not be the cause of harm to his people.[121] We may compare Jesus as the Light of the world, that is, the sun. (e) The qualities of truth and sincerity are absolutely essential for him.[122] Jesus also describes his sovereignty as from heaven and as witnessing to the truth. Thus the dialogues with Pilate portray the ideal monarch, Jesus, speaking with the typical tyrant Pilate. It is exceedingly ironic that it is Pilate, the tyrant, who presents the ideal sovereign to his own people and they reject him (cf. John 12:36b-43).

### Investiture and Homage (John 19:1-4)

From this point forward Pilate proceeds with the "consecration" of the monarch. An important aspect of royalty was its regalia, clothing, of course, being an extension of one's character and an indication of honor. Walbank observes that this was modest in comparison with Eastern monarchies.[123] Monarchs wore the military cloak and boots, the broad-brimmed hat or the helmet,[124] a diadem "consisting of a white or purple and white headband with two loose ends behind."[125] Other appurtenances were crowns, purple robes,[126] a scepter, and a ring with the monarch's seal. The appearance of the king can be seen on coins and through sculptures.

In all four Gospels Jesus undergoes a mock investiture as a king.[127] From an anthropological point of view this is a status reversal rite that brings the recipient a different status and new powers.[128] I offer three examples from the ancient world.[129]

a. The Babylonian or Persian *Sacaea* festival was celebrated in honor of the goddess Anaitus. Berossus *Babyloniaca* 1.6 describes this feast as follows:

> . . . a festival called Sacaea [which] is celebrated in Babylon for a period of five days. . . . During these days it is the custom for masters to be ruled by their slaves; . . . one of the slaves puts on a robe similar to that of a king and manages the affairs of the house.[130]

Here a condemned prisoner dons the royal robes and is permitted mock rule, feasting, and service from the royal concubines for about five days. He is then stripped, scourged, and killed.[131] We have a further reference to this festival in Dio Chrysostom; the context is a fictitious dialogue between Alexander the Great and Diogenes. The feast is designated Sacian and practiced among the Persians. The victim is a prisoner and receives the same mockery together with permission to "dally" with the king's concubines. He explains that the ceremonies show that foolish and wicked people frequently acquire regal power but come to a shameful end. The motto is, "Do not aspire to sovereignty until you acquire wisdom."[132] We note the meaning that Dio Chrysostom gives to the ritual.

b. The Saturnalia. The god Saturn reigned briefly and then abdicated. He had an earthly counterpart in the king elected for a short period during the feast.[133] Athenaeus (*The Deipnosophists* 14.639) mentions the Saturnalia, "when it is customary for the Roman children to entertain the slaves at dinner, while the children take upon themselves the duties of the slaves." The custom also obtained in Greece in Crete at the festival of Hermaea (cf. Plato *Lysis* 206D). A similar festivity is found in Troezen.[134]

c. There is a historical episode recorded in Philo (*Flaccus* 6:36-39): King Agrippa was mocked in Alexandria after receiving the kingship of Judaea from the emperor Caligula. The people ". . . set up Karabas, a lunatic, as mock king, clothed him with a royal robe and crown and a piece of papyrus for scepter. They saluted him as Lord."

Thus this status reversal ritual was very well known to the ancient world. The last example is of peculiar historic interest. But John also has a literary interest, and the whole passion is an example of high, dramatic irony, especially in the investiture.

### *Irony*[135]

John has transformed this ritual into a matter of deep theological import. It is the height (or depth) of the dramatic irony that runs throughout his Gospel. Further, this irony is very important from a readers'-response point of view. M. H. Abrams defines dramatic irony as follows:

> Dramatic irony involves a situation in a play or narrative in which the audi-
> ence shares with the author knowledge of which a character is ignorant: the
> character acts in a way grossly inappropriate to the actual circumstances, or
> expects the opposite of what fate holds in store, or says something that antici-
> pates the actual outcome, but not at all in the way he means it.[136]

This dramatic irony often makes use of a deluded hero who has a
worldview that differs from the circumstances as seen by the author and
the readers. It flatters the intelligence of the reader, for the audience has
information or knowledge of the situation of the hero and can foresee an
outcome that is contrary to what is expected, thus:

> ... ascribing a sharply different sense of some of the character's own state-
> ments; in tragedies this is called tragic irony. The term "cosmic irony" is
> sometimes used to denote a view of people as the dupes of a cruelly mocking
> Fate, as in the novels of Thomas Hardy.[137]

Aristotle (*Art of Rhetoric* 2.2.23) states that "irony shows contempt" and
that "irony is more gentlemanly than buffoonery; for the first is employed
on one's own account, the second on that of another" (*Art of Rhetoric*
3.18.7). Socrates used irony with his students "to nudge and agitate them
into new vision." Irony was both "assassin of pretension and midwife of
truth."[138] Irony depends on the fact that some may fail to understand that
the meaning is hidden from the victim. Those who are "in the know" are
guided by the narrator. Irony creates a bond between the narrator and the
reader.[139] But the narrator must not spoon-feed his audience; he must leave
the interpretation for the reader to determine. He merely drops clues for
the readers to help them to reject the literal or superficial meaning of the
drama. The victims of John's irony are Pilate, the tyrant, and the unbeliev-
ing Jews. The passion becomes the height of the Johannine technique of
irony and misunderstanding. The audience knows that Jesus rose from the
dead, they might also have known of the tragic fall of Jerusalem in 70 C.E.
and of Pilate's disgrace. It is the friends of Jesus who understand the
meaning of this dramatic irony and the true consecration of the true
monarch. Moreover, all this must be seen in the light of John's second reference to "kingdom" (the first being John 3:3, 5) and Jesus' unequivocal
statement that his kingdom is not of this world and that his followers do
not use human war weapons (John 18:36).

### The Presentation of the Sovereign

After this status reversal, Pilate presents the jested king to the Jews. It must
have been a miserable and pathetic sight. But Pilate's words, "Behold, the
man," add another ironic twist to the scene. Some scholars wish to read

the words merely as an expression of pity; Barrett points to myths of the primal man;[140] others remark the son of man or the man of sorrows. Meeks's interpretation seems to be more appropriate; it is a title used among Hellenistic Jews.[141] Meeks compares Zachariah 6:12, cf. also Numbers 24:17. Thus it is possible that Pilate is presenting Jesus to the Jews under a messianic title.[142] MacRae[143] declares this scene the most ironic and theologically profound in John's passion. It is the

> . . . spectacle of the Son of God appearing as man in the lowest degradation of human suffering and humiliation . . . the scandal of the transcendent divinity revealing itself in the paradox of humanity suffering out of the motive of love . . . man's quest for the divine must terminate in the irony of man's supreme act of self-giving in love.

The Jewish retort, "Crucify him, crucify him" (John 19:6) is the antithesis to acclaiming him as monarch but is more understandable in the light of the Qumran evidence of crucifixion as a capital punishment by some Jewish courts. It is the punishment for blasphemy.[144]

### The Problem of Authority (John 19:8-11)
Pilate's second discourse with Jesus (John 19:8-11) addresses the problem of authority. To Pilate's assertion that he has authority to release or sentence Jesus to crucifixion, Jesus replies that all authority comes from above. This is not dissimilar to the ideal monarch who claimed Zeus as his authority; Jesus traces all authority back to God. But in addition, Jesus' words are a confirmation of the logion in the shepherd discourse: no one takes my life from me, I lay it down and take it up of my own volition (John 10:17-18).

### Jesus Placed on the Bēma, or Judgment Seat (John 19:13)
The climax of the mockery comes when Jesus, flogged and mocked, is brought out a second time to the Jews. There is some discussion whether Pilate himself or Jesus sits on the *bēma*. The latter is more likely, perhaps because of Jesus' state of weakness or as a final scornful act by Pilate. Support for this interpretation is found in Justin Martyr.[145]

### The Friend of Caesar (John 19:1)
John 19:12 contains the poignant sentence, "If you release him, you are no friend of Caesar. Everyone who makes himself a king opposes Caesar." The competing powers of Rome and Israel confront each other. This sentence brings the whole theme of friendship and love in the Gospel of John in general and in the Farewell Discourses in particular to a climax. Like Judas, Pilate must make a decision about friendship. In this way we see the

contrast between the earthly friends of a monarch (Caesar) and the friends chosen by the ideal monarch, Jesus. The monarch's court and its personnel were of social and political importance, but most significant were the group of the king's friends, *philoi*.[146] They enjoyed an intimate relationship with the monarch and were the recipient of lands and properties. The status of friend was not handed down to successors but was personally bestowed by each king. The friends formed a council and met daily to advise the king.[147] Included among his friends were artists, philosophers, doctors, etc. The monarch and his friends were a partnership formed for mutual benefit. At times the friends made great sacrifices for the king or their colleagues, even at the risk of their lives. In the Farewell Discourses, Jesus stated that his disciples were no longer servants (slaves) but friends (John 15:12-16). The full import of this makes its impact thus in the light of the friends of the monarch and the Jews' reference to the friends of Caesar. Before his "consecration" as monarch, Jesus carefully chose his friends, his own, and endowed them not with lands but with the inheritance of the Paraclete, the Spirit of truth. Mary, John, Mary the mother of Cleopas, and Mary Magdalene are the friends who attend his "enthronement" on the cross, and who must have been with Joseph of Arimathea when he entombed Jesus with the superabundance of spices like a sovereign (John 19:38-42). These are the friends of Jesus who will accept his sovereignty.

## *The* Doulos Basileus *of the Cynics*

Further insight into the Johannine notion of monarchy may be found, however, by looking through the eyes of the Cynics and the Stoics. For them only the wise person is sovereign. Höistad, discussing Dio Chrysostom's work, focuses on the catalogues of contrasting virtues and vices of the monarch and the tyrant.[148] They are the social and ethical terms that define true monarchy, and many are consonant with Homeric terminology.[149] The catalogues suggests "a relatively fixed and uniform representation" of the sovereign and tyrant. Dio concludes that no one can be a bad king, just as no one can be a bad good person (*Discourses* 4.24). Höistad (189) traces a development in Dio's ideology of king from pre-Stoic to Stoic sources, from the idea of an individual being kingly to the monarch per se being the true king. Underlying the whole concept of the wise person as true monarch is religious motivation; the true monarch reveres the deities and copies their (good) behavior. Epithets for Zeus are used of the monarch.[150] In the Fourth Discourse *On Kingship*, Dio Chrysostom represents Alexander the Great conversing with Diogenes the Cynic. Of the Cynics he says that they strip their wise persons of everything—wealth,

honor, prestige—so that they are revered only for their wisdom and understanding.[151] Alexander was "the most ambitious of men and the greatest
lover of glory" (*Discourses* 4.4–7), he needed his army, cavalry, mercenar-
ies as a security measure, but Diogenes went everywhere unattended and
completely secure (*Discourses* 4.7–8). In John's Gospel, the Jews and the
Romans need their police and their soldiers, but the Johannine Jesus needs
neither. Moreover Dio presents the ideal king as a "solitary, poor and suffering figure."[152] The model for the king is Heracles (*Discourses* 1.59–65),
who suffered poverty, nakedness, homelessness, and pain, but was the son
of Zeus and possessed ideal kingship.[153] Diogenes followed this principle.
Dio Chrysostom (*Discourses* 9.8–9) says that some regarded him as the
wisest of humankind; others thought he was crazy and treated him as a
beggar, insulted him, and threw bones at him as if he were a dog. But he
was like Odysseus. He was a king disguised as a beggar and no one knew
his identity. There are many similar anecdotes about the Cynic bearing
insult or suffering. For example, Diogenes Laertius[154] reports that Antisthenes said, "When men are slandered, they should endure it more courageously than if they were pelted with stones." The Cynic does not meet
violence with violence but with a witty remark or disarming words.[155] Dio
says that the noble person bears all adversities with equanimity, "and while
in their very grip the perfect man is often as sportive as boys with their
dice and their colored balls" (*Discourses* 8.16). It is this noble person who is
truly a sovereign (*Discourses* 9.9). One may compare *Discourses* 9.11, where
Diogenes crowns himself for his victory in moral difficulties. He says:

> There is nothing to prevent the Great King, while wearing a tall tiara upon his
> head, from being a slave and not being allowed to do anything that he does . . .
> But some other man who is regarded as a slave and is so called, . . . wears very
> heavy fetters, [but] will be more free than the Great King (Dio Chrysostom,
> *Discourses* 14.18).

Dio teaches that even if a person is in physical captivity, one can be
king. In a moving passage, he uses the mythological figures of Cronos and
Odysseus to prove his point. Cronos, the king of gods, was bound in fetters
and treated unjustly by one who loved him dearly, who treated him in this
way because he thought it just and profitable. But, says Dio, we fail to recognize the free person and the slave. Perhaps he should wear some distinctive badge.[156]

All this may be summed up in the phrase "servant ruler" (*doulos
archōn*).[157] Höistad (202) summarizes the themes of Dio's suffering king:
he abases himself and performs *ta phaula* as a protest *prō tēn doxan*, is
reviled, suffers physically, endures moral conflict, and is disguised as a
slave. He is like Heracles, who underwent many sufferings.[158] Höistad

dates the theme of suffering king seen in Heracles, Odysseus, and Cyrus to fourth-century Cynicism.[159] The tradition, therefore, of the suffering slave king, is old and was continually developed. The philosopher must submit to menial tasks and mockery; thus he shows that he is the true king. There are frequent anecdotes about this.[160] Höistad also avers that "the theme of the suffering *basileus*, the slave king, was not exclusively, or even in its origin, bound up with the association of Diogenes with Alexander the Great or any other representative of external power." For example, it is found in Antithenes's portrayal of Cyrus. Dio himself goes back to Homer to expound this theory. In *Discourses* 15.29, he argues that the true slave is the one enslaved by a servile nature, not one who is bought by another or the offspring of a slave. "The distinction between slavery and freedom is entirely of a spiritual nature."

John, therefore, in addressing his Hellenistic audience, represents Jesus as the suffering-servant-sovereign who remains sovereign even on the cross. This is ironically confirmed by the title in three languages that Pilate causes to be written (John 19:19-22). When Jesus was taken down from the cross he received a regal burial.

Thus Jesus of Nazareth supersedes the role model even of Diogenes. He is the king who wins "imperishable glory." The reader of John's Gospel sees that Jesus has his sovereignty from God and is guided and nurtured by God; he is the Good Shepherd (John 10); he is the Light of the world (cf. the image of the sun in Dio's discourses); he pursues truth and sincerity and eschews outward pomp. He lays down his life for his sheep, for greater love has no one than to lay down her or his life for a friend. Pilate's answer, "What is truth?" is not merely skeptical but expresses the question posed by the "world" in the Johannine sense.[161] When Pilate says "Behold, the human being," again this is not to be understood just on a superficial level; it is the answer to the question, "What is truth?" Pilate acclaims the person, the offspring of God who determines what is truth and how one lives according to Truth. Pilate does not belong to Jesus' kingdom,[162] yet he recognizes that it cannot harm the Roman Empire.

Over and above representing Jesus as superior to the Cynic monarch, however, John emphasizes that Jesus is Son of God.[163] Although Jesus' status as Son of God may be ambiguous in the Synoptic Gospels, in John's it is explicit throughout[164] and particularly so in the Farewell Discourses.

For we must interpret the passion in the light of the Prologue. It declares the preexistence of the Logos and states that he "was God" (John 1:1). We have seen that the Prologue also presents the Logos as incarnate wisdom who is "the aura of the might of God and a pure effusion of the glory of the Almighty" and the "image of his goodness" (Wisd. 7:25-26). He is the Word who has entered history, time, and tangibility. All the themes of the Prologue are woven in and out of the Gospel material.[165] John the Baptist bears testimony that "this is the Son of God" (although some variants read *elektos*). Jesus refers to himself as the "Son."[166] The Jews claim that Jesus makes himself equal to God (e.g., John 5:18; 6:42), and they take up stones to stone him after he claims priority to Abraham.[167] But it is in the Farewell Discourses that Jesus expounds his unity with the Father. The departure or death of Jesus is the activity of the triune God. She or he who has seen Jesus has seen the Father (14:9-10), they are one in their mutuality and glory. The *egō eimi* sayings are brought to a climax in the garden, and John symbolizes this in his portrayal of the prostration of Jesus' opponents. C.H. Giblin[168] calls this phrase "the humanly unostentatious and divine sovereign *egō eimi*." The two separate confrontations throw into relief the "sovereign freedom" of Jesus and also serve to contrast him with the crowds. M. Sabbe,[169] commenting on the use of the *egō eimi* pronouncement, reminds us that this occurs in Mark 14:44 and parallel, Matthew 26:48. He argues that those who fell prostrate may not have been only the enemies of Jesus. "In that moment of glorification on the verge of his arrest, the challenge of faith is equally offered to the whole world."[170] The trial before Caiaphas is brief (18:13-14 and 19-21). Jesus as "royal Messiah empowered with the divine prerogative of judgment . . . would be an anticlimax in John's Gospel for his Gospel has shown stage by stage Jesus' transcendent messiahship."[171] The Jews openly tell Pilate that Jesus claimed to "make himself the Son of God" (John 19:8). In the light of this material we are justified in seeing John's portrayal of Jesus' crucifixion as the crucifixion of the Son of God in a fuller sense than the persecuted righteous in Wisdom 2:13, 16, 18.

Therefore what the passion shows is, indeed, the human suffering and death of Jesus as a monarch, a sacred and sacrosanct person. As such he challenges certain aspects of the Hellenistic concept of sovereign but more that of imperial Rome, especially under the rule of Domitian. But it is also the suffering and "death" of God as we described his or her pain in chapters 2 and 3.[172] It is the pain (*congoja*) and anguish (*angst*) of one who offers his or her life for his or her friends. Thus the subject of divine sovereignty is addressed. The concept of sovereignty, human and divine, is revolutionized. God's bestowal of freewill on humanity causes God's passion. It allows the possibility of sadism towards God and humanity. The *pathos* of God is designed to lure humankind back to their place beside God. It is the suffering of the Shekinah and the rift in the very being of God. It can be repaired only by human response to God and by God's answer in the Resurrection.

## Feminine Texts in the Passion

We have indicated the possibility of the crucifixion of women in the Greco-Roman world. Theoretically, therefore, it would have been possible for the women disciples of Jesus to have witnessed a female crucifixion at one time or another; hence, those women who attended Jesus during his passion would not have thought of crucifixion as purely male punishment. Further—and I make this suggestion with some reserve—as followers of an alleged revolutionary/blasphemer or sorcerer, would the male and female disciples have run the risk of incurring the same punishment as Jesus as accomplices? This might be indicated in the flight of the disciples, reported in Mark 14:50 and Matthew 26:56.

### The Women and the Maccabean Mother (John 19:25-27)

As we have placed the passion of Jesus against the background of classical heroes, it behooves us to give some attention to the group of women who stood at the foot of the cross. Would a Hellenistic reader have reflected on other heroic women? Although these women do not die for or with Jesus, they have the courage to remain with him, seemingly in the absence of any of the disciples save the beloved disciple. Would Greek women readers or hearers have thought of Alcestis[173] to whom Admetus declares: "You do save me by giving all you love in place of my own life"[174] and "she alone has died in my stead"?[175] Or would Antigone,[176] who wished her death to witness to her religion and duty to the dead, have come to mind? Or might they have remembered Iphigeneia,[177] who professed, "So by my bloodshed and my sacrifice, if need be, shall I cancel what the goddess decreed;"[178] or Macaria in The Children of Hercules,[179] who offered herself as a victim to be sacrificed to secure the success of the Athenian armies; or the much bereaved Hecuba of the Iliad and the Daughters of Troy of Euripides? I do not think this unlikely.

However, the most apt exemplar of the woman (and mother) is the mother of the Maccabees who watched the martyrdom of seven sons. In 2 Maccabees 7 she is described thus: "Filled with a noble spirit that stirred her womanly heart with manly courage, she exhorted each of them in the language of their forefathers [sic] with these words. . . ."[180] She boldly confesses her belief in not only the immortality of the soul but the resurrection of the body (vv. 20-23). She is, therefore, a good type of the mother of Jesus and her friends. However in 4 Maccabees she receives even more laudatory emphasis, e.g., in 4 Maccabees 15:30-32:

More noble than men in fortitude and stronger than heroes in endurance! Like the ark of Noah, carrying the universe in the worldwide cataclysm and stoutly enduring the waves, so did you, guardian of the Law, buffeted on every side in the flood of the passions and by the mighty gales of your sons' torments, so did your perseverance nobly weather the storms that assailed you for religion's sake.

She is compared more than once to Abraham, who was willing to offer his only son, Isaac (Gen. 22). Jonathan A. Goldstein,[181] referring to the mother's speech in 2 Maccabees 7, says that she uses "the technical language of a philosopher." Indeed, both she and the "senior citizen" martyr, Eleazar, are represented as sophists.[182] The author of 4 Maccabees devotes four and a half chapters to her. Here she not only encourages her sons, but some of the guards alleged that she voluntarily threw herself into the fire, "so that no one might touch her body." The author says that her soul was like Abraham's (in the *Akedah*): it did not waver. He has a lengthy panegyric on the triumph of reason over maternal affection (4 Macc. 15). He invokes her:

> O woman who alone among women *brought perfect piety to birth!* . . . like a true daughter of God-fearing Abraham called to mind Abraham's unflinching bravery. O mother of the nation, champion of the Law, defender of true religion, and winner of the prize in the inward contest of the heart. More noble than men in fortitude and stronger than heroes in endurance! (author's italics)

The author speaks about her "bringing her brood of sons to birth into immortal life . . ." (4 Macc. 16:13). Again, we have the birth image to denote attainment of salvation.

### The Group Near the Cross

In the light of this, we approach the little group around the cross (John 19:25-26). According to John, they comprised Jesus' mother; his aunt; Mary, the wife of Clopas; Mary Magdalene; and the beloved disciple. We should perhaps see them *mutatis mutandis* in a similar position to the mother of the Maccabean martyrs. Perhaps we are not to think of weeping women as in Luke 23:27-31 but of women who encouraged their friend (son) to endure his sufferings for the sake of truth.[183] We should note, too, that the mother of Jesus and his aunt go far beyond filial affection. They are friends of Jesus and go to calamity's depths for their friend. Jesus is their hero and friend, too. So the women show *apatheia* and *hypomonē*. They show greatness of soul. But they are witnesses also to the passion of God. They are the true friends of the martyr, like the beloved disciple, Nicodemus, and Joseph of Arimathea, attending his death and caring for the disposal of his body.[184]

In contrast to the Synoptic Gospels, John introduces the women confronting the death of Jesus. They stand near, not at a distance from, the cross.[185] In the Synoptics, Jesus dies alone, but in John, surrounded by a small group of friends. Their proximity to the cross would mean that Jesus could try to converse with them, hence his directives to the beloved disciple and Mary. Richard Atwood[186] thinks that they represent the true believers, and the soldiers the unbelievers. Atwood (61) concludes that the women "play a considerably more crucial and key role than the disciples themselves." The presence of Mary Magdalene seems significant. Not only is she a key witness to the death of Jesus to the resurrection (John 20:1-18), but also there is a possibility that she is a sister of the beloved disciple to whom Mary, his mother, was committed. As was noted above, Vernard Eller[187] has argued fairly cogently that the beloved disciple *may* be identified with Lazarus. At the Last Supper he reclines on Jesus' breast; if he were one of the Twelve this might have caused some jealousy; he seems to have associations with the high priestly court;[188] Lazarus, at whose home Jesus enjoyed hospitality, would be more likely to take care of Jesus' mother; Mary Magdalene announces the news of the resurrection to him as well as Peter; and Jesus' allusion to him in John 21:20-23 seems explicable in this way, that Jesus might have emphasized Lazarus' eventual death even though he had been raised from the dead (John 11). Eller[189] argues that in John it is Mary who anoints Jesus (John 12:1-8) and that Luke comes near to identifying this Mary with Mary Magdalene. In all four Gospels there is agreement about only one of the names of the women near the cross, and this is Mary Magdalene. In the Fourth Gospel she and the beloved disciple are eyewitnesses of the death of Jesus. Mark and Matthew mention Magdalene among the women at the tomb after the death of Jesus. Mark, Luke, and John portray Magdalene at the tomb on Easter morning. In John she has an intimate conversation with the risen Jesus; this is consistent with the close relationship between Magdalene and Jesus suggested by Luke and John. Magdalene carries the good news of the resurrection to the other disciples.[190] Eller notices, too, that John has carefully paired Mary with Lazarus in various episodes, and then Mary and the beloved disciple. He states: "This pattern could hardly be coincidental; it must be an effort to tell us *something*" (70). So the beloved disciple, perhaps Lazarus, and Mary Magdalene, the sister of Lazarus and Martha, become prime examples of the male and female true believers, genuine disciples of Jesus. The scene at the house of Lazarus becomes more intimately associated with the crucifixion and resurrection of Jesus. Mary and the beloved disciple (Lazarus) accompany Jesus throughout the passion up to the resurrection. They are the prototypes of those who become *friends* of God. They exemplify—give role models for—all men and women disciples of Jesus. The fact that Jesus does not name Mary, his mother, but calls her "woman" in John 2:4 and John 19:26, may suggest that she represents all faithful and sorrowing women. Like Eudamidas in Lucian's story, Jesus commends his mother to the beloved disciple, and him to her.[191] The disciple takes her to his own (*eis ta idia*), thus adopting the same love as Jesus for his own.[192]

## The Sword Thrust and the Effusion of Blood and Water (John 19:31-37)

### Symbolism

However, the text of most interest to feminists may be John 19:31-37, especially vv. 34-35, which describe the spear thrust into the side of Christ and the consequent effusion of blood and water (cf. John 7:39). Naturally, blood would not "gush" forth from a corpse.[193] We are, then, meant to understand the text in a highly symbolic way.

Richter[194] points out the serious difficulty in interpreting this pericope and summarizes the work of the principal exegetes.[195] He points to the aorist (*ēlthon*), which indicates one event in the past.[196] He also observes that in the whole of the Johannine corpus only two passages speak of "coming in" in this sense. Jesus comes "in the flesh" in 1 John 4:2 and 2 John 7. Both passages confirm the reality of Jesus' humanity. So the incident of the spear thrust emphasizes the humanity of Jesus. Further, according to ancient thought, blood is the material out of which humankind is made. Waszink[197] observes that the ancients believed that the menstrual blood from which the embryo was formed represented this. The Jewish concept is expressed in Wisdom 7:1-2:

> I too am a mortal man (*anthrōpos*), the same as all the rest, and a descendant of the first man formed of earth. And in my mother's womb (*koilia*) I was molded into flesh (*sarx dekamēniaiō chronō pageis en haimati ek spermatos andros*)... in ten-months' period body and blood, from the seed of man, and the pleasure that accompanies marriage....

E. Schweizer gives examples of texts from antiquity, including Jewish sources, which show the idea that the human is composed half of blood and half of water.[198] Richter also compares 4 Maccabees 9:20, where blood and water issue from a wound: "the heap of coals was quenched by the discharged fluid dropping down."[199]

Richter observes that this fluid also from the martyr's wound comes from a live body. Personally I do not find this example a persuasive parallel. Richter contrasts some docetic texts with this idea.[200] The phantom body of Christ according to the docetics was formed from water,[201] not blood. In the Mandaean texts, Anosch-Uthra (the redeemer) has a body formed of water not blood, her garments are the rain clouds; the *Lügen-propheten* have garments of light, they were not conceived by women from blood and menstruation.[202] We note that the docetics used water, not wine in the Eucharist. Richter then cites patristic texts to show that the blood and water symbolize the true humanity of Jesus.[203] John 19:34b can be understood in a similar way[204] and has an anti-docetic thrust[205] and symbolically affirms that Jesus' body is real flesh and blood.[206] Again we have a childbirth image.

Josef Heer[207] sets our text within its immediate and remote contexts. He divides the pericope in John 19:28-37 as follows: the cry of victory ("it is fulfilled" vv. 28-30b); the transmission of the Spirit (v. 30c); the piercing of the side (vv. 31-34); the testimony of the one who saw (v. 35); the first interpretation (v. 36, "they shall break none of his bones"); the second interpretation (v. 37, "they shall look upon him whom they have pierced"). He notes the importance of the passage as seen from its length, its numerous details, the cry of the Lord, the emphasis on witness, on the confirmation of the reader's faith, and the interpretation in the light of the two biblical quotations. John seems to wish to make this episode a climax. Heer examines these verses in reverse order.

Verse 37 demonstrates that the incident is the fulfillment of prophecy: the Old Testament text gives it an eschatological orientation. The text from Zachariah speaks of the end times, the annihilation of the enemy, the pouring out of the Spirit of compassion and prayer, mourning, and purification. John cites these verses to show that the endtime has come, that God has given the Spirit, and that now one is face to face with the one who is pierced. Heer adds several observations: (a) In interpreting the Johannine text one must go beyond the physical aspect; (b) The piercing of the side is a theological sign.[208] He compares this sign with the symbol of the serpent in the desert (John 3:14), the lifting up of the son of humanity in order to reveal the identify of Jesus (John 8:28) and to draw all to him (John 12:32); (c) The piercing of the side is more than an historical moment, it places not only the crucified, but the resurrected and exalted Lord before the eyes of the believer. The crucified and the exalted are one. The lifting up can bring life to the believer (John 3:14b-d). Jesus dies as the exalted one who gives the Spirit to the community, and so bestows life. All this is seen in the spear thrust. As the believer beholds this scene she or he realizes the love with which Jesus fulfilled his mission: (a) perfected is his loving obedience to the Father; (b) perfected is Jesus' love towards his own.

This is seen in the cry of victory, but there "fulfilled" (v. 30, *tetelestai*) has a double meaning. It completes the statement of the evangelists that Jesus loved his disciples to perfection (John 13:1, *eis telos*). It indicates that the symbol of the footwashing has been wholly enacted in the passion.[209] The believer realizes that Jesus, as the one who is glorified, gives the Spirit. The disciple whom Jesus loved and Jesus' mother represent the community to whom the Spirit is bequeathed. Many opine that the believer sees the piercing and the issue of blood and water from the side of Jesus[210] as an indication of the expiatory and life-giving effect of the death of Jesus. With this I should disagree. The blood and the water are symbolic of delivery in childbirth. The symbolism of the blood and water can be further understood through a comparison with 1 John 5:6-9:

> This is he who came by water and blood,[211] Jesus Christ, not with the water only but with the water and the blood. And the Spirit is the witness, because the Spirit is the truth. There are three witnesses, the Spirit, the water, and the blood: and these three agree. If we receive the testimony of men, the testimony of God is greater; for this is the testimony of God that he has borne witness to his Son.

Our theme does not permit us to engage in a detailed exegesis of this interesting text but rather to see what light it can throw on John 19:34.[212] The text may allude to baptism and the Eucharist (as may John 19:34) or the incarnation or the baptism and death of Jesus or only to the death of Jesus. The mention of the Spirit in the 1 John text would also be consonant with the death of Jesus, because John records that Jesus bowed his head and "transmitted the Spirit" (John 19:30), and the Spirit, like the believer or witness in John 19:35, witnesses to the truth. Brown believes that the text symbolizes the giving of the Spirit to believers through the sacrificial death of Christ.[213]

But for our purposes this pericope is a text dealing with birth. And here we have a fitting analogy to God herself describing herself in labor for the salvation of Israel. The symbol used is the breaking of the amniotic fluid and, as explained above, the blood is uterine blood. So the death of Jesus is intimately related to the symbol of female parturition. Jesus, like Yahweh, gives birth. The pericope also forms an *inclusio* with the birth from above in Jesus' conversation with Nicodemus (John 3:1-16). Nicodemus is also prominent in both texts (cf. John 19:39). It is interesting also that the woman stands at the beginning of the manifestation of Jesus' glory (John 2:4) and at the end (John 19:26), in a way framing the whole Gospel. Through the breaking of the water and the blood comes the birth of the church from the side of Christ. Through death comes life in the deepest sense of the word.[214] From the death of God is born the new humanity. We may compare the famous "Johannine Comma," that is, the variant found in Latin manuscripts of this text which includes a reference to the Trinity: "For there are three who bear witness in heaven, the Father, the Word, and the Holy Spirit, and these three are one. And there are three who bear witness on earth, the Spirit and the water and the blood, and these three are one." This introduces the action and relationship of the whole Trinity in the death and exaltation of Jesus and the bestowal of the Spirit.[215] We may compare the birth pangs of the Messiah and the patristic texts that refer to the passion of Christ as labor in childbirth. Consider Clement of Alexandria (*The Instructor* 1.6): "The Lord Himself brought forth in throes of flesh, which the Lord Himself swathed in his precious blood. . . ." Or Ambrose (*On Virgins* 1:5), who refers to Christ as the "Virgin who bare us." We may also compare Paul, who speaks about being in labor with those to whom he ministered.[216] Thus the water and the blood (blood and water) from the side of Christ complement the image which Jesus uses of suffering in the Farewell Discourses: a woman has pain in childbirth but joy when the child is born. It is in this context that we can understand Jesus' cry of victory, "It is consummated" (John 19:30). The child, new humanity, is born from the throes of the cross and the mother cries out in joy.

### The Syriac Tradition

We must add a note on the interpretation of this text in the Syriac tradition. Sebastian Brock[217] demonstrates how early in the Syriac tradition the lance became associated with the sword guarding paradise (Gen. 3:24). The side of Christ is compared to Adam's side, and in this way the Syriac exegete sees the whole panorama of salvation history. One of Ephraem's hymns (*Hymns on the Crucifixion* 9.2) reads:[218]

> The sword that pierced Christ removed the sword guarding Paradise;
> his forgiveness tore up our document of debt.[219]

Further, the Syriac church recognizes the birthing image which is employed. As Adam's side gave birth to Eve, so the pierced side of Jesus gave birth to the church. Jacob of Serugh, sixth century, writes:

> For from the beginning God knew and depicted
> Adam and Eve in the likeness of the image of his Only-begotten;
> He slept on the cross as Adam had slept his deep sleep,
> his side was pierced and from it there came forth the Daughter of Light,
> water and blood as an image of divine children
> to be heirs to the Father who loves his Only-begotten
>
> . . . . . . . .
>
> Adam's side gave birth to a woman who gives birth to immortals.
> In the crucifixion he completed the types that had been depicted,
> and the hidden mystery that had been covered revealed itself.[220]

Jacob also speaks of baptism as the "second mother":

His side was pierced in his sleep,
he gave birth to the Bride, as happened with Eve...
and from him came forth the Mother who gives birth to all spiritual beings:
... water and blood for the fashioning of spiritual babes
flowed from the side of that Living One who died, in order to bring life to
Adam.[221]

Another Syriac poet, Cyrillona, portrays Christ on the cross as the vine:

The Vine ripened in secret...
The Vine is Christ who came to us,
proffering us the Cluster in his love;
it bowed its head in joy,
for the Cluster to be plucked,
just as our Lord bowed his head...
The sickle lops off the vine-shoot
and streams of water flow,
the sword pierced Christ
and there flowed for us streams of mercy.

Robert Murray[222] uses other Syriac texts to illustrate this allegorization
of the sword thrust. He observes that *rumha* is used both for the sword in
Paradise and for the lance at the crucifixion (cf. the sword piercing Mary's
heart in Luke 2:35).

Blessed be the Merciful One/who saw the *lance*
beside paradise,/ which barred the way
to the Tree of Life./ And he came and took him
a body, that was wounded,/ that by the opening of his side
he might open a way/into paradise.[223]

And

As we left paradise with Adam,
who from paradise had to depart,
now that the lance is removed
through the lance let us gird ourselves and go hence.[224]

Thus the birth image, symbolized by the blood and water from the side
of Christ, was accepted and elaborated by the early Christian tradition. We
are brought back to the concept of redemption as birth.

Mary Grey[225] describes how process theologians see redemption as
based on "the mutuality of divine and human becoming" with a special
emphasis on the "dynamics of love," a phrase peculiarly pertinent to
Johannine thought and our theme of friendship. She refers to Meland,[226]
who discerns a unity between creation and redemption. He explains that

the central concept of redemption is:

> The renewal of the creative act in human life by which the sensitive nature which is God is made formative and fulfilling in our purpose. Whatever happens in life to open up our natures to the tendernesses of life which are of God is redemptive.[227]

Grey (176) wishes to use a new image of redemption, namely, the "birthing of God." She sees the advantage of this image as:
- its origin in mutuality between man and woman;
  - its involvement in productive pain and labor;
    - its engendering of new forms of mutuality.[228]

She quotes Sara Maitland:[229]

> It seems that the creative birthing of God as expressed in Christ's passion . . . can be given a deeper relating if we can learn to hear as holy the bodily experiences of women, and trust the metaphor of God the Mother.

Grey finds this image in the Hebrew Scriptures.[230] Then she refers especially to the Johannine text, John 16:21-22.[231]

In the light of this I suggest that Jesus goes to his passion not as a victim, nor as a scapegoat, nor as a bloody sacrifice, nor to appease a deity, nor to trap or pay a debt to the devil, but as a woman to give birth to her child through blood and water. Neither does he implement this alone but in total mutuality with the Father, in whom and for whom he is glorified, and the Spirit, the *alter Christus.* In John 19:34 the soldier pierces the side of Christ, and water and blood gush out. The re-birthing of God is consummated.

Similar to the Jewish theology of creation and redemption, especially when brought into association with the theology of the Shekinah, Grey sees that there is suffering, anguish, sacrifice, and renunciation as well as joy in God's act of creation and redemption. Redemptive birth, like physical birth, brings about a change in the mother, the family, and the wider human circle: it often calls for a social reorganization. As in human birth there is a "letting go" of the self and a certain distancing preceded by a waiting period, a state of stasis. Yet this very stasis is a period of growth.[232]

> So the static image of Jesus as a perfect man, ultimate symbol of redemption, gives way to the image of the Body of Christ, "enfleshed by a relational Christology which opens us to recognize the way in which human connectedness brings God to the world."[233]

Redemption reveals not only persons as richly related beings but God per se as a richly relating being. In creation, God is Father-Mother, but in redemption she or he is also friend and companion and Mother. This is the position of Jesus at the Last Supper, Mother (John 16:21-22), friend (John 15:15) and com-pan-ion, one who shares bread (John 13).

## *The Johannine Pentecost*

We have one last text upon which to comment,[234] namely, the Johannine Pentecost (John 20:21-23):

> Jesus said to them again, "Peace be with you. As the Father has sent me, even so I send you." And when he had said this, he breathed on them, and said to them, "Receive the Holy Spirit. If you forgive the sins of any, they are forgiven; if you retain the sins of any, they are retained."[235]

First, we note the greeting of "peace." It is a fulfillment of the peace that is above earthly understanding promised in John 14:27 and mentioned again in John 16:33. The greeting appears three times in John 20 (vv. 19, 21, 26). Commenting on this, Carson says that the common word *salom* was a comprehensive term that denoted "the unqualified well-being" that characterizes God's people when the kingdom dawns. Jesus' "peace!" on Easter evening is the complement to "it is finished" on the cross, for God now imparts peace of reconciliation and life.[236]

Second, we note the trinitarian aspect in this text, the Father who sent Jesus, Jesus himself, and the Spirit who is given. In this way our text forms a complement or fulfillment of the Farewell Discourses. The promised Paraclete, the Spirit of truth, comes; Jesus' commission from the Father is now handed on to the disciples (John 17:18; cf. 20:21). De Durant[237] gives a full discussion of patristic texts that comment on John 20:21-23. He observes that Augustine says that the Spirit is given by breathing because the Spirit is consubstantial and coeternal in the Trinity and is not possessed only by the Father but by the Son, too.[238] The Lucan Pentecost represents the coming of the Spirit; but John 20:22, the inspiration of the Spirit.[239]

Third, we notice the context. Jesus, in helping the disciples to identify him, showed them his hands and side (v. 20; cf. Luke 24:39, which reads "hands and feet").[240] This is no mere polemic against docetism but rather John's emphasis that there is an irrefrangable link between the crucifixion and the donation of the Spirit.[241] Thus a reference back to the lance thrust must be intended.[242] The verses tell us that upon seeing the Lord—and his hands and side—they rejoiced, just as the woman rejoices at the birth of her child (John 16:21-22; cf. 14:18). Only the crucified God, not a crucified human being, can confer the Spirit. But this God is also incarnate. Ghiberti[243] states that reminders of John 19 underline the physical aspect of the redemption of the resurrected Lord. The Spirit cannot be given before the glorification of Jesus (John 7:39).[244]

Further, the giving of the Spirit,[245] both from the cross (John 19:30) and through Jesus' breathing on his disciples, is an act of creation or procreation and resurrection. One must read the text against the background of the creation of Adam (Gen. 2:7) and the resuscitation of Israel in the famous vision of the valley strewn with dead bones.[246] The text of Ezekiel refers to the restoration of Israel rather than the resurrection of the dead, but it was easily accommodated to this. Jesus breathes upon the disciples to bring them the life and Paraclete he had promised. It may also be possible that the insufflation reflects the action of the midwife helping the newly born child to breathe. There is, however, no preposition after *enephusensen*. In light of this, Carson[247] asks whether this is a symbolic action anticipating a future bestowal of the Spirit. But he omitted a reference to Wisdom 15:11 which, like our text, does not use the preposition.

> Because he (the potter who makes clay images of gods) knew not the one who fashioned him, and breathed into him a quickening soul *(empneusanta autō psychēn energousan)*, and infused a vital spirit *(ton emphusēsanta pneuma zōtikon)*.[248]

Therefore, Jesus would appear to be giving the Spirit here. It is a divine begetting, the giving of the Paraclete promised in the Farewell Discourses. It is the reification of the whole theology of immanence that Jesus has developed in these discourses.[249] But this text is also consonant with our friendship theme. It indicates an interpenetration of spirits, human and divine. The friend who has gone to calamity's depth for his friends is imparting to them his own Spirit.

Fourth, I add a note on the curious text about the forgiveness and retention of sin (John 20:23). The rabbinic phrase, "binding and loosing," is used here as in Matthew 16:19 and 18:18. B. de Margerie[250] has a full discussion of this phrase in the light of Origen, the *Didascalia*, Jerome, Cyril of Alexandria, Augustine, and Gregory the Great.[251] He has several important reflections. "Binding" does not exclude subsequent reconciliation.[252] Further, the author of the *Apostolic Constitutions* reads "bind" in the light of Ezekiel 18 and 34, which refers to binding what is wounded. The admonition is to bind wounds, cure them, and bring the sinners into the church (*Const. Apost.* II, 20:4). De Margerie finds that the fusion of the medicinal and judicial images are perfect.[253] Cyril of Alexandria also sees two meanings to this text, either keeping those who are not worthy away from divine grace or correcting sinners (by temporal punishment) in order to save them, like Paul in 1 Corinthians 5.[254] The key to Cyril's interpretation is correction, in order to effect reconcilation.[255] Ambrose (*Concerning Penance* 1.2.7–8) criticizes the heretics for binding but not loosing.[256] But in our view, the Johannine text is more understandable in the light of the interpretation of the *Apostolic Constitutions*. Binding is portrayed as a curative method, especially in the light of the text of Ezekiel 34, the exhortation about the shepherds of Israel. This text must lie behind Jesus' teaching about the Good Shepherd (John 10). It throws light on John 20:23. Ezekiel 34:4 and 16 refer to the binding up of the crippled (*suntetrimmenon ou katedēsate* and *to suntetrimmenon katadēsō*). Although John uses the word *kratein*, this can also mean repair, make good (LXX, 4 Kings 12:6), and the cognate *kratēma* can be used of a bandage.[257] The disciples in the name and power of the glorified Lord are to forgive sin and to heal, support, care for the weak and wounded. In this way they continue the work of the Good Shepherd, as Peter is told to do in John 21: "Feed my lambs, feed my sheep."[258] The disciples "loose" by sharing the insufflation of the Spirit as the believer shares the spirit in John 7:38-39, breast-feeding and nourishing. In some cases, however, they must go further and bind wounds before they can adequately nourish and fill with the Spirit.[259] It is for the disciples to "beget" and nourish others with the Spirit, and thus to release them from sin and effect salvation, *shalom*.

Thus our pericope does not end on a negative note, the retention of sin.[260] Rather the redemptive work of Christ is transmitted to the disciples. One notes that the perfect tense is used. This expresses a past action with "enduring results."[261] The sins have been forgiven and/or have been "retained" or "bound up." The perfect refers to the work of Christ through his death and resurrection. United to Christ and his redemptive work, the disciples effect forgiveness in those to whom they minister in Christ's name. Thus they become, as Paul describes them, "ambassadors for Christ":

> All this is from God, who through Christ reconciled us to himself and gave us the ministry of reconciliation; that is, in Christ God was reconciling the world to himself, not counting their trespasses against them, and entrusting to us the message of reconciliation. So we are ambassadors for Christ, God making his appeal through us (2 Cor. 5:18-21).

# 11

# Conclusions

*Artists Confronting the Inconceivable*[1] is the title of a unique book that commemorates *Kristallnacht*, November 9, 1938. It comprises 105 artistic, award-winning works of glass sculpture and expresses the inexpressible—the inconceivable brutality that led to the Holocaust. The editor, Dr. Borowsky, states:

> Seeing the events of the Holocaust through the eyes of artists enlightens the dark side of the world. In our time, it has frequently been their vision that has moved righteous people to think about the implications of the choices they make and the relevance of these choices to society. . . . Glass is a reminder of both the strengths and the fragile qualities that lie within us . . . within civilization itself . . . The artists whose work fill this volume . . . present a mirror that can hallow the past and safeguard the future. . . .[2]

In this book each work provides a profound meditation not only upon the atrocities perpetrated but also upon the courage, resilience, and hope springing up from its own ashes like the fabled phoenix.[3]

The Holocaust and other barbaric events in our own century and in the past not only raise questions about humanity and inhumanity but also about the nature and the comportment of God. Is God dead? Where is God's compassion and omnipotence in such dereliction? God is, indeed, placed on trial, accused of inhumanity and indifference as in Elie Wiesel's play, *The Trial of God*.[4] It is in the light of such accusations, understandably posed, that in this book we have inquired about the *pathos* of God and tried to portray it both from its paternal and maternal aspect. We have complemented this with the quality of friendship. Our findings cause us to ask, Is not God's anguish as acute or more acute than the innkeeper's in Wiesel's play? She or he sees generation after generation of sons and daughters tortured, raped, massacred. God knows full well that this is the consequence of God's own awesome, almost refragable, gift of freewill and individual responsibility. Does God feel guilt or anguish for the divine generosity? But we may question further. Free will or not, should not the witness—and God is omniscient and omnipercipient—to an act of violence try to succor the victim? Does not God play the role of the Gospel good Samaritan? Our results would suggest that the deity plays both roles, those of redeemer and victim. God is omnipotent, but possession of absolute power requires wisdom in administration. God's omnipotence must not trespass on the sacred and mined soil of human adulthood and responsibility. Sometimes we place before God the same temptations that the Gospels of Matthew and Luke show Jesus enduring in the desert: easy miraculous power to solve economic problems (turning stones to bread); dramatic "conjuring" tricks to overawe the credulous crowds (throwing himself from the temple); and the attainment of absolute, unchallenged, political, universal power (all the kingdoms of the world will be yours if you bow down and worship me). God does help individual and corporate victims and grateful tales of delivery ring through the centuries. In our own time we remark the initial defeat of nazism and fascism in Europe, the victory over racism and the change of government in South Africa, the destruction of the Berlin wall, the sowing of the seeds of freedom in Communist countries. The discerning soul can see that good is stronger than evil.[5] God, however, does not come to the rescue by a demonstration of sensational, overwhelming, and irresistible power but by a mother's and a father's love and the even deeper love of a friend. God goes forward to help humankind not by overpowering people but by entering into the very frailty of their nature and into the obscenity of their cruelty until the divine Spirit interpenetrates ours. The Shekinah theology and contemporary Christian theology illuminate this very point. So in the passion of John we have tried to demonstrate Jesus as the true, friendly monarch whose power is wielded in compassionate love and pursuit of truth, not by force of arms. His blood is poured out for his friends but it is a selfless love. We think of George Herbert's *Agony*:

> Love is that liquor sweet and most divine,
> Which my God feels as bloud; but, I as wine.

There is a striking analogy between Wiesel's description of the execution by hanging of the young lad who had "the face of a sad angel" in the concentration camp and the crucifixion of Jesus.

> For more than half an hour he stayed there, struggling between life and death,
> dying in slow agony under our eyes . . .
> Behind me, I heard the same man asking:
> "Where is God now?"
> And I heard a voice within me answer him:
> "Where is He? Here He is—He is hanging here on this gallows. . . ."[6]

In this book we have emphasized that in the crucifixion we truly see the torture of the triune God. So God in Jesus enters into the Holocaust with us, fellow friend, fellow prisoner, fellow God.

But his message goes beyond the crucifixion. It points to the resurrection, a resurrection not only of the future but in the present world with the growth of God's peaceable kingdom. The challenge represented by holocausts is throwing down the gauntlet at the feet of humanity to take up the redemptive love of God. We may not be passive and place the whole onus on God. Redemption is bipolar and mutual. Redemption requires human response.

Another crisis today is the whole question of the status of women, especially in the Roman Catholic Church. Again, the problem is closely entwined with our image of the deity. To their agony women have replied in art (see pp. 60–61 on feminine crucifixes) and poetry. The recapturing of the motherhood of God and of Jesus and the role of divine wisdom has contributed much to encourage women. I hope that this book has cast new light also on the active role of women and the rich feminine imagery in the Gospel of John.[7] This should provide a more feminine approach to the passion and death of Jesus and the bestowal of the Spirit. It also adds another dimension to the symbolism of birth in baptism and nurturing (breast-feeding) in the Eucharist. This imagery was eagerly pursued by the medieval spiritual writers. It is important for women, too, that not only the mother of Jesus and the beloved disciple stand by the cross but also Mary (Magdalene). She is the feminine "beloved disciple." She plays a key role in the great drama of the book of glory. She is the female friend par excellence of the human Jesus. She is a woman of "spunk." Portrayed in art[8] and poetry she is first characterized as a sinner/harlot, albeit also as a symbol of the resurrection but more recently as the clear prototype of the woman disciple.

Finally, what practical result will emanate from our study? Our main thrust has been to grow and develop our concept of the trinitarian God who will lead us to proclaim and implement the true sovereign estate (kingdom) of heaven. The Trinity is the role model of the God of anguish and resilience in the person of Jesus, not only in his death but in his pre- and post-resurrection ministry. We must be avid not only for the peace that passes all understanding but for the unity that goes beyond understanding—the impenetrable, mysterious unity within the Godhead that is the ontological ground of unity within the church and the world, that we may be one even as the triune God is one. Comprehended in this unity is the love of one's enemy. Judas betrayed God, yet Jesus gave him the "morsel" (John 13:26). Luke (Acts 1:18-20) portrays him suffering a death commensurate with his crime. Matthew (Matt. 27:3-10) gentles it. He repented and took his own life. Modern theories of Judas may portray more vividly God's own anguish for Judas and in Judas. This is powerfully conveyed in Francis Thompson's *Hound of Heaven*[9] and also illustrated in the poem *Judas* by Vasser Miller. The first line reads:

Always I (Judas) was on the brink of love. . . .

And the last line—

I hang, a huge teardrop on the cheek of night.[10]

The God of the Old Testament has sometimes won the title "bloodthirsty victor." We seek not to be thirsty for bloodshed, but for life-saving, transfusing blood—an intense longing to see everything in the universe come alive with the sprightliness of the Spirit.

# Appendix

*Feminine Clues in the Gospel of John*

**Anointing of Jesus by Mary (John 12:1-11)**
　　(N. B.: The presence of the two beloved disciples, Mary and Lazarus)
　　This events anticipates:
　　(a) the footwashing
　　(b) the passion
　　(c) the burial with spices
　　(d) the resurrection appearance to Mary

**John 6 and 7:37-39**
**Bread of life discourse** using breast-feeding images and related to gift of Spirit

**John 4**
**Samaritan woman,** Jesus as living water

**John 3:1-14, cf. v. 29**
**Discourse with Nicodemus** on rebirth. Christian initiation as act of birthing with reference to *amniotic* fluid

**John 1:12-13, 18**
**Rebirth,** not by the will of the male, but of God

**John 13**
**Last Supper,** emphasis on Spirit (always feminine in Jewish tradition)

**John 15**
**Jesus as the vine,** which is a feminine image; cf. Ezekiel 19:10-14 "Your mother was like a vine . . ." N.B. the suffering of the vine here; cf. Isaiah 5.

**John 16:21**
The image of the disciples' and Jesus' **suffering as childbirth**

**John 19:34-37**
The piercing of Jesus' side and the gushing forth of blood and *amniotic* fluid; cf. also Genesis 2:21-23

**John 20:23**
**Johannine Pentecost, rebirth** by insufflation of Spirit (feminine in Jewish tradition); cf. Genesis 2:7 and Ezekiel 37:1-14

# Notes

## Introduction

[1] See bibliography.

[2] Cicero, *On Friendship*, 64.

## Chapter 1

[1] In this verse Jesus comes to "exegete," "make known" (*exegeomai*) the Father.

[2] Compare Marcion (c. 160) who rejected the Hebrew Scriptures and saw the Creator God as the demiurge, a God of the Law, who was wholly disconsonant with the God of Love revealed in Jesus Christ.

[3] This is, of course, a biblical study, and I shall trespass little into the field of systematic theology.

[4] We have here a combination of sources, J, E and P.

[5] See Würthwein, "Elijah at Horeb."

[6] For discussions of the reader-response theories see: Preminger and Brogan, *New Princeton Encyclopedia of Poetry*, 1014-17; Makaryk, *Encyclopedia of Contemporary Literary Theory*, 170-74; McKnight, *Post-Modern Use of the Bible*, esp. 115-215.

[7] See McFague, *Models of God*, esp. 157-80.

[8] We cannot deny that throughout the ages the theology of redemption/salvation has been dictated by the prevailing model of God, which is always culturally, socially and politically conditioned, and at times dictated by ecclesiastical concerns. For a critical survey of interpretations of Gen. 1:26-28 see Jónsson, *Image of God*. The concept, "image of God," as it relates to humankind is important for the much neglected text of Sirach.17:1-18.

[9] For a detailed study of terms pertaining to salvation and redemption see Haubeck, *Loskauf durch Christus*. For a short study of words in the New Testament see Cowen, *Salvation*.

[10] See Perkins, *Resurrection*, esp. 14-30 and 257-83.

[11] See Mertens, *Not the Cross*, esp. 133-53.

[12]For a study of the notion of "salvation" in the New Testament see Lyonnet, *Sin, Redemption, and Sacrifice*, 64-70.

[13]See Gunton, *Actuality of Atonement*.

[14]McIntyre, *Shape of Soteriology*. For a systematic treatment of the history of soteriology see Hillenbrand, *Heil in Jesus Christus*.

[15]Compare Kelly, *Early Christian Doctrines*, 163. LaCugna, *God for Us*, 358-9.

[16]McIntyre, *Shape of Soteriology*, 2-3.

[17]Therefore the theology of the Eucharist fuses with the theology of redemption.

[18]I will discuss use of the term "atonement."

[19]McIntyre, 10, italics mine.

[20]McIntyre, 16.

[21]McIntyre, 15.

[22]See Gunton, *Actuality of Atonement*.

[23]Although notice his persistence in mentioning the resurrection in his predictions of his passion.

[24]See also the author's *Bonded with the Immortal*, 194-97.

[25]The present author would consider that the obligation lay only in God's faithfulness to the covenant that God will keep even unto death.

[26]McIntyre 26-52. See also Mertens, *Not the Cross*, 48-58, who discusses redemption, reconciliation, propitiation, liberation, sacrifice and sacrificer.

[27]See also Durken, *Sin, Salvation and the Spirit*. Especially important are parts 1 and 3: Pfeifer, "Experience of Sin," 3-20; Schüssler Fiorenza, "'For the Sake of Our Salvation . . .,'" 21-39; Maly, "Sin and Forgiveness," 40-48; Stock, "Concept of Redemption," 49-64; Vawter, "Salvation Is a Family Affair," 65-70; Murphy, "Wisdom and Salvation," 177-183; Hellwig, "Central Scandal of the Cross," 187-194; and Ellis, "Wisdom of the Cross," 324-333. See also Beardslee, *et al.*, *Biblical Preaching*; Haubeck, *Loskauf durch Christus*; Hanson, *Paradox of the Cross*; Hillenbrand, *Heil in Jesus Christus* (although this is mainly systematic theology); Hultgren, *Christ and His Benefits*; Kettler, *Vicarious Humanity*; Mertens, *Not the Cross*; Nelson, *Salvation and Secularity*.

[28]See Haubeck, *Loskauf durch Christus*, for a linguistic analysis of words related to "ransom."

[29]See Mertens, *Not the Cross*, who emphasizes the whole life of Christ rather than only his death as redemptive.

[30]See Lyonnet, *Sin, Redemption, and Sacrifice*, 80 ff., who also argues that in many cases no price *per se* is paid.

[31]See Mann, *Mark*, 410-20.

[32]Lyonnet, *Sin, Redemption, and Sacrifice*, 80.

[33]Stock, "Concept of Redemption," 49.

[34]The concept is linked to some extent to Rom. 8:3. Note that the female devil is usually identified with Lilith.

[35]We may compare Thomas Aquinas: "Christ therefore is not said to have offered his blood. . . to the devil, but to God" (*Summa Theologica* 3, a. 48, 4 *ad* 3, Blackfriars trans.).

[36]Compare Brown and Parker, "For God so Loved the World?," 5-6, who comment on Gregory of Nyssa and repudiate presenting the death of Jesus as "divine trickery."

[37]Others argued that God sent the Logos in the likeness of sinful flesh to deceive the devil, or that the evil one lost his puissance through his abuse of power.

[38]Compare also Gregory of Nyssa, *Catechetical Oration* 22. (see Augustine *On the Trinity* 13.16 ff.)

[39]He also refers to the idea of "debt" in *Against the Arians* 20 and applies Isa. 53:3-10 to the interpretation of the death of Jesus when he answers the criticism of the Jews (*Against the Arians* 34).

[40]See the classic work of Aulén, *Christus Victor*, for a critical, if biased, survey of the doctrines of redemption from a Reformed perspective.

[41]Marcion (d. ca. 160) led a schismatic congregation in Rome, and taught a theological system closely related to gnosticism. He rejected the entire Hebrew Scriptures, and accepted a severely expurgated New Testament. For him the God of the Old Testament was different from the God of the New Testament.

[42]Jerome, *Ad Gal*, 2, col 385, line 42 and 3, col 433, line 36 (PL 26). Although he does say that Christ offered himself as a victim and redeemed us with his blood (col. 437, line 16.; cf. *Ad Eph*, 1, col. 480, line 37; 482, line 14 and 39 etc).

[43]We find similar statements in Augustine: "He came and found us lying down in sin and penalty; he took our penalty only, but cancelled both the sin and penalty" (Augustine, *Guelferbytine Sermon* 31.1, in *PL Supplement* 2.633). After Augustine, Christian writers continued to interpret 2 Cor. 5:21 as showing Christ offered as a sin offering.

[44]One could hardly call our society "non-militant" but few today would espouse the idea of sacred warfare within which God plays an active part.

[45]See especially Sabourin, *Rédemption Sacrificielle*. Forestell, *Word of the Cross*, 76, points out that Deut. 24:16 prohibits substitutive death.

[46]So also Eusebius, *Proof of the Gospel* 1.10. Cf. Greg. Naz. *Or.* 45

[47]Sabourin, *Rédemption sacrificielle*, 205.

[48]Derrett, *The Victim*. See the contrary view in Forestell, *Word of the Cross*.

[49]Anselm, *Why did God Become Human?* (*Cur Deus Homo?*) 1.8.

[50]Sabourin, *Rédemption sacrificielle*, 216.

[51]Sabourin, quoting Anselm, *Why did God Become Human?* 2.11.

[52]Sabourin, 219.

[53]Peter Lombard, *Commentary on the Letter to the Romans*, PL 191.1386B (on Rom. 5:8-10).

[54]See Milgrom, *Leviticus 1-16*, 1040-46. Milgrom refers to Levine, *Presence of the Lord*, 82, who opines that the Azazel rite "epitomizes the demonic character of the Day of Atonement" (1042).

[55]Milgrom, 1041.

[56]The sins are those performed with a "high hand" (arrogantly).

[57]Milgrom, *Leviticus 1-16*, 1042, citing Levine.

[58]Note the ten methods by which impurity was removed among the Hittites (Milgrom, 1072).

[59]Milgrom, 1045. See also 1071-79 for purification rites in the Ancient Near East.

[60]I am using the English translation of his works, which will be available to my readers.

[61]Girard, *Things Hidden*, 25.

[62]Girard, 3-47.

[63]Girard, 9.

[64]Girard, 23.

[65]Girard, 24.

[66]Girard, 25.

[67]Girard, 27.

[68]Girard, 32.

[69]Girard, 12.

[70]In Hamerton-Kelly, *Violent Origins*, 9. Mack then critiques Girard's theory, and also discusses Walter Burkert's theory of the hunt (22-32) and Smith, *Map is not Territory* and *Imagining Religion*.

[71]See Girard, *Scapegoat*, and also Perera, *Scapegoat Complex*.

[72]Girard, 41.

[73]Girard, 42.

[74]Girard, *Things Hidden*. Girard sees the rending of the temple veil in Mark 15:38 and Lk 23:45 as symbolic of the end of the sacrificial system. Oddly, Girard does not mention the cleansing of the Temple, or the position of that episode in the Gospel of John.

[75]Girard, 182.

[76]Girard, 181.

[77]Girard, 182.

[78]Girard, 183.

[79]Girard, 213.

[80]One could claim the same for God's rejection of Abraham's willingness to offer his son Isaac.

[81]Girard, 204.

[82]Girard, 207.

[83]Girard, 211.

[84]Girard, *Scapegoat,* 112-24. He also associates this with the sign of Jonah (Matt. 12:38-40 and Luke 11:29-30) that is, Jonah is sacrificed for the safety of his fellow travelers (117).

[85]Girard, *Things Hidden,* 224-31.

[86]See also Girard, *Violence and the Sacred*; Juilland, *To Honour René Girard*; Hamerton-Kelly, *Violent Origins* (esp. 73-145, "Generative Scapegoating"); and Hamerton-Kelly, *Sacred Violence* (see esp. 77-81, which discusses Jesus' death on the cross in terms of the scapegoat theory and esp. Gal. 4:4-5; pp. 94-95, Adam scapegoating God; 138-39, God scapegoating Jesus for humanity's sin; and 179, the church as victim).

[87] Schwager, *Brauchen Wir Einen Sündenbock?* (*Must There be Scapegoats?*).

[88]Schwager, 43-53.

[89]Schwager, 55-71.

[90]Schwager, 55.

[91]Schwager, 57.

[92]Schwager, 71-81.

[93]Schwager, 86.

[94]Schwager, 91-109.

[95]Schwager, 117.

[96]Schwager, 119.

[97]Schwager, 134.

[98]Schwager, 135.

[99]Schwager, 137.

[100]Schwager, 193.

[101]Schwager, 194.

[102]See Müller, *Die Geschichte der Christologie* and "Die Bedeutung des Kreuzestodes Jesu."

[103]For a full discussion of the Pauline concept of atonement and reconciliation see Breytenbach, *Versöhnung.* He finds that *diallagē* and *katallagē* are often interchangeable and are used in the context of persons or parties previously hostile, changing to a relationship of freedom, peace, harmony and friendship. They can also be used in a political context where former enemies become *friends.* Often there is a group, either of relatives or others, who are representatives of the parties (82-83). These words stand in a close relationship to *eirēnē, eirēneusis, symbasis, spondē, eirēneuein, symbibaxein, spondas poiein* (104). He discusses particularly 2 Cor. 5:11-6:10, and emphasizes that God takes the initiative and changes hostility into friendship (135). Redemption has a cosmic dimension (129). The much

debated verse 2 Cor. 5:21, that Christ was made sin for us, does appear uncharacteristic of Paul. Breytenbach thinks that Paul may have used some traditional (pre-Pauline) material. This might explain the lack of a subject for *epoiēsen* (137-9). "Christ made sin for us" can be taken in various senses. Most probably God allows Christ to assume the judgement and curse of sin. He also discusses Rom. 5:1-11 esp. 5:9-11 and concludes that the atonement brings a new relationship between humankind and God through grace; this new relationship is possible through the death of Jesus, which robs sin of its power and creates a friendship between God and humanity. Paul does use cultic terminology: Christ's death is expiatory but he seems to be using earlier material and in spite of the terminology he re-interprets Christ's death, freeing it from its original, cultic context (170) and extends it to embrace the entire world (176). Jesus' death is understood in the light of Isa. 52:13-53:12 (LXX), the death of the righteous which effects atonement for sin. But Breytenbach does not wish to associate the Pauline *katallassein* concept with *kpr* in the Old Testament (see 220-24). After an examination of the pertinent terms he concludes that in the New Testament *lytron, apolytron, lytrōsis, lytrōtēs* and *antilytron* refer mainly to messianic liberation, in which no payment is required.

[104]Philosopher and theologian, 1079-1142.

[105]See my discussion of this text in *My Enemy Is My Guest*.

[106]For a short introduction to Liberation Theology see Boff and Boff, *Introducing Liberation Theology*.

[107]Tamayo-Acosta, *Para comprender*, 59. This is a useful book which discusses the history of liberation theology and individual theologians. There is a good bibliography for each chapter.

> . . . momento reflexivo de la profecía, que arranca de la realidad humana, social, histórica, para pensar desde un horizonte mundial las relaciónes de injusticia que se ejercen desde el centro contra la periferia de los pueblos pobres.

[108]See Sölle, *Christ the Representative*, 113-49.

[109]See Healey, *Fifth Gospel*.

[110]See Farrell, "Christa," 11. The artist is Edwina Sandys. Reaction to this work was varied but vehement. Christa is symbolic of the many ways in which woman has been crucified metaphorally through the ages.

[111]Crumlin, *Images in Australian Art*.

[112]Thiel and Helf, *Christliche Kunst in Afrika*. Since writing this manuscript I have discovered a number of female crucifixes.

[113]Brown and Bonn, *Christianity, Patriarchy, and Abuse*.

[114]Elizabeth Bettenhausen, "Foreword," in Brown and Bohn, *Christianity, Patriarchy, and Abuse*, xi-xii.

[115]Brown and Parker, "For God so Loved," in Brown and Bohn, *Christianity, Patriarchy, and Abuse*, 2-3.

[116]Brown and Bonn 10.

[117]Brown and Parker seem to understand "atonement" in a very narrow sense.

[118]Brown and Bonn, 26.

[119]Brown and Parker, "For God so Loved," 27. The present writer does not necessarily concur.

[120]Brock, "And a Little Child," in Brown and Bohn, *Christianity, Patriarchy, and Abuse*, 52.

[121]Brock, 58.

[122]Brock, 59.

[123]Fortune, "Transformation of Suffering," in Brown and Bohn, *Christianity, Patriarchy, and Abuse*, 141.

[124]Fortune, 142, quoting Beverly Wildung Harrison, *When Bad Things Happen to Good People* (Boston: Beacon Press, 1985) 18-19.

[125]Grey, *Feminism*, 13-14; cf. Schillebeeckx, *Jesus*, 676.

[126]Grey, 16.

[127]Grey, 19.

[128]If woman must refuse to be a victim, we should also refuse to see Christ as victim.

[129]Grey, 22.

[130]Grey, 23.

[131]Grey, 40.

[132]Grey, 42.

[133]Whitehead, *Process and Reality*, 525-26, quoted by Grey, *Feminism*, 44.

[134]McFague, *Body of God*.

[135]Grey, 95.

[136]Grey, 97.

[137]Grey, 98.

[138]Grey, 99.

[139]Grey, 100.

[140]Grey addresses the idea of atonement which, in general, she finds unsatisfactory for women because it is inclined to emphasis the "victim" motif.

[141]Grey, 159.

[142]Meland, *Faith and Culture*, 176.

[143]Grey, 163.

[144]Grey rebukes Meland for his oversight of sexism and the "fact that divine tenderness is barred from society's structures as long as the myth of the eternal feminine sees tenderness as a personal and private feminine quality" (Grey, *Feminism*, 163-64).

[145]Grey, 166.

[146]Grey, 164.

[147]Grey, 167.

[148]Grey, 165.

[149]Compare Brown and Parker, "For God so Loved," 10-11.

[150]Grey, 178.

[151]Readers should also consult Searching the Scriptures vol I (1995), vol. II (1994) ed. by Elisabeth Schüssler Fiorenza (New York: Crossroad, 1994 and 1995).

## *Chapter 2*

[1]The suggested date of the fall of Masada is now 74 C.E.

[2]See Abraham J. Heschel, *The Prophets*. (New York: Harper and Row, 1962), chapter 16 on the wrath of God.

[3]Heschel, 221-321.

[4]Heschel, 225.

[5]Heschel, 226.

[6]Heschel, 226.

[7]Heschel, 231.

[8]Heschel, 23.

[9]Compare also Heschel, *Prophets*, chapter 14 for a discussion of the repudiation of divine pathos and the assertion of the indignity of passivity.

[10]Jack Miles, *God: A Biography* (New York: Alfred A. Knopf, 1995). See also Karen Armstrong, *A History of God: The 4,000-Year Quest of Judaism, Christianity and Islam* (New York: Alfred A. Knopf, 1993).

[11]Miles, 21.

[12]Miles, 86, 87.

[13]Miles, 197.

[14]Miles, 197.

[15]Although whether God is the agent of this tragedy can be questioned.

[16]Miles, 202.

[17]Isa. 40:1-2.

[18]Miles, 263-68, cf. 294-302.

[19]Miles, 398.

[20]See Giuseppe Marco Salvati, *Teologia Trinitaria Della Croce*. (Torino, Elledici, 1987), 111-17.

[21]P. Kuhn, *Gottes Selberniedrigung in der Theologie der Rabbinen.* (Munich, 1968).

[22]Kuhn, 31-39.

[23]Kuhn, 45-46.

[24]Kuhn, 56-58.

[25]Kuhn, 65-67.

[26]Kuhn, 85-88.

[27]Kuhn, 152-6.

[28]Kuhn, 213.

[29]Kuhn, 412.

[30]Goldberg, 13-430. Goldberg, *Untersuchungen über die Vorstellung von der Shekhinah.*

[31]Goldberg, 89-91, 171-74.

[32]Goldberg, 125-41.

[33]Goldberg, 142-60.

[34]Goldberg, 160-69.

[35]Goldberg, 174.

[36]Kuhn, *Gottes Selbsterniedrigung,* 28; Scholem, *Von der mystischen Gestalt,* 135 ff.

[37]Kuhn, *Gottes Selbsterniedrigung,* 89 ff.; Scholem, *Von der mystischen Gestalt,* 144 f.

[38]Cf. the link between glory and suffering in the Gospel of John.

[39]Michael E. Lodahl, *Shekhinah Spirit, Divine Presence in Jewish and Christian Religion.* A Stimulus Book, (New York: Paulist, 1992), 3.

[40]Lodahl, 44.

[41]Lodahl, 53-54.

[42]Lodahl, 54.

[43]Lodahl, 60.

[44]Lodahl, 60. The phrase, "One Who Calls," he borrows from John Cobb.

[45]Lodahl, 61.

[46]Lodahl, 83.

[47]Lodahl, 83.

[48]Lodahl, 86. Cf. Bloom, *Kabbalah and Criticism,* 28.

[49]Lodahl, 89.

[50]Lodahl, 89.

[51]Lodahl, 94.

[52]Lodahl, 95.

[53]Cf. the response of Mary in Luke 1:38.

[54]Lodahl, 107.

[55]Lodahl, 117.

[56]Quoted by Lodahl, 113.

⁵⁷Lodahl, 121.

⁵⁸Theopassianism and theopaschites refer to those who believe that God (the first person of the Trinity) suffered. It is usually applied to a group which formed about 519 C.E. at Constaninople. They defended the formula "One of the Trinity was crucified."

⁵⁹Monophysites taught that in the person of the incarnate Christ there was only the divine nature. They formed a distinct body after the Council of Chalcedon (451) which defined the dyophysite doctrine.

⁶⁰Peter the Fuller, d. 488, was the monophysite patriarch of Antioch.

⁶¹Quoted by Torrance, "Does God Suffer?"

⁶²A branch of Monarchianism which arose in the early third century taught that God the Father suffered as the Son. It is sometimes known as Sabellianism.

⁶³The principal objection was his denial of the Trinity.

⁶⁴Torrance, "Does God Suffer?" 348, n. 9, quotes another canon from Rome which declared that Christ "sustained the suffering of the cross to as great an extent as was in accordance with the flesh."

⁶⁵Torrance, "Does God Suffer?" 349, n.11, also notes that in discussing the impassibility or passibility of God one would be obliged to consider the influence of neo-Platonism in Plotinus. I add that it is useful to peruse his treatise, *On the Impassibility of Things without Body* where Plotinus discusses (1) the impassibility of the soul (chs. 1-5) and (2) the impassibility of matter (chs. 6-19), matter is "receptacle," "nurse" and "mother" (19).

⁶⁶Jüngel, *Doctrine of the Trinity*, 15.

⁶⁷Moltmann, *Trinity and the Kingdom*, 21-60.

⁶⁸Moltmann, 21.

⁶⁹Moltmann, 22.

⁷⁰Moltmann, 23.

⁷¹Moltmann, 24.

⁷²Moltmann, 25.

⁷³Torrance, 366.

⁷⁴Moltmann, 368.

⁷⁵Moltmann, 36-42.

⁷⁶Unamuno, *Del sentimiento trágico de la vida*, (*The Tragic Sense of Life*).

⁷⁷For a good critical edition see Unamuno, *El cristo de Velazquez*, in the bibliography.

⁷⁸Unamuno, *The Tragic Sense of Life*, 223.

⁷⁹Moltmann, 41.

⁸⁰Moltmann, 42.

⁸¹Unamuno, 188.

⁸²Unamuno, 213.

⁸³Unamuno, 223.

[84]Unamuno, 224.

[85]Unamuno, 225.

[86]Moltmann, *Trinity and the Kingdom*, 43.

[87]Moltmann, 44, citing Berdyaev.

[88]Moltmann, quoting Berdyaev.

[89]Moltmann, 46, italics mine.

[90]Barth, *Church Dogmatics* 2/2.166, quoted by Moltmann, 52.

[91]Moltmann, *Trinity and the Kingdom*, 56, caps. mine.

[92]Moltmann, 57.

[93]Moltmann, 59.

[94]Rolt, *The World's Redemption*, 95.

[95]Hinton, *Mystery of Pain*, 40. The book is published anonymously. Quoted by Moltmann, *Trinity and the Kingdom*, 32.

[96]Moltmann, *Trinity and the Kingdom*, 33.

[97]Moltmann, *The Crucified God*.

[98]Moltmann, *Trinity and the Kingdom*, 202, citing von Balthasar, "Mysterium Paschale," in Balthasar, *Mysterium Paschale*.

[99]Moltmann, 203.

[100]Moltmann, 243.

[101]Moltmann, *The Crucified God*, 244. Cf. Salvati, *Teologia Trinitaria della croce*,123-34.

[102]Moltmann, *Crucified God*, 276.

[103]Moltmann, *Crucified God*, 246.

[104]Moltmann, *Crucified God*, 248.

[105]First alluded to in *Models of God*, 71, and then developed into an entire book, *Body of God*, esp. 159-91.

[106]*Body of God*, 171-74.

[107]McFague, *Body of God*, 169.

[108]McFague, *Models*, 72-73.

[109]McFague, *Models*, 73.

[110]McFague, *Models*, 77. Compare Sirach 17.

[111]Grey, *Feminism*, 128, speaks about the transforming of power into "mutuality-in-relation".

[112]See the remarkable portrayals of holocaust suffering in *Artists Confronting the Inconceivable* ed. Irvin J. Borowsky. (Philadelphia: American Interfaith Institute, 1992).

## *Chapter 3*

[1]Cf. Numbers 11:12-13.

[2]Carl Jung (quoted by Schmitt, "Motherhood of God," 567) says: "The

city is a maternal symbol, a woman who harbors the inhabitants in herself like children. . . . The Old Testament treats the cities of Jerusalem, Babylon, etc., just as if they were women." Schmitt thinks that Jung was influenced by the Bible itself.

[3]Benjamin, "Israel's God."

[4]*The Literal Meaning of Genesis*, 1.18.36.

[5]Schökel, "La Simbola Biblica della Salvezza."

[6]*Theogony*, 176-78

[7]Cf. John 15:1.

[8]Schökel, "La Simbola Biblica della Salvezza," 40-42.

[9]Schökel, 45.

[10]Schökel, 43.

[11]Schökel, 44.

[12]Romans 8:19-23.

[13]For a full critical survey of the interpretation of humanity made in God's image and likeness see Jónsson, *The Image of God.*

[14]Claus Westermann, *Genesis 1-11.* (Augsburg, Minneapolis, 1984), 146.

[15]See Westermann, 1984, 148-158.

[16]Westermann, 1984, 152.

[17]See Mollenkott, *Divine Feminine*, 83-91. This is a useful book, but relies rather heavily on secondary sources.

[18]One notes that the targum has added "father" to the text so that Moses (and God) are not referred to as feminine and that the word "strength" has been substitued for "bosom."

[19]Blenkinsopp, "Deuteronomy," 108.

[20]The Targum reads, "Like *pangs upon* a woman in travail *my judgment will be revealed upon them.* . . ."

[21]This would seem to point to the community rather than God. The LXX has, "I have endured like a travailing (woman)."

[22]Gruber, "Motherhood of God in Second Isaiah," 353.

[23]Gruber, 355.

[24]Gruber, 354, n.11.

[25]Lamaze, *Painless Childbirth*, 88-91.

[26]Temkin, ed., Soranus of Ephesus, *Gynaecology*, 6.70b.

[27]Gruber, "Motherhood of God in Second Isaiah," 355, n.15. He quotes Jelliffe, *Human Milk in the Modern World*, 156: "Apart from such operant conditioning to the pleasurable sensations resulting from the infant's sucking, hormonal differences, including increased levels of prolactin, may also affect the woman's 'motherliness' and her attachment to the baby." See also Daniel Rancour-Laferrière, *Signs of the Flesh. An Essay on*

*the Evolution of Hominid Sexuality.* New York: Mouton deGruyter, 1985, especially 196-214, 260-267.

[28]Gordis, "Studies in the Book of Amos," 1:211.

[29]Gruber, "Motherhood of God in Second Isaiah," 356, n. 16.

[30]Stuhlmueller, "Deutero-Isaiah and Trito-Isaiah," 340.

[31]Although some would call this Third Isaiah.

[32]So Mollenkott, *Divine Feminine,* 33, God delivers the child, cleanses the mother and places the infant at her breast.

[33]Compare also Ps. 18:6, where the "cords" of the nether-world surely refer to the cord of the fetus.

[34]Mollenkott, *Divine Feminine,* 33.

[35]Mollenkott, 34-35.

[36]The sapiential literature has a strong attraction for feminists. See, e.g., Aldredge-Clanton, *Search for the Christ-Sophia;* Johnson, *She Who Is,* 87-89, 94-100; Cady, Ronan and Taussig, *Sophia;* Schüssler Fiorenza, *In Memory of Her,* 130-140; Robinson, "Jesus as Sophos and Sophia," 11-12; Suggs, *Wisdom, Christology, and Law,* 66-71; Christ, *Jesus Sophia;* Engelsmann, *Feminine Dimension;* Schneiders, *Women and the Word;* Cady, Ronan and Taussig, *Wisdom's Feast;* Matthews, *Sophia Goddess of Wisdom.*

[37]Proverbs 9:1-12.

[38]We should compare also Job 28.

[39]Although by the command of God (Sirach 24:8).

[40]vv. 13-21.

[41]vv. 28-31.

[42]vv. 22-27.

[43]Philo uses the concept of the Logos (*The Worse Attacks the Better,* 83; *On the Special Laws,* 1.40).

[44]Isis was said to be in the rays of the Sun (Winston, *Wisdom of Solomon,* 187).

[45]The Logos is the image of God (Philo, *On Flight and Finding* 101; *On the Confustion of Tongues* 146).

[46]Winston, *Wisdom of Solomon,* 179-180.

[47]Winston, 178.

[48]*Sifre Deut.* 30b and *BT Hullin* 91b.

[49]Plutarch, *Isis and Osiris* 372E.

[50]No. 1380, second century.

[51]Cf. the many names used of Wisdom in Philo *Allegorical Interpretation* 1.43; cf. *On Dreams* 2.254.

[52]Wisdom 7:27.

[53]Wisdom 10:1-19:22, although there is a long digression on idolatry in Wisdom 13-15:17.

[54]Corrington, *Her Image of Salvation,* 103-23.

[55]Proverbs 1:20-21 and 8:1-3.

[56]Lang, *Wisdom and the Book of Proverbs.*

[57]Corrington, 55-59.

[58]Corrington, 60.

[59]One must recall that Jesus was the "Son of David" i.e. Solomon.

[60]In the Wisdom book *passim.*

[61]Lang, *Wisdom and the Book of Proverbs,* 66.

[62]See Nicole Loraux, "What is a Goddess?" in *A History of Women* ed. Pauline Schmitt Pantel. (Cambridge, Mass.: Belknap Press, 1992), 11-44.

[63]See Tran and Labrecque, *Isis Lactans.*

[64]Corrington, *Her Image of Salvation,* 90.

[65]Witt, *Isis in the Greco-Roman World,* 138, quoted by Corrington, *Her Image of Salvation,* 91-92. See also Price, *Kourotrophos.*

[66]For further details pertinent to "salvation" and Isis see Corrington, *Her Image of Salvation,* 89-98.

[67]Corrington, 73.

[68]Livy *From the Founding of the City* 1.58-60; Corrington, 73; We may consult also Pseudo-Hesiod's *Catalogue of Women;* and in Hesiod (LCL 57), 154-219.

[69]Paul speaks of his being in labour with his converts (Gal. 4:19). The idea of breastfeeding as a symbol for teaching Christians occurs in 1 Cor. 3:2; 9:7; Heb. 5:12-13 and 1 Pet. 2:2.

[70]*The Literal Meaning of Genesis,* 1.18.36.

[71]*Letters,* 46; See also Bradley, "Patristic Background of the Motherhood Similitude," 107, n. 42.

[72]For a translation of many of these texts see Robinson, ed., *Nag Hammadi Library in English,* rev. ed.

[73]See also King, ed., *Images of the Feminine in Gnosticism.*

[74]Pagels, 48-69. I have consulted her references and list the following which may be of interest to my readers. The quotations have been changed to NHLE 3rd. ed. (1988): there are some significant differences. I wish to thank my graduate assistant, Ms. Susan L. Graham, who worked diligently on the revised texts.

[75]Quoted by Pagels, *Gnostic Gospels,* 49.

[76]Pagels, 50.

[77]Cf. Schökel, "La Simbola Biblica della Salvezza," above.

[78]Pagels, 51.

[79]*Apocryphon of John* (longer rec.) 2.9-15. Robinson, ed., *Nag Hammadi Library,* 105; cf. Pagels, *Gnostic Gospels,* 52.

[80]Robinson, ed., *Nag Hammadi Library,* 107.

[81]Origen, *Commentary on the Gospel of John* 2.12; so also the *Gospel of Philip* 59.35-60.1.

[82]*Refutation*, 5.12.

[83]I have been unable to check this reference.

[84]*Trim. Prot.* 45.2-10; *Nag Hammadi*, 519.

[85]*Thunder*, 13.16-16.25; *Nag Hammadi*, 297-99.

[86]Pagels, *Gnostic Gospels*, 57.

[87]Until recent discoveries some scholars suggested that the Odes were Gnostic, but see Charlesworth, "Odes of Solomon," 725.

[88]*Ode*, 19, lines 1-5. Charlesworth, 752.

[89]Lines 5-6; Charlesworth, 765.

[90]Cabassut, "Une dévotion médiévale," 234-245.

[91]Bradley, "Patristic Background of the Motherhood Similitude," 103.

[92]Bradley, 103.

[93]*Against Heresies*, 3.24. Later the side of Christ is associated with the nourishment from his breasts.

[94]Wilkin, p. xiv.

[95]Clement, *Who is the Rich Person Who Shall Be Saved?*, 37.

[96]Augustine, *Expositions on the Book of Psalms*, on Ps. 58, serm. 1.10.

[97]*Expositions on the Book of Psalms*, on Ps. 30, narr. 2, serm. 1.9.

[98]*Sermon*, 105.8.11.

[99]*Expositions on the Book of Psalms*, on Ps. 47.5.

[100]Cf. John 20:23.

[101]*Tractate on the Gospel of John* 104; cf. also 16.2; 18.1 and 21.1. This is in the context of the beloved disciple reclining on the breast of Jesus.

[102]*Expositions on the Book of Psalms*, on Ps. 26, narr. 2.18. See Bradley, "Patristic Background of the Motherhood Similitude," 101-113.

[103]McHugh, ed., *Ambrose of Milan. Seven Exegetical Works*, 269.

[104]*Postilla on Isaiah*, 49.15.

[105]*Postilla on Isaiah*, 66.13.

[106]*Visa Quarta*, coll. 1. See Bradley, "Patristic Background of the Motherhood Similitude," 110.

[107]Bynum, *Jesus as Mother*. This was originally an article.

[108]See Cabassut, "Une dévotion médiévale," 234-45.

[109]Bynum, *Jesus as Mother*, 112.

[110]Bynum, *Holy Feast*, 260-276.

[111]I use the text of Colledge and Walsh, eds., *Julian of Norwich: Showings*.

[112]*Showings*, 60.

[113]Readers might be interested in Berliner, "'God is Love.'" He discusses female and angelic illustrations of Jesus.

## *Chapter 4*

[1]Moltmann, *Passion for Life*, refers to Hegel's designation of friendship

as "the concrete concept of freedom" (52). Friendship has also been called the "soul of socialism" which without friendship degenerates into a "soulless bureaucracy" (53). Moltmann believes that Jesus' friendship with the outcast was based on his joy in God and in human existence (55).

²Mark 8:31-33; 9:30-32; 10:32-34 and parallels. Only Matt. 20:19 mentions crucifixion.

³Two thousand Jews were crucified by Quintilius Varus in 13 B.C.E. (Josephus *Jewish Antiquities* 17.295).

⁴Fulda, *Das Kreuz und die Kreuzigung*; Hengel, *Crucifixion* and Fr. transl. *La Crucifixion*; Merino"El suplicio de la Cruz"; Kuhn, "Die Kreuzesstrafe." Kuhn covers patristic evidence. He differs from Hengel's view at various points. N.B. his detailed bibliography.

⁵Originally my studies were directed to three forms of protracted death, crucifixion, impalement and *apotympanismos*, but I have decided to treat all these under the heading "crucifixion," as my aim is anthropological and theological, not historical.

⁶Fastening the victim through five clamps to a board, usually set on the ground. Death might not ensue for ten days or more.

⁷Fulda, *Das Kreuz und die Kreuzigung*, 113-16: ". . . dies bestand in der Verbindung möglichst grosser Schmerzen mit möglichst arger Beschimpfung . . ." (107). Other forms of execution were beheading, burning, strangulation etc.

⁸Cf. Cicero, *Against Verres* 2.5.66.169 and Valerius Maximus 2.7.12.

⁹Fulda, 753-55. The word *oiktristos* is used frequently.

¹⁰See Malina, *New Testament World*.

¹¹A word study of crucifixion, impalement and hanging would include: Latin *crux, crucifigo, patibulum, furca*; Greek, *proseloun, stauros, stauroun, anartaō, anaskolopizō, kremannumi, sanis*; Semitic roots, *tlh, tullu*.

¹²*Letters*, 101.14.

¹³See Kuhn, "Die Kreuzesstrafe," 758-75.

¹⁴See below for the crucifixion of women.

¹⁵Compare Malina and Neyrey, *Calling Jesus Names*, 88-91 (on status-degradation rituals).

¹⁶Plautus, *Miles Gloriosus*, or *The Braggart Warrior*, 372-373.

¹⁷At first I was puzzled by this statement, for it seemed to me that money would not benefit a dead man. However, a note in Barkan seems to shed light on this. He quotes Athenaeus:

Among the Romans twenty pounds are offered to any who will brave decapitation with an axe on condition that their heirs receive the prize. And often when too many are enrolled they dispute which of them has the best right in each case to have his head cut off (Athenaeus, *Deipnosophists* 4.154C).

[18]Cf. Terence, *The Lady of Andros*, 621.

[19]For labeling in the anthropological sense see Malina and Neyrey, *Calling Jesus Names*, 95-97.

[20]*Against Verres*, 2.5.63.163-64.166.

[21]*Against Verres*, 66.169.

[22]*Against Verres*, 2.5.66.169-170, italics mine. Transl. LCL.

[23]See Neyrey, "Nudity."

[24]It was so even among the Hellenistic Jews (cf. 1 Macc. 1:14; 2 Macc. 4:9-15).

[25]See Isa. 20:4 which describes the procession of naked prisoners, "naked, barefoot, with buttocks uncovered." Neyrey compares 2 Sam. 10:4; 1 Chron. 19:4 and Job 12:17, 19.

[26]Neyrey, "Nudity."

[27]Hengel, *Crucifixion*, 67, n.2.

[28]*Mekhilta Makshirin*, 3.14-15.

[29]". . . they stripped off the old man's clothes, though he was still adorned with the beauty of his piety" (4 Macc. 6:2; in Charlesworth, ed., *Old Testament Pseudepigrapha*, 2.551).

[30]Neyrey, "Nudity."

[31]Cf. "When [the condemned person] was at a distance of four cubits from the place of stoning they stripped off his garments. They covered a man in front and a woman both in front and behind: this is the view of R. Judah: but the Sages say, A man is stoned naked, but a woman is not stoned naked" (*B. T. Sanhedrin* 6.3).

[32]Fulda, *Das Kreuz und die Kreuzigung*, 1O2.

[33]Fulda, 89.

[34]Plutarch, *Parallel Lives: Coriolanus*, 24.

[35]Fulda, 90.

[36]Fulda, 96.

[37]Hengel, *Crucifixion*, 62. I was unable to find the reference to this.

[38]Fulda, *Das Kreuz und die Kreuzigung*, 97, remarks that at times the crime was branded on the forehead of the victim.

[39]Suetonius, *Life of Domitian*, 10.

[40]Suetonius, *Life of Caligula*, 32; see also Horace, *Epodes*, 4.11.

[41]Malina and Neyrey, *Calling Jesus Names*, 3-42.

[42]*Patibulo adfixus in isdem anulis quos acceptos a Vitellio gestabat.* Tacitus, *History* 4.3.2.

[43]Ibid. 38-39, points out that from a sociological point of view "labeling a person" not only causes other members of society to despise the victim but provokes sharp reaction and thus leads to internal and external conflict.

[44]"The vulture hurries from dead cattle and dogs and gibbets to bring some of the carrion to her offspring" (Loeb). *vultur iumento et canibus crucibus relictis ad fetus properat partemque cadaveris adfert* (Juvenal, *Satires* 14.77-78; 83-85).

[45]*Parallel Lives: Galba*, 28.

[46]*The Civil Wars*, 1.120, Hengel, *Crucifixion*, 55.

[47]*Scriptores Historiae Augustae: Life of Severus Alexander* 23:8. (Attributed to Aelius Lampridius).

[48]Tacitus, *Annals* 14.45.

[49]Cf. Isa. 13:20-22; 34:11, 14; Jer. 9:10; Bar. 4:35 and Rev. 18:2.

[50]Fulda, *Das Kreuz und die Kreuzigung*, 140.

[51]Ezra 6:11.

[52]Fulda, 109.

[53]Strictly speaking this would be impalement.

[54]Cf. Tacitus, *Annals* 15.44 for similar torture practised on Christians.

[55]Hengel, 2.

[56]Seneca, *To Marcia on Consolation*, 20.3.

[57]Josephus, *Jewish Wars* 5.449-51.

[58]Fulda, *Das Kreuz und die Kreuzigung*, 116-26, who discusses composite crosses.

[59]Catullus (*Epigrams* 107) says: "*effossos oculos vorat atro gutture corvus, intestina canes, caetera membra lupi.*" Compare Martial, *On the Spectacles* 7.

[60]Suetomics, *Life of Colba* 9.

[61]Fulda, *Das Kreuz und die Kreuzigung*, 157.

[62]Sophocles, *Antigone* 255-6. See Cicero *Treatise on the Laws* 2.57, who refers to the turf which must be thrown over the bones after cremation. See also *Treatise on the Laws* 2.67 for a reference to Plato's restrictions with regard to funeral rites. See Plato *Laws* 12.958D-960C, e.g., bodies may not be buried near tilled land.

[63]Seneca, *On the Happy Life* 19.

[64]For crucifixion among non-Romans see Kuhn, "Die Kreuzesstrafe," 704-6.

[65]Merino, "El suplicio de la Cruz," 40.

[66]Cf. Merino, 37.

[67]Col. 64. Maier, ed., *Temple Scroll*.

[68]The *Sifre* commenting on Deut. 21:22 says that not all those condemned to death were crucified, only those who had blasphemed God but the crucifixion must not last more than a day (Merino, "El Suplicio," 38). But the Talmud speaks clearly about hanging the person after she or he is dead (*B. T. Sanhedrin* 46b) although this same reference may refer to the

crucifixion (or impalement) of women (probably witches) at Askelon. The Mishnaic text reads:

> They hanged a man [with his face] towards the people and a woman with her face to the gallows; this is the opinion of R. Eliezer; but the Sages say, The man is hanged, but the woman is not hanged. R. Eliezer said [to them], But did not Simon ben Shetach hang women in Askelon? (*B. T. Sanhedrin* 6.4).

For a full discussion about the eighty women executed by Simon ben Shetach see Hengel, *Rabbinische Legende.* Hengel examines the three texts which relate to these women but comes to the conclusion that they were not witches and, indeed, the incident may concern effeminate men rather than women.

[69]Merino, "El Suplicio," 48-69.

[70]Maier, ed., *Temple Scroll*, 133-34.

[71]See also Fitzmyer, "Crucifixion in Ancient Palestine."

[72]In Akkadian *tullu* (sometimes under the form *thw*); in Hebrew *tlh*; in Aramaic *slb*; Greek *kremazō.*

[73]Philo, *On the Special Laws* 3.151-152.

[74]We may also compare: ". . . and all souls in this condition (loving the body) depend on and hang from lifeless things, for, like men [sic] crucified (*anaskolopisthentes*) and nailed (*proselontai*) to a tree, they are affixed to perishable materials till they die (*On the Posterity and Exile of Cain*, 61).

[75]I wish to thank Kathleen Corley for her insightful observations on a paper on this subject read at the Context meeting in Portland, Oregon, 1995. I was not able to incorporate all her suggestions but hope to pursue more research on this topic. Dr. Corley suggested that I look into the social status of the women mentioned and also that I begin with the Gospel material concerning the women who stood near the cross.

[76]Mark 8:34; 10:21; Matt. 10:38; 16:24; Luke 9:23; 14:27. N.B. the addition of "daily" (*kath'ēmeran*) in Luke 9:23.

[77]Although she wears a loin cloth.

[78]Farrell, "Christa," 11.

[79]The figure looks pregnant, but I am not sure that the artist meant to draw attention to this.

[80]Crumlin, *Images in Australian Art* 158-159.

[81]Thiel and Helf, *Christliche Kunst in Afrika*, 91.

[82]Doris Jean Dyke, *Crucified Woman*. United Church Publishing House: Toronto, Canada, 1991.

[83]Quoted by Dyke, *ibid.*, 41 from a quotation by Bobbie Crawford, "A Female Crucifix," in *Daughters of Sarah*, vol 14, no. 6 (November/December, 1988, Chicago), 26.

[84]This was originally a paper presented to the Mid-West Society of Biblical Literature.

[85]Fulda, *Das Kreuz und die Kreuzigung*, 89-90, observes that the "cross" did not always comprise a vertical and horizontal shaft, the word *crux* and its cognates can mean a simple pole. See also the diagrams in Fulda's monograph.

[86]Dr. Corley suggested that I should look into the social status of the women victims. I far as I can see there was not such an emphasis upon crucifixion as a *slave* punishment. High born women seem to have been victims as well.

[87]There is now some doubt about the Spartan women warriors.

[88]See Driver and Miles, *Babylonian Laws*.

[89]Driver and Miles, *Babylonian Laws*, 108-9; cf. Josh. 10:26 and 2 Sam. 4:12.

[90]Driver and Miles, 313.

[91]Driver and Miles, 456.

[92]Leyes Asirias, Tabla A, col. vii, lines 92-97; cf. Cardascia, *Les lois assyriennes*, 244, par. 53.

[93]Driver and Miles, 314, aver that she might have been impaled after death.

[94]Goldstein, *I Maccabees*, 227, points out that hanging *kremasai* was also the punishment inflicted on the pupils of forbidden philosophers.

[95]Goldstein, 227.

[96]Josephus, *Jewish Antiquities* 12.256.

[97]Josephus, *Jewish Wars* 2.253-255.

[98]*Jewish Wars* 2.293.

[99]*Jewish Wars* 2.301.

[100]*Jewish Wars* 2.305.

[101]*Jewish Wars* 2.307-8, italics mine.

[102]Josephus, *Jewish Antiquities* 18.65–79.

[103]*Jewish Antiquities* 18.80.

[104]This refers to two texts. First, "hanging" *hoka* with reference to Num. 25:4 where Moses orders the execution of those who have submitted to the rites of Baal of Peor (And hang them (the guilty) up unto the Lord in the face of the sun). It is difficult to decide whether this includes woman as well as men and women. The second text is 2 Sam. 21:6 'And we will hang them up [*we-hoka'ah*] unto the Lord in Gibeah.' This text is followed by the curious statement: "And it is written, *And Rizpah the daughter of Aiah took sack-cloth, and spread it for her upon the rock, . . .* (as a protection against birds of prey)."

[105]In Epstein, ed., *Babylonian Talmud*, Tractate *Sanhedrin*, n.2.

[106]*B. T. Sanhedrin* 46a, commenting on, "Thou shalt hang him . . .," says that "him" refers to a male who has attained thirteen or more years but adds that the hanging in *B. T. San.* 46a is certainly far less than Roman cru-

cifixion because the body is hung after death and for a much shorter time, but this comment may be anachronistic.

[107]Hengel, *Rabbinische Legende*, 18-21.

[108]He examines all the three references to this incident, *Sifre Deut.* 21; *Hag.* 77d and *Sanh.* 23d and Rashi on *Sanh.* 11b. The case has four historic points: 1) the subject, Simeon b. Shetah; 2) the place, Askalon; 3) the object, women in the plural; and 4) the predicate, hanging. Although all three versions are independent they stand in similar traditions. In *Jerusalem Hagigat* 77d (2.2) Simeon is in danger of hell fire if he does not execute the witches; here we find ourselves in the world of popular legend interwoven with multi-cultural magic. Simeon with the help of eighty young men brings the witches up from their cave and crucifies them. Obviously, this tale does not come from scholarly circles. The Sanhedrin text is based on Exod. 22:17 "Do not permit a sorceress to live." Hengel accepts the literary analysis of Jacob Neusner (*Rabbinische Legende*, 18-21, 27; Neusner, *Rabbinic Traditions*, 90-103). Simeon was a representative of early Pharisaism and the arch-enemy of Janneus. He was obviously a powerful personality although Josephus gives him scant attention.

With regard to Askalon Hengel (36-37) argues that it was the last bulwark of heathenism in the Holy Land. Even in Roman times it retained its status of *civitas foederata et libera*. There was mutual hatred between the citizens of Askalon and the Jews. Hengel (41-44) thinks it is extremely unlikely that Simeon could have been responsible for a mass execution in Askalon.

[109]Hengel, 54-56.

[110]Hengel, 58-61.

[111]In private correspondence, Prof. Hengel recommended his article to the present writer and stated that he did not know of other cases of the crucifixion of women, but his correspondence took place about six years ago (before the availability of the *Thesaurus Linguae Graecae* on CD Rom).

[112]Tacitus, *Annals* 14.43.

[113]Tacitus, *Annals* 14.45. "He was answered by a din of voices, expressing pity for the numbers, the age, or the sex of the victims, and for the undoubted innocence of the majority" (LCL).

[114]Tacitus, *Annals* 14.45.

[115]Apuleius, *Golden Ass* 4.24.

[116]It is in this context that Apuleius relates the story of Psyche's search for Cupid.

[117]Apuleius, *Golden Ass* 6.31-32.

[118]Petronius flourished in the reigns of Claudius (41-54 c.e.) and Nero (54-68 c.e.). He was governor of Bithynia and at one time a consul.

[119]This one of the Milesian tales attributed to Aristeides of Miletus.

They were popular romantic tales which were forerunners of the medieval romances.

[120]*Satyricon*, 111-113.

[121]"*Debuit patris familiae corpus in monumentum referre, mulierem affigere cruci*" (Petronius, *Satyricon* 113). A variant reads: . . . *itaque ne te putes nihil egisse, si magistratus hoc scierint, ibis in crucem, polluisti sanguine domicilium meum ante hunc diem inviolatum.* . . . (Petronius, *Satyricon* 112-113).

[122]*Lysistrata*, 678-679.

[123]Seel, ed., *Justini. Epitoma Historiarum Philippicarum.*

[124]Yet, when the matter became known, the people rushed together and Agathocles was killed and also out of vengeance for the death of Eurydices the women were submitted to crucifixion. When the death of the king and the punishment of the concubines had, as it were, atoned for the infamy of the kingdom, the Alexandrians sent embassadors to the Romans and besought them to take responsibility for the safety of the king's son (minor) and protect the kingdom of Egypt, which they said had already been split by a contract made between Philip and Antiochus.

There is now a translation by R.Develin, Scholars' Press, 1995.

[125]Dio Cassius, *Roman History* 62.7.2-3.

[126]*Kai autos meta teknōn hepta kai gunaikos aichmalōtos lēphtheis anestaurōthē.* Diodorus Siculus, *The History* 2.1.10.

[127]*The History*, 2.18.1.

[128]*The History*, 18.16.

[129]*The History*, 26.23.1-4.

[130]*The History*, 35.12.1.3.

[131]*The History*, 19.67.2.3.

[132]Pseudo-Plutarch, *Concerning Rivers* (*De Fluviis*), in Müller, ed., *Geographi Graeci Minores*, 637-665.

[133]Ps.- Plutarch, *Concerning Rivers*, 1.4.

[134]Hengel, *Crucifixion*, 11-14.

[135]Hengel, 12, n.2.

[136]See Nauck, *Tragicorum Graecorum Fragmenta*, 397 ff.

[137]According to the Elder Pliny (*Natural History* 35.199), Manilius of Antioch was brought to Rome as a slave in 90 B.C.E., but this cannot be verified. See the detailed discussion in the introduction to the Loeb edition: Goold, ed., Manilius. *Astronomica*, (Astronomy) xi.

[138]See Manilius, *Astronomy* 5.538-557. Bruce Malina tells me that this is not the correct constellation.

[139]Compare Nauck, *Tragicorum Graecorum Fragmenta*, 392, quoting Eratosthenes *Catast.* 17.

[140]Manilius also adds. "The person who is born when Andromeda rises

will prove to be merciless in executing punishment:From the same constellation comes the figure of the executioner, ready to take money for a speedy death and the rites of a funeral pyre . . . in short he is the man who could have looked unmoved on Andromeda herself fettered to the rock (pendentem e scopulis ipsam spectare puellam)."

[141]Achilles Tatius, *The Adventure of Leucippe and Clitophon*, 3.6.3-4.

[142]Compare Nauck, *Tragicorum Graecorum Fragmenta*, 393-94, no. 115, where Andromeda is described as *Thanatou thlēmon mellousa tuchein*.

[143]Cf. the sacrifice of Jephtha's daughter (Judg. 11), although we do not know the mode of execution.

[144]Keramopoullos, *Apotympanismos*, 74-76.

[145]Blandina was a martyr of Lyons who died in 177 C.E.. Her story is recounted in the *Letter of the Churches of Lyons and Vienne* (Eusebius *Ecclesiastical History* 5.1.1-5.28). Her fellow believers saw Christ in her.

[146]The text is in Musurillo, *Acts of the Christian Martyrs*.

[147]Musurillo, 75.

## *Chapter 5*

[1]See Pitt-Rivers, *Fate of Shechem*, 89-105, cited by Herman, *Ritualised Friendship*, 32. Amiable relations are divided into two pedigrees. Kinship includes real kinship, adoptive kinship and ritual kinship and Friendship includes ritualised friendship and unritualised friendship. See also Gould,and Kolb, *Dictionary of the Social Sciences*, under "kinship" and "kinship system," 116-369, but especially "kinship terminology," 368.

[2]The epistles of John are not my immediate concern.

[3]Zizioulas, *Being as Communion*. LaCugna, *God for Us*, 351-55.

[4]Sallie McFague, *Models of God*, Philadelphia: Fortress, 1987, 157-180.

[5]McFague, 157-180.

[6]McFague, 157. This may provide a partial answer to our initial question concerning the necessity of Christ's death (*dei*). McFague (157) quotes C.S. Lewis, "Friendship is unnecessary, like philosophy, like art, like the universe itself. . . ." She quotes *The Four Loves* (New York: Harcourt, Brace and Co)., 1960, 103.

[7]McFague, 159.

[8]D. Bonhoeffer, *Letters and Papers from Prison*, rev. ed. (New York: Macmillan Co., 1967), 192-93 calls friendship "the rarest and most priceless treasure".

[9]Compare Ian B. Sloan, "Ezekiel and the Covenant of Friendship" *BTB* 22 (4, 1992) 149-154 who discusses Ezek 34:25; 37:26 and Isa. 54:10 but both MT and LXX read "covenant of peace."

[10]Quoted by Meilaender, 32-33.

[11]Daniel Day Williams, *The Spirit and the Forms of Love*. (New York and Evanston: Harper and Row, 1968), 3.

[12]McFague, *Models*, 160, she compares Dante's *Divine Comedy*.

[13]See LaCugna, *God for Us*, 270-278.

[14]Cited by McFague, 157.

[15]McFague, 162.

[16]McFague, 158 does recognize the difficulty over deciding whether human nature is basically aggressive and hostile or natural benevolent. She suggests that the latter may well be true of Christianity.

[17]McFague, 160.

[18]McFague, 162.

[19]McFague, 162 states that one does not open the door even slightly for an adversary.

[20]Although, of course, the symbol of marriage for God's relationship to Israel and the church is mentioned in both Testaments.

[21]See Meilaender, *Friendship*, 31.

[22]McFague, *Models of God*, 164.

[23]Cf. Davies, *Gospel and the Land*.

[24]McFague, *Body of God* and Carter Heyward, *Redemption of God*.

[25]I discuss this on pp. 147-53.

[26]McFague, *Models of God*, 166-67.

[27]Wren, "Sexism in Hymn Language," 8, quoted by McFague, *Models of God*, 220, n. 34. We may contrast Byron's play, *Cain* where Lucifer pours scorn on the "loneliness of God":

> . . . But let him
> Sit on his vast and solitary throne,
> Creating worlds, to make eternity
> Less burthensome to his immense existence
> And unparticipated solitude.
> Let him crowd orb on orb, he is alone
> Indefinite, indissoluble tyrant (lines 147-151).

[28]McFague, *Models of God*, 168.

[29]McFague, 171.

[30]Page, *Ambiguity*, 189-90.

[31]Page, 192. Page observes, too, that there is no generation gap with God: she or he is always our contemporary:

> . . . quality and force of his [*sic*] relationship. . . Recognition, however, alters one' s whole perspective: the world no longer fills the horizon but is contained within his [*sic*] relating, indeed exists because of that relationship. In that case

action, thought and being have point not only as a struggle for survival, the making of order or the promotion of pleasure or justice, but as a response to divine possibility. Because that possibility is offered through a relationship which God has with every part of creation. . . .(190).

[32]Campbell, *Rediscovering Pastoral Care*, 93; cited by Hunt, 194.

[33]Hunt, 195.

[34]Whitehead's phrase, see Hunt, 131.

[35]Hunt, 194. McFague, *Models of God*, 172-74, points out the importance of the meal. See the author's, *My Enemy is My Guest*, 259-91.

[36]I omit a specific discussion of friendship in the Old Testament, for it is bound up in the covenant relationship.

[37]See Culpepper, *Johannine School.*

[38]Aristotle says that happiness consists in life and activity (*Nichomachaean Ethics* 9.5).

[39]I wish to thank the members of the SBL Consultation on Hellenistic Moral Philosophy and Early Christianity for permitting me to peruse their papers. References will be to the typescript. This will be edited by John Fitzgerald and published by Scholars' Press. The papers are: D.L. Balch, "Friendship in the Historian Dionysius of Halicarnassus"; K.G.Evans, "Friendship in the Documentary Papyri: An Analysis of Its Role in the Daily Life of Greek and Roman Egypt"; B. Fiore, "The Theory and Practice of Friendship in Cicero"; R.F.Hock, "Friendship in the Greek Romances;" A.C.Mitchell, "'Greet the Friends by Name': New Testament Evidence for the Greco-Roman *Topos* on Friendship;" E.N. O'Neil, "Plutarch on Friendship;" R.I. Pervo, "With Lucian: Who Needs Friends? Lucian's Story of Friendship (The *Toxaris*);" F.M. Schroeder, "Friendship in Aristotle and the Peripatetic Tradition;" G.E.Sterling, "The Bond of Humanity: Friendship in Philo of Alexandria;" J.C.Thom, "'Harmonius Equality' The Topos of Friendship in Neopythagorean Writings."

The most well-known works on this subject are: Plato, *Lysis, Symposium* and *Phaedrus*; Aristotle, *Nichomachean Ethics, Eudemian Ethics, Great Ethics (Magna Moralia)*; Cicero, *On Friendship; The Supreme Good*; Plutarch, *Moralia: How to Tell a Flatterer from a Friend, On Brotherly Love, On Having Many Friends, How to Profit by One's Enemies*; Lucian *Toxaris, or Friendship*; Xenophon *Memorabilia of Socrates* 2; Isocrates *Oration* 1 (*To Demonicus*); Seneca *Moral Essays* 9 (On Philosophy and Friendship); Gellius *Attic Nights* 1; Aspasius, *On the Nichomachean Ethics*; Epictetus *Discourses*. This is not a comprehensive list and there are, of course, many *obiter dicta* on friendship scattered throughout classical works.

[40]I use the text of Dillon and Hershbell: *Iamblichus: Pythagorean Way of Life.*

[41]Iamblichus, *Pythagorean Way of Life* 30-32.

[42]Women and slaves could become members of the Pythagorean communities. See Iamblichus *Pythagorean Way of Life* 170 for the education of his daughter, and 173 referring to a slave mastering the teaching of Pythagoras.

[43]Dillon and Hershbell, *Iamblichus*, 2.

[44]Compare Plato, *Republic* 464D: ". . . they have nothing in private possession but their bodies, but all else in common?" But Plato carries the idea of "all in common" further than Pythagoras.

[45]Iamblichus, *Pythagorean Way of Life*, 167.

[46]N.B., Acts 4:32: the community was one *kardia kai psychē mia*.

[47]*Pythagorean Way*, 168.

[48]*Pythagorean Way*, 169. "Seeing, then, that he made humans friends with animals because they consist of the same elements as we do, and share in the more basic level of life with us, how much more did he thereby institute familiarity among those sharing the same kind of soul (*homoeidous psychēs kekoinōnēkosi kai tēs logikēs tēn oikeiōsin*), even the rational!"

[49]Pythagoras, 179.

[50]*Pythagorean Way*, 229, (cf. 69-70).

[51]This is repeated in the *Pythagorean Way* 69, which also includes precepts concerning the purification of the soul from disturbing emotions so that the divine may be kindled in it. He also speaks about the divine "eye" (*theion omma*).

[52]*Pythagorean Way*, 229-30. Trans. Dillon and Hershbell. Some of this material is attributed to Aristoxenus, see their 227, n. 2.

[53] *Vide infra*

[54]Pizzolato, *L'idea di amicizia*.

[55]Pizzolato, 19.

[56]Empedocles's concept of friendship is influenced by his cosmology. For Empedocles, *philia* indicates the principle of cohesion which preserves all the elements, while hatred is the force which disintegrates them. Friendship is also important for the unity in the political realm. However, for Empedocles friendship is a cosmic force, not a human factor and, as such, necessarily, it is not the fruit of freewill. Even so Socrates is able to use this concept in his discussion of friendship and he passes from cosmological interests to anthropological (24-25).

[57]Pizzolato, 19.

[58]*Agōna te kai philoneikian*. Compare Iamblichus, *Pythagorean Way*, 101.

[59]Note the emphasis placed on trust and/or faith in the Gospel of John. *Pistein eis* (to believe in) may indicate trust as well as belief. Forestell, *Word of the Cross* (105), observes that *pistein eis* is based on the Hebrew *ha'amin*

*be* "with a stronger sense of the complete, personal and all-embracing commitment to another person." See Barr, *Semantics,* 161-205.

[60]*Hōrismena kai nenomismena* 233.

[61]*Kakian megalēn te kai anepanorthoton.*

[62]234-36. Iamblichus also tells the stories of Cleinias of Tarentum and Thestor of Posidonia (*Pythagorean Way of Life* 239) to illustrate the lengths to which friendship will go.

[63]Probably composed by Iamblichus (Dillon and Herschbell, *Iamblichus,* 235, n.9).

[64]Iamblichus *Pythagorean Way* 240, italics mine.

[65]Iamblichus tells the story of a Pythagorean who fell ill during a journey. When he was near death he told the innkeeper to hang a symbol on a tablet outside and the person who recognized it would pay his deceased friend's debts to the innkeeper (*Pythagorean Way* 238). So it happened.

[66]Iamblichus, *Pythagorean Way* 20-21.

[67]Theognidos of Megara (544 B.C.E.) discusses friendship under the aegis of nobility and seems to treat it almost as an aristocratic monopoly. But he himself did not enjoy the support of his friends when he was sent into exile (Pizzolato, *L'idea di amicizia,* 22-24).

[68]For a consideration of friendship in Homer and Hesiod see Pizzolato, *L'idea di amicizia,* 12-18.

[69]Compare Isocrates (ps.) *Oration 1: To Demonicus* 24 on putting your friends to the test. A friend should be willing to stay with you in adversity and not envy you in good fortune.

[70]We, of course, reconstruct Socrates' thoughts from the Platonic dialogues and Xenophon, especially *Memorabilia* II, 4-6.

[71]Xenophon, *Memorabilia* 2.4.1-2.

[72]Xenophon, *Memorabilia* 2.4.6-7.

[73]Xenophon, *Memorabilia* 2.5.3: "others (friends) I would sacrifice any sum and take any trouble to have among my friends."

[74]Xenophon, *Memorabilia* 2.6.5.

[75]See Fraisse, *Philia,* 123-68; and Price, *Love and Friendship,* 1-102.

[76]One must read the *Lysis* together with the *Symposium* and the *Phaedrus* for a full discussion of the norms of attraction as a nostalgia for the absolute which is illuminated by beauty (*Phaedrus* 250D-251B; Pizzolato, *L'idea di amicizia,* 45).

[77]Pizzolato, *L'idea di amicizia,* 33.

[78]Pizzolato, 35.

[79]*Lysis* 215A and B.

[80]*Odyssey* 17.218; cf. John 12:32; Lysis 214 A, B.

[81]On this point Socrates disagrees. He argues that opposites become friends, e.g., the poor friends of the rich. He states that the good, the bad

and what is neither good nor bad are mutually attracted.

[82]*Lysis* 221E-222A. It is difficult to draw fine lines between friendship and love. See Pizzolato, *L'idea di amicizia,* 40-45.

[83]*Lysis* 210B.

[84]*Lysis* 214E; cf. Hillel's golden rule and also Matt. 7:12.

[85]Plato *Symposium* 213A.

[86]Compare Xenophon, *Memorabilia of Socrates* 2.6.14-20, where there is a discussion of the possibility of making a friend of a bad person.

[87]Plato, *Lysis* 219C.

[88]In a similar way *erōs* in the *Symposium* (203C-E) is considered to be of the same nature as philosophia because she stands between ignorance and wisdom.

[89]Plato *Lysis* 219D.

[90]Plato, *Lysis* 222A-B.

[91]Plato, *Alc.* I 126C. Compare Plato in *Epistles* 7.323D-352A.

[92]Plato, *Laws* 3.701D; Pizzolato, *L'idea di amicizia,* 46.

[93]Plato, *Laws* V, 729B-730B; VI, 757A-C.

[94]Dawe, "Fresh Look."

[95]See Sakenfeld, *Meaning of Hesed;* Lofthouse, "*ḥen* and *ḥesed*"; Glueck, *Ḥesed in the Bible,* 35-37; Hills, "*ḥesed* of Man"/"*ḥesed* of God" (quoted by Sakenfeld, 10-11); McCarthy, *Treaty and Covenant* and *Old Testament Covenant;* Moran, "Ancient Near Eastern Background;" Hillers, *Covenant;* Mendenhall, "Covenant Forms."

[96]Plato *Lysis* 214C-D.

[97]Meilaender, *Friendship,* 32-33.

[98]See Neumann, "Diotima's Concept of Love."

[99]However, Plato uses *erōs,* not *agapē.*

[100]It is not known whether she was an historical character.

[101]*Symposium* 178C; cf. 1 Cor. 13.

[102]*Symposium* 179.

[103]But compare Cornford, *Unwritten Philosophy,* 72, who points out that she is really a *daimon. Erōs* is "desire."

[104]*Symposium* 180B.

[105]*Symposium* 181A.

[106]*Symposium* 188D, italics mine. Then *Symposium* 189E discusses the original and androgynous person.

[107]*Symposium* 203A.

[108]*Symposium* 205C.

[109]*Symposium* 206A.

[110]Compare Cornford, *Unwritten Philosophy,* 73: Beauty is like a birth-goddess: she gives relief to travail.

[111]*Symposium* 206A.

[112]*Symposium* 206C.

[113]*Symposium* 209A.

[114]*Symposium,* 206C4-E1.

[115]Neumann, "Diotima's Concept of Love," 39-40.

[116]Neumann, 44.

[117]*Symposium* 209D. Cornford (*Unwritten Philosophy,* 75-76) points to three types of immortality, perpetuating race, fame and thoughts. But *Erōs'* passion is for immortality in the eternal sphere.

[118]*Symposium* 210B-C.

[119]*Symposium* 210E-211A.

[120]*Symposium* 212.

[121]See Spicq, *Agape in the New Testament.*

[122]Cornford, *Unwritten Philosophy,* 77, states "For Plato believed that the goal of philosophy was that man should become a god, knowing good and evil with such clearness and certainty as could not fail to determine the will infallibly."

[123]Gal. 5:22-23.

[124]Cf. Phil. 4:8-9.

[125]John 3:1-15.

[126]Plato *Symposium* 179A.

[127]Plato *Symposium* 180A.

[128]Compare Fascher, "Platon und Johannes." He discusses discipleship and approaches to death.

[129]Plato, *Phaedo* 62C.

[130]Plato, *Phaedo* 108C.

[131]John 14:8-11.

[132]See also Fraisse, *Philia,* 189-266; and Price, *Love and Friendship,* 103-61.

[133]In this chapter I do not intend to discuss the subject of patrons and clients although they would seem to fall into the category of friends based on utility. See Moxnes, "Patron-Client Relations." Jesus and the early Christian community are set in the context of patron-broker-client. It is my opinion that John transcends these relationships.

[134]For further analysis see Fraisse, *Philia,* 287-318.

[135]I agree with B. Fiore when he states that friendship was a public rather than private affair in the ancient world (Fiore, "Sage in Select Genres," 1).

[136]A discussion of Greek homosexual friendship does not come within the purview of this book.

[137]Pizzolato, *L'idea di amicizia,* 47.

[138]Aristotle *Politics* 1253a. Note the discussion whether God needs friends (Aristotle *Eudemian Ethics* 7.12.1245b.)

[139]Aristotle *Nichomachean Ethics* 8.1.1155a.

[140]Although Pizzolato, *L'idea di amicizia*, 51, points out that the terms used of friendship are never clearly defined.

[141]*Nichomachaean Ethics*, 8.3.7-9 (1156b 18-33).

[142]Pizzolato (50) notes the difference between *philēsis* which is *pathos*, and friendship which is a disposition.

[143]*Nichomachean Ethics*, 9.9-10.

[144]Ibid. 9.9.10. Compare Pizzolato, *L'idea di amicizia*, 20, who points out the Pythagorean maxim that a friend is a "second self" (Iamblichus *Pythagorean Way of Life* 33).

[145]Compare Pizzolato, *L'idea di amicizia*, 59-60, for the discussion of loving the self and the distinction from egocentricism in the light of seeing that two friends have one soul.

[146]*Nichomachean Ethics*, 8.3-7. As in Hebrew and Greco-Roman thought, the blood is the source of life in John's Gospel. As we shall see below, blood is a vital source of nourishment, it contains the essence of vitality. Cf. John 6.

[147]*Nichomachean Ethics*, 8.5.5.(1157b29-32.)

[148]Pizzolato, *L'idea di amicizia*, 55. However, see Rader, *Breaking Boundaries*, esp. Ch. 1, "Heterosexual Friendship: Distinctive Phenomenon within Early Christian Societies" and Ch. 2, "Normative Greco-Roman and Judaic Male/Female Relationships."

[149]*Nichomachean Ethics*, 8.6-7.

[150]*Nichomachean Ethics*, 8.11.

[151]*Nichomachean Ethics*, 8.14.3.

[152]*Nichomachean Ethics*, 8.7.1.

[153]*Nichomachean Ethics*, 8.7.6.

[154]*Nichomachean Ethics*, 8.6.3.

[155]*Nichomachean Ethics*, 8.7.

[156]*Nichomachean Ethics*, 8.9.12.

[157]*Nichomachean Ethics*, 9.4.5 Aristotle maintains that there can be no true friendship with slaves (*Nichomachaean Ethics*, 8.11.6-7).

[158]*Nichomachean Ethics*, 8.5.5.

[159]*Nichomachean Ethics*, 9.4.5-6.

[160]Aristotle, *Great Ethics* 2.16.1213a.

[161]See *Nichomachean Ethics* 9.8.

[162]*Nichomachean Ethics*, 9.3.3.

[163]In *Eudemian Ethics* 1.13, Aristotle says that animals die for their young.

[164]Cf. John 8:50.

[165]Cf. John 1:17. We note also the happiness does not consist in self-sufficiency. This is true of God and humanity.

[166]Theophrastus wrote three works on friendship but they are not

extant. However, we do have some information about his *philia* philosophy from Gellius and Diogenes Laertius. He emphasized *syngeneia, oikeiōsis* and the virtues associated with friendship and companionship (see Pizzolato, *L'idea di amicizia*, 66-69).

[167]Pizzolato, 71.

[168]Epicurus *Principal Doctrines* 30 in Diogenes Laertius *Lives and Opinions of Eminent Philosophers* 10.154.

[169]See Eusebius' remarks in *Preparation for the Gospel* 14.5 and Cicero, *The Supreme Good* 1.65.

[170]Pizzolato, *L'idea di amicizia*, 78.

[171]Plutarch *That Epicurus Actually Makes a Pleasant Life Impossible* 28.5.1105E.

[172]Fiore, "Sage in Select Genres," 9, n. 8.

[173]See O'Connor, "Invulnerable Pleasures."

[174]In Diogenes Laertius *Lives and Opinions of Eminent Philosophers* 10.120. Compare Seneca, *Letter 35: On the Friendship of Kindred Minds*, 3. Here Seneca urges Lucilius to concentrate upon study in order to develop himself. Seneca makes a distinction between love and friendship. At times love can cause harm but friendship is always helpful. Seneca speaks of receiving strength from Lucilius' youth. He asks him to give himself "as a gift of great price" (*ingens munus*) to him.

[175]*Memorabilia of Socrates* 1.2.14; 4.2.40. See Fiore, "Sage in Select Genres," 10-12, See Fiore also on the philophronetic letter.

[176]Fiore, 10, n. 11.

[177]O'Connor, "Invulnerable Pleasures," 168. For further material on Epicurean friendship see Fraisse, *Philia*, 287-330.

[178]See Meeks, *First Urban Christians*, 31, 75-80, 93, 158; and Banks, *Paul's Idea of Community*, women would also be active in the community.

[179]Diogenes Laertius *Lives and Opinions of Eminent Philosophers* 7.174.

[180]Plutarch, *Against the Stoics on Common Conceptions* 1039b.

[181]Compare Jesus' logic on "Love your neighbor as yourself" (Matt. 19:19; 22:34).

[182]Pizzolato, 82.

[183]Yet, on the other hand, there is a certain "depersonalization" in the Stoic idea of friendship (Pizzolato, 88).

[184]See Cicero, *Treatise on the Laws* 1.49 and *The Supreme Good* 2.70.

[185]O'Connor, 84.

[186]Yet Middle Stoicism tended to be somewhat exclusive.

[187]For an interesting collection of texts eulogizing benefactors see Danker, *Benefactor*.

[188]Cf. Cicero, *In Defense of L. Cornelius Balbus* 29: *amicitia foedere coniuncta*.

[189]Cf. John 19:12.

[190]See Pizzolato, 95-99, for friendship as it is portrayed in the Roman theatre.

[191]*On Friendship* 5.17.

[192]Compare his sentiments about the deceased Scipio throughout this treatise.

[193]*On Friendship*, 4.15

[194]9.29. Cicero thinks that the friendship of utility is of "low pedigree", the "daughter of poverty" (Cicero *On Friendship* 9.31).

[195]*On Friendship*, 1.

[196]Fiore, 22, 50, 49.

[197]Dugas, *L'amitié antique*. I have not been able to procure this book yet.

[198]*On Friendship* 9.32.

[199]*On Friendship* 9:32.

[200]Although see Neyrey, *Ideology of Revolt*. He focuses on controversies within the Johannine community.

[201]Culpepper, *Johannine School*.

[202]For better or for worse, Philo had an incalculable influence on the early Christian writers. Christians seem to have preferred the use of the word *agapē* to *erōs*, *philia* and *storgē* (affection), (Pizzolati, *L'idea*, 217-218). Hence the infrequency of *philia* and its cognates in the New Testament. *Agapē* approximates the Hebrew `*ahaba*. *Agapē* especially refers to the love radiating from God. In Latin, *caritas* was preferred to *amor*. It has a less sensual meaning.

[203]I shall not examine the Hebrew Scriptures but here I note the following. Lev. 19:18 "Love your neighbor as yourself". This principle can be the basis of "friendship." It suggests a parity among humans. This friendship in the Law and the Prophets focuses on the Covenant in virtue of election. God is called "father", "mother," "lover". LXX of Exod. 33:11 (2) speaks of Moses face to face with God as a friend (see the *targumim*). Although *philos* may not occur frequently in LXX yet we have outstanding examples of friendship: Jonathan and David (1 Sam. 18:1-3); 2 Sam. 1:26; Ruth and Naomi; Ps. 40:10; Sirach 22:2; Deut. 13:7; Sirach 6:11 (2); Sirach 6:5-17; Prov. 27:5-6; Sirach 27:22; Sirach 6:16-17; Job 6:14. Friendship in the Hebrew Scriptures (Old Testament) is radically ontological. One important aspect of friendship is hospitality (cf the tragic cry of Cain in Gen. 4:15); compare also Gen. 18-19 and Isa. 41:8). Abraham is called a friend of God by virtue of his justification by faith (Gen. 15:6). It is not a friendship of parity.

[204]See Sterling, "Bond of Humanity."

[205]. . . *theophilēs* . . . *philanthropos*; *On the Virtues* 77.

[206]*ho gennētēs* (85).

207 *On Flight and Finding,* 58.

208 *On Noah's Work as a Planter,* 90.

209 *On Noah,* 91.

210 *Every Good Man is Free,* 44.

211 *On the Virtues* 35, cf. 179.

212 *On the Special Laws,* 1.317.

213 Philo's treatment of Gen. 15 is wholly allegorical, and does not appear to add much to our present enquiry.

214 Friendship vocabulary in Philo includes: *homonoia, symphōnia, koinōnia, hetairia, synētheia.*

215 *On the Special Laws* 1.68, italics mine.

216 On Abraham, 194-195. Cf. Sterling, "Bond of Humanity," 1-2.

217 *On Abraham,* 196-197.

218 *On Abraham,* 198.

219 Philo also introduces the *topos* of friendship in his work on Joseph. He speaks of the brothers of Joseph as "partners in the board and salt which men have devised as the symbols of true friendship" (*On Joseph* 210).

220 *On Dreams* 1.231-232.

221 Exod. 33:11.

222 He states that the most precious possessions of life are "mercy, neighborliness (*koinōnia*), charity, magnanimity, a good report and good fame" (Philo, *On the Virtues* 84).

223 *On the Virtues* 102-103. The laws speak of "the friendliness shown by him who loves the incomer even as himself" (Philo *On the Virtues* 84).

224 *On the Virtues,* 179; cf. *On the Special Laws* 1.51-52. "Now as friends it would be a great hardship to deprive them of the necessities of life and by so doing lay nothing by which may be of service to meet the uncertainty of the future. It is a very admirable saying of the ancients that in joining friendship we should not ignore the possibility of enmity, and conduct our quarrels with future friendship in view, so that every one in his own nature lays by something to ensure his safety. . ." (152).

225 Rader, *Breaking Boundaries,* 25, n. 24, citing Ferguson, *Moral Values.*

## *Chapter 6*

1 For the Lukan scene in the garden, see the author's *My Enemy is My Guest,* 116-22.

2 Cf. Seneca *On Tranquillity of Mind.* He identifies this with the Greek *euthymia* "well-being" of soul (2.3).

3 Ford, "Hellenistic Monarchy." Material from this is incorporated in this book.

4 Although *timē* seems to denote human honor and *doxa* has a much

wider span of meanings.

[5]Iamblichus, *Pythagorean Way of Life*, 229-30. See the whole quotation on page 77.

[6]See particularly Kuhn's discussion of Celsus and Origen's dialogue in "Die Kreuzesstrafe," 744-45.

[7]See the author's *My Enemy is My Guest*, Maryknoll, N.Y.: Orbis Books, 1984, 108-135.

[8]Culpepper, *Johannine School*. He considers the Pythagorean, Platonic, Stoic, Epicurean and Philonic schools as well as those of Qumran, Hillel and Jesus. Curiously he omits a full discussion of the Cynic School. See also Cullmann, *Johannine Circle*, 30-62.

[9]Moreau, *Stoïcisme, epicurisme, tradition hellénique*, 7.

[10]Moreau, 7-8.

[11]Moreau, 8-9.

[12]In the interests of space I omit for the time being the concept of *kabod* in the Hebrew Scriptures.

[13]von Rad, "*dokeō, doxa, doxazō . . . ,*" 235.

[14]See the classic, Zeller, *Stoics, Epicureans and Sceptics*. Paquet, *Les Cyniques Grecs*.

[15]For a concise overview of Stoic thought see Colish, *Stoic Tradition*; Kimpel, *Stoic Moral Philosophies*; Long, *Soul and Body in Stoicism*; Bodson, *La morale sociale*; Forschner, *Die stoische Ethik*; Hülser, *Die Fragmente zur Dialektik der Stoiker*.

[16]Deissmann and Schneider suggested that *doxa* had originally the meaning of "light" or "radiance" and as such was used as a woman's name. However, there is slender evidence for this.

[17]Deissmann and Schneider, 239.

[18]For a full discussion of glory in John's Gospel see Evans, *Word and Glory*, 81-83, where he discusses "glory" and the exodus covenant tradition.

[19]See Paquet, *Les Cyniques Grecs*.

[20]See Inwood, *Ethics and Human Action*.

[21]See, for example, Cicero *The Supreme Good* (*De finibus*).

[22]Cf. Colish, *Stoic Tradition*, 45.

[23]This can be important for the soteriological aspect of John's Gospel.

[24]For further discussion of goals (*telos, skopos*) see Forschner, *Die stoische Ethik*, 171-82.

[25]*Discourses* 3.24.40.

[26]Epictetus *Fragments* 36 (LCL).

[27]*On Moral Duties* 1.13.

[28]See, for example, Cicero *The Supreme Good* 3.16 (Cato as "wise"); 2.89 (Cato's preference for the simple life).

[29]John 1:14, 17; 3:21; 4:23, 24; 5:33; 8:32.

[30]John 8:40-46; 14:6, 17; 16:7, 13; 17:17, 19.

[31]The Stoics expounded on many role models, for example, Heracles and Socrates. Rôle modeling is, of course, an important anthropological study in itself.

[32]See Fascher, "Platon und Johannes," 79-86.

[33]Seneca, *Moral Epistles* 114.24. Quoted by Arnold, *Roman Stoicism*, 239.

[34]Epictetus, *Discourses* 1.18.21.

[35] *How to Profit by One's Enemies* 4 (*Moralia* 88B).

[36]See Bodson, *La morale sociale*, 68-81. See also Cicero, *On Fate*.

[37]Inwood, *Ethics and Human Action*, 110.

[38] *On the Happy Life*, 15.7.

[39]Inwood, 110-11.

[40]Inwood, 184-85. On Cicero's ethics, see Colish, *Stoic Tradition*, 126-58; and Valente, *L'éthique stoïcienne chez Cicéron*. Cicero takes Stoicism as the foundation of his ethics but is by no means uncritical of the stoic ethical system. With regard to this, see *Paradoxes of the Stoics, On Old Age, On Friendship* and *On Moral Duties* (Colish, 128). In *Paradoxes of the Stoics*, he considers six theses: (1) virtue is the only good; (2) virtue alone is sufficient for happiness; (3) all vices and virtues are equal; (4) all fools are madmen; (5) only the sage is free; (6) only the wise man is rich. For Cicero freedom is "power to live as one wills" (Colish, 131). "The sage alone is free because his will, enlightened by his judgment, freely chooses the good. Everyone else is a slave, regardless of his social status." (Colish, 131; Cicero *Paradoxes of the Stoics* 33-40. See also Arnold, *Roman Stoicism*, 210-11, cf. John 13, the footwashing).

[41]A dyad is a "personal relationship which links two ACTORS" (Seymour-Smith, *Dictionary of Anthropology*, 86).

[42]Not, of course, in the Stoic sense that he can choose to commit suicide.

[43]Neyrey, *Ideology of Revolt*, 61-62.

[44]Neyrey, 63.

[45]Neyrey, 64.

[46]Neyrey, 65.

[47]Compare Cicero's *On Moral Duties*, although his view of decorum was, at times, much disputed.

[48]Some scholars might like to see Stoic influence in John's use of Logos in the Prologue to his Gospel.

[49]Antipater of Tarsus, quoted by Arnold, *Roman Stoicism*, 228.

[50]Epictetus, *Discourses* 3.13.2, italics mine.

[51]This is very different from the cry of desolation in Mark 15:34 and Matt. 27:48.

[52]On this point Moreau, *Stoïcisme, epicurisme, tradition hellénique*, 9 mentions Cleanthes' Hymn to Zeus.

[53]Seneca, *Letters* 47.1, italics mine.

[54]*Letters* 47.4.

[55]See Colish, *Stoic Tradition*, 37-38.

[56]Moreau, *Stoïcisme, epicurisme, tradition hellénique*, 7.

[57]Schneiders, "The Foot Washing."

[58]Schneider, 86.

[59]Est enim amicitia nihil aliud, nisi omnium divinarum humanarumque rerum cum benevolentia et caritate consensio (Cicero, *On Friendship* 6.20, cf. 4.15). J.G.F. Powell, ed., *Cicero: Laelius, On Friendship and the Dream of Scipio* (Warminster, England: Aris & Phillips, 1990) 37.

[60]Colish, *Stoic Tradition*, 135.

[61]See Amand de Mendieta, *Fatalisme et liberté*.

[62]Inwood, *Ethics and Human Action*, 48.

[63]Aulus Gellius (*Attic Nights*) quoted in Inwood, 48.

[64]Moreau, *Stoïcisme, epicurisme, tradition hellénique*, 19.

[65]Colish, *Stoic Tradition*, 42.

[66]Colish, 43.

[67]For example, in *To Serenus on the Firmness of the Wise Person* (*passim*).

[68]Colish, 44.

[69]Cf. also the Hebraic tradition as, for example, see in Prov. 8-9.

[70]Colish, *Stoic Tradition*, 46, cf. Prov. 8-9.

[71]Colish, 47.

[72]Colish, 48.

[73]Epictetus, *Discourses* 1.2.24; *Man.* 50-51; Colish, *Stoic Tradition*, 48.

[74]*Letters* 13.1-3, and 110:3; *To Helvia on Consolation* 2.3; *To Marcia on Consolation* 5:5; *On Providence* 1.6, 2.4-12, 4.1-5, 4.11.

[75]*Tusculan Disputations* 2.14-32, 3.1.2., 3.17-37, 5.28.82.

[76]Colish, *Stoic Tradition*, 142.

[77]However, on the other hand one should not seek to prolong life like Maecenas (see Horace *Odes* 2.17). Seneca calls the prayer of Maecenas for a longer life a pitiable prayer:

> Thence came that most debased of prayers, in which Maecenas does not refuse to suffer weakness, deformity, and as a climax the pain of crucifixion (*novissime acutam crucem*) provided only that he may prolong the breath of life amid these sufferings: Fashion me with a palsied hand,/ Weak of foot, and a cripple:/ Build upon me a crook-back'd hump;/ Shake my teeth till they rattle;/ All is well, if my life remains./ Save, oh, save it, I pray you,/ Though I sit on the piercing cross (*vel acuta Si sedeam cruce, sustine*). (Seneca, *Letters*. 101.10-11.)

[78]Colish, *Stoic Tradition*, 49-50. See also Droge and Tabor, *A Noble Death*. Much of this book concerns suicide, which does not come within my purview. I shall discuss the martyrdom aspect below.

[79]Colish, *Stoic Tradition*, 50; 8. Marcus Aurelius *Meditations* 2.17, 3.7, 3.16.

[80]See Colish, *Stoic Tradition*, 142.

[81]Epictetus, *Discourses* 1.29.29.

[82]*Mors non est gloriosa, sed fortiter mori gloriosum est.*

[83]Epictetus, *Discourses* 82.10, 12, 14, 17.

[84]*Tetelestai*, John 19:30.

[85]See Kotzé, "John and Reader's Response;" Minear, "Audience of the Fourth Evangelist."

[86]Benz, *Der gekreuzigte Gerechte.*

[87]Plato, *Republic* 2.362A.

[88]There is a similar passage in Plato's *Gorgias*:

> . . . If a man be caught criminally plotting to make himself a despot, and be straightway put on the rack and castrated and have his eyes burnt out, and after suffering himself, and seeing inflicted on his wife and children, a number of grievous torments of every kind, he be finally crucified (*anaschinduleuthēsetai*, literally, impaled) or burnt in a coat of pitch, will he be happier than if he escape and make himself despot, and pass his life as the ruler in his city, doing whatever he likes, and envied and congratulated by the citizens and the foreigners besides? (Gorgias, or, *On Rhetoric* 473C).

We may compare Luke 23:47 and Acts 3:14-15. (2.366 B).

[89]*Discourses*, 1.2.1-2. See also Plato *Republic* 2.366C-D and Cicero *The Republic* 3.27.

[90]Arnold, *Roman Stoicism*, 410.

[91]I have concentrated on the Stoic wise person but reference could be made to differing concepts in the various philosophical schools. See Gammie and Perdue, eds., *The Sage in Israel*. Especially important in this volume are: Kerferd, "The Sage in Hellenistic Philosophical Literature," who discusses the sage in Stoicism (320-322) in Epicureanism (322-324), the elusive sage (324-325); the sage among the Peripatetics, Pythagoreans, Cynics, and Later Sophists (325-328); and Gammie, "The Sage in Hellenistic Royal Courts," who discusses the various meanings of "friends of the king" (151-153); and Fiore, "The Sage in Select Genres."

[92]Harris, "The Female 'Sage'."

[93]Camp, "The Female Sage."

[94]She studies especially the two wise women in 2 Samuel and Jer. 9:16 [17], cf. Exod. 35:25, and refers particularly to Brenner (The Israelite Woman) and her own essay "The Wise Women in 2 Samuel: a Role Model for Women in Early Israel."

[95]See also Brooten, *Women Leaders.*

[96]Ménage, *History of Women Philosophers.*

[97]Zedler, xi.

[98]Zedler, xii.

[99]Ménage, 45.

[100]Ménage, 46.

[101]See Pliny, *Letters* 3.11; 6.24, 5.7; 7.19, 9.13; Dio Cassius, *Roman History* 60.

[102]Bassler, "The Widows' Tale." See also the author's article, "The 'Call-girl' in Antiquity."

[103]See also Davies, *Revolt of the Widows*.

[104]Bassler, 25.

[105]Bassler, 26.

[106]Wider, "Women Philosophers," 27.

[107]Diogenes Laertius, *Lives and Opinions of Eminent Philosophers* 8.42.

[108]*Pythagorean Way of Life*, 92.

[109]See Festugière, *Epicurus and His Gods*, 27-50. Wider, 27.

[110]See Meeks, "The Image of the Androgyne."

[111]*Advice to Bride and Groom* 48.145B-E.

[112]Lutz, *Musonius Rufus*, 43-44.

[113]Wider, "Women Philosophers."

[114]Wider, 29.

[115]*Parallel Lives: Pericles* 24.5-6.

[116]According to Diogenes Laertius, *Lives and Opinions of Eminent Philosophers* 2.72, 2.81.

[117]*Lives and Opinions of Eminent Philosophers* 6.97-98.

[118]Wider, 51; see the Elder Pliny, *Natural History*, Pref. 29.

[119]*Lives and Opinions of Eminent Philosophers* 3.46. Plutarch adds Boïdion.

[120]I have been unable to verify this reference.

[121]Wider, "Women Philosophers," 22.

[122]See Richeson, "Hypatia of Alexandria," this reference on 79.

[123]Wider, "Women Philosophers," 52.

[124]In *Life of Isidorus* 31.29-30. Damasicius *Life of Isidorus* 31.33-38, quoted by Wider, "Women Philosophers," 53.

[125]Quoted by Wider, "Women Philosophers," 53-54.

[126]Rist, M. "Hypatia," 216, suggests that her expertize in astronomy may have aroused suspicions.

[127]See the highly laudatory portrayal of Sara as wise woman in the *Genesis Apocryphon* 19-20 (Vermès, *Dead Sea Scrolls* 253-254).

[128]Sandra Schneider, "Women in the Fourth Gospel" in *The Gospel of John as Literature. An Anthology of Twentieth-Century Perspectives* ed. Mark W. G. Stibbe. New York: E.J. Brill, 1993, 123-143.

[129]E.g., ". . . the Samaritan Woman (4.7-31) who realistically negotiates

an incredible range of emotions from suspicion, to almost brassy defiance.
. ." (129). Schneider, 129-130.

[130]Schneider, 130.

[131]Schneider, 131.

[132]Schneider, 130.

[133]Since writing this section Maria Dzielska's *Hypatia of Alexandria*, trans. F. Lyra, Cambridge: Harvard University Press, 1995 came into my hands.

## *Chapter 7*

[1]I do not wish to make this merely a word study. Clusters of words pertinent to friendship have been used in the consideration of classical texts above and in the consideration of John's text.

[2]On redemption during the earthly ministry of Jesus see Mertens, *Not the Cross*, 133-53, and Schwager, *Must There be Scapegoats?*, 41-75.

[3]In this essay I focus upon the Gospel of John but further study would necessitate a perusal of the Johannine epistles.

[4]Nygren, *Agape and Erōs*. However, this study has received some negative criticism in recent years.

[5]Nygren, *Agape and Erōs*, 210.

[6]Meilaender, *Friendship*, 11.

[7]Note the importance that John places on wisdom and knowledge (of God).

[8]I have used the Greek and Latin retrieval programs. The Perseus program gave the following synonyms for friend and friendship: *bēltistos* (dear friend, best friend), *xēnios* (guest-friend, bound by treaty of hospitality); *xynēmōn* (joint partner); *doruxenos* (spear friend, ally); *hetaîros* (companion, friend); *paranymphos* (friend of bridegroom); *pēpōn* (cooked by the sun, metaphorically a term of endearment; *proxenos* (protector, patron, broker, public guest friend); *prosetairozomai* (take as a friend); *thōps* (false friend, flatter); *synēbos* (young comrade); *tân* (my good friend); *arthmios* (united, peaceful relationships, friendship); *arthmos* (league or friendship); *dexiōma* (acceptable thing, pledge of friendship, offer of right hand); *diallassō* (interchange, reconcile, change from enmity to friendship); *philios, philia, philikōs, philotēs, philotēsios* (friend, friendship); *katallagē* (change from enmity to friendship), *systasis* (bringing together—of god and humans); *chrēstophilia* (friendship of good persons, trusty friend). These were collected for me by Mr. Richard Rivera.

[9]*telos eusebeias philia pros theon  culmen autem pietatis amicitia ad deum*, 86b.

[10]Diogenes Laertius, *Lives and Opinions of Eminent Philosophers* 10.120.

[11]But see Graefe, *Der Gespaltene Erōs*, who considers both the positive and negative aspects of *Erōs*.

[12]I shall discuss these more fully in my examination of the Farewell Discourses.

[13]Eltester, "Der Logos und sein Prophet," 109-34, argues for a scheme of redemptive history in the Prologue, but it would seem that it is easier to see allusions to the incarnation especially in vv. 9, 11, 14 (cf. Borgen, "Observations," 289).

[14]For the structure of the Prologue see especially Culpepper, "The Pivot of John's Prologue." He finds it to have a chasitic structure with the pivot not in v. 14 but 12b (becoming children of God) so that as *tekna theou* the Johannine community identifies itself as the heir of Israel. The designation is rooted in the Old Testament, especially the wisdom tradition.

[15]Bultmann, *The Gospel of John*, esp. 25-36.

[16]Talbert, "Myth of a Descending-Ascending Redeemer."

[17]E.g., Latin literature: Ovid, *Metamorphoses* 8.626-721; Tacitus, *Histories* 4.83-84; Virgil, *Fourth Eclogue*: ". . . iam nova progenies caelo demittitur alto" (7); Horace, *Odes* 1.2.

[18]Prov. 8:22-36; Sirach 24; Bar. 3:27-4:4; Wisd. 6:18-20; 7:27; 8:10, 13, 17; 9:10, 18, cf. 10:1, 4, 6, 13, 15; 4 Esd. 5:9-10 (the withdrawal of wisdom) and 2 Bar. 48:36 (departure of wisdom).

[19]Talbert, 422.

[20]Tob. 12:14-15a; *Joseph and Aseneth* 14-17; *Testament of Job* 2.27; *Apocalypse of Moses* (where angels descent to redeem Adam's soul) 33.1-5; *Testament of Abraham* 7.3-17; *Prayer of Joseph* used by Origen. He finds parallel examples in Philo and the *Apostolic Constitutions* 8.12, 6-27.

[21]Talbert, 430.

[22]Justin Martyr, e.g., *Dialogue with Trypho* 38, 48, 56, 59, 61, 126, 128; *Shepherd of Hermas* Parables 5.6.3-8; *Sybilline Oracles* 8; Tertullian *Against Hermogenes* 18, *Against Praxeas* 16, *On the Flesh of Christ* 6; *Odes of Solomon* 12, 22, 23.

[23]Talbert, 435-38.

[24]Meeks, "The Man from Heaven."

[25]Meeks, 44.

[26]Meeks, 47.

[27]Meeks, 50, n.17. He notes that the *katabasis* of the Spirit (John 1:32) is from the synoptic baptism scene of Jesus, but John omits the actual baptism.

[28]Meeks, 50.

[29]I shall discuss a "trinitarian" approach when I examine the Farewell Discourses.

[30]Davies, *Rhetoric and Reference*, 121.

[31]Davies, 122.

[32]For the atoning aspect of a martyr's death, either of a man or a woman, see Frend, *Martyrdom and Persecution*, 36, 64, 150, 152, 182, 290. The words *hilastērion* and *antipsychos* (ransom) are used. See also Williams, *Jesus' Death*, 102-35.

[33]John 1:12-13; cf. Plato, *Symposium* 209. We may compare Philo who said of converts that they become "dearest friends", "closest kinsfolk" and soul mates.

[34]Cf. the conversation with Nicodemus: John 3:1-21; John 16:21 and John 20:22-23.

[35]It can also mean honored guest. In the LXX it translates *chekh* and is used to express marital relationships; cf. Deut. 13:7; 28:54; Sirach 9:1, and also devoted care of a child (Num. 11:12; 1 Kings 3:20; 17:19; Judg. 4:16; Isa. 49:22; 2 Sam. 12:3). It is also used of membership of community (2 Clement 4.5). Compare also the mother of the Maccabean martyrs who speaks about the "bosom of Abraham" (*Pesaim* 108b; *Kid* 72a/b the dying patriarch in bosom of Abraham. Cf. *Apostolic Constitutions* 8.41.2 where the righteous rest in the bosoms of Abraham, Isaac and Jacob).

[36]Targumim are the translations of Hebrew Scriptures into vernacular, especially those into Aramaic. The process of translation often involved considerable paraphrase and interpretive license. These were recited orally from memory in the synagogue services.

[37]Midrashim are rabbinic commentaries on Hebrew Scriptures, originally transmitted orally, until their collation into written form early in the Christian Era.

[38]Evans, *Word and Glory*, 114-24.

[39]Evans, 133.

[40]They were only using *Targum Onqelos* and *Targum Pseudo-Jonathan*. *Memra* is much more frequent in *Targum Neofiti*. Borgen, "Observations on the Targumic Character."

[41]Evans, *Word and Glory*, 124-25.

[42]McNamara, *Targum and Testament*, 101-2. See also his "*Logos* of the Fourth Gospel," 115-17.

[43]Evans, *Word and Glory*, 77-99. We may compare the phrase "in the beginning" in Genesis and John, and the activity of God—especially the deity's relationship to speech, light and darkness, life and creation of humanity. We think back to Philo and his interpretation of this creation text against the background of God's intimate friendship with humanity. A comparison with Exod. 33-34 finds the following as the background to vv. 14-18: the contrast between Moses and Jesus and the giving of the Torah on Sinai; grace is received in place of Law, that is, the new covenant.

[44]Exod. 33: 22-23 "I will cover you with my hand until I have passed . . . so that you may see my back; but my face is not to be seen."

[45]One notes the variants in v. 18.

[46]Evans, *Word and Glory*, 81: *pros* as "facing [God]". "Full of grace and truth" can be compared with Exod. 34:6, "abounding in steadfast love and faithfulness" (Hebr. *ḥesed*).

[47]Koester, *The Dwelling of God*, 102.

[48]Evans, *Word and Glory*, 137-40.

[49]And throughout Wisdom 10.1-19.22; cf. John 12:40; cf. also 1 Enoch 42:1-3.

[50]For a discussion of the School of Religion approach see John Ashton. He expounds Job 28, Prov. 8-9 and 30:1-4; Deut. 30:11-14; Bar. 3:9-4:4; Sirach and Wisdom and 1 Enoch 42:1-2.

[51]For a convenient chart of the development of these themes in the rest of the Gospel see Carson, *The Gospel According to John*, III (adapted from Robinson, *Twelve More New Testament Studies*, 68).

[52]Scott, *Sophia and the Johannine Jesus*.

[53]Scott, 13-14.

[54]Scott, 29. Schnackenburg, *Gospel According to St. John*, 1.492, observes that John may have used the masculine Logos as "more fitting than the feminine noun Sophia to present his pre-existing and incarnate Christ."

[55]Scott, *Sophia and the Johannine Jesus*, 43, quotes Engelsmann, *Feminine Dimension*, 28, to the effect that the goddess is called "virgin" not in the sense of *virgo intacta* but because she is not under the control of a male figure.

[56]Scott, *Sophia and the Johannine Jesus*, 50-52.

[57]Camp, "Wisdom and the Feminine," 291.

[58]Johnson, "Jesus, the Wisdom of God," 267.

[59]Johnson, 267. When we turn to Philo we find much more caution with regard to feminine Sophia, she is delegated to heavenly realms and the Logos takes her place and descends to the earth (Philo, *On Dreams* 2.242).

[60]Scott, 81. In Wisdom of Solomon she is given prominence, possibly to discourage devotion to the goddess Isis.

[61]Scott, 94.

[62]Scott, 94-112.

[63]Scott, 113.

[64]Scott, 115. He examines the "I am" sayings. He comments on the hospitality of Wisdom (Prov. 9:15) and sees some parallel with John 6:35-59, the Bread of Life discourses. He finds an affinity between Sirach. 29:21; 24:30 and John 20:29. Wisdom is associated with light in Sirach. 2:13 and Wis. 7:29-30. The door of the sheepfold could be anticipated in Wisdom as

"door" (Prov. 8:34-35): she is the door to knowledge and salvation (Scott, 122); Wisdom also is (or leads to) "life" ( Prov. 3:16; 8:35; 9:11; Wisd. 8:13) although not "resurrection."

[65]Johnson, "Jesus, the Wisdom of God," 28.

[66]Scott, 174-184.

[67]Scott, 184-198.

[68]Scott, 198-216.

[69]Scott, 216-234.

[70]Tobin, "Prologue of John."

[71]Particularly C.H. Dodd, *The Interpretation of the Fourth Gospel.* Cambridge: CUP, 1968 *passim.*

[72]Collins, "Aristobulus," 834-35.

[73]Tobin, "Prologue of John," 257.

[74]Tobin, 259.

[75]*On the Confusion of Tongues* 40-41.

[76]Tobin, 261.

[77]Tobin, 264. Compare John 20:22.

[78] (Philo *On the Confusion of Tongues* 63; cf. John 1:12, 13). In Philo, Wisdom is seen as the "first-born mother of all things" (*Questions and Answers on Genesis* 4.97), and "daughter of God" (*Questions and Answers on Genesis* 4.97, 4.243; *On Flight and Finding* 50-52). Cf. also *The Worse Attacks the Better* 54: "If you accord a father's honor to Him who created the world, and a mother's honor to Wisdom, through whom (*di'hēs*) the universe was brought to completion, you will yourself be the gainer."

[79]*On the Confusion of Tongues* 28, 146.

[80]Philo, *On Flight and Finding* 19, 101.

[81]Philo, *On Dreams* 1.39, 230.

[82]*On the Cherubim* 35.127; cf. *On Flight and Finding* 18: 95.

[83]*On the Creation* 8.30, 33.

[84]*On the Confusion of Tongues* 28, 146.

[85]Philo, *Questions and Answers on Genesis* 2.62.

[86]*On the Posterity and Exile of Cain* 48.169.

[87]E.g., Philo, *Questions and Answers on Exodus* 2.13.

[88]Philo, *Questions and Answers on Exodus* 2.68.

[89]Evans, *Word and Glory,* 107.

[90]Evans, 123.

[91]See *On the Creation* 134-135; *Allegorical Interpretation* 1.31-32, 53-55, 88-89, 90-96.

[92]The ritual is found in the covenant-making and its memorials. See Hermann, *Ritual Friendship.*

[93]Compare the *Memra* in the *targuimim* and the Logos in Wisd. 18:15-16.

[94]The judicious choice and testing of a friend over time is discussed by several classical writers.

[95]Fiore, "Sage in Select Genres," 8, n.4, italics mine.

[96]*On Friendship* 64, italics mine.

[97]Although Jesus does call Philip (John 1:43).

[98]Culpepper, *Johannine School*, 215-46, although he points out some important differences from the philosophical schools that he discussed in the earlier part of his book.

[99]Meeks, "The Man from Heaven." 50-51.

[100]Maher, ed., *Targum of Pseudo-Jonathan, Genesis*, 100.

[101]McNamara, ed., *Targum Neofiti 1: Genesis*, 140.

[102]Meeks, "The Man from Heaven." 51.

[103]See the works of J. Galot, *Etre né de Dieu, Analecta Biblica* 37 (Rome: Biblical Institue Press, 1969); P. Hofrichter, *Nicht aus Blut sonder monogen aus Gott geboren.* (Würzburg: Echter, 1978); Antonio Vicent Cernuda, " La doble generaciön de Jesucristo según John. 1, 13. 14" *EstBibl* 40 (1982) 313-344; "La doble generacíon de Jesucristo según John. 1,13,14" *EstBiblc* 40 (1982) 313-344 and "La huella cristolde Jesucristo según John. 1,13,14" Jesucristo según John. 1, 13. 14" *EstBiblc* 40 (1982), 313–44 and "La huella cristólogica de Jn 1,13 en el siglo II y la insólita audacia de esta fórmula joanea." *EstBiblc* 43 (1985), 275-320. in which he discusses the gnostic reaction to Irenaeus. For a full discussion see e.g., L. Sabourin, "Who was Begotten . . . of God" (John 1:13) *BTB* 6 (1976) 86-90 who argues that the singular reading may be origin; Michael Mees, " Joh 1,12.13 nach frühchristlicher Überlieferung" *BZ* 29 (1985) 107-15 who discusses the patristic evidence, Origen, Epiphanius, Ps. Athanasius, Tertullian, Aphraat, Clement of Alexandria, Justin, Irenaeus, Hippolytus, Cyprian and Ignatius; John W. Pryor, " Of the Virgin Birth or, the Birth of Christians? The Text of John 1:13 Once More" *NovTest* 3 27 (4, 1985), 296-318 who critiques the exegesis of Harnack, Galot and Hofrichter. On page 296 note 1 he lists proponents for the singular but he shows that there are not adequate grounds to reject the plural reading.

[104]See Bassler, "Mixed Signals," 635-46, for a discussion of other texts where Nicodemus appears. She sees Nicodemus as an essentially an ambiguous figure.

[105]See Schenke, "Der 'Dialog Jesu mit den Juden'," for a reconstruction of this pericope together with other texts of John which show Jesus in dialogue with the Jews. See also Pazdan, "Nicodemus and the Samaritan Woman," in which she compares and contrasts the two pericopes 3:1-21 and 4:1-42 and sees them as the central panel of a triptych framed by 1:19-2:25 and 4:43-6:69.

[106]Lindars, *The Gospel of John*, 149.

[107]Meeks, "The Man from Heaven," 52.

[108]Meeks, 54.

[109]A text approaching our passage is found in Eccl. 11:5 (the previous verse mentions the wind and sowing): "Just as you know not how the breath of life fashions the human frame in the mother's womb, So you know not the work of God which he is accomplishing in the universe."

[110]Plato, *Symposium* 208-210.

[111]See the more negative approach of Graefe, *Der Gespaltene Erōs*, 106-19.

[112]Compare John 1:49-51.

[113]Parallel ideas occur Philo, especially in his long and diffuse commentary on Gen. 15, *Who is the Heir.*

[114]*Symposium* 179B.

[115]*Symposium* 179A-B.

[116]Witherington, "The Waters of Birth."

[117]E.g., *Mishna, Tractate Abot* 3.1; 4 Ezra 8:8.

[118]Pope, *Song of Songs,* 496-97.

[119]Witherington, "The Waters of Birth," 156.

[120]Stol and Wiggerman, *Zwangerschap en gebooorte,* 59ff., cited by Pamment and Witherington (158).

[121]Witherington, 159.

[122]Witherington, 160.

[123]Lindars, "John and the Synoptic Gospels." See the parallel columns from 287.

[124]However, Lindars (Ibid. 293) asserts that John obtained the saying from a source independent of Matthew.

[125]Lindars, 290.

[126]Lindars, 291.

[127]Grese, "'Unless One is Born Again'."

[128]Odeberg, *The Fourth Gospel Interpreted.*

[129]Meeks, "The Man from Heaven."

[130]Meeks, "The Man from Heaven," 52.

[131]Grese, "'Unless One is Born Again'," 679-84.

[132]487-509, quoted by Grese, 682, italics mine.

[133]Grese finds the closest parallel to John 3 in the *Corpus Hermeticum* 13.

[134]Grese, 691.

[135]Grese, 683.

[136]For a discussion of this see Klaiber, "Der irdische und der himmlische Zeuge."

[137]Grese, "'Unless One is Born Again'," 689.

[138]Grese, 692.

[139]I do not address myself to John 4: feminist scholars have given this text a great deal of attention. See the bibliography listed in van Belle, *Johannine Bibliography*, 213-18.

[140]For the important role of women in the Gospel of John see Brown, "Roles of Women."

[141]This account does not differ significantly from the Synoptic accounts (Matt. 14:13-31; Mark 6:30-44; Luke 9:10-17) save that the people attempt to make Jesus king (v. 15).

[142]Many scholars argue that vv. 52-59 are an addition to the text.

[143]Compare *Ketubot* 59b, that the duties of a wife include grinding and baking.

[144]Sandelin, 21.

[145]B. Lang, *Frau Weisheit. Deutung einer biblischen Gestalt* (Dusseldorf, 1975) 124. There is now an English edition, *Wisdom and the Book of Proverbs*. He cites Lang.

[146]It is the LXX which adds sacrificial details (see Sandelin, *Wisdom as Nourisher*, 73-81).

[147]See Mollenkott, *Divine Feminine*, 60-68, who discusses God as female homemaker. Lang, 23.

[148]Lang, *Wisdom and the Book of Proverbs*, 90-95.

[149]Lang, 96.

[150]Thus he offers a different interpretation from Sandelin (96). We note that Jesus is hostess in a desert place rather than a seven pillared house. Is this part of John's irony?

[151]He discusses the various Hebrew manuscripts (Sandelin, *Wisdom as Nourisher*, 27-28).

[152]That is his mother, although this might mean "first wife," but the parallelism suggests rather the former (Sandelin, 37).

[153]Sandelin refers to Gruber, "Motherhood of God"; Winter, *Frau und Göttin*; and Schmitt, "Motherhood of God." Num. 11:12; Deut. 32:18; Isa. 49:14f., 66:13; cf. Ps. 27:10.

[154]Sandelin discusses other passages which present Wisdom as a female teacher (Sirach 4:11 and Sirach 51; Sirach 1:11-20 and 6:18-37;. He also discusses the Qumran fragment (see Sanders, ed., *Psalms Scroll*, 42, Plate XIII) whose sense is ambiguous but appears to refer to Wisdom as both nurse and mother (Sandelin, *Wisdom as Nourisher*, 44).

[155]Sandelin also discusses Ps. 154 (found at Qumran, which is influenced by the Syriac version). This is the first text that witnesses to Wisdom present at an actual meal and the context might be the Essene community meal. She is present at the meal, primarily as a Teacher. But the psalm also alludes to her as hostess and nourisher.

[156]*Every Good Person is Free* 1-6; cf. *On the Special Laws* 1.321.

[157]*Every Good Person is Free* 13.

[158]*On the Creation* 158, cf. *Allegorical Interpretation* 3.161 and *On the Creation* 158.

[159]*On the Sacrifices of Abel and Cain* 78f.

[160]*Allegorical Interpretation* 3.52.

[161]*Allegorical Interpretation* 1.59.

[162]*On the Posterity and Exile of Cain* 122f. There are a number of other metaphors for Wisdom as nourisher (Sandelin, *Wisdom as Nourisher*, 89).

[163]*On the Migration of Abraham* 37. Sandelin, 89-92.

[164]Cf. Exod 17:6; Num 20:11; 1 Cor 10:1-4.

[165]*Allegorical Interpretation* 3.161ff., 169ff., and *On Flight and Finding* 137ff.

[166]Cf. *Allegorical Interpretation* 2.86.

[167]Cf. *On the Sacrifices of Abel and Cain* 86.

[168]*Allegorical Interpretation* 2.82; *On the Cherubim* 8-10; *The Worse Attacks the Better* 124. See Sandelin, 98-99 for Wisdom as wife; 100 for Wisdom as a stream; 103-6 the Word/Wisdom as cupbearer; 108 the association of light and nourishment; 115-28 Wisdom as the royal road.

[169]Sandelin, 105.

[170]The concept of Jesus coming down from heaven is close to Wisdom, who was sent by God from heaven (Sirach 24:3-11 and Wisd. 9:10). The phrase "bread of life" occurs in *Joseph and Aseneth* (Sandelin, 179), thus in an early Jewish literary text. Jesus' description of the "bread of life" coming down from heaven is probably reminiscent both of John 3:13 and Num. 11:9.

[171]The bread from heaven which Moses gave to the Israelite may mean the Law (*On the Change of Names* 258ff.; cf. John 1:17). The manna also signifies the Law in rabbinic sources (e.g., *Med Ex* 13.17).

[172]Sandelin, 184.

[173]For good discussions of the *targumic* material behind this text see Borgen, *Bread from Heaven*; Malina, *Palestinian Manna Tradition*; and Muñoz, Léon, "El sustrato targúmico."

[174]This is suggested by "bleeding host" stories which are found in the Coptic, Latin and other traditions. This is to misunderstand the body of Christ in the Eucharist which can be none other than the resurrected presence of the savior.

[175]*The Worse Attacks the Better* 115ff.

[176]Cf. *On Drunkenness* 31, *On the Confusion of Tongues* 49.

[177]I have not be able to find the phrase "flesh and blood".

[178]Bynum, *Holy Feast and Holy Fast*, 65 and 330.

[179]See Mollenkott, *Divine Feminine*, 44-47 (cf. Ps. 102:6, which may or

may not refer to a pelican). The Latin *Bestiary* (a very popular work in the Middle Ages) says of the pelican that ". . . the parents . . . kill them. Three days afterwards, the mother pierces her breast, opens her side, and lays herself across her young, pouring out her blood over the dead bodies.

> In the same way, Our Lord Jesus Christ . . . begets and calls us into being out of nothing. We, on the contrary, strike him in the face. . . . That was why he ascended into the height of the cross, and, his side having been pierced, there came from it blood and water for our salvation and eternal life. (cited in Mollenkott).

[180]Since I wrote this section I have received some very helpful information of Rabbi Marc Bregman. He refers to Dr. Shmuel Kottek's work on "Breast-Feeding in Jewish Sources- History and Halakhah" *Assia* 4 (1983), 275-286. He refers to a paragraph on "Mother's Milk: Source and Nature." I wish to thank Professor James Vanderkam for translating a modern Hebrew article on lactation for me.

[181]57, note 3, see also *Tos Nid* II.

[182]Kottek then mentions *Mishnah Makhshrin* that links Milk and Blood, and also passages in the Tosephot and in Maimonides, Laws of Impurity of Goods 10:5.

[183]Dr. Bregman refers me also to Steinberg's *Encyclopaedia of Medical Halahah*, which I have been unable to obtain yet. For male lactation see Rancour-Laferriere, *Signs of the Flesh*, 213.

[184]Kottek, S. "Breast Feeding in Ancient Jewish Sources" *Korot*, vols. 27-28, 1980, 46-57.

[185]Rancour-Laferriere, 293.

[186]Bynum, *Jesus as Mother*, 132.

[187]Bynum, 133.

[188]*Etymologiae* 11.1.77, transl. Brehaut, *Encyclopedist*, 217. I have quoted from Wood, "The Doctors' Dilemma," 719. The author discusses the difficulties of the ecclesiastical doctors, especially Albert the Great and Thomas Aquinas, the difficulty of reconciling Mary's immaculate conception, her lactation and, as some averred, her lack of menstruation. The difficulty arose in that they could not conceive of one who did not menstruate being able to provide milk!

[189]Quoted by McLaughlin, "Survivers and Surrogates," 115.

[190]*Gynaecology* 8-11.

[191]Cf. the texts from Gnosticism and the *Odes of Solomon* above (pp. 46–47).

[192]*Against Heresies* 3.24.1. The same quotation appears in chapter 4. Later the side of Christ is associated with the nourishment from his breasts.

[193]See Bradley, "Patristic background."

[194]Compare also *Enarrationes in Psalmos* on Pss. 8; 26; 30; 32; 58; 64.

[195]Ambrose, *Concerning Virgins* 1.5.22, PL 16,195.

[196]*Homilies on the Gospel of Matthew* 76.5. The idea of suckling from the breasts of Christ is also found in commentaries on the Apocalypse of John in expositions of the vision of Christ in Rev. 1, where he wears a golden girdle round his breasts. I am pursuing some research on this.

[197]See Bynum, *Holy Feast*, chap. 9, "Woman as Body and as Food"; chap 10, "Women's Symbols."

[198]Corrington, "Milk of Salvation."

[199]Corrington, 398.

[200]Philostratus, *Life of Apollonius of Tyana* 8.7.4; Homer, *Odyssey* 9.27; Euripides, *Daughters of Troy* 566.

[201]Price, *Kourotrophos*, 1-2.

[202]Price, 1.

[203]Price, 3.

[204]Price, 2-9.

[205]Tran, *Isis Lactans.*

[206]Tran, 1. In the Egyptian iconography the birth of the king may sometimes be depicted through the throne and thus Isis becomes the mother of the Pharaoh. At times it is difficult to distinquish the Virgin Mary with Christ from Isis with Horus (Corrington, "The Milk of Salvation," 399).

[207]Corrington, 399.

[208]Formula from the *mammisi* at the Temple of Sobek and Horus at Kom Ombo, quoted by Corrington, 399-400.

[209]Corrington, 400.

[210]Price, *Kourotrophos*, 201.

[211]Corrington, 202.

[212]Kloppenborg, "Isis and Sophia," 78. See also Mack, *Logos und Sophia*; and Schüssler Fiorenza, Elisabeth. "Wisdom Mythology and the Christological Hymns of the New Testament," pages 17-41 in *Aspects of Wisdom in Judaism and Early Christianity.* Robert L. Wilken, editor. Studies in Judaism and Christianity in Antiquity 1, (Notre Dame: University of Notre Dame Press), 1975.

[213]Cf. the work translated by Vanderkam, note 180.

[214]*On Drunkenness* 31.10; 33, but also see "right reason" (*orthos logos*) as nurse.

[215]Corrington, "The Milk of Salvation," 406-7.

[216]See Dio Chrysostom, *Discourses* 33.7, 44.

[217]Compare also Paul in 1 Cor. 3:2; 1 Pet. 2:2-3; and 1 Thess 2:7. See Malherbe, "Gentle as a Nurse."

[218]Corrington, "The Milk of Salvation," 407-13, also asks why lactation

was predicated of the Father/Son/Spirit rather than Mary, who is rarely seen suckling the child Jesus in the first five centuries of the Christian era; instead, male characteristics are attributed to her.

[219]Adolf de Ceuleneer, "La Charité romaine dans la littérature et dans l' art." *Acad. Royale d' archaeologie de Belgique*, 67 (1919) 175-206.

[220]de Ceuleneer, 181.

[221]de Ceuleneer, 182.

[222]*Natural History* 7:36.

[223]de Ceuleneer, 182-3.

[224]*Dionys*, 26: v. 101ff.

[225]Cf. Hosea 11.1-7.

[226]Found in Papyrus 66.

[227]See Juan B. Cortéz, "Yet Another Look at John 7, 37-38." *CBQ* 29 (1967) 75-86, on the punctuation (77-78) and the grammatical argument (78).

[228]Cortéz, 78-79.

[229]He also comments on contemporary rabbinic parallels (Cortéz, 80).

[230]Cortéz, 80.

[231]See also Sandro Leanza, Testimonianze della Tradizione Indiretta su Alcuni Passi del N.T. (Gion. vii, 37-38 e altri passi." *Rivista Biblica* 15 (1967) 407-18), who directs his study especially to the baptismal significance of our texts as seen in New Testament and patristic texts.

[232]John 3:18,36; 6:35,47; 11:25; 14:12 and 12:44.

[233]Zane C. Hodges, "Rivers of Living Water-John 7:37-39." *Biblio. Sacra* 3.136 (1979), 239-248.

[234]Compare also Luis F. Ladaria, "Juan 7, 38 en Hilario de Poitiers. Un analisis de Tr.Ps. 64,13-16." *Estudios Eclesiasticos* 52 (1977) 123-128 who in explaining Ps. 64 refers to John 7:38. It is accommodated to the fertility of the earth at the time of God's visitation. Hilary combines John 4:14 and 7:38, and shows that the Spirit is called "river." The second time Hilary quotes the texts, he refers it to the gifts of the Spirit, but the river does not come from the human being but from God.

[235]Cf. Leanza, 81. Cf. also Miguel Balagué, "Flumina de ventre credentis (John 7, 38)." *Estudios Biblicos* 26 (1967), 187-201, this reference 192-93 who, as well as searching for the Hebrew Scriptures behind this passage also discusses the Feast of Tabernacles (199-200).

[236]M. Miguens, "El Agua y el Espíritu en John 7,37-39." *Estudios Biblicos* 31 (1972) 369-98.

[237]Miguens, 374-375.

[238]Miguens, 375-379.

[239]Miguens, 379-384.

[240]Miguens, 383.

[241] Since I completed this book, Judith E. McKinlay's *Gendering Wisdom the Host, JSOT,* no 216 (Supplement Series) Sheffield: Sheffield Academic Press, 1996, has appeared

## *Chapter 8*

[1] I cannot discuss the resurrection fully in this monograph but hope to do so in the future.

[2] The text is symbolic, it illustrates the fact that the disciples looked upon Jesus as sovereign. See de Kruijf, "More than Half a Hundredweight."

[3] Farmer, "Palm Branches in John 12:13."

[4] The rare word *baion* (palm) is found in 1 Macc. 4:52-59.

[5] The title occurs only on the lips of Jesus except here and in Acts 7:56.

[6] Cf. 4 Macc 14:13.

[7] *To Marcella* 16; Josephus *Jewish Antiquities* 15.27 of enticing (*helkusai*) Anthony into sexual pleasures.

[8] Muñoz in *Gloria de la Shekina,* 225.

[9] Odeberg, *The Fourth Gospel,* 166 n.1.

[10] ". . . es idiomaticio en la literatura rabínica para expresar la experiencia religiosa." E.g., *Canticles Rabbah* 1.25. (In rabbinic literature this is an idiom expressing religious experience).

[11] Forestell, *Word of the Cross.*

[12] Müller, *Die Geschichte der Christologie.* This differs from Müller's thesis of a vicarious and expiatory aspect of Jesus' death as seen in John 1:29; 3:16; 10:11, 15, 17; 11:50.

[13] Forestell, 2.

[14] Forestell, 40.

[15] Forestell, 43.

[16] Forestell, 46-47.

[17] Forestell, 60-61.

[18] Forestell, 119-20.

[19] Later I should like to consider whether the washing of feet could be a "ritualistic admission of defeat" (see Herman, *Ritualised Friendship,* 57).

[20] For the relationship of the footwashing to the Synoptic Gospels see Sabbe, "The Footwashing in John 13," 279-308 and Keinknecht, "Johannes 13," 361-88, see esp. 370-71 and 380 for useful charts. I shall not discuss the structure or composite character of the pericope of Jesus washing the feet of his disciples text but I refer the reader to Frédéric Manns, M. Sabbe, Fernando F. Segovia, G. Richter, and E. Lohse. Manns, "Le Lavement des Pieds," works particularly with the *inclusiones,* parallelism and the concentric structure in the text and discerns that the structure throws

into high relief laying down one's life and Jesus' return to the Father as a new Exodus. The washing is a prophetic gesture. He studies the *Targumim* and *Midrash* of Gen. 18:4 (Abraham washing his guest's feet) which associate the text with the passover, the Messiah and give it an eschatological interpretation. Sabbe, "The Footwashing in John 13," studies especially the stylistic features of the pericope (283-87). He also discusses the use of *trogō (291)*. Segovia, "John 13, 1-20, The Footwashing," gives a good summary of the exegesis of the text and harmonizing and redactional approaches. Richter, *Die Fusswaschung*, gives a history of the exegesis of this passage from the Latin Fathers to the twentieth century. Also see Lohse, *Die Fusswaschung (Joh 13:1-20)*.

[21]Richter, "Die Deutung des Kreuzedtodes Jesus," 21.

[22]Richter, 25. Cf. Beutler, "Die Heilsbedeutung des Todes Jesu," 188-89.

[23]I cannot agree with thesis of J. Duncan M. Derrett. Derrett, *The Victim.*

[24]Or, "to the end."

[25]Ball, "S. John and the Institution."

[26]Ball, 61.

[27]Ball, 63. Augustine, *Homilies on the Gospel of John* 62.5 disagrees. Origen, *Commentary on the Gospel of John* 32.13.30/24.16 (see G.C.S. *Origenes* IV, 468).

[28]*Teleō* is used with reference to the candidates in the mystery religions.

[29]In John it is not a Passover celebration.

[30]Compare Socrates in Plato's *Apology*. See also Segovia, *Farewell of the Word*, 1-48, for a critical survey of John 13-17 as a Farewell Speech in the Greco-Roman tradition.

[31]Grossouw, "A Note on John XIII 1-3," sees a refusal to undergo the washing as refusing "to have faith in the sense of Jesus' crucifixion", that is, a flight from the *scandalum crucis.*

[32]He sees the word *poiein* as a Johannine expression for the eschatological work of Jesus.

[33]Cf. Hultgren, "The Johannine Footwashing."

[34]Levine, "Symbolism of the *Pedilavium*."

[35]Levine, 24.

[36]Hayward, ed., *Targum of Jeremiah.*

[37]Schneiders, "The Foot Washing."

[38]Cf. Malatesta, "Entraide fraternelle," but he speaks of the footwashing as a supreme act of love, the manifestation of the compassion of God, but he does not actually express himself in terms of friendship.

[39]See Beutler's discussion (190-92) of *huper* in John 11:50-52 and 18:14; cf. 1 John 2:2; 4:20 (check), "Die Heilsbedeutung des Todes Jesu." He considers 6:51c as post-Johannine (191).

[40]Lucian, *Toxaris, or Friendship* 27-34. I agree with Pervo (21) that these

tales contain a great deal of irony and may, indeed, be a critique of male friendship depicted in romantic novels.

[41]Von Rohden, "Die Handlungslehre," 83.

[42]See Kathleen E. Corley, *Private Women, Public Meals.* Peabody, Mass.: Hendrickson, 1993, 102-106 for an analysis of the Markan account, she sees the unnamed woman as an "excellent example of Markan discipleship."

[43]Elisabeth Schüssler Fiorenza, *In Memory of Her*, N.Y.: Crossroad, 1992, 330-331.

[44]He continues: Höhepunkt der Hausgemeinschaft ist die Tischgemeinschaft der *Bundesfreunde.* Wenn Jesus zu Petrus sagt: "Wasche ich dich nicht, so hast du keinen Anteil an mir," dann steckt darin ein *Bundesultimatum: Freund oder Feind:* Jünger, den ich erwähle, oder feindlich Fremder, der mich verleugnet und den ich verleugne." *Sind die zwölf Jünger der Erstling einer Freundwelt Gottes,* die durch Jesus Fusswachung aus der Bundesfremde der nächsten Stunden, aus Untreue und Feindschaft in gerreinigt *Bundesfreundschaft* (15,15) hinübergezogen (12,32) werden? (83, italics mine).

[45]Hultgren, 541.

[46]*Joseph and Aseneth* 20.4-5.

[47]Hultgren, 542.

[48]Hultgren sees "being clean" (John 13:10-11) as a necessary preparation for salvation.

[49]Herman, *Ritualised Friendship.*

[50]Aristotle saw great difficulty in persons from different social classes becoming friends.

[51]Herman, 10.

[52]Compare Judas Iscariot's interest in money.

[53]Herman, 11. See Polybius, *Histories* 20.5-6; Xenophon, *History of the Affairs of Greece* 4.1.39.

[54]Herman, 41-43.

[55]Herman, 16.

[56]These friendships were often arranged with people who lived at considerable distances from the beneficiary party.

[57]Cf. Aristotle, *Great Ethics* 2.1211a46.

[58]Herman, 43.

[59]Herman, 44.

[60]Isocrates, *Oration 4: To Panegyricus* 43. Herman, *Ritualised Friendship,* 46, remarks that war was often the context of these friendships.

[61]Herman, 46-54.

[62]See Xenophon, *History of the Affairs of Greece* 4.1.29-31.

[63]Herman, 50.

⁶⁴This gift-giving differed from ordinary gift bestowal in the following features: the counter gift must be presented promptly; the gifts of benefactor and beneficiary must be commensurate; the gift must possess both utilitarian and symbolic value; they were not at all commercial, rather "They filled a psychological need, the need to translate every state or quality into a symbol. . . ." and they created an obligation which, ideally, would be permanent (Herman, *Ritualised Friendship*, citing Finley, *World of Odysseus*, 123).

⁶⁵See Finley, *World of Odysseus*, 89, 99-104. Finley (100) says, "Guest-friend and guest-friendship were far more than sentimental terms of human affection. In the world of Odysseus they were technical names for very concrete relationships, as formal and as evocative of rights and duties as marriage."

⁶⁶Herman, *Ritualised Friendship*, 50, quoting Finley, *World of Odysseus*, 123. Sometimes there was a blood bond, where the parties drank blood (Herman, 54). See Tegnaeus, *Blood-Brothers*.

⁶⁷Tegnaeus, *Blood-Brothers*. (New York: Philosophical Library,1952). His discussion of the classical texts is on pages 19-23. The original texts include: Herodotus, *Hist*, 3.8;4.70; Lucian,*Toxaris*, . . . Sallust, *Catilina*, 22; Dio Cassius, 37.46a; Plutarch, *Vita de Cicero*, 10.14; Florus, *Hist*, 4.1; Tertullian, *Apol* 9; Valerius Maximus, 9. 11,2.3.; Diodorus Siculus, II, 562f..

⁶⁸Nicol, "Jesus' Washing the Feet."

⁶⁹Aeschines, *Against Ctesiphon* 224.

⁷⁰Thom, p. 12.

⁷¹Diogenes Laertius, *Lives and Opinions of Eminent Philosophers* 8.33.

⁷²Diogenes Laertius, *Lives and Opinions of Eminent Philosophers* 8.35.

⁷³Vernard Eller, *The Beloved Disciple, His Name, His Story, His Thought*. Grand Rapids, Michigan: Eerdmans, 1987.

⁷⁴Eller, *Beloved*, 58, also suggests that he was the author of the Fourth Gospel.

⁷⁵Eller, 54.

⁷⁶Eller, 55.

⁷⁷Eller, 57.

⁷⁸Eller, 60.

⁷⁹Eller remarks that it would be very natural to see Jesus giving his mother into the care of a close friend.

⁸⁰Compare Perkins, *Love Commandments*, 104-11.

⁸¹See Keinknecht, "Johannes 13," 376, for a discussion of the relationship between Luke 22:24-27 and John 13:34f.

⁸²Sabbe, "The Footwashing in John 13," 298-305. Sabbe points out the parallelism between the foot washing and John 12:1-8, the woman anointing Jesus. He finds linguistic affinity, a parallelism in the behaviour of

Judas, the sympotic nature of the scenes and a similarity in the two narratives' perspective towards Jesus' death. The washing may anticipate the future martyrdom of the disciples. He concludes:

> The symbolism of the anointing, an act of love and servitude of the woman, simultaneously also "done" in the perspective of Jesus' death, is continued in the symbolism of the footwashing, an ultimate act of love and servitude of Jesus *who will lay down his life for his friends.*

[83]Segovia, "John 13, 1-20, The Footwashing," 38.

[84]Segovia, 43.

[85]Robinson, *Twelve More New Testament Studies*, 77-80.

[86]A direct contradiction of Dan. 7:13.

[87]Robertson, 79. Herald Weiss compares five passages from Philo with the footwashing. Unwashed feet are a sign of moral turpitude. Weiss argues that in the Hellenistic synagogues, footwashing was thought to provide sanctification by the Spirit, and to open the soul to divine revelation. He asserts that the footwashing is related to the anointing of Jesus' feet by Mary. In John, it is the feet which are anointed, and it serves as a preparation for the triumphal entry. Weiss argues that by washing the feet of the disciples, Jesus prepares them for martyrdom: "He is symbolically announcing their burial, but he is also preparing them to have a vision of God as they walk with washed feet in the temple of God. Weiss also finds a correspondence with John 21 where Peter's martyrdom is predicted (Weiss, 320).

[88]Cf. also Malatesta, "Entraide fraternelle."

[89]Jesus included Iscariot in the footwashing, thus manifesting love for an "enemy."

[90]Weiss, 88.

[91]Cf. Beutler, "Die Heilsbedeutung des Todes Jesu," 194.

[92]See above 26–29.

## Chapter 9

[1]I was unable to procure Guiseppe Ferraro, *Mio-Tuo: Teologia del possesso reciproco del Padre e del Figlio nel Vangelo di Govanni.* Vatican City: Libreria Editrice Vaticana, 1994.

[2]I regret that I use such anachronistic language as "Trinity" and "persons" but these terms do enable me to link the biblical text with select systematic theological works. Compare Gruenler, *Trinity in the Gospel of John.* The book is useful but not detailed.

[3]Käsemann, *The Testament of Jesus,* 56-73.

[4]LaCugna, *God for Us,* 352.

[5]John 12:33 and 18:32 (signifying by what manner he would die) appear to be *obiter dicta* by the evangelist or redactor (cf. 11:51; 18:14).

[6]Compare Andrei Rubler, *The Holy Trinity*, Tetreyekor Gallery, Moscow. The icon depicts the Trinity as three persons. Doug Adams, *Transcendence of the Human Body in Art*, New York: Crossroad, 1991, (49) says that "Rubler's icon then invites movement into more dynamic relationships within the community." All the figures are looking away from themselves and it is impossible to fix one's gaze on only one.

[7]Johnson, *She Who Is*, 218.

[8]Compare John 8:42 (for I came from God).

[9]We might also understand the Father's sending of the Son in this way (John 3:17, 34; 5:36; 6:29, 57; 7:29; 8:42; 10:36; 11:42; 17:3,8; 18:1, 21, 23, 25; 20:21).

[10]LaCugna, *God for Us*, 228, refers to John 17:20-21, but the actual word *perichorēsis* is not found.

[11]LaCugna, 210.

[12]Rahner, *The Trinity*, 35-36.

[13]Kasper, *The God of Jesus Christ*, 275.

[14]Unamuno, *Del sentimiento trágico de la vida*; see also Engl. trans. *The Tragic Sense of Life*.

[15]The word "know" belongs to covenant vocabulary. Note how Jesus stresses knowledge and recognition in the Farewell Discourses.

[16]LaCugna, *God for Us*, 222.

[17]LaCugna, 257.

[18]LaCugna, 224, quoting MacMurray, *The Self as Agent* and *Persons in Relation*.

[19]LaCugna, *God for Us*, 228.

[20]LaCugna, but she cites only this Johannine text.

[21]John 15:5-9.

[22]Or reciprocal, having the same relationship, interchange of feeling between two parties.

[23]See especially Segovia, *Love Relationships*, which, though devoting itself mainly to the *agapē* in Johannine epistles, has an important section on the Gospel (81-172, esp. 133-72). The book has an excellent critique of secondary sources.

[24]In John 17:9-10 there is a mutuality of possession between the Father and the Son.

[25]See Moltmann, *Trinity and the Kingdom*, 30-36.

[26]Moltmann, 245.

[27]The genuine person originates in the mother-child relationship.

[28]Moltmann, 257.

[29]Cited by LaCugna, *God*, 259.

[30]LaCugna, 249.

[31]Hence the patron-client relationship is not pure friendship.

[32]LaCugna, 258, italics mine.

[33]Johnson, *She Who Is*, 217.

[34]Johnson.

[35]Johnson, 260, notes that MacMurray does not distinguish between "a community of persons" and "communion among persons." Zizioulas implements this.

[36]MacMurray, *Persons in Relation*, 164, quoted by LaCugna, *God for Us*, 259.

[37]Zizioulas, *Being as Communion*, 49-65.

[38]LaCugna, *God for Us*, 263.

[39]Zizioulas, *Being as Communion*, 49.

[40]LaCugna, *God for Us*, 265.

[41]Hardy and Ford, *Praising and Knowing God*.

[42]LaCugna, *God for Us*, 338.

[43]See Sobrino, *Christology at the Crossroads*, 214-18; Boff, *Jesus Christ, Liberator*, 111-17; Hellwig, *Jesus, the Compassion of God*, 85-95; Moltmann, *The Crucified God*, 149-53.

[44]See the interpretation of Jesus' cry of abandonment on the cross by Hans Urs von Balthasar, "Nell'abbandono da parte di dio del Figlio sulla croce, si è resa visibile l'opposizione economica più alta tra le persone divine" in *Mysterium paschale*, 341, quoted by Salvati, *Teologia Trinitaria della croce*, 23, n. 57.

[45]LaCugna, *God for Us*, 350.

[46]Moltmann, *Trinity and the Kingdom*, 152.

[47]Johnson, 198, 199.

[48]Johnson, 207, italics mine. See especially Salvati, *Teologia Trinitaria della croce*. He refers to the cross as . . . "quale momento di massima concentrazione, teologica, la fede trinitaria . . ." (81).

[49]Johnson, *She Who Is*, 208.

[50]Johnson, *She Who Is*, 216.

[51]John 14:16-17, 26; 15:26-27; 16:7b-11, 12-15.

[52]Johnson, *Spirit-Paraclete*.

[53]Johnson, *Spirit-Paraclete*, 35, remarks the use of the unusual personal verbs and, we add, the pronouns.

[54]Johnson, *She Who Is*, 196.

[55]Simoens, *La gloire d'aimer*.

[56]See Betz, *Der Paraklet*, esp. 117-92.

[57]Moltmann, *Trinity and the Kingdom*, 27-28.

[58]Moltmann, 42.

[59]Moltmann, 55.

[60]Moltmann, 56.

[61]Fernando Segovia suggests that the mutual love of the *philoi* is founded on the belief in the reality of Jesus' death, that is, "correct belief is the highest example of brotherly love" (127).

[62]Sandvik, "Joh. 15 als Abendmahlstext."

[63]Cf. *Didache* 9:2 and 10:2 "the holy vine of David."

[64]*Jewish Antiquities*, 15:395. Sandvik, 324.

[65]N.b. the allusion to Friend in Isa. 5 (three times in v. 1).

[66]Sometimes the image was associated with the tree of life.

[67]E.g., 1 QS 8.5, 11.3ff.; 1 QH 6.15ff.

[68]In John 2:21, *sōma* not *sarx*, stands for Jesus as temple.

[69]Sandvik, "Joh. 15 als Abendmahlstext," 327.

[70]Dodd, *Interpretation*, 411.

[71]Dodd, 140. Cf. Segovia, *Farewell of the Word*, 135.

[72]Carson, *Gospel According to John*, 510-24.

[73]See Segovia, *Farewell of the Word*, 125-31.

[74]See Segovia, 132.35.

[75]Bauckham, "Parable of the Vine."

[76]For a discussion of the literary *Gattung* of this text see Borig, *Der Wahre Weinstock*, 21-23. He does not accept the vine as either a parable or an allegory but rather as a *Bildrede* (22).

[77]Ps. 80:9-16; Isa. 5:1-7, 27:2-6; Jer. 2:21, 12:10-13; Ezek. 15:1-8, 17:1-21, 19:10-14; Hos. 10:1-2.

[78]Borig, 103. Cf. also Rom. 15:12, Acts 13:22, Rev. 22:16.

[79]See Goodenough, "Symbolism, Jewish," 569-70.

[80]Skehen and DiLella, *The Wisdom of Ben Sira*, 334.

[81]See Fournier-Bidox, "L'Arbre et la demeure."

[82]Schnackenberg, *Gospel According to St. John*, 3:107.

[83]Philo, *On Dreams*, 2.171 and *On the Change of Names*, 224.

[84]Sandelin, *Wisdom as Nourisher*, 93.

[85]For Philo, Wisdom is also the tree of life which gives power to life (*Allegorical Interpretation* 3.52). As we have said, Philo describes the tree of life as "virtue in the most comprehensive sense" (*Allegorical Interpretation* 1.59). It offers immortality (*On the Migration of Abraham* 37).

[86]Bauckham, "Parable of the Vine." Like Carson I do not agree with the literary genre, parable, proposed by Bauckham (144-148).

[87]There is a similar metaphor in *Odes of Solomon* 38.17-19 where, again, the planting of the Lord's vine is described.

[88]The reference to "inheritance" probably alludes to Isa. 60:21 where God's plantation inherits the land. Compare John 13:9 (*mēros*).

[89]Quoted from Bauckham, "Parable of the Vine," 89; cf. John 13:8.

[90]*Shepherd of Hermas Simile* 5.2.3-5, cf. 1 QH 8.24-25.

[91]See Borig, *Der wahre Weinstock*, 135-65.

[92]Quoted by Schnackenberg, *Gospel According to St. John*, 3:105.

[93]*Ginza*, 59.39-60.2.

[94]Borig, *Der wahre Weinstock*.

[95]Schnackenberg, *Gospel According to St. John*, 3:105, does not think that there is a great deal of correspondence between John 15 and the Mandaean vine imagery.

[96]Cf. Segovia, *Farewell of the Word*, 136, who recognizes the importance of this background yet feels that the Jewish background is more favorable.

[97]Borig, *Der wahre Weinstock*, 43.

[98]Borig, 63.

[99]Borig, 81.

[100]Borig, 199-221.

[101]Borig, 202.

[102]Borig, 202-3.

[103]Borig, 211.

[104]Borig, 211, n. 23.

[105]Borig, 222-223.

[106]John 14:7, cf. 1 John 4:13, 3:24.

[107]Borig, 225.

[108]Borig, 229.

[109]Borig, 230.

[110]Borig, 232. "Die Immanenz ist das Heil, hineingegeben in die Gemeinschaft der Brüder mit dem Sohn, die als solche aufgenommen ist in die göttliche Liebesgemeinschaft als ihr Urbild und ihren Grund."

[111]Borig, 241.

[112]Borig, 244.

[113]Borig, 246.

[114]Cf. the vine image in Isa. 5:1-10.

[115]John 2:4; 4:21-23; 5:25, 28; 7:30; 8:20; 12:23, 27; 13:1; 16:21, 32; 17:1 and perhaps 19:27.

[116]As quoted in Brownlee, "Messianic Motifs," 23-24. The text then describes the delivery of the woman pregnant with the asp. N.B. in line 9 there is a change from the singular to the plural, mothers and children.

[117]Holm-Nielsen, *Hodayot*, 54.

[118]Cf. Isa. 37:3b "Children are at the point of birth, but there is no strength to bring them forth," and 2 Sam. 22:5-7. Holm-Nielson, 54.

[119]Betz thinks that the woman is the community and he compares 7:20-22 where the psalmist is breast-feeding, and those suckling are his students. Holm-Nielsen thinks that this "approaches the grotesque."

[120]So Chamberlain, "Another Qumran Thanksgiving Psalm," and "Further Elucidation." See also Dupont-Sommer, "La mère du Messie."

[121]Baumgarten and Mansoor, "Studies in the New *Hodayot* II," 180ff.

[122]Holm-Nielsen, *Hodayot,* 55, lists those who understands this hymn as referring to an individual (Brownlee, Dupont-Sommer, M. Black and Licht) and those who interpret the text as referring to the messianic birth pangs in the eschatological era (Gaster, Silberman, Betz, Chamberlain, Mowinckel, Bardtke, Otzen, Woude and G. Hinson).

[123]Jeremias, *Der Lehrer der Gerechtigkeit,* does not discuss this text with respect to the Teacher of Righteousness. Brownlee, 26.

[124]Brownlee, "Messianic Motifs," 27.

[125]Brownlee, 27-28.

[126]Brownlee, 29.

[127]Nancy Klenk Hill, "Savior as Woman" ("Jesus Death in Childbirth").,*Crosscurrents* 39 (1, 1989), 1-9.

[128]I am not quite comfortable with the term "chiasmus" here.

[129]Hill, 2.

[130]Hill, 5.

[131]Hill, 7.

## Chapter 10

[1]Although glorious death in battle was especially emphasized in antiquity (see Williams, *Jesus' Death,* 144-46).

[2]In this same text Plato dreams of an army comprised of lovers and their favorites "in mutual rivalry of honor."

[3]Plato, *Symposium* 179C.

[4]*Symposium* 179E.

[5]This discourse on heroic love even unto death leads to Plato's reflection on the pregnancy of the soul, nurturing others in godly pursuits. He gives as examples Lycurgus and Solon.

[6]*Letters On Philosophy and Friendship* 9.10.

[7]Epictetus *Discourses* 2.7.3. On the theme of dying for a friend see also Plutarch, *Moralia: On Having Many Friends* 93E; Lucian, *Toxaris, or Friendship* 10.58-60; Achilles Tatius, *The Adventures of Leucippe and Clitophon* 3.22.1.

[8]Hengel, *The Atonement,* 6-15.

[9]This is a fictitious dialogue between Mnesippus and Toxaris where they compete with each other in telling stories of outstanding friendships. They limit themselves to five examples each (Lucian, *Toxaris or Friendship* 11).

[10]For the romance genre of these stories, see Hock, "Friendship in the Greek Romances," forthcoming.

[11]Lucian, *Toxaris* or *Friendship* 5-6. Lucian is, of course, dealing mainly with mythological or romantic material.

[12]Lucian, *Toxaris,* 6.

[13] *Toxaris* or *Friendship* 10.

[14] *Toxaris*, 36.

[15] Compare Heimann, "Ritualized Friendship," 37.

[16] *Toxaris*, 44.

[17] See 48 for the ceremony of the hide. *Toxaris*, 46.

[18] *Toxaris*, 53.

[19] Although Macentes may have died of his wounds.

[20] *Toxaris* 57-60.

[21] *Toxaris*, 61-62.

[22] See also the cases described in Droge and Tabor, *A Noble Death*: Achilles and Ajax (17-20), but these were cases of suicide.

[23] See Droge and Tabor on Plato's views (20-22), Aristotle (22-23), the Cynics (23-26), Epicureans (26-29), Stoics (29-39), Neo-Platonists (39-42).

[24] cf. Seneca *Letter* 70.17-18 and Plato *Gorgias* 527E.

[25] Cf. Plato, *Crito* 47B. Cf. also 4 Macc. 5:23-24, 6:10, 16:16, but especially 17:11-16.

[26] Cf. Epictetus *Discourses* 4.1.161. Cf. also 4 Macc. 17:23-24.

[27] See Xenophon *Memorabilia of Socrates*.

[28] *Lives of the Sophists* 8.

[29] cf. *Crito* 51B-C.

[30] See also Williams, *Jesus' Death*, 141-44 for the influence of Socrates' death. He quotes Jaeger, *Paideia*, 11 (13 in the 1943 edition):

> Socrates is one of the imperishable figures who have become symbolic. The real man . . . shed most of his personality as he entered history and became for all eternity a 'representative man'. It was not really his life or his doctrine . . . which raised him to such eminence, so much as the death he suffered for the conviction on which his life was founded.

[31] See Ruth E. Harder, *Die Frauenrollen bei Euripides*, Stuttgart: J. B. Metzlerschen and Poeschel, 1993.

[32] Cited by Williams, *Jesus' Death*, 159, from Schmitt, *Freiwilliger Opfertod bei Euripides*, 2.

[33] Anderson, "4 Maccabees," esp. 537-39. See also Hadas, ed., *Third and Fourth Books of Maccabees*. See further Renehan, "Greek Philosophic Background." *4 Maccabees*.

[34] 538.

[35] Cf. also Wisd. 3:4-6 which, speaking of the death of the righteous ones, uses the analogy of a whole burnt offering.

[36] Williams, *Jesus'Death*, 174.

[37] Williams, 175.

[38] Williams, 178-79.

[39]Williams, 186-87.

[40]Williams, 188.

[41]Williams, 194.

[42]Williams, 539.

[43]See David Winston, *The Wisdom of Solomon.* Anchor Bible Commentary, 43 (Garden City, New York: Doubleday, 1979), 111-150.

[44]See Attridge, *Hebrews,* 305-58.

[45]Williams, *Jesus' Death,* 138-141.

[46]Cf. John's use of *doxa* in the book of glory.

[47]Höistad, *Cynic Hero,* 61.

[48]Williams, 139.

[49]Cf. Philo *Every Good Person is Free* 106-9 and Plutarch *Moralia: Concerning Talkativeness* 505D. Diogenes Laertius *Lives and Opinions of Eminent Philosophers* 9.26-27 and 58-59.

[50]Droge and Tabor, *A Noble Death,* 123.

[51]Seeley, *Noble Death,* 145.

[52]Seeley, 150.

[53]*On Providence* 1.5.

[54]Thom, 21.

[55]Iamblichus, *Pythagorean Way of Life* 240.

[56]Williams, *Jesus' Death,* 203-29. But cf. Acts 8:32-36. 229.

[57]Forestell, *Word of the Cross.*

[58]Richter, "Die Deutung des Kreuzestodes Jesus;" Nicholson, *Death as Departure,* points out that some would wish to centre the discussion of the nature of Jesus' death around the *hyper* sayings (John 6:51; 10:11, 15; 11:50, 51, 52; 15:13; 17:19; 18:14), but this is to judge John from the point of view of the Synoptics.

[59]Käsemann, *The Testament of Jesus.*

[60]Käsemann, 4.

[61]Käsemann, 7.

[62]Appold, *The Oneness Motif.*

[63]Müller, "Die Bedeutung des Kreuzestodes Jesu." Cf. also Müller, *Die Geschichte der Christologie,* 22-36, where he argues that John 1:14, 16 refers to the earthly ministry of Jesus, the glory of the Logos in the performance of the signs.

[64]Nicholson, *Death as Departure,* 9.

[65]See Table 5 (52) for the distribution of descent language and Table 6 (58) for the distribution of the departure and ascent language. 21.

[66]3:14, 8:28, 12:32-34.

[67]Nicholson, 75-144.

[68]Nicholson, 81-82.

[69]Nicholson, 163.

[70]Much of this material is now published in *BBT*. Blank, "Die Verhandlung."

[71]Dauer, *Die Passionsgeschichte*.

[72]Meeks, *The Prophet-King*.

[73]Boismard and Lamouille, *L'Évangile de Jean*.

[74]De la Potterie, *The Hour of Jesus*. This dramatic structure is all the more striking because on the cross it would appear that Jesus is still wearing the purple, regal cloak.

[75]See Culpepper, *Anatomy of the Fourth Gospel*.

[76]Walbank, *The Hellenistic World*, 62-100. 62.

[77]Walbank, 64.

[78]Walbank, 63.

[79]I think particularly of the Egyptian queens.

[80]Walbank, *The Hellenistic World*, 74.

[81]Walbank, 74.

[82]Walbank, 76.

[83]However, one may compare and contrast Aristotle *Politics* 3.14.1.1284B.

[84]Walbank, 78.

[85]Dio Chrysostom, *Discourses* 1-4.

[86]The monarch was often seen as the "living law," although she or he must abide by the Torah.

[87]Walbank, 76.

[88]283.

[89]Walbank, *The Hellenistic World*, 79.

[90]Malina and Neyrey, "Honor and Shame."

[91]Plutarch, *Parallel Lives: Pyrrhus* 14.

[92]Diogenes Laertius, *Lives and Opinions of Eminent Philosophers* 4.44-47.

[93]Diogenes Laertius, *Lives and Opinions of Eminent Philosophers* 7.177.

[94]P. Jones, *The Roman World of Dio Chrysostom*.

[95]Jones, 115.

[96]Rostovtzeff, *Social and Economic History*, 120, quoted in Jones' *Roman World*, 115.

[97]Jones, 116.

[98]It is, therefore, not surprising that John in writing his account of the passion chose a dialogue between the representative of a tyrant (Pilate) and an ideal king (Jesus) as a vehicle to convey his ideas of ideal monarchy and true glory.

[99]Cf. the anecdote in Cicero *Tusculan Disputations* 5.32.91f.

[100]Höistad, *Cynic Hero*, 207.

[101]Hölstad, 207.

[102]See 213-214 for contrast between Diogenes and Alexander.

[103]Höistad, 184-89.

[104]B.A. Mastin, "The Imperial Cult and the Ascription of the Title *theos* to Jesus (John XX.28). *Studia Evangelica* 6 (=TU 112), ed. E.A. Livingstone, Berlin: Berlin Akademie, 1973, 353-65.

[105]Domitian's claim to divinity has been questioned by A.A.Bell, "The Date of John's Apocalypse." *NTS* 25 (1978-79) 93-102.

[106]Dio Cassius, *Roman History*, 67:8, 1.

[107]51:20, 6-8.

[108]Especially if John 21 is an appendix added later.

[109]Mastin, 364.

[110]Mastin, 365.

[111]John 12:13, John emphasizes the "king" motif more than the Synoptics.

[112]Aristeas, 258.

[113]Aristeas, 265.

[114]See esp. Meeks, *The Prophet-King*, 307-12.

[115]See Simonis, *Die Hirtenrede im Johannes-Evangelium*, and Kiefer, *Die Hirtenrede*.

[116]Höistad, 194.

[117]*On Mercy* 3.1, 11.4, 17.3, 24.2, 26.1 and 5.

[118]Dio Chrysostom, *Discourses* 1.1-14.

[119]Dio Chrysostom, *Discourses* 1.21.

[120]Dio Chrysostom, *Discourses* 1.22.

[121]Dio Chrysostom, *Discourses* 1.24; cf. *Discourses* 3.72-82.

[122]Dio Chrysostom, *Discourses* 1.26.

[123]Walbank, *The Hellenistic World*, 67.

[124]See Aymard, *La civilisation iranienne*, 401 (1.8); Bikerman, *Institutions des Seleucides*, 32 (E 6); Préaux, *Le monde hellénistique*, 1.210 (A 48).

[125]Walbank, *The Hellenistic World*, 67. On diadem see Ritter, *Diadem und Konigsherrschaft*, 1.62. Polybius *The Histories* 30.2.4. See also plates.

[126]See Reinhold, *History of Purple*.

[127]In John there appear to be two occasions upon which Jesus was mocked (Brown, *John* vol 2, 888). In the first Jesus is mocked as a prophet, in the second as monarch. N.B. the useful chart on the accounts of the mockery (*Brown*, 887).

[128]See Turner, *The Ritual Process*.

[129]Reference are found in Flint, "The Psalters at Qumran."

[130]Burstein, *Babyloniaca of Berossus*, 7, cited from paper of Flint, "The Psalters at Qumran," 5.

[131]Burstein observes that the *Sacaea* festival is not actually mentioned and he suggests that Berossus may be referring to the Persian substitute-king ritual.

[132]Dio Chrysostom *Discourses* 4.66-69.

[133]See Lucian, *Saturnalia* 2; 4; 7; 9; 13 and Martial, *Epigrams* 12.62.9-26.14:72.2; Virgil, *Aeneid* 8.3819-3827; Virgil, *Georgics* 2.536-540; Tacitus, *Annals* 13.15; Seneca, *Letter 18: On Festivals and Feasting* 1-14; Horace, *Satires* 2.7.1-5; Plutarch, *Parallel Lives: Sulla 18.5;* Dio Cassius, *Roman History* 60.19; Athenaeus, *The Deipnosophists* 14.44; Livy, *From the Founding of the City* 2.21.1, 22.1.19; compare also Fowler, *Roman Festivals.*

[134]We may compare also Plutarch *Parallel Lives: Pompey 24.6-8:* Mediterranean pirates mocking Romans.

[135]See G. MacRae, "Theology and Irony in the Fourth Gospel" in Stibbe, *Gospel of John,* 103-113. See 105 n. 2 for a reference to the Socratic origin of Johannine irony.

[136]Cited in Duke, *Irony in the Fourth Gospel,* 11-12.

[137]Baldick, ed., *Concise Oxford Dictionary of Literary Terms,* s.v. "irony."

[138]Duke, *Irony in the Fourth Gospel,* 9.

[139]Duke, 30.

[140]Barrett, *Gospel According to St. John,* 450.

[141]Meeks, *Prophet-King,* 70-71.

[142]Brown, *Gospel According to John,* 876.

[143]MacRae, "Theology and Irony" 111-112.

[144]See the full discussion by Merino, "El suplicio de la Cruz."

[145]See de la Potterie, "Jesus roi et juge."

[146]Walbank, *The Hellenistic World,* 68.

[147]Walbank, 69.

[148]Höistad, *Cynic Hero.* 184-95.

[149]Höistad, 188.

[150]Höistad, 194.

[151]Dio Chrysostom *Discourses* 4.2.

[152]Höistad, 195.

[153]cf. Epictetus *Discourses* 3.26.32.

[154]*Lives and Opinions of Eminent Philosophers* 6.7.

[155]Höistad, 198.

[156]Dio Chrysostom *Discourses* 14.21-24.

[157]Höistad, 201.

[158]Höistad, 195.

[159]Höistad, 204.

[160]Höistad, 198.

[161]Schwank, "'Was ist Wahrheit?'," 492.

[162]Ehrman, "Jesus' Trial."

[163]Raymond E. Brown, "Does the New Testament Call Jesus God?" in *Jesus God and Man.* London: 1968, 1-38.

[164]We look at the Gospel as a whole, not from the redactional point of view.

[165]See the chart in Carson, *Gospel According to John*, 11.

[166]e.g., John 3:16-17 cf. also vv. 31-36; although these appear to be the words of the Baptist; 5:19-47.

[167]8:39-59 cf. 10:31-33.

[168]Giblin, "Confrontations," 218.

[169]Sabbe, "The Arrest," 218-19.

[170]Comp. e.g., 12:31f., 12:35ff.

[171]Giblin, "Confrontations," 225.

[172]Compare Richter, "Blut und Wasser," 78, Jesus from the beginning of the garden scene is portrayed in a heroic fashion. Richter in this work discusses the objections of Celsus to a God who suffered.

[173]Euripides *Alcestis.* See Williams, *Jesus' Death*, 158-59.

[174]Euripides *Alcestis* 340-341.

[175]See Williams, 160-61, for examples from Latin literature. Cf. Williams, 159, from Schmitt, *Freiwilliger Opfertod bei Euripides*, 2. Euripides *Alcestis* 434; cf. 524, 383.

[176]See Williams, *Jesus' Death*, 151-53.

[177]See Williams, 153-56.

[178]Euripides, *Iphigeneia in Aulis* 1484-86.

[179]See Williams, 157-58.

[180]2 Macc. 7:21. See the whole paragraph vv. 20-23.

[181]Goldstein, *II Maccabees*, 312-13.

[182]See Renehan, "Greek Philosophic Background."

[183]Mary seems to have been a faithful disciple of Jesus (John 2:12).

[184]Cf. Antigone.

[185]Compare Ps. 37 (38):12 and 87 (88):9.

[186]Richard Atwood, *Mary Madalene in the New Testament Gospels and Early Tradition*, European University Studies, vol. 457, (Berlin and New York: Peter Lang, 1993), 48-53.

[187]Vernard Eller, *The Beloved Disciple. His Name, His Story, His Thought*, (Grand Rapids, Michigan: Eerdmans, 1987). The material of this book is interesting but the colloquial literary style is somewhat of a deterrent. For the identity of the beloved disciples see especially 70-73.

[188]Eller, *Beloved*, 54-59 argues that he, like Nicodemus, may have belonged to the Jewish intelligentsia.

[189]Eller, 64-70.

[190]See Eller's chart (*Beloved*, 62-63).

[191]We might compare Heb. 11:35, where the eulogy of faithful men and women changes from military heroes to women who are said to have "received their dead by resurrection." Attridge cites the widow of Zarephat (1 Kings 17:17-24); the Shunammite woman (2 Kings 4:18-37; cf. also Luke 7:11-17, 11:1-40, Acts 7:36-43).

[192]Although *Ta idia* is neuter in John 19:27.

[193]Pennells, "The Spear Thrust," discusses in detail the various manuscript and patristic traditions, some of which suggest that the spear thrust was made *before* the death of Jesus.

[194]Richter, "Blut und Wasser."

[195]For bibliography see Richter, 120-21, nn.1-24. See also Malatesta, "Blood and Water," who gives a survey of the interpretations of this text.

[196]Richter, 122.

[197]Article, "Blood" in *RAC.*

[198]Cited by Richter, 136.

[199]*tois tōn ichōrōn esbennuto stalagmois* . . .

[200]Richter, 129-30.

[201]Richter, "Blut und Wasser," 130, n. 65, points out that according to Irenaeus (*Against Heresies* 3.11.3), many Valentinians believed that the Logos was delivered from Mary like water through a reed.

[202]Also the ancients believed that the gods and goddesses did not have ordinary blood, but blood mixed with water (see Brown, *Gospel According to John,* 947). Richter, 130.

[203]137-38, Irenaeus *Against Heresies* 4.33.2; Origen *Commentary on the Gospel of John* 2.8; Novatian *Treatise on the Trinity* 10.

[204]Richter, "Blut und Wasser," 134.

[205]Richter, 135.

[206]We could also see the blood in the light of Exod. 24:8: the blood which sealed the first covenant (cf. Mark 14:24; Matt. 26:28; Luke 22:20; 1 Cor. 11:25).

[207]Heer, "Das johanneische Bild."

[208]With which one could compare the "signs" in the book of signs.

[209]Heer surmises that one can see the two dimensional love of Jesus in the form of the cross, the vertical to the Father and the horizontal to humankind. I am not certain that I agree with him here.

[210]Heer mentions that according to rabbinic thinking this is the essential part of the human body. He does not give the rabbinical reference.

[211]Some variants add a reference to the Spirit.

[212]The reader is referred to Brown, *Epistles of John,* 572-89, 594-99 and the bibliography pertinent to this (602-3). See also Bultmann, *Johannine Epistles,* 79-82, but especially 81 for a discussion of the "Johannine Comma."

[213]Brown, *Epistles of John,* 580.

[214]Heer does not think that this allusion is primarily to baptism or to the crucifixion; rather it alludes to the meaning of his coming, to bring Light (12:46) and Life (10:10) into the world and to rescue it (12:47).

[215]See Thiele, "Beobachtungen."

[216]e.g., Gal. 4:19; 1 Cor. 3:2, 9:7; cf. Heb. 5:12-13 and 1 Pet. 2:2.

[217]Brock, "Mysteries."

[218]I quote from Brock.

[219]Cf. Ephraem *Hymns on the Nativity* [*De Nat.*] 8.4.

[220]Brock, "Mysteries," 464. Sometimes the text of John 19:34 was linked with John 7:37-38 (the waters flowing from the heart of the believer and/or Christ).

[221]Brock, 465.

[222]Murray, "The Lance."

[223]Ephraem, *Hymns on the Nativity* [*De Nat.*] 8.4; in Murray, "The Lance," 225.

[224]Ephraem, *Harm.* 49.23-28; in Murray, "The Lance," 226.

[225]Grey, *Feminism*.

[226]Meland, *Faith and Culture*, 176.

[227]Meland; Grey, *Feminism*, 161.

[228]Grey, 177.

[229]Maitland, "Ways of Relating."

[230]Hos. 13:13, Mic. 4:10, Isa. 13:8, Jer. 4:31, Isa. 42:14-16; cf. also Jer. 31:15-22 and 31:2.

[231]Brown, *Gospel According to John*, 732, refers to Brownlee who suggests that the child is the risen Christ born from the community. I was not, however, able to locate his reference.

[232]Grey, *Feminism*, 188.

[233]Grey, 190.

[234]I do not intend to examine John 21, even though the use of love is prominent, because it would appear that this text is an addition to the Gospel.

[235]Giuseppe Ghiberti ("Il Dono Dello Spirito e I Poteri di Giov. 20, 21-23." In P-R. Tragan, ed. *La Parabole du 'Pasteur' et ses explications. Jean 10, 1-18. La genèse, les milieux littéraires* (Studia Anselmiana, 67), Rome: Ed. Anselmiana, 1980, 183-220) sees this pericope not only as the main point of this chapter but of the entire Gospel (185). He sees an analogy between the Nicodemus pericope and this one (186-7): he also compares 4:14 and 7:38f.

[236]Beasley-Murray, 379 quoted by Carson *John*, 646.

[237]M. G. de Durand, "Pentecôte Johannique et Lucanienne." *Bulletin de littérature eccelésiastique* 79 (1970) 97-126.

[238]See de Durand. "Pentecôte," 100-101.

[239]de Durand, 102.

[240]See Frans Neirynck, "Lc 24, 36-43. Un Récit Lucanien." *Mélanges offertes à Dom Jacques Dupont*, Lectio Divina 123; Paris: Cerf, 1985 655-80.

[241]It appears rather inconsistent to see Jesus transmitting the Spirit in John 19:30, and then breathing the same Spirit into the disciples on Easter

Sunday. Yet the text nicely complements the feminine creative activities of John 19 with creation. Jesus, like God breathes upon the clay to make Adam.

[242]In v. 20, we may also have an oblique reference to the pregnant mother image of John 16:21.

[243]Ghiberti, "Il dono dello spirito" 188.

[244]See M.-G. de Durand, who discusses Augustine's idea of the two glorifications of Jesus, one at the resurrection followed in John by the donation of the Spirit and one at the ascension followed in Luke by the donation of the Spirit.

[245]Luke has a different day for Pentecost, the Jewish Feast of Pentecost which commemorated the Covenant on Mt. Sinai, was celebrated fifty days after Passover.

[246]Cf. also Tob. 6:8 (S) and 11:11 (S); Job, 4:21; Sir. 43:4; Nah. 2:1 and Ezek. 21:31 and 22:20 (of God's wrath blowing like a furnace). Ezek. 37:5, 9-10 cf. 1 Kgs. 17:21, Elijah reviving the boy; Sir. 43: 4 of the sun breathing out heat; and Wisd. 15:11.

[247]Carson, *Gospel according to John*, 652-3.

[248]Although the dative may serve for both uses of the verb.

[249]Compare Vasclin Kesich, "Resurrection, Ascension, and the Giving of the Spirit." *Greek Orthodox Theological Review* 25 (1980) 249-60.

[250]Bertrand de Margerie, "La Mission Sacerdotale de Retenir Les Péchés en Liant les Pécheurs: Intérêt actuel et justification historique d'une exégèse tridentine." *Revue des Sciences Religieuses* 58 (1984) 300-17.

[251]de Margerie, 301-314.

[252]de Margerie, 302. Or there is a possibility of it meaning "reprimand" (303)?

[253]de Margerie, 303.

[254]Cyril, *In Jo 20:23* MG 74, 721.

[255]de Margerie, 305-6.

[256]de Margerie, 307.

[257]Gal. 18 (2) 538, see also L & S under *krateō*. See also Lampe, *Patristic Greek Lexicon* under *krateō*, C.

[258]Ghiberti discusses the Johannine concept of sin, it is lack of belief in Christ, belonging to the wrong "camp," being in darkness rather than light.

[259]One thinks also of swaddling an infant (Gr. *sparganoō, spargavizō*, swaddle, wrap up, Hebr. *htl* entwine enwrap). See Ezek 16:4 cf 30:21; Job 38:9 and Wisd 7:4. See Moshe Greenberg, *Ezekiel, 1-20* ABC 22, 1983, 274-5 and the bibliography there cited.

[260]Although it is the sins rather than the sinners which are forgiven and/or retained.

[261]Julius Robert Mantey, "Distorted Translations in John 20:23;

Matthew 16:18-19 and 18:18." *RExp* 78 (1981) 409-414 and also "Evidence that the Perfect Tense in John 20:23 and Matthew 16:19 is Mistranslated." *JournEvTheolSoc* 16 (1973) 129-138.

## *Chapter 11*

[1]*Artists Confronting the Inconceivable*, Award Winning Glass Sculpture. Ed. Irvin J. Borowsky (Philadelphia: American Interfaith Institute, 2nd printing 1993).

[2]Borowsky, Foreword.

[3]See, for example, Lioubon Savalyeva's *Sorrow*, two figures of intense sorrow, one standing and the other seated (pages 32-33). Their bodies are shot through with light. The artist comments, "There is still room in their hearts for tomorrow." Also Jan-Willem van Zijst, *Rosenhoet*, the crown of thorns which represents the brutal treatment of the innocent. The artist observes that it is "a timeless image that links sharp glass shards, man in his time and fragments in space." It contains both life and death, love and hate.

[4]Compare Elie Wiesel, *The Trial of God* (as it was held on February 25, 1649, in Shamgorod) (New York: Random House, 1979). In this play God is placed on trial after the pogrom on the village of Shamgorod. The innkeeper, Berish, is his chief accuser. The pogrom took place on the wedding day of his daughter. He was forced to watch her gang-raped, which led to a deep psychological condition. Only Satan, disguised as the Stranger, Sam, will act as defendant for God.

[5]Remark, for example, the words of a survivor of Auschwitz: "Under the pressure of a concentration camp you grew more closely attached to people than you would have done otherwise in such a short time" (Ella Lingens-Reiner, *Prisoners of Fear* 1948), quoted in *The Oxford Book of Friendship*, edited by D.J. Enright and David Rawlinson. (New York: OUP, 1992), 256.

[6]Elie Wiesel, *Night*, trans. by Stella Rodway (New York: Hill and Wang, ET, 1960), 71.

[7]See Appendix I.

[8]See Jane Dillenger, "The Magdalen: Reflections on the Image of Saint and Sinner in Christian Art." Pp. 28-50 (ch. 2) in her *Image and Spirit in Sacred and Secular Art*. New York: Crossroad, 1990. Dillenberger discusses the figure of Magdalen in Picasso's *Crucifixion*, 1930.

[9]See *A Dictionary of Biblical Tradition in English Literature*, edited by David Lyle Jeffrey, (Grand Rapids, Mich.: Eerdmans, 1992), art.: Judas Iscariot.

[10]In *Chapters into Verse*. Vol. 2, edited by Robert Atwan and Laurance (Wieder. New York: OUP, 1993), 191.

# Bibliography

Aldredge-Clanton, Jann. *The Search for the Christ-Sophia. An Inclusive Christology for Liberating Christians.* Mystic, Conn.: Twenty-Third Publications, 1994.

Amand de Mendieta, Emmanuel. *Fatalisme et liberté dans l'antiquité grecque: Recherches sur la survivance de l'argumentation morale antifataliste de Carneade chez les philosophes grècques et les théologiens chrétiens des quatre premiers siècles.* Amsterdam: A. M. Hakkert, 1973.

Anderson, H. "4 Maccabees (First Century A.D.)." Vol. 2, pp. 531–564 in *The Old Testament Pseudepigrapha.* Edited by James H. Charlesworth, 2 vols. Garden City, N.Y.: Doubleday, 1985.

Appold, Mark L. *The Oneness Motif in the Fourth Gospel: Motif Analysis and Exegetical Probe into the Theology of John.* Wissenschaftliche Untersuchungen zum Neuen Testament, 2/1. Tübingen: J.C.B. Mohr, 1976.

Aquinas, Thomas, *Summa Theologiae.* Vol. 34: 3a. 46–52. London: Blackfriars; Eyre & Spottiswoode, 1963.

Arnold, Edward V. *Roman Stoicism, Being Lectures on the History of the Stoic Philosophy.* Cambridge: The University Press, 1911.

Ashton, John. "The Transformation of Wisdom: A Study in the Prologue of John's Gospel." *New Testament Studies* 32 (1986): 161–286.

Attridge, Harold W. *The Epistle to the Hebrews.* Hermeneia, A Critical and Historical Commentary on the Bible. Philadelphia: Fortress Press, 1989.

Atwood, Richard, *Mary Magadalene in the New Testament Gospels and Early Tradition.* European University Studies, vol 457, Berlin and New York: Peter Lang, 1993.

Aulén, Gustaf. *Christus Victor: An Historical Study of the Three Main Types of the Idea of Atonement.* Translated by A. G. Hebert, New York: Macmillan, 1969.

Aymard, André. *La civilisation iranienne.* Paris: Payot, 1952.

Baldick, Chris, editor. *The Concise Oxford Dictionary of Literary Terms.* Oxford: Clarendon Press, and New York: Oxford University Press, 1990.

Balagué, Miguel, "Flumina de ventre credentis (John 7, 38)." *Estudios Biblicos* 26 (1967) 187–201.

Ball, R. M. "S. John and the Institution of the Eucharist." *Journal for the Study of the New Testament* 23 (1985): 59–68.

Balthasar, Hans Urs von. *Mysterium Paschale*, translated by Aidan Nichols. Vol. 3, Ch. 9 of *Mysterium Salutis Grundriss heilsgeschichtlicher Dogmatik*. Edinburgh: T & T Clark, 1990.

Banks, Robert J. *Paul's Idea of Community: The Early House Churches in Their Historical Setting*. Grand Rapids, Mich.: Eerdmans, 1980. Reprinted. Peabody, MA: Hendrickson, 1994.

Bardtke, Hans. "Considérations sur les cantiques de Qumrân." *Revue biblique* 53 (1956): 220–233.

_____. "Das Ich des Meisters in den Hodajoth von Qumrân." *Wissenschaftliche Zeitschrift der Karl-Marx-Universität Leipzig* 6 (1956–1957) 93–104.

_____. *Die Handschriftenfunde am Toten Meer: Die Sekte vom Qumrân*. Berlin: Evangelische Haupt-Bibelgesellschaft, 1958.

_____. "Die Loblieder von Qumrân." *Theologische Literaturzeitung* 81 (1956): cols. 149–154, 589–604, 715–724; 82 (1957): cols. 339–348.

Barr, James. *The Semantics of Biblical Language*. London: SCM Press and Philadelphia: Trinity Press International, 1991.

Barrett, Charles K. *The Gospel According to St. John: An Introduction with Commentary and Notes on the Greek Text*. Second edition. Philadelphia: Westminster Press, 1978.

Barth, Karl. *Church Dogmatics*. Edited by G. W. Bromiley and T. F. Torrance. Second ed. 4 vols. Edinburgh: T. and T. Clark, 1936–69.

Bassler, Jouette M. "Mixed Signals: Nicodemus in the Fourth Gospel." *Journal of Biblical Literature* 108 (1989): 635–646.

_____. "The Widows' Tale: A Fresh Look at 1 Tim 5:3–16." *Journal of Biblical Literature* 103 (1984): 23–41.

Bauckham, Richard. "The Parable of the Vine: Rediscovering a Lost Parable of Jesus." *New Testament Studies* 33 (1987): 84–101.

Baumgarten, Joseph and Menahem Mansoor. "Studies in the New *Hodayot* (Thanksgiving Hymns) I." *Journal of Biblical Literature* 74 (1955): 115–24.

_____. "Studies in the New *Hodayot* (Thanksgiving Hymns) II." *Journal of Biblical Literature* 74 (1955): 188–95.

_____. "Studies in the New *Hodayot* (Thanksgiving Hymns) III." *Journal of Biblical Literature* 75 (1956): 107–113.

_____. "Studies in the New *Hodayot* (Thanksgiving Hymns) IV." *Journal of Biblical Literature* 76 (1957): 139–148.

Beardslee, William A., *et al.*, editors. *Biblical Preaching on the Death of Jesus*. Nashville, Tenn.: Abingdon Press, 1989.

Benjamin, Don C. "Israel's God: Mother and Midwife." *Biblical Theology Bulletin* 19 (1989): 115–120.

Benz, Ernst. *Der gekreuzigte Gerechte bei Plato, im Neuen Testament und in der alten Kirche.* Wiesbaden: F. Steiner/Mainz; Verlag der Akademie der Wissenschaften und der Literatur, 1950.

Berliner, Rudolf. "'God is Love'." In *Essays in honor of Hans Tietze, 1880–1954,* edited by E. Gobrich, J. S. Held and Otto Kurz, pp. 143–160 Wildenstein: Gazette des Beaux-Arts, 1950–1958.

Betz, Otto. "Die Geburt der Gemeinde durch den Lehrer (Bemerkungen zum Qumranpsalm 1 QH III, 1 ff.)" *New Testament Studies* 3 (1957): 314–326.

_____. *Der Paraklet: Fürsprecher im häretischen Spätjudentum, in Johannes-Evangelium und in neu gefunden gnostischen Schriften.* Arbeiten zur Geschichte des Spätjudentums und Urchristentums, 2. Leiden: E. J. Brill, 1963.

Beutler, Johannes. "Die Heilsbedeutung des Todes Jesu im Johannesevangelium nach Joh 13, 1–20." Pp. 188–204 in *Der Tod Jesu: Deutungen im Neuen Testament,* edited by Karl Kertlege. *Quaestiones Disputatae* 74. Freiburg: Herder, 1976.

Bikerman, Elias Joseph. *Institutions des Seleucides.* Paris: P. Geuthner, 1938.

Black, M. "Messianic Doctrine in the Qumran Scrolls." *Studia Patristica* 1; Texte und Untersuchungen 63 (1958): 441–459.

Blenkinsopp, Joseph. "Deuteronomy," Pp. 94–109 in *The New Jerome Biblical Commentary,* edited by Raymond E. Brown, Joseph A. Fitzmyer and Roland E. Murphy. Englewood Cliffs, NJ: Prentice Hall, 1990.

Bloom, Harold. *Kabbalah and Criticism.* New York: Continuum Publishing Company, 1983.

Bodson, A. *La morale sociale des derniers Stoïciens, Sénèque, Epictète et Marc Aurèle.* Bibliothèque de la faculté de philosophie et lettres de l'Université de Liège, 176. Paris: Les Belles Lettres, 1967.

Boff, Leonardo. *Jesus Christ, Liberator: A Critical Christology for Our Time,* translated by Patrick Barnes. Maryknoll, N.Y.: Orbis Books, 1978.

Boff, Leonardo and Clodovis Boff. *Introducing Liberation Theology.* Maryknoll, New York: Orbis Books, 1987.

Boismard, M.-É., and Arnaud Lamouille. *L'Évangile de Jean.* Paris: 1977.

Bonhoeffer, Dietrich. *Letters and Papers from Prison.* Rev. ed. Eberhard Bethge. New York: Macmillan, 1967, 1971.

Borgen, Peder. "Observations on the Targumic Character of the Prologue of John." *New Testament Studies* 16 (1970): 288–295.

Borig, Rainer. *Der wahre Weinstock: Untersuchungen zu Jo 15, 1–10.* Studien zum Alten und Neuen Testament, 16. Munich: Kösel, 1967.

Brenner, Athalya. *The Israelite Woman: Social Role and Literary Type in Biblical Narrative.* Sheffield: JSOT Press, 1985.

Brooten, Bernadette. *Women Leaders in the Ancient Synagogues: Inscrip-

*tional Evidence and Background Issues.* Brown Judaic Studies 36. Chico, Calif.: Scholars, 1982.

Bradley, Ritamary. "Patristic Background of the Motherhood Similitude in Julian of Norwich." *Christian Scholar's Review* 8 (1978): 101–113.

Breytenbach, Cilliers. *Versöhnung. Eine Studie zur paulinischen Soteriologie.* Wissenschaftliche Monographien zum Alten und Neuen Testament 60. Neukirchener: Neukirchen-Vluyn, 1989.

Brock, Rita Nakashima. "And a Little Child Will Lead Us: Christology and Child Abuse." Pp. 42–60 in *Christianity, Patriarchy and Abuse,* edited by Joanne Carlson Brown and Carole R. Bohn. New York: Pilgrim, 1990.

Brock, Sebastian. "The Mysteries Hidden in the Side of Christ." *Sobornost* 7 (1977–78): 462–472.

Brodie, Thomas. *The Gospel According to John: A Literary and Theological Commentary.* New York: Oxford University, 1993.

Brown, Joanne Carlson and Carole R. Bohn, editors. *Christianity, Patriarchy, and Abuse: A Feminist Critique.* New York: Pilgrim, 1990.

Brown, Joanne Carlson and Rebecca Parker. "For God so Loved the World?" pages 1–30 in *Christianity, Patriarchy and Abuse,* edited by Joanne Carlson Brown and Carole R. Bohn. New York: Pilgrim, 1990.

Brown, Raymond E. *The Community of the Beloved Disciple.* New York: Paulist, 1979.

————. *The Gospel According to John: Introduction, Translation, and Notes.* 2 vols. Anchor Bible Commentary, vols. 29–29A. Garden City, N.Y.: Doubleday, 1966–1970.

————. "Roles of Women in the Fourth Gospel." Pp. 112–144 in *Woman: New Dimensions,* edited by Walter J. Burghardt. New York: Paulist, 1977.

Brownlee, William Hugh. "Biblical Interpretation among the Sectaries of the Dead Sea Scrolls." *Biblical Archaeologist* 14 (1951): 54–76.

————. *The Dead Sea Manual of Discipline: Translation and Notes.* Bulletin of the American Schools of Oriental Research, Supplemental Studies 10–12. New Haven, Conn.: American Schools of Oriental Research, 1951.

————. "Messianic Motifs of Qumran and the New Testament." *New Testament Studies* 3 (1956–1957): 12–30, 195–210.

Bruce, Frederick F. *The Gospel of John: Introduction, Exposition, and Notes.* Grand Rapids, Mich.: W. B. Eerdmans, 1983.

Bultmann, Rudolf. *The Gospel of John: A Commentary,* translated by G. R. Beasley-Murray from the Supplemented edition. Philadelphia: Westminster, 1971.

Burstein, Stanley Mayer. *The Babyloniaca of Berossus.* Malibu, Calif.: Undena Publications, 1978.

Byron, George Gordon. *Cain: A Dramatic Mystery in Three Acts.* New York and London: G. P. Putnam's Sons, 1923.

Bynum, Caroline Walker. *Jesus as Mother, Studies in the Spirituality of the High Middle Ages.* Berkeley: University of California, 1984.

Cabassut, André. "Une dévotion médiévale peu connue: la dévotion à Jésus notre mère." *Revue d'ascetique et de mystique* 25 (1949) 234–245.

Cady, Susan, Marian Ronan and Hal Taussig. *Sophia: The Future of Feminist Spirituality.* San Francisco: Harper and Row, 1988.

Cady, Susan, Marian Ronan and Hal Taussig. *Wisdom's Feast: Sophia in Study and Celebration.* San Francisco: HarperSanFrancisco, 1989.

Camp, Claudia V. "The Female Sage in Ancient Israel and in the Biblical Wisdom Literature." Pp. 185–203 in *The Sage in Israel and the Ancient Near East,* edited by John G. Gammie and Leo G. Perdue. Winona Lake, Ind.: Eisenbrauns, 1990.

_____. Wise Women in 2 Samuel: A Role Model for Women in Early Israel?" *Catholic Biblical Quarterly* 43 (1981): 14–29.

Campbell, Alastair V. *Rediscovering Pastoral Care.* London: Darton, Longman and Todd, 1981 (a later edition, 1986).

Cardascia, Guillaume. *Les lois assyriennes: Introduction, traduction, commentaire.* Paris: Cerf, 1969.

Carson, Donald A. *The Gospel According to John.* Grand Rapids, Mich.: W. B. Eerdmans, and Leicester, UK: Inter-Varsity, 1991.

_____. "Recent Literature on the Fourth gospel." *Themelios* 9 (1983): 8–18.

Chamberlain, John V. "Another Qumran Thanksgiving Psalm." *Journal of Near Eastern Studies* 14 (1955): 32–41.

_____. "Further Elucidation of a Messianic Thanksgiving Psalm from Qumran," *Journal of Near Eastern Studies* 14 (1955): 181–182.

Charlesworth, James H. "Odes of Solomon." Vol. 1, pages 725–771 in *The Old Testament Pseudepigrapha,* edited by James H. Charlesworth. 2 vols. Garden City, N.Y.: Doubleday, 1985.

_____. Editor. *The Old Testament Pseudepigrapha.* 2 vols. Garden City, N.Y.: Doubleday, 1985.

Christ, Felix. *Jesus Sophia: Die Sophia-Christologie bei den Synoptiken.* Abhandlungen zur Theologie des Alten und Neuen Testaments, 67. Zurich: Zwingli-Verlag, 1970.

Colish, Marcia L. *The Stoic Tradition from Antiquity to the Early Middle Ages.* 2 vols. Studies in the History of Christian Thought, 34–35. Leiden: Brill, 1985.

Colledge, Edmund and James Walsh, editors. *Julian of Norwich: Showings. The Classics of Western Spirituality.* New York: Paulist Press, 1978.

Collins, A. Y. "Aristobulus." Vol. 2, pages 831–842 in *The Old Testament*

*Pseudepigrapha*, edited by James H. Charlesworth. 2 vols. Garden City, N.Y.: Doubleday, 1985.

Cornford, Francis M. *The Unwritten Philosophy and other Essays*. Cambridge: Cambridge University, 1950.

Corrington, Gail Paterson. *Her Image of Salvation: Female Saviors and Formative Christianity*. Louisville, KY: Westminster/John Knox, 1992.

Cortéz, Juan B. "Yet Another Look at John 7, 37–38." *CBQ* 29 (1967): 75–86.

Cowen, Gerald. *Salvation: Word Studies from the Greek New Testament*. Nashville: Broadman, 1990.

Crumlin, Rosemary, with Judith Ryan. *Images of Religion in Australian Art*. Kensington, N.S.W.: Bay Books, 1988.

Cullmann, Oscar. *Baptism in the New Testament*. Repr. Studies in Biblical Theology 1. Philadelphia: Westminster, 1978.

————. *The Johannine Circle*, translated by John Bowden. Philadelphia: Westminster, 1976.

Culpepper, R. Alan. *Anatomy of the Fourth Gospel: A Study in Literary Design*. Foundations and Facets, New Testament. Philadelphia: Fortress, 1983.

————. *The Johannine School: An Evaluation of the Johannine School Hypothesis Based on an Investigation of the Nature of Ancient Schools*. Society of Biblical Literature Dissertation Series, 26. Missoula, Mont.: Scholars, 1975.

————. "The Pivot of John's Prologue." *New Testament Studies* 27 (1980–81): 1–31.

Danker, Frederick W. *Benefactor, Epigraphic Study of a Graeco-Roman and New Testament Semantic Field*. St. Louis, Missouri: Clayton Publishing House, 1982.

Dauer, Anton. *Johannes und Lukas: Untersuchungen zu den johanneisch-lukanischen Parallelperikopen Joh 4, 46–4/Lk 7, 1–10 – Joh 12, 1–8/Lk 7, 36–50; 10, 38–42 – Joh 20, 19–29/Lk 24, 36–49*. Würzburg: Echter, 1984.

Davies, Margaret. *Rhetoric and Reference in the Fourth Gospel*. JSNT Supplement Series 69. Sheffield: JSOT Press, 1992.

Davies, Stevan L. *The Revolt of the Widows: The Social World of the Apocryphal Acts*. Carbondale: Southern Illinois University; London: Feffer and Simons, 1980.

Davies, W. D. *The Gospel and the Land: Early Christianity and Jewish Territorial Doctrine*. Berkeley: University of California, 1974; repr. Sheffield: JSOT Press, 1994.

de Margerie, Bertrand, "La Mission Sacerdotale de Retenir Les Péches en Liant Les Pécheurs: Intérêt Actuel et Justification Historique d'"Une Exégèse Tridentine. *Revue des Sciences Religieuses* 58 (1984): 300–17.

Donald D. Dawe. "A Fresh Look at Kenotic Christologies." *Scottish Journal of Theology* 15 (1962): 337–49.

Derrett, J. Duncan M. *The Victim: The Johannine Passion Narrative Reexamined.* Shipston-on-Stour, Warwickshire: Peter I. Drinkwater, 1993.

Dillon, John M., and Jackson P. Hershbell, editors. *Iamblichus. On the Pythagorean Way of Life.* Texts and Translations 29, Graeco-Roman Religion Series 11. Atlanta, GA: Scholars, 1991.

Dodd, C. H. [Charles Harold]. *Historical Tradition in the Fourth Gospel.* Cambridge: Cambridge University, 1963.

_____. *Interpretation of the Fourth Gospel.* Cambridge: Cambridge University, 1953 and 1955.

Dods, Marcus. *The Gospel of St. John.* 2 vols. The Expositor's Bible 27–28. London: Hodder and Stoughton, 1891–1892.

Driver, G. R., and John C. Miles. *The Babylonian Laws.* 2 vols. Oxford: Clarendon, 1952–55.

Droge, Arthur J. and James D. Tabor. *A Noble Death: Suicide and Martyrdom among Christians and Jews in Antiquity.* San Francisco: HarperSanFrancisco, 1992.

Dugas, Ludovic. *L'amitié antique après les moeurs populaires et les thèmes des philosophes.* Rev. ed. Paris: Librairie Felix Alcan, 1914.

Duke, Paul D. *Irony in the Fourth Gospel.* Atlanta: John Knox, 1985.

Dupont-Sommer, André. "Le Livre des Hymnes découvert près de la mer Morte (1 QH)." *Semitica* 7 (1957): 1–120.

_____. "La mère du Messie et la mère de l'Aspic dans un hymne de Qoumran," *Revue de l'Histoire des Religions* 147 (1955) 174–188.

Durand, M.-G. "Pentecôte johannique et Pentecôte lucanienne chez certain Pères." *Bull Litt Ecclés* 79 (1970): 97–126.

Durken, Daniel O.S.B., editor. *Sin, Salvation and the Spirit: Commemorating the Fiftieth Year of The Liturgical Press.* Collegeville, Minn.: Liturgical, 1979.

Dyke, Doris Jean, *Crucified Woman.* Toronto: United Church Publishing House, 1991.

Ehrman, Bart D. "Jesus' Trial before Pilate: John 18:28–19:16." *Biblical Theology Bulletin* 13 (1983): 124–31.

Eller, Vernard, *The Beloved Disciple, His Name, His Story, His Thought.* Grand Rapids, Mich.: Eerdmans, 1987.

Ellis, Peter F. *The Genius of John: A Composition-Critical Commentary on the Fourth Gospel.* Collegeville, Minn.: Liturgical, 1984.

_____. "Salvation through the Wisdom of the Cross (1 Cor 1:10–4:21)." Pp. 324–333 in *Sin, Salvation and the Spirit: Commemorating the Fiftieth Year of The Liturgical Press.* Daniel Durken, O.S.B., editor. Collegeville, Minn.: Liturgical, 1979.

Eltester, Walter. "Der Logos und sein Prophet." Pp. 109–34 in *Apophoreta: Festschrift für E. Haenchen zu seinem 70 Geburtstag. Beihefte zur Zeitschrift für die neutestamentliche Wissenschaft*, 30. Berlin: Topelmann, 1967.

Engelsmann, Joan Chamberlain. *The Feminine Dimension of the Divine.* Philadelphia: Westminster, 1979.

Evans, Craig A. *Word and Glory: On the Exegetical and Theological Background of John's Prologue.* JSNT Supplement Series, 89. Sheffield: JSOT, 1993.

Farmer, William R. "Palm Branches in John 12:13." *Journal of Theological Studies* n.s. 3 (1952): 62–66.

Farrell, Michael J. "Christa." *National Catholic Reporter* 21, 23 (April 5, 1985): 11–12.

Fascher, E. "Platon und Johannes in ihrem Verhältnis zu Sokrates und Christus." *Das Altertum* 14,2 (1968): 79–86.

Fee, Gordon D. "Once More- John 7:37–39." *ET* 89 (1977–78): 116–118.

Ferguson, John. *Moral Values in the Ancient World.* London: Methuen, 1958.

Festugière, A.-J. *Epicurus and his Gods.* Oxford: Basil Blackwell, 1955.

Finley, M. I. *The World of Odysseus.* Rev. ed. New York: Viking, 1977.

Fiore, Benjamin. "The Sage in Select Hellenistic and Roman Literary Genres (Philosophic Epistles, Political Discourses, History, Comedy, and Romances)." Pp. 329–341 in *The Sage in Israel and the Ancient Near East*, edited by John G. Gammie and Leo G. Perdue. Winona Lake, Ind.: Eisenbrauns, 1990.

Fitzmyer, Joseph A. "Crucifixion in Ancient Palestine, Qumran Literature, and the New Testament." *Catholic Biblical Quarterly* 40 (1978): 493–513.

Flint, Peter W. "The Psalters at Qumran and the book of Psalms." Ph.D. diss. University of Notre Dame, 1993.

Ford, Josephine Massyngbaerde. *Bonded with the Immortal: A Pastoral Introduction to the New Testament.* Wilmington, Del.: Michael Glazier, 1987.

_____. "The 'Call-girl' in Antiquity and her Potential for Mission." *Proceedings of the Eastern Great Lakes and Midwest Biblical Societies* 12 (1992): 105–116.

_____. "Hellenistic Monarchy and the Passion according to John." Paper presented at the Congreso Internacional Sobre La Interpretación Socio-histórica del Nuevo Testamento. Madrid, Spain, May, 1991,

_____. *My Enemy is My Guest: Jesus and Violence in Luke.* Maryknoll, N.Y.: Orbis Books, 1984.

Forestell, J. Terence. *Word of the Cross: Salvation as Revelation in the Fourth Gospel.* Analecta Biblica 57. Rome: Biblical Institute, 1974.

Forschner, Maximilian. *Die stoische Ethik: Über den Zusammenhang von*

*Natur-, Sprach- und Moralphilosophie im altstoischen System.* Stuttgart: Klett-Cotta, 1981.

Fortune, Marie F. "The Transformation of Suffering: A Biblical and Theological Perspective." Pp. 139–47 in *Christianity, Patriarchy and Abuse,* edited by Joanne Carlson Brown and Carole R. Bohn. New York: Pilgrim, 1990.

Fournier-Bidoz, Alain. "L'Arbre et la demeure: Siracide xxiv 10–17." *Vetus Testamentum* 34 (1984): 1–10.

Fowler, W. Warde. *The Roman Festivals of the Period of the Republic: An Introduction to the Study of the Religion of the Romans.* London: Macmillan, 1933.

Fox, Matthew. *Breakthrough, Meister Eckhart's Creation Spirituality, in New Translation.* Garden City, N.Y.: Doubleday, 1980.

_____. *Meditations with Meister Eckhart.* Santa Fe, N.M.: Bear & Co., 1983.

_____. "The Spiritual Journey of the Homosexual . . . and Just about Everyone Else." Pp. 189–204 in *A Challenge to Love: Gay and Lesbian Catholics in the Church,* edited by Robert Nugent. New York: Crossroad, 1983.

Fraisse, Jean Claude. *Philia: La notion d'amitié dans la philosophie antique: essai sur un probleme perdue et retrouvé.* Paris: J. Vrin, 1974.

Frend, W. H. C. *Martyrdom and Persecution in the Early Church: A Study of a Conflict from the Maccabees to Donatus.* Oxford: Basil Blackwell, 1965; New York: New York University Press, 1967

Fulda, Hermann. *Das Kreuz und die Kreuzigung, eine antiquarische Untersuchung.* Breslau: W. Koebner, 1878.

Gammie, John G. and Leo G. Perdue, editors. *The Sage in Israel and the Ancient Near East.* Winona Lake, Ind.: Eisenbrauns, 1990.

Gammie, John G. "The Sage in Hellenistic Royal Courts." Pp. 147–153 in *The Sage in Israel and the Ancient Near East,* edited by John G. Gammie and Leo G. Perdue. Winona Lake, Ind.: Eisenbrauns, 1990.

Gaster, Theodor H. *The Dead Sea Scriptures in English Translation.* Rev. ed., Garden City, N.Y.: Anchor Books, 1964.

_____. "A Qumran Reading of Deuteronomy xxxiii, 10." *Vetus Testamentum* 8 (1958): 217–219.

Ghiberti, Guiseppe, "Il Dono dello Spirito e I Poteri di Giov. 20,21–23." Pp. 183–220 in *Segni e sacramenti nel Vangèlio di Giovanni,* edited by Pius-Ramon Tragan. *Studia Anselmiana* 66; Sacramentum 3 Roma: Editrice Anselmiana, 1977.

Giblin, Charles Homer. "Confrontations in John 18,1–27." *Biblica* 65 (1984) 210–232.

Girard, René. *The Scapegoat,* translated by Y. Freccero. Baltimore: Johns Hopkins University, 1986.

_____. *Things Hidden Since the Foundation of the World*, translated by Stephen Bann and Michael Metear. Stanford, Calif.: Stanford University, 1987.

_____. *Violence and the Sacred*, translated by Patrick Gregory. Baltimore: Johns Hopkins University, 1972.

Glueck, Nelson. * esed in the Bible*, translated by Alfred Gottschalk; edited by Elias L. Epstein. Cincinnati: Hebrew Union College, 1967.

Gnilka, J. *Johannesevangelium*. Würzburg: 1983.

Goldberg, A. M. *Untersuchungen über die Vorstellung von der Shekhinah in der frühen rabbinischen Literatur*. Berlin: Walter de Gruyter, 1969.

Goldstein, Jonathan A. *I Maccabees: A New Translation with Introduction and Commentary*. Anchor Bible Commentary 41. Garden City, N.Y.: Doubleday, 1976.

_____. *II Maccabees: A New Translation with Introduction and Commentary*. Anchor Bible Commentary 41A. Garden City, N.Y.: Doubleday, 1983.

Goodenough, Erwin Ramsdell. "Symbolism, Jewish." Vol. 15, Pp. 569–578 in *Encyclopaedia Judaica*. Jerusalem: Keter and New York: Macmillan, 1971.

Goold, George P., editor. *Manilius. Astronomica*. Loeb Classical Library. Cambridge, Mass.: Harvard University, 1977.

Gordis, Robert. "Studies in the Book of Amos." Vol. 1, pp. 201–264 in *American Academy for Jewish Research Jublilee Volume*. 2 vols., edited by Salo W. Baron and Isaac E. Barzilay. Jerusalem: American Academy for Jewish Research; New York: Columbia University Press (distrib.), 1980.

Gould, Julius, and W. L. Kolb, editors. *A Dictionary of the Social Sciences*. Glencoe, NY: The Free Press, 1964.

Grese, William C. "'Unless One is Born Again': The Use of a Heavenly Journey in John 3." *Journal of Biblical Literature* 107 (1988): 677–693.

Grey, Mary C. *Feminism, Redemption, and the Christian Tradition*. Mystic, Conn.: Twenty-Third Publications, 1990.

Grossouw, Willem K. M. "A Note on John XIII 1–3." *Novum Testamentum* 8 (1966): 124–131.

_____. *Revelation and Redemption: A Sketch of the Theology of St. John*, translated by Martin W. Schoenberg. Westminster, M.d.: Newman, 1955.

Gruber, Mayer I. "The Motherhood of God in Second Isaiah." *Revue biblique* 90 (1983): 351–359.

Gruenler, Royce Gordon. *The Trinity in the Gospel of John: A Thematic Commentary on the Fourth Gospel*. Grand Rapids, Mich.: Baker, 1986.

Gundry, Robert H. "'In My Father's House are Many *Monai*' (John 14, 2)." *Zeitschrift für die neutestamentliche Wissenschaft* 58 (1967): 68–72.

Gunton, Colin E. *The Actuality of Atonement: A Study of Metaphor, Rationality, and the Christian Tradition.* Grand Rapids, Mich.: W. B. Eerdmans, 1989.

Haacker, Klaus. *Die Stiftung des Heils: Untersuchungen zur Struktur der johanneischen Theologie.* Arbeiten zur Theologie, 47. Stuttgart: Calwer, 1972.

Hadas, Moses, editor. *The Third and Fourth Books of Maccabees.* Jewish Apocryphal Literature. New York: Ktav, 1973.

Haenchen, Ernst. *Das Johannesevangelium: Ein Kommentar.* Tübingen: J. C. B. Mohr Paul Siebeck, 1980.

————. *John: A Commentary*, translated and edited by Robert W. Funk, and Ulrich Busse Hermeneia, A Critical and Historical Commentary on the Bible. Philadelphia: Fortress, 1984.

Hamerton-Kelly, Robert G. *Sacred Violence. Paul's Hermeneutic of the Cross.* Minneapolis: Fortress, 1992.

Hamerton-Kelly, Robert G., editor. *Violent Origins: Walter Burkert, René Girard, and Jonathan Z. Smith on Ritual Killing and Cultural Formation.* Stanford, Calif.: Stanford University, 1987.

Hanson, Anthony T. *The Paradox of the Cross in the Thought of Paul.* Sheffield: JSOT Press, 1987.

Harder, Ruth E. *Die Frauenrollen bei Euripides.* Stuttgart: Metzlerschen und Poeschel, 1993.

Hardy, Daniel W., and David F. Ford. *Praising and Knowing God.* Philadelphia: Westminster, 1985.

Harris, Rivkah. "The Female 'Sage' in Mesopotamian Literature (with an appendix on Egypt)." Pp. 3–17 in *The Sage in Israel and the Ancient Near East*, edited by John G. Gammie and Leo G. Perdue. Winona Lake, Ind.: Eisenbrauns, 1990.

Harrison, Jane. *Prolegomena to the Study of Greek Religion.* Metuchen, NJ: Scarecrow, 1961.

Haubeck, Wilfrid. *Loskauf durch Christus: Herkunft, Gestalt und Bedeutung des paulischen Loskaufmotivs.* Giessen: Brunnen, 1985.

Hayward, Robert, editor. *The Targum of Jeremiah: Introduction, Translation and Commentary.* Wilmington, Del.: Michael Glazier, 1986; repr. Collegeville, Minn.: Liturgical, 1987.

Healey, Joseph. *The Fifth Gospel: The Experience of Black Christian Values.* Maryknoll, N.Y.: Orbis Books, 1981.

Heer, Josef "Das johanneische Bild des Durchbohrten in seiner soteriologischen Bedeutung." Pp. 37–54 in *Christusglaube und Christusverehrung: Neue Zugange zur Christusfrommigkeit*, edited by Leo Scheffczyk. Aschaffenburg: Paul Pattloch, 1982.

Hellwig, Monika E. "The Central Scandal of the Cross: From Sin to Salvation," pages 187–94 in *Sin, Salvation and the Spirit: Commemorating the Fiftieth Year of The Liturgical Press*. Daniel Durken, O.S.B., editor. Collegeville, Minn.: Liturgical, 1979.

_____. *Jesus, the Compassion of God: New Perspectives on the Tradition of Christianity*. Theology and Life Series, 9. Wilmington, Del.: Michael Glazier, 1983.

Hengel, Martin. *La Crucifixion*. French trans. Paris: Cerf, 1981.

_____. *Crucifixion in the Ancient World and the Folly of the Message of the Cross*. E.T. Philadelphia: Fortress, 1977.

_____. *Rabbinische Legende und frühpharisäische Geschichte: Schimeon b. Schetach und die achtzig Hexen von Askalon*. Abhandlungen der Heidelberger Akademie der Wissenschaften, Philosophisch- historische Klasse, 1984/2. Heidelberg: Carl Winter, Universitätsverlag, 1984.

Herman, Gabriel. *Ritualised Friendship and the Greek City*. Cambridge and New York: Cambridge University, 1987.

Heschel, Abraham. *The Prophets*. 2 vols. New York: Harper & Row, 1969–71.

Hill, Nancy K. "Jesus' Death in Childbirth." *Cross Currents* 11 (1953): 1–9.

Hillenbrand, Karl. *Heil in Jesus Christus. Der Christologische Begründungszusammenhang im Erlösungsverständnis und die Rückfrage nach Jesus*. Würzburg: Echter, 1982.

Hillers, Delbert R. *Covenant: The History of a Biblical Idea*. Baltimore, Md.: Johns Hopkins University, 1969.

Hills, S. "The *esed* of Man in the Old Testament" and "The *esed* of God." Two-part paper delivered at the Biblical Colloquium meeting. Pittsburgh, November 29, 1957.

Hinson, Glenn. "Hodayoth III, 6–18: In What Sense Messianic?" *Revue de Qumrân* 2 (1959/60): 183–204.

Hinton, James. *The Mystery of Pain: A Book for the Sorrowful*. London: K. Paul, 1892.

Hock, Ronald F. "Friendship in the Greek Romances," SBL seminar paper. Forthcoming, Scholar's.

Hodges, Zane C. "Rivers of Living Water—John 7:37–39." *BiblSacr* 136 (1979): 239–248.

Höistad, Ragnar. *Cynic Hero and Cynic King: Studies in the Cynic Conception of Man*. Uppsala: Carl Bloms Boktryckeri A.-B., 1948.

Holm-Nielsen, Svend. *Hodayot: Psalms from Qumran*. Acta Theologica Danica 2. Aarhus: University Press, 1960.

Hülser, Karlheinz. *Die Fragmente zur Dialektik der Stoiker*. 4 vols. *Neue Sammlung der Texte mit deutscher Übersetzung und Kommentaren*. Stuttgart: Frommann-holzboog, 1987– .

Hultgren, Arland J. *Christ and His Benefits: Christology and Redemption in the New Testament.* Philadelphia: Fortress Press, 1987.

_____. "The Johannine Footwashing (13.1–11) as Symbol of Eschatological Hospitality." *New Testament Studies* 28 (1982): 539–546.

Inwood, Brad. *Ethics and Human Action in Early Stoicism.* Oxford: Clarendon, 1985.

Jaeger, Werner. *Paideia: The Ideal of Greek Culture, Vol. 2: In Search of the Divine Centre.* Third English edition, translated by Gilbert Highet. New York: Oxford University, 1946.

Jelliffe, E. F. Patrice. *Human Milk in the Modern World.* Oxford: Oxford University, 1978.

Jeremias, Gert. *Der Lehrer der Gerechtigkeit. Studien zu Umwelt des Neue Testaments* 2. Göttingen: Vandenhoeck and Ruprecht, 1963.

Johnson, Elizabeth A. "Jesus, the Wisdom of God: A Biblical Basis for Non-Androcentric Christology." *Ephemerides theologicae lovanienses* 61 (1985): 261–294.

_____. *She Who Is: The Mystery of God in Feminist Theological Discourse.* New York: Crossroad, 1992.

Jonge, Marinus de. *Jesus: Stranger from Heaven.* SBL Sources for Biblical Study 11. Missoula, Mont.: Scholars, 1977.

Jónsson, Gunnlaugus A. *The Image of God: Genesis 1:26–28 in a Century of Old Testament Research.* Coniectanea biblica. Old Testament Series 26. Lund: Almqvist & Wiksells International, 1988.

Johnston, George. *The Spirit-Paraclete in the Gospel of John.* Society for New Testament Studies Monograph Series 12. Cambridge: Cambridge University, 1970.

Juilland, A., editor. *To Honour René Girard. Stanford French and Italian Studies* 34. Saratoga, Calif.: Anima Libri, 1986.

Jüngel, Eberhard. *The Doctrine of the Trinity: God's Being is in Becoming,* translated by Horton Harris. *Monograph Supplements to the Scottish Journal of Theology* 4. Grand Rapids, Mich.: W. B. Eerdmans; Edinburgh: Scottish Academic Press, 1976.

Käsemann, Ernst. *The Testament of Jesus: A Study of the Gospel of John in the Light of Chapter 17,* translated by Gerhard Krodel. London: SCM, Philadelphia: Fortress, 1968.

Kasper, Walter. *The God of Jesus Christ,* translated by Matthew J. O'Donnell. New York: Crossroad, 1984.

Keinknecht, Karl Theodor. "Johannes 13, die Synoptiker und die »Methode« der johanneischen Evangelienüberlieferung." *Zeitschrift für Theologie Kirche* 82 (1985): 361–388.

Kesich Veselin. "Resurrection, Ascension, and the Giving of the Spirit."

*Greek Orthodox Theological Review* 25 (1980): 249–60.

Kelly, John N. D. *Early Christian Doctrines*. Fifth edition. London: A.C. Black, 1977.

Keramopoullos, Antonios D.…*Ὁ Ἀποτυμπανισμος. Συμβολη ἀρχαιολο-γικη εἰς την ἱστοριαν ποινικου κικαιου και την λαογραφιαν . . .[Apotimpanismos.]* Library of the Archaeological Society of Athens 22. Athens: Archaeological Society, 1923.

Kerferd, George B. "The Sage in Hellenistic Philosophical Literature (399 B.C.E.–199 C.E.)." Pp. 319–328 in *The Sage in Israel and the Ancient Near East*, edited by John G. Gammie and Leo G. Perdue. Winona Lake, Ind.: Eisenbrauns, 1990.

Kettler, Christian D. *The Vicarious Humanity of Christ and the Reality of Salvation*. Lanham, Md.: University Press of America, 1991.

Kiefer, Odo. *Die Hirtenrede. Analyse und Deutung von Joh 10, 1–18*. Stuttgarter Bibelstudien 23. Stuttgart: Katholisches Bibelwerk, 1967.

Kimpel, Ben. *Stoic Moral Philosophies: Their Counsel for Today*. New York: Philosophical Library, 1985.

King, Karen L., editor. *Images of the Feminine in Gnosticism*. Philadelphia: Fortress, 1988.

Klaiber, Walter. "Der irdische und der himmlische Zeuge. Eine Auslegung von Joh 3.22–36." *New Testament Studies* 36 (1990): 205–233.

Koester, Craig R. *The Dwelling of God: The Tabernacle in the Old Testament: Intertestamental Jewish Literature, and the New Testament*. Catholic Biblical Quarterly Monograph Series 22. Washington, D.C.: Catholic Biblical Association of America, 1989.

Kotzé, P. P. A. "John and Reader's Response." *Neotestamentica* 19 (1985): 50–63.

Kruijf, Theo C. de. "More than half a hundredweight of Spices (John 19:39 NEB): Abundance and Symbolism in the Gospel of John." *Bijdragen* 43 (1982): 234–239.

Kuhn, Peter. *Gottes Selbsterniedrigung in der Theologie der Rabbinen*. Munich: Kosel-Verlag, 1968.

Kysar, Robert. *The Fourth Evangelist and His Gospel*. Minneapolis: Augsburg, 1975.

————. *John*. Augsburg Commentary on the New Testament. Minneapolis, Minn.: Augsburg, 1986.

LaCugna, Catherine Mowry. *God for Us. The Trinity and Christian Life*. San Francisco and New York: HarperSanFrancisco, 1991.

Ladaria, Luis F. "Juan 7, 38 en Hilario de Poitiers. Un analisis de Tr. Ps. 64, 13–16." Estudios Eclesiasticos 52 (1977): 123–128.

Lamaze, Fernand. *Painless Childbirth: Psychoprophylactic Method*, translated by L. R. Celestin. Chicago: H. Regnery, 1970; New York: Pocket Books, 1972 (later edition, 1977).

Lang, Bernhard. *Wisdom and the Book of Proverbs: An Israelite Goddess Redefined.* New York: Pilgrim, 1986.

Langbrandtner, Wolfgang. *Weltferner Gott oder Gott der Liebe: Der Ketzerstreit in der johanneischen Kirche: Eine exegetisch-religionsgeschichtliche Untersuchung mit Berücksichtigung der koptisch-gnostischen Texte aus Nag-Hammadi.* Beiträge zur biblische Exegese und Theologie 6. Frankfurt-am-Main: Peter Lang, 1977.

Leanza, Sandro,"Testimoninze della Tradizione Indiretta su Alcuni Passi del N.T. (Giov.vii, 37–38 et altri passi)." *Rivista Biblica* 15 (1967): 407–18.

Levine, Baruch A. *In the Presence of the Lord: A Study of Cult and Some Cultic Terms in Ancient Israel.* Leiden: E. J. Brill, 1974.

Levine, Etan. "On the Symbolism of the *pedilavium*" *American Benedictine Review* 33 (1982): 21–29.

Lewis, C. S. *The Four Loves.* New York: Harcourt, Brace and Co., 1960.

Licht, Jacob. *Megillat haHodayot.* [In Hebrew; English title: *The Thanksgiving Scroll: A Scroll from the Wilderness of Judea: Text, Introduction, Commentary and Glossary.*] Jerusalem: Bialik Institute, 1957.

Lindars, Barnabas. *The Gospel of John.* New Century Bible. London: Oliphants, 1972.

————. "John and the Synoptic Gospels: A Test Case." *New Testament Studies* 27 (1981): 287–294.

Lodahl, Michael E. *Shekhinah Spirit: Divine Presence in Jewish and Christian Religion.* New York: Paulist, 1992.

Lofthouse, W. F. "en and esed in the Old Testament" *Zeitschrift für die alttestamentliche Wissenschaft* 51 (1933): 29–35.

Lohmeyer, Ernst. *Gottesknecht und Davidssohn.* Second edition. Forschungen zur Religion und Literatur des Alten und Neuen Testaments, n.f. 43. Göttingen: Vandenhoeck und Ruprecht, 1953.

Lohse, Eduard. *Die Fusswaschung (Joh 13:1–20). Eine Geschichte ihrer Deutung.* Doctoral diss. Erlangen, 1967.

Long, Anthony A. *Soul and Body in Stoicism: Protocol of the Thirty–sixth Colloquy, 3 June 1979.* Berkeley Calif.: Center for Hermeneutical Studies, 1980.

Lutz, Cora Elizabeth. *Musonius Rufus: The Roman Socrates.* Yale Classical Studies 10. New Haven: Yale University, 1947.

Lyonnet, Stanislaus. *Sin, Redemption, and Sacrifice.* Analecta Biblica 48. Rome: Biblical Institute, 1970.

MacRae, George, "Theology and Irony in the Fourth Gospel." Pp. 103–113 in *The Gospel of John as Literature: an anthology of twentieth-century perspectives,* edited by Mark W. A. Stibbe, Leiden; New York: E. J. Brill, 1993.

McCarthy, Dennis J. *Old Testament Covenant: A Survey of Current Opinion.*

Richmond, Va.: John Knox, 1972.

_____. *Treaty and Covenant: A Study in Form in the Ancient Oriental Documents and the Old Testament. Analecta Biblica* 21. Rome: Pontifical Biblical Institute, 1963; rev. edition, 1981.

McFague, Sallie. *The Body of God: An Ecological Theology.* Minneapolis: Fortress Press, 1993.

_____. *Models of God.* Philadelphia: Fortress Press, 1987.

McHugh, Michael P., editor. *Ambrose of Milan. Seven Exegetical Works.* Fathers of the Church 65. Washington, D.C.: Catholic University of America, 1972.

McIntyre, John. *The Shape of Soteriology: Studies in the Doctrine of the Death of Christ.* Edinburgh: T & T Clark, 1992.

McKnight, Edgar V. *Post-Modern Use of the Bible: The Emergence of Reader-Oriented Criticism.* Nashville: Abingdon, 1988.

McKnight, Edgar V., editor. *Reader Perspectives on the New Testament.* Semeia 48 (1989).

MacMurray, John. *Persons in Relation.* Vol. 2 of *The Form of the Personal.* New York: Harper and Brothers, 1961.

_____. *The Self as Agent.* Vol. 1 of *The Form of the Personal.* New York: Harper and Brothers, 1957.

McNamara, Martin. "*Logos* of the Fourth Gospel and *Memra* of the Palestinian Targum (Ex 12:42)." *Expository Times* 79 (1967–8): 115–117.

_____. "To Prepare a Resting-Place for You." A Targumic Expression and John 14:2f." In *Milltown Studies* 3 (1979): 100–108.

_____. *Targum and Testament: Aramaic Paraphrases of the Hebrew Bible: A Light on the New Testament.* Grand Rapids, Mich.: Wm. B. Eerdmans, 1972.

Maher, Michael., editor. *Targum of Pseudo-Jonathan, Genesis.* Collegeville, Minn.: Liturgical, 1992.

Maier, Gerhard. *Johannes-Evangelium. 1 Teil.* Stuttgart: Hänssler-Verlag, 1984.

Maier, Johann, editor. *The Temple Scroll: An Introduction, Translation, and Commentary. JSOT Supplement Series* 34. Sheffield: JSOT Press, 1985.

Maitland, Sara. "Ways of Relating." *The Way* 26 (1986) 124–33.

Makaryk, Irena R., editor. *Encyclopedia of Contemporary Literary Theory: Approaches, Scholars, Terms.* Toronto: University of Toronto, 1993.

Malatesta, Edward. "Entraide fraternelle par la communion avec Jésus," *Christus* 23 (1976) 209–223.

Malina, Bruce J. *The New Testament World: Insights from Cultural Anthropology.* Rev. edition. Louisville, Ken.: Westminster/John Knox, 1993.

Malina, Bruce J. and Jerome H. Neyrey. *Calling Jesus Names: The Social Value of Labels in Matthew.* Sonoma, Calif.: Polebridge, 1988.

Maly, Eugene H. "Sin and Forgiveness in the Scriptures." Pp. 40–48 in *Sin, Salvation and the Spirit: Commemorating the Fiftieth Year of The Liturgical Press*, edited by Daniel Durken, O.S.B. Collegeville, Minn.: Liturgical, 1979.

Mantey, Julius R. "Distorted Translations in John 20:23; Matthew 16:18–19 and 18:18." *RExp* 78 (1981): 409–414.

—————. "Evidence that the Perfect Tense in John 20:23 and Matthew 16:19 is Mistranslated." *Journ Evang Theo Soc* 16, 3 (1973): 129–138.

Matthews, Caitlin. *Sophia Goddess of Wisdom: The Divine Feminine from Black Goddess to World-Soul.* London: Mandala (HarperCollins), 1991.

Mann, Christopher S. *Mark.* Anchor Bible Commentary 27. Garden City, N.Y.: Doubleday, 1986.

Manns, Frédéric "Le Lavement des Pieds. Essai sur La Structure et la Signification de Jean 13." *Revue des sciences religieuses* 55 (1981): 149—69.

Martyn, J. Louis. *History and Theology in the Fourth Gospel.* Second Edition. Nashville: Abingdon, 1979.

Meeks, Wayne A. *The First Urban Christians: The Social World of the Apostle Paul.* New Haven: Yale University, 1983.

—————. "The Image of the Androgyne: Some Uses of a Symbol in Earliest Christianity." *History of Religions* 13 (1974): 165–208.

—————. "The Man from Heaven in Johannine Sectarianism." *Journal of Biblical Literature* 91 (1972): 44–72.

—————. *The Prophet-King.* Supplements to Novum Testamentum 14. Leiden: E. J. Brill, 1967.

Meilaender, Gilbert C. *Friendship, a Study in Theological Ethics.* Notre Dame, Ind.: University of Notre Dame, 1981, 1985.

Meland, Bernard E. *Faith and Culture.* Chicago: Illinois University Press, 1955; repr. Carbondale, Ill.: Southern Illinois University, 1972.

Ménage, Gilles. *The History of Women Philosophers*, translated by Beatrice H. Zedler. Lanham, Md.: University Press of America, 1984.

Mendenhall, G. E. "Covenant Forms in Israelite Tradition." *Biblical Archaeologist* 17 (1954): 50–76.

Merino, Luis Diéz. "El suplicio de la Cruz en la literatura Judia Interestamental (Dt 21:22–23, John 15:31, 40 Nah I,6–8, Temple Scroll, Targumîm." *Studium Biblicum Franciscanum, Liber Annuus* 26 (1976): 31–120.

Mertens, Herman-Emiel. *Not the Cross, But the Crucified: An Essay in Soteriology.* Louvain Theological and Pastoral Monographs 11. Louvain: Peeters, 1992.

Miguens, M. "El Agua y el Espíritu en John 7, 37–39." *Estudios Biblicos* 31 (1972): 369–98.

Milgrom, Jacob. *Leviticus 1–16.* Anchor Bible Commentary 3. Garden

City, N.Y.: Doubleday, 1991.

Minear, Paul S. "The Audience of the Fourth Evangelist." *Interpretation* 31 (1977): 339–354.

Mollenkott, Virginia Ramey. *The Divine Feminine. The Biblical Imagery of God as Female.* New York: Crossroad, 1993.

Moltmann, Jürgen. *The Crucified God: The Cross of Christ as the Foundation and Criticism of Christian Theology,* translated by R. A. Wilson and John Bowden. New York: Harper and Row, 1974.

_____. *The Trinity and the Kingdom: The Doctrine of God,* translated by Margaret Kohl. San Francisco: Harper and Row, 1981; repr. Philadelphia: Fortress, 1993.

Mondragón, Juan Carlos. *El evangelio según San Juan: Estudio de quatro episodoros.* Montevideo, Uruguay: Fundación de Cultura Universitaria, 1997.

Montaigne, Michel de. *Essays,* translated by Jacob Zeitlin. New York: Alfred A. Knopf, 1934.

Moran, William L. "The Ancient Near Eastern Background of the Love of God in Deuteronomy." *Catholic Biblical Quarterly* 25 (1963): 77–87.

Moreau, Joseph. *Stoïcisme, epicurisme, tradition hellénique.* Paris: J. Vrin, 1979.

Mowinckel, Sigmund. "Some Remarks on Hodayot 39, 5–20," *Journal of Biblical Literature* 75 (1956): 265–76.

Moxnes, Halvor. "Patron-Client Relations and the New Community in Luke-Acts" Pp. 241–270 in *The Social World of Luke-Acts: Models for Interpretation,* edited by Jerome H. Neyrey. Peabody, Mass.: Hendrickson, 1991.

Müller, K., editor. *Geographi Graeci Minores.* 2 vols. Paris: Firmin-Didot, 1882; repr. Hildesheim: Olms, 1965.

Müller, Ulrich B. "Die Bedeutung des Kreuzestodes Jesu im Johannesevangelium: Erwägungen zur Kreuzestheologie im Neuen Testament." *Kerygma und Dogma* 21 (1975): 49–71.

_____. *Die Geschichte der Christologie in der johanneischen Gemeinde.* Stuttgarter Bibelstudien 77. Stuttgart: Katholisches Bibelwerk, 1975.

Muñoz Léon, Domingo. Gloria de la Shekina en los Targumim del Pantateuco. Madrid, 1977..

Murphy, Roland E., O. Carm. "Wisdom and Salvation." Pp. 177–183 in *Sin, Salvation and the Spirit: Commemorating the Fiftieth Year of The Liturgical Press,* edited by Daniel Durken, O.S.B. Collegeville, Minn.: Liturgical, 1979.

*Murray, Robert. "The Lance Which Re-opened Paradise: A Mysterious Reading in the Early Syriac Fathers," Orientalia Christiana Periodica* 39 (1973): 224–34.

Musurillo, Herbert. *The Acts of the Christian Martyrs.* Oxford: Oxford

University, 1972.

Nauck, August. *Tragicorum Graecorum Fragmenta.* Second edition. Lipsiae: B. G. Teubner, 1889.

Neirynck, Frans, "Lc 24, 36–43, Un Récit Lucanien." Pp. 655–80 in *Mélanges Offertes à Dom Jacque Dupont.* Lectio Divina 123. Paris: Cerf, 1985.

Nelson, Wesley W. *Salvation and Secularity, A Reexamination of the Message of the Apostles and Its Significance for Our Day.* Chicago: Covenant, 1968.

Neumann, Harry. "Diotima's Concept of Love." *American Journal of Philology* 86 (1965): 33–59.

Neusner, Jacob. *The Rabbinic Traditions about the Pharisees before 70.* 3 vols. Leiden: E. J. Brill, 1971.

Neyrey, Jerome H. *An Ideology of Revolt: John's Christology in Social-Science Perspective.* Philadelphia: Fortress, 1988.

————. "Nudity." Pp. 119–25 in *Biblical Social Values and Their Meaning: A Handbook,* edited by John J. Pilch and Bruce J. Malina. Peabody, Mass.: Hendrickson, 1993.

Nicol, George G. Jesus' Washing the Feet of the Disciples: A Model for Johannine Christology" *ET* 91 (1979–80): 20–21.

Nicholson, Godfrey Carruthers. *Death as Departure: The Johannine Descent-Ascent Schema.* SBL Dissertation Series 63. Chico, Calif.: Scholars, 1983.

Nygren, Anders. *Agape and Erōs.* Rev. ed., translated by Philip S. Watson. London: SPCK, 1953; New York: Harper and Row, 1969.

O'Connor, David K. "The Invulnerable Pleasures of Epicurean Friendship." *Greek, Roman and Byzantine Studies* 30 (1989): 165–86.

Odeberg, H. *The Fourth Gospel Interpreted in its Relation to Contemporaneous Religious Currents in Palestine and the Hellenistic-Oriental World.* Uppsala: Almqvist & Wiksells, 1929; reprinted Chicago: Argonaut, 1968; Amsterdam: B. R. Gruner, 1974.

Otzen, Benedikt. "Die neugefundenen hebräischen Sektenschriften und die Testamente der zwölf Patriarchen." *Studia Theologica* 7 (1953): 125–157.

Paquet, Léonce. *Les Cyniques Grecs: Fragments et témoignages.* Ottawa: Université d'Ottawa, 1988.

Page, Ruth. *Ambiguity in the Presence of God.* London: SCM, 1985.

Pagels, Elaine. *The Gnostic Gospels.* New York: Random House, 1979.

Pazdan, Mary Margaret. "Nicodemus and the Samaritan Woman: Contrasting Models of Discipleship," *Biblical Theology Bulletin* 17 (1987): 145–48.

Pennells, Stephen. "The Spear Thrust (Mt 27.49b,v.l./John 19.34)." *Journal for the Study of the New Testament* 19 (1983): 99–115.

Perera, Sylvia Brinton. *The Scapegoat Complex: Toward a Mythology of Shadow and Guilt. Studies in Jungian Psychology by Jungian Analysts* 23. Toronto: Inner City Books, 1986.

Perkins, Pheme. *The Gospel According to St. John: A Theological Commentary.* Chicago: Franciscan Herald, 1978.

————. *Love Commandments in the New Testament.* New York: Paulist, 1982.

————. *Resurrection: New Testament Witness and Contemporary Reflection.* London: Geoffrey Chapman; Garden City, N.Y.: Doubleday, 1984.

Pfeifer, Claude, O.S.B. "The Experience of Sin, Salvation and the Spirit as a Prerequisite for the Understanding of Scriptures." Pp. 3–20 in *Sin, Salvation and the Spirit: Commemorating the Fiftieth Year of The Liturgical Press,* edited by Daniel Durken, O.S.B. Collegeville, Minn.: Liturgical, 1979.

Pinto da Silva, Alcides, "L'Interpretazione di Giov. 7, 37–39." Pp. 859–64 in *Credo in Spiritum Sanctum* 2. *Atti del Congresso Teologico Internazional di Peneumatologia; Teologia e Filosofia* 6; Vat. City: Libreria editrice Vaticana, 1983.

Pitt-Rivers, Julian Alfred. *The Fate of Shechem: or, The Politics of Sex: Essays in the Anthropology of the Mediterranean.* Cambridge Studies in Social Anthropology 19. Cambridge: Cambridge University, 1977.

Pizzolato, Luigi. *L'idea di amicizia nel mondo antico classico e cristiano.* Torino: Giulio Einaudi, 1993.

Potterie, Ignace de la. *The Hour of Jesus: The Passion and Resurrection of Jesus According to John.* ET New York: Alba House, 1989.

————. "Jesus roi et juge d'après John 19:13: Ἐκάθισεν ἐπὶ βήματος." *Biblica* 41 (1960): 217–247.

————. *Studi di cristologia Giovannea.* Genoa: Marietti, 1986.

————. *La vérité dans saint Jean.* Analecta Biblica 73–74. Rome: Pontifical Biblical Institute, 1977.

Préaux, Claire. *Le monde hellénistique.* 2 vols. Nouvelle Clio, 6. Paris: Presses Universitaires de France, 1978.

Preminger, Alex and T. V. F. Brogan. *The New Princeton Encyclopedia of Poetry and Poetics.* Princeton, N.J.: Princeton University, 1993.

Price, A. W. *Love and Friendship in Plato and Aristotle.* Oxford: Clarendon Press and New York: Oxford University, 1989.

Price, Theodora Hadzisteliou. *Kourotrophos: Cults and Representations of the Greek Nursing Deities.* Studies of the Dutch Archaeological and Historical Society 8. Leiden: E. J. Brill, 1978.

Rader, Rosemary. *Breaking Boundaries: Male/Female Friendship in Early Christian Communities.* New York: Paulist, 1983.

Rahner, Karl. *The Trinity,* translated by Joseph Donceel. New York: Herder and Herder, 1970.

Reinhold, Meyer. *The History of Purple as a Status Symbol in Antiquity.* Collection Latomus 116. Brussels: Latomus, 1970.

Renehan, Robert. "The Greek Philosophic Background of Fourth Maccabees." *Rheinisches Museum für Philologie* 115 (1972): 223–238.

Ricardo Foulkes, B. "'Mi reino no es de este mundo.' Estudio exegético de John 18.36," *Vida y Pensamiento* 3 (1983): 43–51.

Richeson, A. W. "Hypatia of Alexandria." *National Mathematics Magazine* 15 (1940): 74–82.

Richter, Georg. "Blut und Wasser aus der durchbohrten Seite Jesu (Joh 19,34b)." Pp. 121–142 in *Studien zum Johannesevangelium,* edited by Josef Hainz. Biblische Untersuchungen 13. Regensburg: Pustet, 1977.

_____. "Die Deutung des Kreuzedtodes Jesus in der Leidensgeschichte des Johannesevangeliums (Jo 13:19)." *BL* 9 (1968): 21–36.

_____. "Die Fleischwerdung des Logos im Johannesevangelium." *Novum Testamentum* 13 (1971): 81–126; and 14 (1972) 257–76.

_____. *Die Fusswaschung im Johannesevangelium. Geschichte ihrer Deutung.* Biblische Untersuchungen 1. Regensburg: Friedrich Pustet, 1967.

Rist, J. M. "Hypatia." *The Phoenix* 19 (1965): 214–225.

Ritter, Hans Werner. *Diadem und Konigsherrschaft. Vestigia* 7. Munich: Beck, 1965.

Robinson, James M. "Jesus as Sophos and Sophia: Wisdom Tradition and the Gospels." Pp. 1–16 in *Aspects of Wisdom in Judaism and Early Christianity,* edited by Robert L. Wilken. Studies in Judaism and Christianity in Antiquity 1. Notre Dame, Ind.: University of Notre Dame, 1975.

Robinson, James M., editor. *The Nag Hammadi Library in English.* Rev. edition. New York: HarperCollins, 1990.

Robinson, John A. T. *Twelve More New Testament Studies.* London: SCM Press, 1984.

Rohden, W. von. "Die Handlungslehre nach Joh. 13," *Theologische Versuche* 7 (1976), 81–90.

Rolt, Clarence Edwin. *The World's Redemption.* London: Longmans & Co., 1913.

Rostovtzeff, Michael I. *The Social and Economic History of the Roman Empire.* 2 vols. Second edition. Oxford: Clarendon Press, 1957.

Ruhl, Franz, and Otto Seel, editors. *Epitoma Historiarum Philippicarum Pompei Trogi: Accedunt prologi in Pompeium Tragum M. Juniani Justini.* Bibliotheca scriptorum Graecorum et Romanorum Teubneriana. Stuttgart: B. G. Teubner, 1985.

Sabbe, M. "The Arrest of Jesus in John 18, 1–11 and its Relation to the Synoptic Gospels." Pp. 203–234 in *L'Évangile de Jean: Sources, rédaction, théologie,* edited by Marinus de Jonge. *Bibliotheca Ephemeridum theologicarum Lovaniensium* 44. Gembloux: J. Duculot, 1977.

_____. "The Footwashing in John 13 and its Relation to the Synoptic

Gospels." *Ephemerides Theologicae Lovanienses* 58 (1982): 279–308.

Sabourin, Léopold, S.J. *Rédemption sacrificielle: Une enquête exégètique. Studia recherches de philosophie et théologie publiées par les Facultés de Montréal* 11. Bruges: Desclée de Brouwer, 1961.

Sakenfeld, Katherine D. *The Meaning of Hesed in the Hebrew Bible: A New Inquiry.* Harvard Semitic Monographs 17. Missoula, Mont.: Scholars, 1978.

Salvati, Giuseppe Marco. *Teologia Trinitaria della croce.* Scuola Superiore di Theologia della Croce 6. Turin: Editrice Elle di Ci, 1987.

Sandelin, Karl-Gustav. *Wisdom as Nourisher: A Study of an Old Testament Theme, Its Development within Early Judaism, and Its Impact on Early Christianity.* Acta Academiae Aboensis, Series A, Humaniora, 64/3. Abo: Abo Akademi, 1986.

Sandvik, Björn. "Joh. 15 als Abendmahlstext" *Theologische Zeitschrift* 23 (1967): 323–328.

SBL Consultation on Hellenistic Moral Philosophy and Early Christianity. It is hoped that these will be published in the near future. The papers are:

> D. L. Balch. "Friendship in the Historian Dionysius of Hali-carnassus."K. G. Evans. "Friendship in the Documentary Papyri: An Analysis of Its Role in the Daily Life of Greek and Roman Egypt."
>
> B. Fiore. "The Theory and Practice of Friendship in Cicero."
>
> R. F. Hock. "Friendship in the Greek Romances."
>
> A. C. Mitchell. "'Greet the Friends by Name': New Testament Evidence for the Greco-Roman *Topos* on Friendship."
>
> E. N. O'Neil. "Plutarch on Friendship."
>
> R. I. Pervo. "With Lucian: Who Needs Friends? Lucian's Story of Friendship (The *Toxaris*)."
>
> F. M. Schroeder. "Friendship in Aristotle and the Peripatetic Tradition."
>
> G. E. Sterling. "The Bond of Humanity: Friendship in Philo of Alexandria."
>
> J. C. Thom. "'Harmonious Equality' The Topos of Friendship in Neopythagorean Writings."

Schenke, Ludger. "Der 'Dialog Jesu mit den Juden' im Johannesevangelium: Ein Rekonstruktionsversuch." *New Testament Studies* 34 (1988): 573–603.

Schillebeeckx, Edward. *Jesus: An Experiment in Christology.* E. T. New York: Crossroad, 1979.

Schmitt, Johanna. *Freiwilliger Opfertod bei Euripides.* Religionsgeschichtliche Versuche und Vorarbeiten 17/2. Giessen: A. Topelmann, 1921.

Schmitt, John J. "The Motherhood of God and Zion as Mother" *Revue biblique* 92–94 (1985): 557–69.

Schnackenberg, Rudolf. *The Gospel According to St. John*. 3 vols., translated by Cecily Hastings, *et al*. Herder's Theological Commentary on the New Testament. New York: Crossroad, 1968–1982.

Schneiders, Sandra M. "The Foot Washing (John 13:1–20): An Experiment in Hermenutics." *Catholic Biblical Quarterly* 43 (1981): 76–92.

_____. *Women and the Word: The Gender of God in the New Testament and the Spirituality of Women*. New York: Paulist, 1986.

Schökel, Alonso. "La Simbola Biblica della Salvezza." Pp. 39–66 in *La Ragione e i simboli della salvezza oggi. Atti del quarto Colloquio su filosofia e religione*; Macerata, 12–14 maggio 1988. Giovanni Ferretti, editor. Genova: Marietti, 1990.

Scholem, Gershom G. *Major Trends in Jewish Mysticism*. Third revised ed. New York: Shocken Books, 1954, 1961.

_____. *Von der mystischen Gestalt der Gottheit: Studien zu Grundbegriffen der Kabbala*. Zürich: Rhein-Verlag, 1962.

Schüssler Fiorenza, Elisabeth. "'For the Sake of Our Salvation . . . .' Biblical Interpretation as Theological Task." Pp. 21–39 in *Sin, Salvation and the Spirit: Commemorating the Fiftieth Year of The Liturgical Press*, edited by Daniel Durken, O.S.B., editor. Collegeville, Minn.: Liturgical, 1979.

_____. *In Memory of Her: A Feminist Theological Reconstruction of Christian Origins*. New York: Crossroad, 1987, 1992.

Schwager, Raymund. *Brauchen Wir Einen Sündenbock? Gewalt und Erlösung in die biblische Schriften*. Munich: Kösel, 1978.

_____. *Must There be Scapegoats?* translated by M. L. Assad. San Francisco: Harper and Row, 1987.

Scott, Martin. *Sophia and the Johannine Jesus*. Sheffield: JSOT Press, 1992.

Segovia, Fernando F. *The Farewell of the Word, The Johannine Call to Abide*. Minneapolis: Fortress, 1991.

_____. "John 13, 1–20, The Footwashing in the Johannine Tradition," *Zeitschrift für die neutestamentliche Wissenschaft* 73 (1982): 31–51.

_____. *Love Relationships in the Johannine Tradition*. SBL Dissertation Series 58. Missoula, Mont.: Scholars, 1982.

_____. "The Theology and Provenance of John 15:1–17," *Journal of Biblical Literature* 101, 1 (1982) 115–128.

Seymour-Smith, Charlotte. *Dictionary of Anthropology*. Boston: G.K. Hall, 1986.

Silberman, Lou H. "Language and Structure in the Hodayot (1 QH 3(37))." *Journal of Biblical Literature* 75 (1956): 96–106.

Silberman, Lou H., editor. *Orality, aurality and Biblical Narrative. Semeia* 39. Atlanta, GA: Scholars, 1987.

Simoens, Yves. *La gloire d'aimer: Structures stylistiques et intérpretatives dans le discours de la Cène (John 13–17). Analecta Biblica* 90. Rome: Biblical Institute, 1981.

Simonis, Adrian J. *Die Hirtenrede im Johannes-Evangelium: Versuch einer Analyse von Johannes 10,1–18 nach Entstehung, Hintergrund, und Inhalt. Analecta Biblica* 29. Rome: Pontifical Biblical Institute, 1967.

Skehan, Patrick W., and Alexander A. DiLella. *The Wisdom of Ben Sira: A New Translation with Notes, Introduction and Commentary. Anchor Bible Commentary* 39. Garden City, N.Y.: Doubleday, 1987.

Sloan Ian B. "Ezekiel and the Covenant of Friendship." *BTB* 22, 4 (1992) 149–154.

Smalley, Stephen S. *John, Evangelist and Interpreter.* Exeter: Paternoster Press, 1978.

Smith, Dwight Moody. *The Composition and Order of the Fourth Gospel.* Yale Publications in Religion 10. New Haven: Yale University, 1965.

_____. *Johannine Christianity: Essays on Its Setting, Sources, and Theology.* Columbia, S.C.: University of South Carolina, 1984.

Smith, Jonathan Z.. *Imagining Religion: From Babylon to Jonestown. Chicago Studies in the History of Judaism.* Chicago: University of Chicago, 1982.

_____. *Map is not Territory: Studies in the History of Religions. Studies in Judaism in Late Antiquity* 23. Leiden: Brill, 1978

Sobrino, Jon. *Christology at the Crossroads: A Latin-American Approach,* translated by John Drury. Maryknoll, N.Y.: Orbis Books, 1978.

Sölle, Dorothee. *Christ the Representative: An Essay in Theology after the Death of God.* E.T. Philadelphia: Fortress, 1967.

Spicq, Ceslas. *Agapē in the New Testament,* translated by Marie Aquinas Richter and Mary Honoria Richter. St. Louis: B. Herder, 1963.

Stock, Augustine, O.S.B., "The Development of the Concept of Redemption." Pp. 49–64 in *Sin, Salvation and the Spirit: Commemorating the Fiftieth Year of The Liturgical Press,* edited by Daniel Durken, O.S.B. Collegeville, Minn.: Liturgical, 1979.

Stol, Marten and F. A. M. Wiggerman. *Zwangerschap en gebooorte bij de Babyloniërs en in de Bijbel.* Ex Oriente Lux 23. Leiden: E. J. Brill, 1983.

Stuhlmeuller, Carroll, "Deutero-Isaiah and Trito-Isaiah." Pp. 329–348 in *The New Jerome Biblical Commentary,* edited by Raymond E. Brown, Joseph A. Fitzmyer and Roland E. Murphy. Englewood Cliffs, N.J.: Prentice Hall, 1990.

Suggs, M. Jack. *Wisdom, Christology, and Law in Matthew's Gospel.* Cambridge: Mass.: Harvard University, 1970.

Talbert, Charles H. "The Myth of a Descending-Ascending Redeemer in Mediterranean Antiquity." *New Testament Studies* 22 (1976): 418–440.

Tamayo-Acosta, Juan-José. *Para comprender La Teología de la Liberaciin.* Estella, Navarra, Spain: Editorial Verbo Divino, 1990.

Tegnaeus, Harry. *Blood-Brothers: An Ethno-Sociological Study of the Institutions of Blood-Brotherhood, with Special Reference to Africa.* New York: Philosophical Library, 1952.

Temkin, Owsei, editor. *Soranus of Ephesus: Gynaecology.* Publications of the Institute of the History of Medicine, The Johns Hopkins University. Baltimore: John Hopkins University, 1956.

Thiel, Josef Franz, and Heinz Helf. *Christliche Kunst in Afrika.* Berlin: Dietrich Reimer, 1984.

Thistlethwaite, Susan Brooks. *Metaphors for the Contemporary Church.* New York: Pilgrim, 1984.

Tobin, Thomas H. "The Prologue of John and Hellenistic Jewish Speculation." *Catholic Biblical Quarterly* 52 (1990): 252–269.

Torrance, Alan. "Does God Suffer? Incarnation and Impassibility." Pp. 345–368 in *Christ in our Place, The Humanity of God in Christ for the Reconciliation of the World,* edited by Trevor Hart and Daniel P. Thimell. Exeter, UK: Paternoster; Allison Park, Penn.: Pickwick Publications, 1989.

Tran, V. tam Tinh, with Yvette Labrecque. *Isis Lactans. Corpus des monuments greco-romains d' Isis allaitant Harpocrate.* Études préliminaires aux religions orientales dans l'Empire romain 37. Leiden: E. J. Brill, 1973.

Turner, Victor W. *The Ritual Process: Structure and Anti-Structure.* Ithaca, N.Y.: Cornell University Press, 1969, 1977.

Unamuno, Miguel de. *The Agony of Christianity,* translated by Anthony Kerrigan. *Bollingen Series* 85. Princeton: Princeton University, 1974.

_____. *El Cristo de Velazquez,* edited by Victor Garcia de la Concha. Clásicos castellanos, n.s. 3. Madrid: Espasa-Calpe, 1987.

_____. *Del sentimiento trágico de la vida en los hombres y en los pueblos.* Akal bolsillo 113. Madrid: Akal, 1983.

_____. *The Tragic Sense of Life in Men and Nations,* translated by Anthony Kerrigan. Bollingen Series 85/4. Princeton: Princeton University, 1972.

Valente, Milton P. *L'éthique stoïcienne chez Cicéron.* Paris: Librairie Saint-Paul, 1956.

Vawter, Bruce, C.M. "Salvation Is a Family Affair." Pp. 65–70 in *Sin, Salvation and the Spirit: Commemorating the Fiftieth Year of The Liturgical Press,* edited by Daniel Durken, O.S.B. Collegeville, Minn.: Liturgical, 1979.

von Rad, Gerhard. "$\delta o \kappa \acute{e} \omega, \delta \acute{o} \xi \alpha, \delta o \xi \acute{a} \zeta \omega. \ldots$" Vol. 2, pp. 232–254 in *Theological Dictionary of the New Testament,* edited by Gerhard Kittel and Gerhard Friedrich, translated by Geoffrey W. Bromiley. Grand Rapids,

Mich.: Wm. B. Eerdmans, 1964.

Vouga, François. *La cadre historique et l'intention théologique de Jean*. Paris: Beauchesne, 1977.

Walbank, Frank William. *The Hellenistic World. Cambridge Ancient History* 7/1. Cambridge: Cambridge University, 1984.

Wasznik, J. H. "Blut." Vol. 2, cols. 459–474 in *Reallexikon für Antike und Christentum*. Stuttgart: Anton Hiersemann, 1954.

Weiss, Herold. "Footwashing in the Johannine Community." *Novum Testamentum* 21 (1979): 298–325.

Whitehead, Albert North. *Process and Reality: An Essay in Cosmology*. Rev. edition, edited by David Ray Griffin and Donald W. Sherburne. New York: The Free Press, 1978.

Wider, Kathleen. "Women Philosophers in the Ancient Greek World: Donning the Mantle." *Hypatia* 1 (1986): 21–62.

Williams, Daniel Day. *The Spirit and the Forms of Love*. New York: Harper and Row, 1968.

Williams, Sam K. *Jesus' Death as Saving Event: The Background and Origin of a Concept. Harvard Dissertations in Religion* 2. Missoula, Mont.: Scholars, 1975.

Winston, David. *The Wisdom of Solomon*. Anchor Bible Commentary 43. Garden City, N.Y.: Doubleday, 1979.

Witacre, R. A. *Johannine Polemic*. Society for Biblical Literature Dissertation Series, 67. Chico, Calif.: Scholars, 1982.

Witherington, Ben III. "The Waters of Birth: John 3.5 and 1 John 5.6–8." *New Testament Studies* 35 (1989): 155–160.

Witt, Reginald E. *Isis in the Greco-Roman World*. London: Thames and Hudson and Ithaca, N.Y.: Cornell University, 1971.

Woude, A. S. van der. *Die Messianischen Vorstellungen der Gemeinde von Qumrân. Studia Semitica Nederlandica* 3. Assen: Van Gorcum, 1957.

Wren, Brian. "Sexism in Hymn Language." *News of Hymnody Quarterly* 7 (July 1983): 8.

Würthwein, Ernst. "Elijah at Horeb: Reflections on 1 Kings 19.9–18." Pp. 152–166 in *Proclamation and Presence: Old Testament Essays in Honour of Gwynne Henton Davies*, edited by John I. Durham and J. R. Porter. Richmond, Va: John Knox, 1970.

Zahn, Theodor. *Das Evangelium des Johannes*. Wuppertal: R. Brockhaus, 1983.

Zeller, Eduard. *The Stoics, Epicureans and Sceptics*, translated by Oswald J. Reichel. London: Longmans, Green, and Co., 1892.

Zizioulas, John D. *Being as Communion: Studies in Personhood and the Church*. Contemporary Greek Theologians 4. Crestwood, N.Y.: St. Vladimir's Seminary, 1985.

# Scripture and
# Ancient Source Index

## Other Ancient Sources

# Author Index

## Modern Authors

Abrams, M. H., 183
Anderson, H., 173, 269, 279
Appold, M. L., 175, 270, 279
Atwood, R., 192, 274

Ball, R. M., 138-39, 259, 279
Balthasar, H. U. von, 218, 264, 279
Barrett, C. K., 185, 272, 279
Barth, K., 33, 218, 279
Bassler, J. M., 104, 245, 252, 279
Bauckham, R., 160–61, 266, 279
Baumgarten, J., 166, 267, 279
Beasley-Murray, 276
Benz, E., 102, 279, 244
Bettenhausen, E., 19, 214
Blank, 176
Bloom, H., 28, 216, 281
Boismard, M.-È., 176, 270, 281
Borig, R., 162–64, 265–66, 282
Borowsky, 202, 218, 277
Bradley, R., 47, 221–22, 256, 282
Brock, R. N., 20, 282, 214
Brock, S., 48, 196, 275, 282
Brown, R. E., 195, 253, 272–73, 275, 282
Brownlee, W. H., 166, 267, 282
Buber, M., 27, 29
Bultmann, R., 111–12, 175, 283, 247, 275
Bynum, C. W., 48–49, 129, 222, 255–56, 283

Camp, C. V., 103, 282, 245, 249
Campbell, A. V., 76, 282, 232
Carson, D. A., 160, 199–200, 249, 265–66, 273, 276, 282
Clines, 59
Cohen, A., 27, 29
Corrington, G. P., 44–45, 131, 220–21, 256–57, 284
Cortéz, J. B., 134, 257, 284
Culpepper, R. A., 90, 94, 284, 232, 239, 241, 247, 251, 270

Dalman, 114
Dauer, A., 176, 270, 284
Davies, M., 59, 284, 231, 245, 248
Dawe, D. D., 80, 235
De Cueleneer, 133, 257
De Durand, 199, 276
De La Potterie, 176, 270, 272
de Margerie, B., 200, 277, 285
Derrett, D. M., 12, 210, 259, 285
Dillenberger, 278
Dillenger, J., 278
Dodd, C. H., 160, 250, 265, 285
Driver, G. R., 62, 226, 285
Dugas, L., 89, 285
Dussel, E., 18
Dyke, D. J., 61, 226, 285

Eller, V., 144–45, 192, 261–62, 274, 285
Evans, C. A., 114, 248–49, 251

Fackenheim, E., 27, 29,

317

## Ancient Authors

# Subject Index

abandonment 34 (Jesus' cry on cross); 50 (by God); 154 (cry of omitted by John); 156 (Father and Son suffer); 264 (interpretation of cry of).

abortion 62 (impalement for); 71 (crucifixion as punishment for).

Abuse 19 (patriarchy and); 51 (and crucifixion); 55 (when carrying cross); 58 (class of); 67 (Nero and children); 71 (of child); 100(Jesus' solidarity with abused); 129 (of Eucharist); 210 (Satan's abuse of power of); 214 (patriarchy and).

affection 32 (of God as friend, Unamuno); 45 (of Isis); 75 (of friends); 79 (not reciprocal); 85 (benefactor and recipient); 86 (none in recipient); 88 (in Epicurean teaching); 89 (equal among friends); 90 (God implants in soul); 91 (Abraham for Isaac); 97 (*oikeiosis* and); 100 (of friends); 118 (mutual); 130 (and lactation); 133 (filial and Roman charity); 137 (of Maccabean mother); 142 (and ritual friendship); 144 (of Jesus for Bethany family); 180 (of ideal king); 191 (of Maccabean mother); 239 (relationship to *agape*) 261 (and guest friendship).

akedah 91 (Philo discusses); 191 (and Maccabean mother).

Alcestis 83 (Plato refers to); 168 (Christ in light of); 169 (cited by Hengel); 172

(and Euripides); 190 (as background to women at cross); 273 (Euripides).

alienation 17 (and wrath of God); 28 (self–alienation in God).

amniotic fluid 38 (protecting fetus); 122–24 (in Nicodemus text); 195 (and sword thrust); 207 (in structure of Gospel).

androgynous 25 (God becomes); 46 (Gnostic concept); 235 (in *Symposium*).

animals 233 (Pythagorean friendship with); 237 (die for young).

anointing 136 (of Jesus' feet); 140 (Mary's mirror image of Jesus' foot-washing); 143 (Judas present at); 176 (by Mary); 207 (in structure of Gospel); 262 (comparison with foot-washing).

*apotympanismos* 51 (capital punishment); 57 (burial disallowed); 66 (in *Lysistrata*); 69 (and Prometheus); 70 (in Andromeda); 71 (monograph on); 168 (and shame); 223 (protracted death); 230 (monograph).

appeasement 13 (of God); 18 (no trace in Liberation Theology).

*ars moriendi* 172 (in Hellenic culture).

atonement 8 (effected by death of Christ); 14 (Day of); 16 (Day of); 17 (result of sacrifice); 20 (desire to obliterate idea); 21 (Grey's concept); 209 (Gunton); 211 (demonic element in

world of); 108 (Jesus friend of sinners);139 (footwashing and remission
of); 144 (of Judas as guest-friend); 157
(Paraclete will convict world of); 173
(martyrdom expiating); 200–01
(binding and loosing of); 209 (experience of, forgiveness of).
slave 12 (to sin); 17 (slavery of sin); 18
(chosen people fr. slavery); 27 (in
Egypt); 43 (in Egypt); 47 (Christ
became); 52–56 (crucifixion punishment for); 62 (women and children
sold into); 64–65 (all slaves killed for
guilt of one); 71 (Blandina); 75
(enslaved body of world); 99
(Stoics–slaves human); 139 (and footwashing); 146 (all must become); 179
(Alexander s. of glory); 182 (wise person does not receive title "master"
from slaves); 183 (Sacaea festival children serve slaves);187 (king with
regalia may be slave); 188 (true s. one
enslaved by servile nature); 229
(Manilius); 233 (members of
Pythagorean communities); 237
(Aristotle, no friendship with slaves);
242 (only sage is not a s.).
sorcery 59, 71.
Spirit 21 (bonding of women and experience of); 24 (basic to *pathos*); 27
(way of speaking about nearness of
God); 34 (reaches out to the forsak-
en); 38 (in analogy with fetus in
uterus); 39 (at creation); 46–47 (in
Gnosticism); 74 (in definition of
friendship); 76 (God's presence with
us); 81 (seeks enjoyment of freedom);
83 (as Love) 90 (and penetration of
spirits and community); 96 (of
Truth); 98 (convicting world; eternal
life of); 121 (agent of birth); 123 (and
1 Jn 3:5); 129–131 (and breastfeeding); 147 (conventicle of); 148 (Spirit
seeks out darkest places to give them
light); 149 (of Truth); 153–55 (role in
ecstasy and community); 156–9
(promise of); 186 (Jesus gives inheritance of); 196 (bestowal of); 200 (giv-

ing from cross and in Pentecost); 205
(life–giving); 257 (lactation predicated of); 262 (and footwashing); 276
(gift of).
status reversal 182, 183, 184.
submission 19, 139.
substitution 11, 12, 62.
sword thrust 193, 197.
*symbolon* 143.

temple 11, 26, 59, 63, 114, 125, 126, 133,
134, 136, 159, 160, 203, 211, 225, 226,
256, 262, 265.
theophany 6, 41.
transformation 21, 25, 214, 279.
travail 39, 41, 42, 43, 164, 165, 167, 219,
236.
Trinity 13 (Christ offered the price to
the Trinity); 32 (suffering precedes
incarnation); 34 (suffering of); 38
(fetus in uterus image of); 48–49 (and
lactation), 74–75 (friendship and the
image of God); 131 (streams of water-
ing); 147–67 (and Farewell Discourses); 204 (role model of God of
anguish); 263 (Rubler's icon).
*tsimtsum* 28.

unmoved mover 30.
utility 84, 87, 89, 236, 239.

veil 150, 211.
vicarious 23, 45, 70, 137, 138, 172, 174,
209, 258.
victim 12–14 (Christ as v.); 15–17,
(scapegoat v.); 19–20 (feminist objection to Christ as victim); 76 (suffer
with victims of estrangement); 183
(Sacaea festival); 184 (and irony); 190
(Macaria offered herself as); 203 (God
playing role of).
vine 116, 126, 159, 160, 161, 162, 163,
164, 197, 265, 266, 267, 280.
violence 14–19 (sacred); 38 (mother
protects child); 77 (Pythagoras, no
violence to people and animals); 142
(and ritual friendship); 187 (Cynic
non–resistance); 212–13 (reconcilia-